KU-714-692

THE HAMLYN ENCYCLOPEDIA OF
GOLF

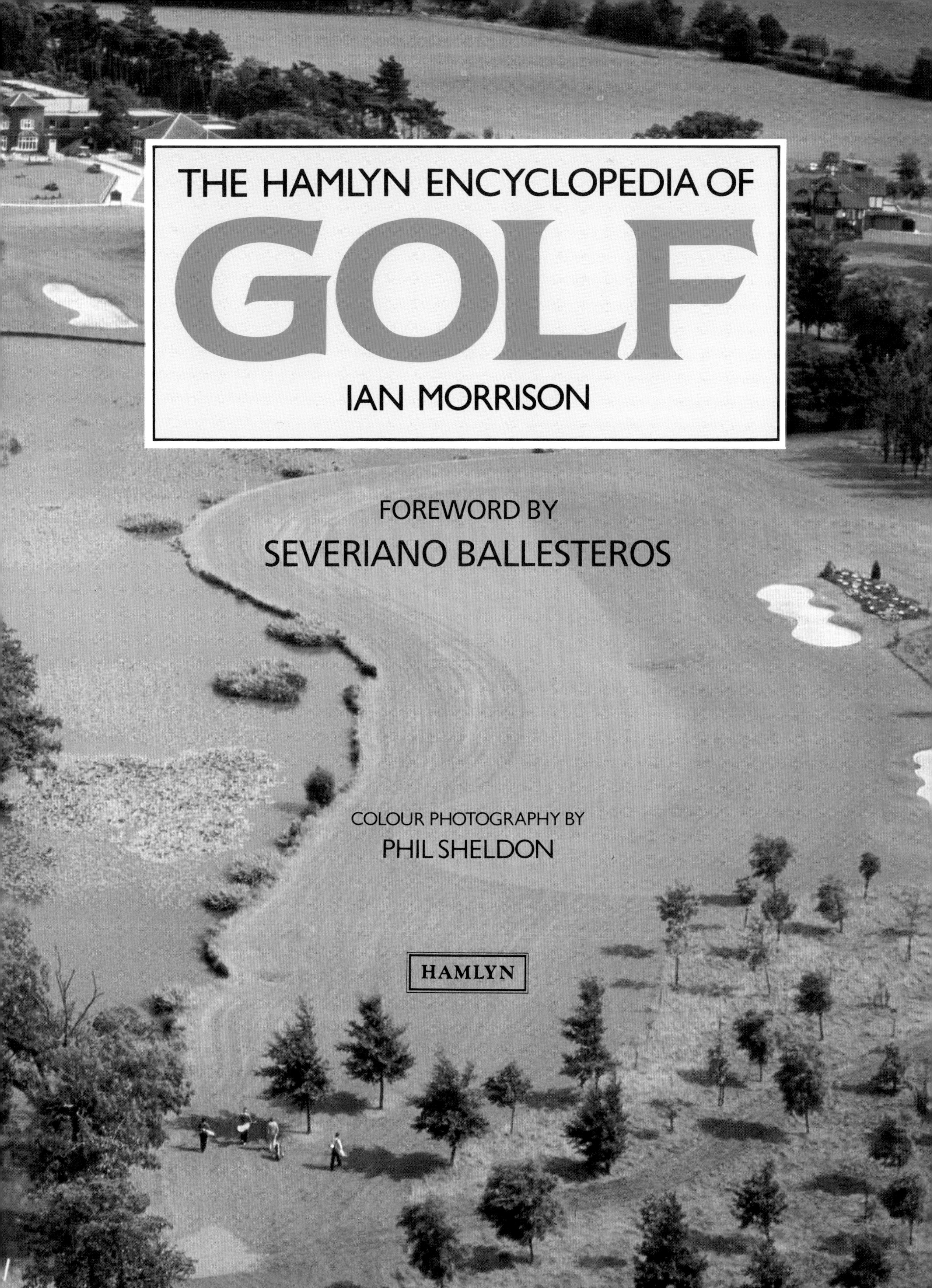

THE HAMLYN ENCYCLOPEDIA OF GOLF

IAN MORRISON

FOREWORD BY

SEVERIANO BALLESTEROS

COLOUR PHOTOGRAPHY BY

PHIL SHELDON

HAMLYN

Published in 1986 by
Hamlyn Publishing,
Bridge House, London Road,
Twickenham, Middlesex, England

ISBN 0 600 50218 X

Printed in Spain

Acknowledgments

The author would like to thank John Pennington of Runcorn Golf Club for his assistance.

All photographs supplied by Ad. Lib. Photo Agency.
Colour photography by Phil Sheldon.
Black and white photographs: BBC Hulton Picture Library: pages 41, 153 top, 156; Cowrie/St Andrews University: pages 23, 68, 96, 133; Tony Duffy: page 89; Lawrence N. Levy: page 71; Bert Neale: pages 24, 25, 33, 37, 52, 53 bottom, 56, 69, 84, 85, 120, 128, 129, 137, 145, 149, 160; Royal and Ancient Club: page 64; Phil Sheldon: pages 11, 53 top, 112, 153 bottom; United States Golf Association: pages 117, 155, 172.

Foreword

Over the past twenty or so years, golf has, along with many other sports, grown at a tremendous rate. Television has to take a lot of the credit for the increased development—a great deal of money has been injected into golf, making it one of the most prestigious sports in terms of prize money. Another important factor is that, due to increased media coverage, many more people are playing golf—long gone are the days when it was regarded as a sport for the wealthy.

But golf's history stretches way before the last twenty years. Indeed, it is second to none in the sporting world. For instance, you will discover in this book that Mary Queen of Scots was so addicted to golf that she was on the links within two weeks of her husband's death.

Although much has changed in the way of techniques and equipment, the object of the game has always been the same—to get that white ball into the hole. This may sound simple, and many of today's golfers make it look easy; in practice it is anything but! As any professional or high-handicap golfer knows, there is no such thing as an easy round of golf.

While I cannot guarantee that this marvellous book will make you a better player, I can assure you that the array of biographies, features, anecdotes and results will provide lasting enjoyment and interest for anyone who wants to find out more about the fascinating sport of golf.

Ace
The American term for a hole-in-one.

Address the Ball
To take up a preparatory position with a club in order to play a shot. A player is said to have addressed the ball once he has adopted his stance and has grounded the club. He is not allowed to ground a club in a bunker.

Air Shot
A stroke which completely misses the ball. Even though the ball is not moved, the player must count it and include it in the score. Also known as a fresh-air shot.

Albatross
A score of three strokes below par for a hole. All below-par scores have names connected with birds. As three under par is the biggest below-par score possible it is named after an appropriately large bird—the albatross. Thus, for example, if a par 5 is holed out in two strokes the player is deemed to have scored an albatross. The expression originated in the United States, although nowadays it is more usually referred to there as a double-eagle.

Perhaps the most famous albatross was in the 1935 US Masters at Augusta, Georgia. Gene Sarazen holed out at the par-5 15th hole with a four wood. The shot put Sarazen in the running for the title. He drew with Craig Wood and then went on to beat him in a play-off.

The last albatross in the British Open was at the 526-yd (480-m) 17th at Royal Birkdale in 1983 when Bill Rogers (US) holed out. Rogers was the first man since Johnny Miller, in 1972, to perform this feat.

The longest albatross in the British Open was achieved by Johnny Miller (US) in the 1972 championship at Muirfield when he holed out at the 558-yd 6th (510-m) hole.

The longest albatross in championship golf is credited to Billy Casper (US) who holed out at the 580-yd (530-m) 14th hole at Crans-sur-Sierre during the 1971 Swiss Open.

Taiwan's Tze-Chung Chen, in 1985, registered the first albatross in the long history of the US Open, when he did so during his opening round at Oakland Hills.

Alliss, Peter
Born in 1931 in Berlin, where his father, Percy, was the professional at the Wannsee Club, Peter Alliss came to England as a youngster. He was a boy international at 15 but shortly afterwards turned professional. He had to wait ten years for his first big win, the 1956 Spanish Open at El Prat. Two years later he enjoyed his most successful season by winning the Spanish, Portuguese and Italian Opens.

Like his father he gained Ryder Cup honours, representing Great Britain and Northern Ireland eight times during 1953–69. His Ryder Cup baptism, however, was a nightmare. He required four putts from the edge of the green at the 36th hole at Wentworth and lost his singles match to Jim Turnesa by one hole. Great Britain lost the cup by just one match.

Although he had a textbook swing and a great natural talent, he was often let down by his inconsistent putting which cost him many more titles.

In 1970 Alliss moved from Dorset, where he had been the professional at Parkstone, to take up a similar appointment in his 'native' Yorkshire at Moor Allerton, Leeds. By this time he was carving out a career as a leading coach, course designer and commentator for the BBC, where he took over from Henry Longhurst.

Career highlights
- Spanish Open 1956, 1958
- Italian Open 1958
- Portuguese Open 1958
- Brazilian Open 1961
- British Open (best) jt 2nd – 1962
- Ryder Cup (Great Britain) 1953, 1957, 1959, 1961, 1963, 1965, 1967, 1969

Aluminium Shafts
In the 1960s many manufacturers fitted aluminium shafts to their new clubs but these failed to become popular with professional players and consequently never caught on. The fact that they were heavier than traditional steel-shafted clubs was a major factor in their unpopularity.

Amateur
According to the rules of golf an amateur is a person who 'plays the game as a non-remunerative or non-profit-making sport'. The rules governing the amateur status of players, as approved by the Royal and Ancient Golf Club, are very strict indeed, with automatic suspension for contravention of any of them.

Amateur Championship, The
In 1877 the Royal and Ancient Club was asked if it was interested in setting up an open championship for amateurs—it was not. Eight years later Thomas Owen Potter of Hoylake went ahead and organized the first British Amateur Championship on the Royal Liverpool links. A field of 44 lined up and the first winner was Allan MacFie, a Scottish member of the host club. The Royal and Ancient was approached once more and, following the success of the Hoylake tournament, realized it had made a mistake in declining the 1877 offer. Since 1886 the championships have taken place under the auspices of the Royal and Ancient. However, the R & A did not recognize the 1885 winner, MacFie, in their list of champions until 1922 when his name was added.

Up to 1983 the format of the championship had altered very little. It was always a match-play event and the changes in format were as follows.

1885–95 All matches over 18 holes.
1896–1955 Final over 36 holes; all other matches over 18 holes.
1956–57 Quarter-finals, semi-finals and final over 36 holes; other matches over 18 holes.
1958 Semi-finals and final over 36 holes; other matches over 18 holes.
1959–65 Final over 36 holes; all other matches over 18 holes.
1966 All matches, including the final, played over 18 holes.
1967–82 Final over 36 holes; other matches over 18 holes.
1983– All competitors play two stroke-play rounds. The lowest 64 scorers then take part in match-play competition, all matches, except the final, being over 18 holes. The final is over 36.

Like the British Open, the Amateur Championship is normally held on a links course. In 1964 and 1977, however, the venue was the inland course at Ganton, Yorkshire.

Winners

Year	Name and Club	Venue	Score
1885	A. F. MacFie (Royal Liverpool)	Hoylake	7 & 6
1886	H. G. Hutchinson (Royal and Ancient)	St Andrews	7 & 6
1887	H. G. Hutchinson (Royal and Ancient)	Hoylake	1 hole
1888	J. Ball, Jnr (Royal Liverpool)	Prestwick	5 & 4
1889	J. Laidlay (Hon. Company)	St Andrews	2 & 1
1890	J. Ball, Jnr (Royal Liverpool)	Hoylake	4 & 3
1891	J. Laidlay (Hon. Company)	St Andrews	20th hole
1892	J. Ball, Jnr (Royal Liverpool)	Sandwich	3 & 1
1893	P. C. Anderson (St Andrew's University)	Prestwick	1 hole
1894	J. Ball, Jnr (Royal Liverpool)	Hoylake	1 hole
1895	L. M. B. Melville (Royal and Ancient)	St Andrews	19th hole
1896	F. G. Tait (Black Watch GC)	Sandwich	8 & 7
1897	A. J. T. Allan (Edinburgh University)	Muirfield	4 & 2
1898	F. G. Tait (Black Watch GC)	Hoylake	7 & 5
1899	J. Ball, Jnr (Royal Liverpool)	Prestwick	37th hole
1900	H. H. Hilton (Royal Liverpool)	Sandwich	8 & 7
1901	H. H. Hilton (Royal Liverpool	St Andrews	1 hole
1902	C. Hutchings (Royal Liverpool)	Hoylake	1 hole
1903	R. Maxwell (Tantallon)	Muirfield	7 & 5
1904	W. J. Travis (US)	Sandwich	4 & 3
1905	A. G. Barry (St Andrews University)	Prestwick	3 & 2
1906	J. Robb (Prestwick St Nicholas)	Hoylake	4 & 3
1907	J. Ball, Jnr (Royal Liverpool)	St Andrews	6 & 4
1908	E. A. Lassen (Royal Lytham)	Sandwich	7 & 6
1909	R. Maxwell (Tantallon)	Muirfield	1 hole
1910	J. Ball, Jnr (Royal Liverpool)	Hoylake	10 & 9
1911	H. H. Hilton (Royal Liverpool)	Prestwick	4 & 3
1912	J. Ball, Jnr (Royal Liverpool)	Westward Ho!	38th hole
1913	H. H. Hilton (Royal Liverpool)	St Andrews	6 & 5
1914	J. L. C. Jenkins (Troon)	Sandwich	3 & 2
1915–19	Not held		
1920	C. J. H. Tolley (Rye)	Muirfield	37th hole
1921	W. I. Hunter (Walmer and Kingsdown)	Hoylake	12 & 11
1922	E. W. E. Holderness (Walton Heath)	Prestwick	1 hole
1923	R. H. Wethered (Worplesdon)	Deal	7 & 6
1924	E. W. E. Holderness (Walton Heath)	St Andrews	3 & 2
1925	R. Harris (Royal and Ancient)	Westward Ho!	13 & 12
1926	J. Sweetser (US)	Muirfield	6 & 5
1927	W. Tweddell (Stourbridge)	Hoylake	7 & 6
1928	T. P. Perkins (Castle Bromwich)	Prestwick	6 & 4
1929	C. J. H. Tolley (Rye)	Sandwich	4 & 3
1930	R. T. Jones, Jnr (US)	St Andrews	7 & 6
1931	E. Martin Smith (Royal St George's)	Westward Ho!	1 hole
1932	J. de Forest (Addington)	Muirfield	3 & 1
1933	Hon. M. Scott (Royal St George's)	Hoylake	4 & 3

Year	Name and Club	Venue	Score
1934	W. Lawson Little (US)	Prestwick	14 & 13
1935	W. Lawson Little (US)	Lytham	1 hole
1936	H. Thomson (Williamwood)	St Andrews	2 holes
1937	R. Sweeny, Jnr (Royal and Ancient)	Sandwich	3 & 2
1938	C. R. Yates (US)	Troon	3 & 2
1939	A. T. Kyle (Sand Moor)	Hoylake	2 & 1
1940–45	Not held		
1946	J. Bruen (Cork)	Birkdale	4 & 3
1947	W. P. Turnesa (US)	Carnoustie	3 & 2
1948	F. R. Stranahan (US)	Sandwich	5 & 4
1949	S. M. McCready (Sunningdale)	Portmarnock	2 & 1
1950	F. R. Stranahan (US)	St Andrews	8 & 6
1951	R. D. Chapman (US)	Porthcawl	5 & 4
1952	E. Harvie Ward (US)	Prestwick	7 & 5
1953	J. B. Carr (Sutton)	Hoylake	2 holes
1954	D. W. Bachli (Australia)	Muirfield	2 & 1
1955	J. W. Conrad (US)	Lytham	3 & 2
1956	J. C. Beharrell (Little Aston)	Troon	5 & 4
1957	R. Reid Jack (Dullatur)	Formby	2 & 1
1958	J. B. Carr (Sutton)	St Andrews	3 & 2
1959	D. Beman (US)	Sandwich	3 & 2
1960	J. B. Carr (Sutton)	Portrush	8 & 7
1961	M. F. Bonallack (Thorpe Hall)	Turnberry	6 & 4
1962	R. D. Davies (US)	Hoylake	1 hole
1963	M. S. R. Lunt (Moseley)	St Andrews	2 & 1
1964	G. J. Clark (Whitley Bay)	Ganton	39th hole
1965	M. F. Bonallack (Thorpe Hall)	Porthcawl	2 & 1
1966	R. Cole (South Africa)	Carnoustie	3 & 2
1967	R. B. Dickson (US)	Formby	2 & 1
1968	M. F. Bonallack (Thorpe Hall)	Troon	7 & 6
1969	M. F. Bonallack (Thorpe Hall)	Hoylake	3 & 2
1970	M. F. Bonallack (Thorpe Hall)	Newcastle, Co. Down	8 & 7
1971	S. Melnyk (US)	Carnoustie	3 & 2
1972	T. W. B. Homer (Walsall)	Sandwich	4 & 3
1973	R. Siderowf (US)	Porthcawl	5 & 3
1974	T. W. B. Homer (Walsall)	Muirfield	2 holes
1975	M. M. Giles III (US)	Hoylake	8 & 7
1976	R. Siderowf (US)	St Andrews	37th hole
1977	P. McEvoy (Copt Heath)	Ganton	5 & 4
1978	P. McEvoy (Copt Heath)	Troon	4 & 3
1979	J. Sigel (US)	Hillside	3 & 2
1980	D. Evans (Leek)	Porthcawl	4 & 3
1981	P. Ploujoux (France)	St Andrews	4 & 2
1982	M. Thompson (Middlesbrough)	Deal	4 & 3
1983	A. P. Parkin (Newtown)	Turnberry	5 & 4
1984	J. M. Olazabal (Spain)	Formby	5 & 4
1985	G. McGimpsey (Bangor, Co. Down)	Dornoch	8 & 7

Most wins
8 – John Ball, Jnr (Royal Liverpool) 1888–1912

Most finals
10 – John Ball, Jnr (Royal Liverpool) 1887–1912

Most consecutive wins
3 – Michael Bonallack (Thorpe Hall) 1968, 1969, 1970

Biggest winning margin (final)
14 & 13 – W. Lawson Little (US) beat J. Wallace (Prestwick) 1934

First US winner
Walter Travis 1904

First European winner
José-Maria Olazabal (Spain) 1984

Winners of Amateur Championship and British Open
John Ball, Jnr
Harold Hilton
Bobby Jones (US)
(Ball and Jones won both in the same year)

Amateur Internationals

See Home Internationals.

Aoki, Isao

A professional since 1964, Isao Aoki began his rise to stardom in 1973 when he won the Japan Professional title for the first time. Three years later he was the leading money winner in his home country with nearly 42 million yen to his credit.

Aoki's unusual but effective putting style was seen by British crowds in the mid-1970s. In 1978 he obtained what was then the best ever placing by a Japanese golfer

A former leading European player, Peter Alliss is now regarded as a great tutor, author and television commentator.

in the British Open when he finished joint 7th. Later that year he gained the biggest prize of his career when he beat New Zealand's Simon Owen 3 and 2 at Wentworth to win the World Match-Play title.

Aoki reached the Wentworth final the following year and, although he had to be content with second place to the American, Bill Rogers, it was still a very profitable tournament for him. His hole-in-one against David Graham won him a furnished flat at Gleneagles worth £55,000.

His success story continued into the 1980s. After finishing second to Jack Nicklaus (his playing partner in all four rounds) in the 1980 US Open he took part in the British Open at Muirfield and equalled the championship record 63 in the third round.

Career highlights

World Match-Play Championship 1978 (winner), 1979 (runner-up)
British Open (best) jt 7th – 1978, 1979
US Open best position 2nd

Approach Shot

A shot made from the fairway, or rough, towards the green.

Apron

The area around the green, cut shorter than the fairway but not as short as the green itself.

Armour, Tommy

The Edinburgh-born Tommy Armour travelled to the United States with the Great Britain Walker Cup team in 1922 and stayed. He then went on to enjoy a successful professional career.

In 1926 he created a unique piece of golfing history by playing in the unofficial Ryder Cup match *against* Britain, and in 1927 he won the first of his three major tournaments, the US Open, after a play-off against Harry Cooper at Oakmont.

His second major was in 1930 when he beat Gene Sarazen at the final hole, thanks to a 14-ft putt, to win the US PGA championship at Fresh Meadow. Then, in 1931, he returned to his native Scotland to win the first British Open to be held at Carnoustie.

He was a great teacher of the game and his skills were sought after by the famous amateur champion, Bobby Jones, and by the former US president, Richard Nixon. His techniques often found their way into print and his golfing books were much prized. The achievements of Tommy Armour were all the more remarkable considering that he lost an eye during the First World War.

Career highlights

US Open 1927
US PGA 1930
British Open 1931
Canadian Open 1927, 1930, 1934
Walker Cup (Great Britain) 1922
Ryder Cup (United States) 1926

Japan's Isao Aoki has every reason to kiss the ball. It had just won a flat and furnishings valued at £55,000 for holing-in-one during the 1979 World Match-Play Championship at Wentworth.

Artisan Golfer

A working golfer who, in return for performing duties around the golf course, is allowed to play on the course at restricted times at a reduced fee. Most leading golf clubs have artisan members, who often have their own small club-house facilities at some distant part of the course.

The first artisan club, the Bulwell Forest Artisan Club, Nottingham, was founded in 1887.

The Artisan Golfer's Association was formed in 1921, with the objective of co-ordinating the existing artisan clubs and encouraging the formation of new ones. An Artisan Championship has been held since 1924.

Attendances

See Gate Money.

Augusta National

Perhaps the best known course in the United States, the Augusta National in Georgia was the realization of a dream of the US champion, Bobby Jones, and his friend, Clifford Roberts. They engaged the services of the Scottish golf-course designer, Dr Alistair Mackenzie, who completed the Augusta course in 1931. Mackenzie also designed the Cypress Point course.

Augusta is now the home of the US Masters. The first Masters was held there in 1934 and won by Horton Smith.

The club was called the Augusta National because the intention was, and still is, to draw members from all over the United States.

It is one of the most beautiful courses in the world, each hole being named after the flower, shrub or tree that can be found along its borders. They are as follows:

Australian Open

Winners

Year	Name	Venue	Score
1904	Hon. M. Scott (*)	The Australian	324
1905	D. Soutar	Royal Melbourne	330
1906	C. Clark	Royal Sydney	322
1907	Hon. M. Scott (*)	Royal Melbourne	318
1908	C. Pearce (*)	The Australian	311
1909	C. Felstead (*)	Royal Melbourne	316
1910	C. Clark	Royal Adelaide	311
1911	C. Clark	Royal Sydney	321
1912	I. Whitton (*)	Royal Melbourne	321
1913	I. Whitton (*)	Royal Melbourne	302
1914–19 not held			
1920	J. Kirkwood	The Australian	290
1921	A. Le Fevre	Royal Melbourne	295
1922	C. Campbell	Royal Sydney	307
1923	T. Howard	Royal Adelaide	301
1924	A. Russell (*)	Royal Melbourne	303
1925	F. Popplewell	The Australian	299
1926	I. Whitton (*)	Royal Adelaide	297
1927	R. Stewart	Royal Melbourne	297
1928	F. Popplewell	Royal Sydney	295
1929	I. Whitton (*)	Royal Adelaide	309
1930	F. Eyre	Metropolitan	306
1931	I. Whitton (*)	The Australian	301
1932	M. J. Ryan (*)	Royal Adelaide	296
1933	M. L. Kelly	Royal Melbourne	302
1934	W. J. Bolger	Royal Sydney	283
1935	F. McMahon	Royal Adelaide	293
1936	G. Sarazen	Metropolitan	282
1937	G. Naismith	The Australian	299
1938	J. Ferrier (*)	Royal Adelaide	283
1939	J. Ferrier (*)	Royal Melbourne	285
1940–45 Not held			
1946	H. O. Pickworth	Royal Sydney	289
1947	H. O. Pickworth	Royal Queensland	285
1948	H. O. Pickworth	Kingston Heath	289
1949	E. Cremin	The Australian	287
1950	N. von Nida	Kooyonga	286
1951	P. Thomson	Metropolitan	283
1952	N. von Nida	Lake Karrinyup	278
1953	N. von Nida	Royal Melbourne	278
1954	H. O. Pickworth	Kooyonga	280
1955	A. D. Locke	Gailes	290
1956	B. Crampton	Royal Sydney	289
1957	F. Phillips	Kingston Heath	287
1958	G. Player	Kooyonga	271
1959	K. Nagle	The Australian	284
1960	B. Devlin (*)	Lake Karrinyup	282
1961	F. Phillips	Victoria	275
1962	G. Player	Royal Adelaide	281
1963	G. Player	Royal Melbourne	278
1964	J. Nicklaus	The Lakes	287
1965	G. Player	Kooyonga	264
1966	A. Palmer	Royal Queensland	276
1967	P. Thomson	Commonwealth	281
1968	J. Nicklaus	Lake Karrinyup	270
1969	G. Player	Royal Sydney	288
1970	G. Player	Kingston Heath	280
1971	J. Nicklaus	Royal Hobart	269
1972	P. Thomson	Kooyonga	281
1973	J. Snead	Royal Queensland	280
1974	G. Player	Lake Karrinyup	279
1975	J. Nicklaus	The Australian	279
1976	J. Nicklaus	The Australian	286
1977	D. Graham	The Australian	284
1978	J. Nicklaus	The Australian	284
1979	J. Newton	Metropolitan	288
1980	G. Norman	The Lakes	284
1981	B. Rogers	Melbourne	282
1982	R. Shearer	The Australian	287
1983	P. Fowler	Kingston Heath	285
1984	T. Watson	Royal Melbourne	281
1985	G. Norman	Royal Melbourne	212(a)
1986	B. Shearer	Royal Melbourne	267

(a) over 54 holes

(*) denotes amateur

Most wins

7 – Gary Player (1958–74)

Lowest score (72 holes)

264 – Gary Player (Kooyonga, 1965)

1st – Tea Olive	10th – Camellia
2nd – Pink Dogwood	11th – White Dogwood
3rd – Flowering Peach	12th – Golden Bell
4th – Crab Apple	13th – Azalea
5th – Magnolia	14th – Chinese Fir
6th – Juniper	15th – Firethorn
7th – Pampas	16th – Red Bud
8th – Yellow Jasmine	17th – Nandina
9th – Carolina Cherry	18th – Holly

Length 6905 yd (6314 m)
Par 72
Course record 63 – Nick Price (1986)

64 – Hale Irwin (1975)
64 – Gary Player (1978)
64 – Miller Barber (1979)

Australian Open

The first Australian Open was held at the Australian Golf Club, Kensington, Sydney, in 1904 and won by the British Walker Cup player, the Hon. Michael Scott.

Apart from 1936, when Gene Sarazen won the title, the championship was not well supported by leading international stars in the years before the Second World War.

Gary Player has been the competition's outstanding performer in the postwar years, winning the title on seven occasions. In 1965 he registered a championship record of 264, aided by two rounds of 62.

B

Back Door Shot

A putt that rolls round the hole and enters it from the back. Also known as a tradesman's entrance shot.

Back Nine

The last nine holes of a round of golf. Also known as the second nine, inward half, or in.

The lowest score for the back nine in the British Open is 30, which was achieved by the following players:

Eric Brown	1958	Lytham
Phil Rodgers	1966	Muirfield
Lee Trevino	1972	Muirfield
Arnold Palmer	1977	Turnberry
Dennis Watson	1980	Muirfield
Tom Watson	1980	Muirfield

Backspin

A motion imparted to a ball which causes it to spin backwards when it hits the green. The backspin shot is played with a lofted club and, at the moment of contact between club and ball, the front of the ball is spinning upwards and the back downwards. The art of applying backspin to a ball is not easy, and one the ordinary player finds difficult.

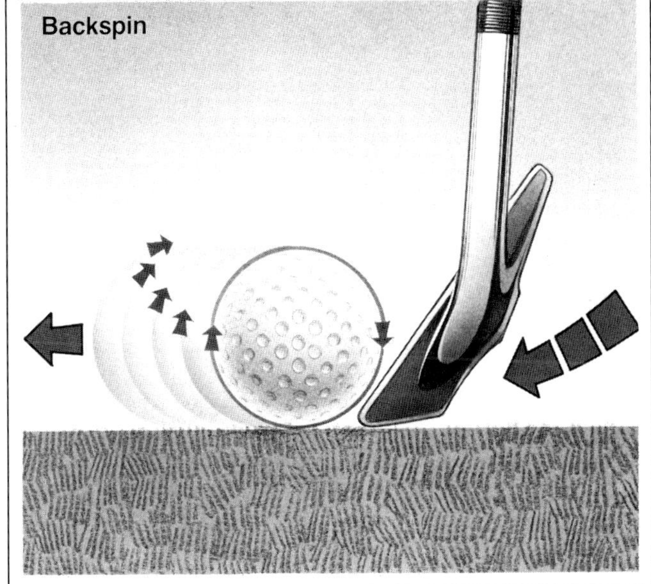

Backswing

The backward movement of the club away from the ball before the downward stroke and eventual striking of the ball. The backswing is a vital part of the golf stroke and an uneven backswing will have disastrous effects on the outcome of the stroke.

Baffy

A hickory-shafted wooden club used in the 19th century. Its present-day counterpart would probably be a No 4 wood.

Ball

Although it is believed that the first known golfers, in the early 15th century, played with wooden golf balls, three other types of ball have been widely used over the past 400 years. The first was the 'feathery' which was probably in use in the 15th century, although there is no recorded reference to it. Consisting of a leather casing stuffed with feathers, each ball was hand-made. Because of this not all balls were the same size or weight, or even the same shape.

The biggest breakthrough came in 1848 when the Rev. Robert Peterson invented the 'gutty', so named because it was made out of a brownish-red gum substance, found in Malaya, called gutta-percha. Although Peterson is credited with the invention of the new ball, it is said that a member of the staff of the firm W. T. Henley actually manufactured the first gutty, which was used at the Blackheath Club.

One advantage the gutty enjoyed over the feathery was that it could be made perfectly round. It had a flat surface and, after making contact with the club, entered into a 'true' flight. Gutties did, however, have a tendency

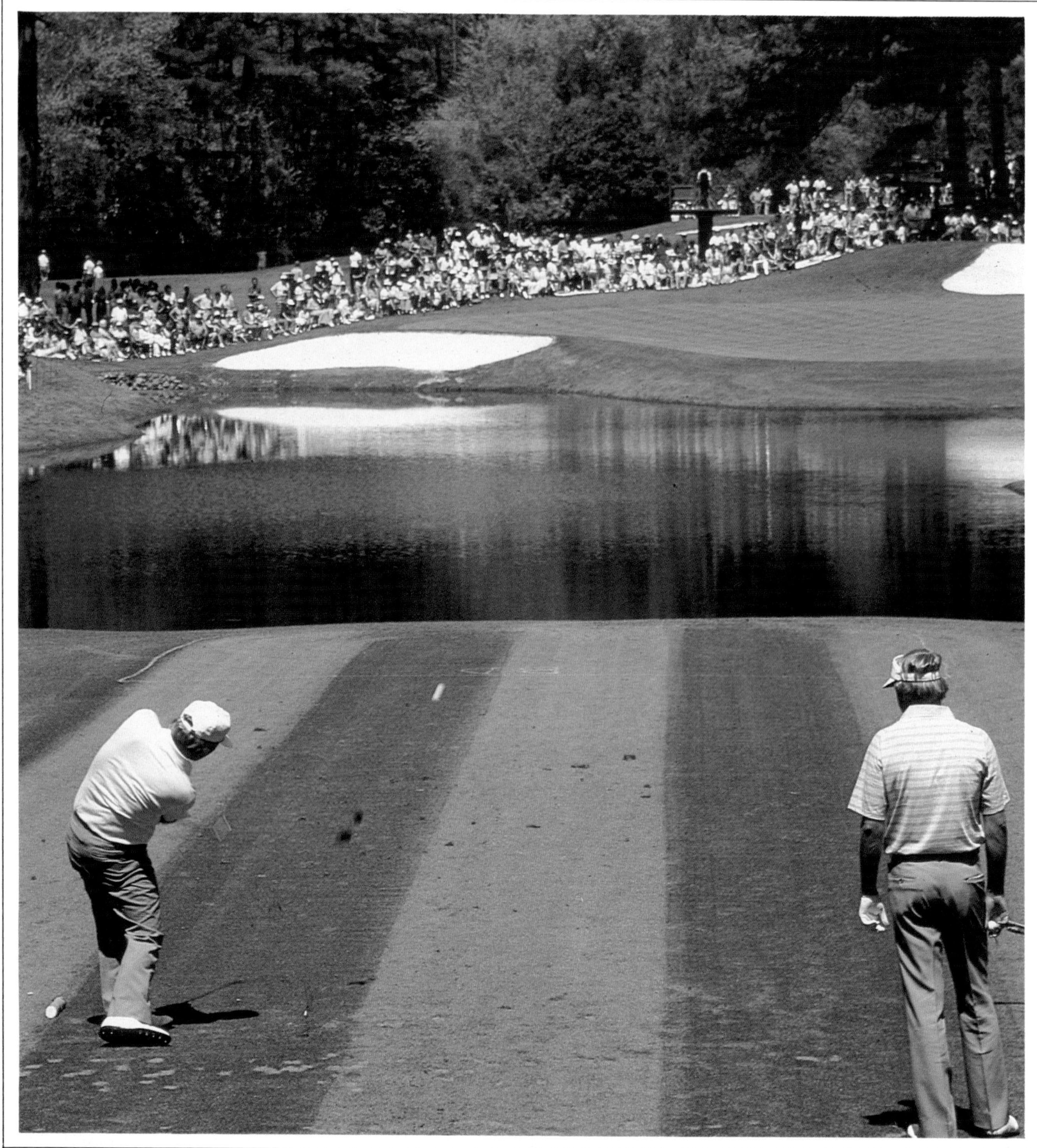

Perhaps the most beautiful golf course in the world, the Augusta National in Georgia. The 16th hole, seen here, is one of its most spectacular.

to just fall from the sky like a shot bird, without completing their proper trajectory. Towards the end of each round this problem seemed to cure itself and the experts soon realized that the damage caused by the club head actually improved the flight of the ball. As a result artificial damage marks were put on each ball, and so was born the dimple.

The gutty was superseded at the end of the 19th century by the rubber-cored ball. Invented by an American, Coburn Haskell, it was made of elastic thread wound around a central rubber core and covered in plastic coating. The new ball proved its superiority over the gutty in 1902 when Alex Herd out-drove his opponent to win the British Open with it.

Surprisingly, legislation governing the size and weight of golf balls was not enacted until 1920 when the Royal and Ancient and the US PGA agreed the weight should not be greater than 1.62 oz (45.93 g) and the diameter not less than 1.62 in (41.15 mm).

In 1931 the US PGA changed its regulations to allow for a ball of 1.55 oz (43.9 g) in weight, with a diameter of 1.68 in (42.67 mm). This ball, however, was found to be too light and the following year the weight was increased back to its previous weight.

The first British tournament to use the American-size ball, as an experiment, took place at Wentworth in 1960 and was won by Christy O'Connor, Snr. In 1964 the British PGA adopted a rule stating that all tournaments held under their auspices should use the larger ball. This experiment was for one year only, and did not include amateur events nor the British Open. The rule was reintroduced in 1968 and is still in force today. The Royal and Ancient decreed that, as from the 1974 championship, the larger ball would be compulsory in the British Open. It is estimated that over 300 million golf balls are sold world-wide each year.

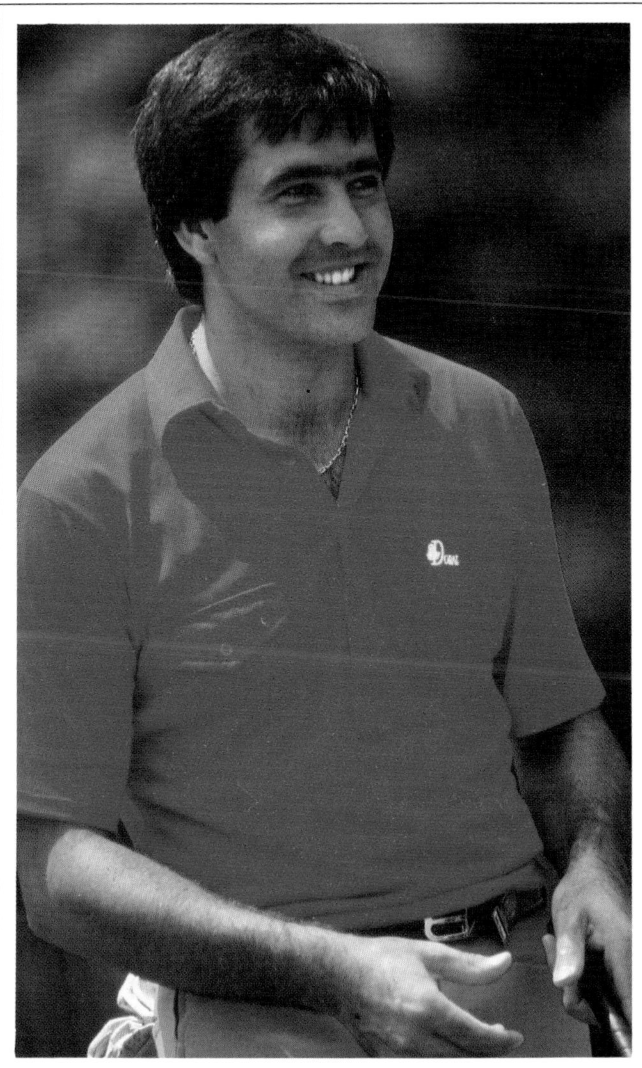

Seve seems to have plenty to smile about during the 1981 US Open at Merion.

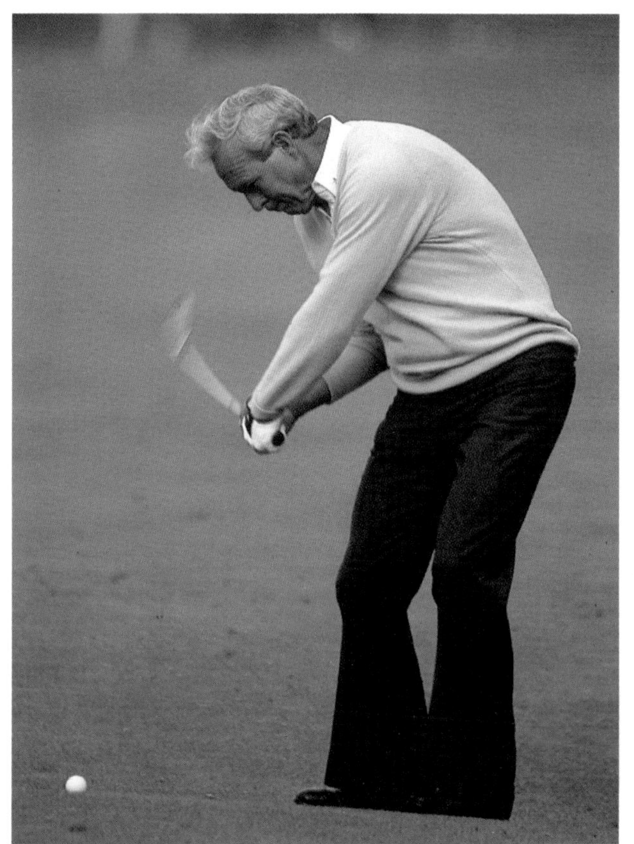

What better player to display the backswing than Arnold Palmer.

Ball, John

John Ball was brought up with golf in his blood. He was born in 1861 in Hoylake where his father owned a local hotel which became the Royal Liverpool Club's first headquarters. In 1877, at the age of 15, he appeared in his first British Open at Musselburgh and finished sixth.

Between 1888 and 1912, despite spending three years in the army, he won the British Amateur Championship a record eight times. In 1890 he became the first amateur to win the British Open and he was also the first Englishman to gain the title.

Ball was one of the first stylists and his swing was a classic of its day. He carried on playing in his later years, and took part in his last amateur championship in 1921—surviving five rounds—at the age of 60. He retired shortly afterwards to his farm in Wales, where he died in 1940.

Career highlights

British Open 1890
Amateur Championship 1888, 1890, 1892, 1894, 1899, 1907, 1910, 1912

Ballesteros, Severiano

Spain's Severiano Ballesteros is undoubtedly the greatest golfer to have emerged from Europe, and his victories all over the world have made him one of the sport's most popular players.

This picture clearly shows how golf balls have developed over the years.

He first appeared on the European PGA Tour in 1974 and finished the season in 118th place with winnings of just £2,915. The following year he was up to 26th, and then, in 1976, 1977 and 1978 he topped the European Order of Merit. Although he has not topped it since, he has constantly figured in the top ten. He has also figured prominently in the United States Order of Merit where he has played a lot of golf. That came to an end in 1985 when the US PGA Tour refused to renew his ticket because he did not play in the required 15 tournaments.

Since his inaugural professional win, in the 1976 Dutch Open, Seve has gone on to win the Open championships of France, Switzerland, Japan, Scandinavia, Kenya, Germany, Ireland as well as the British Open twice. In addition he has won the US Masters twice, the World Match-Play title four times, the Sun City Million Dollar Challenge twice, and many more.

As a 19-year-old, Ballesteros first attracted attention in Britain during the 1976 Open at Birkdale when he tied for second place with Jack Nicklaus, behind the eventual winner Johnny Miller. Three years later, at Lytham, Seve won the first of his two cherished British Open titles when he beat Nicklaus and Ben Crenshaw by three strokes. His second success in the Open was at St Andrews, in 1984, when he beat off a strong challenge from fellow-European Bernhard Langer to win by two strokes.

The pleasant Spaniard, from Pedrena in Northern Spain, received his professional player's card in January 1974 and, at the age of 16 years and eight months, was Spain's youngest ever professional. He followed the footsteps of his elder brother Manuel who had been a professional since 1969. Seve is, on his day, by far the best golfer in the world, and is capable of playing every shot in the book . . . and a few more that he has invented!

Career highlights

British Open 1979, 1984
US Masters 1980, 1983
World Match-Play 1981, 1982, 1984, 1985
Ryder Cup 1979, 1983, 1985

Baltusrol

Founded in 1895, the Baltusrol club at Springfield, New Jersey, is one of the oldest golf clubs in the United States. It was named after a farmer, Baltus Roll, who was murdered in the locality in 1825.

The venue for most leading American tournaments, it staged its first, the US Ladies' Championship, in 1901. It has housed the US Open a record six times, the last occasion being in 1980 when Jack Nicklaus broke US Open records for the lowest 18, 36, 54 and 72 holes.

The original course was ploughed up in the 1920s to make way for two courses—the Upper and Lower. Both have been used for the US Open, the shorter Upper course just once—in 1936.

The fourth hole on the Lower course is regarded as one of the finest in the United States, and the 623-yd (570-m) par-5 17th is the longest hole ever to have been seen in the US Open.

Lower course

Length 7022 yd (6421 m)
Par 70
Course record 63 – Tom Weiskopf (US Open, 1980)
63 – Jack Nicklaus (US Open, 1980)

Belfry, The

Now the headquarters of the PGA, the Belfry, near Sutton Coldfield, Warwickshire, was officially opened only in 1977. Prior to that it had been a hotel at which many golfers stayed when playing in nearby tournaments. The transformation of the 15 adjacent potato fields into one of Britain's top inland courses is remarkable. There are two courses at the Belfry—the Derby course and the larger, championship Brabazon course. The latter was designed by David Thomas and, unlike most British courses, it contains water. The 18th hole is one of the most picturesque final holes on a British golf course.

The first major tournament to be held at the Belfry was the 1978 Hennessy Cognac Cup. The State Express Classic had its home there between 1979 and 1983 and in 1984 the Lawrence Batley Classic moved from Bingley to the Belfry. But, without any doubt, the greatest moment at the course came in 1985 when Tony Jacklin captained the European team to victory in the Ryder Cup for the first time in 28 years.

Brabazon course
Length 7176 yd (6562 m)
Par 72
Course record 63 – Eamonn Darcy (State Express Classic, 1983)

Benson and Hedges International Open

Held every year since 1971, the Benson and Hedges International Open has its home at Fulford near York. However, in 1979 international golf was taken to Cornwall and played on the St Mellion course.

The event began its life as the Benson and Hedges Tournament. It became the Benson and Hedges Festival in 1972, acquiring its current title in 1977.

During the 1985 event the Welsh player, Ian Woosnam, equalled the world record of eight consecutive birdies in one round and eventually finished second to Sandy Lyle. Ten years earlier the American, Doug Sanders, had hit a championship best 62 in the third round.

Winners

Year	Name	Venue	Score
1971	A. Jacklin	Fulford	279
1972	J. Newton	Fulford	281
1973	V. Baker	Fulford	276
1974	P. Toussaint	Fulford	276
1975	V. Fernandez	Fulford	266
1976	G. Marsh	Fulford	272
1977	A. Garrido	Fulford	280
1978	L. Trevino	Fulford	274
1979	M. Bembridge	St Mellion	272
1980	G. Marsh	Fulford	272
1981	T. Weiskopf	Fulford	272
1982	G. Norman	Fulford	283
1983	J. Bland	Fulford	273
1984	S. Torrance	Fulford	270
1985	A. W. Lyle	Fulford	274

Most wins
2 – Graham Marsh (1976, 1980)

Lowest score (72 holes)
226 – Vicente Fernandez (Fulford, 1975)

Best-ball

Describes a match in which one player competes against two or three others. The single player's score is matched

A great amateur golfer, John Ball was one of the first golf stylists, with a swing that was the classic of its day.

with the best individual total at each hole of the other players. It can be used for both stroke- or match-play competition.

Better Ball

Describes a four-ball match in which the lowest scoring ball of each pair of partners counts at each hole. It can apply to either stroke- or match-play conditions.

Bing Crosby Pro-Am

Now part of the US professional circuit, the Bing Crosby Pro-Am was first instituted in 1936 and played at the Rancho Santa Fe club in California. After the war Crosby joined the Cypress Point club and made it the event's new home. It soon outgrew Cypress Point and had to be moved to its present site at Pebble Beach, also in California. The profits from the tournament go to charities, many of which have benefited over the years.

Winners (since 1970)

1970	B. Yancey	278	1978	T. Watson	280
1971	T. Shaw	278	1979	L. Hinckle	284
1972	J. Nicklaus	284	1980	G. Burns	286
1973	J. Nicklaus	282	1981	J. Cook	209(a)
1974	J. Miller	208(a)	1982	J. Simons	274
1975	G. Littler	280	1983	T. Kite	276
1976	B. Crenshaw	281	1984	H. Irwin	278
1977	T. Watson	273	1985	M. O'Meara	283

(a) over 54 holes

Most wins

4 – Sam Snead (1937, 1938, 1941, 1950)

Lowest score (72 holes)

273 – Tom Watson (1977)

Birdie

A score of one stroke under par for a hole. The expression originated in the United States in the early part of the 20th century and is reputed to have been first used by Ab Smith. While playing at Atlantic City he put his second shot at a par 4 just inches away from the hole. He turned to his two playing partners and said: 'That was one bird of a shot.'

Some records involving birdies:

Most successive birdies in one round

8 – Bob Goalby (US): St Petersburg Open, Pasadena, 1961

8 – Fuzzy Zoeller (US): Quad Cities tournament, Oakwood, 1976

8 – Severiano Ballesteros (Spain): Italian Open, Milan, 1985

8 – Ian Woosnam (GB): Benson and Hedges International Open, Fulford, 1985

Most birdies in one round

11 – Jimmy Martin (GB): Swallow-Penfold Tournament, Stoneham, 1961 (Martin also registered one eagle)

Most birdies in one round in British Open

10 – Christy O'Connor, Jnr: Sandwich, 1985

Bisque

A form of handicapping which enables a player to take a stroke at the hole of his choice. Rather than take advantage of the stroke index system which, on occasions, can be of no use, players agree before each match how many bisques, or strokes, a player is allowed. He may use them at any hole and may use more than one per hole. The advantage of the bisque handicap is that a player can choose to use it after he has completed the hole, but before the beginning of the next. This system is beneficial under match-play conditions because a player can use one of his bisques to turn a halved-hole into a win. The bisque system is used only in friendly matches and not in competitive play.

Blaster

The blaster was a lofted club formerly used for 'blasting' the ball out of a bunker or from difficult lies. It was the forerunner of the sand wedge.

Bobby Jones Award

An annual award made by the US Golf Association to a person who has displayed distinguished sportsmanship in golf. Named after one of the finest and most sporting golfers ever, it was first presented in 1955.

Recipients

1955	Francis Ouimet	1971	Arnold Palmer
1956	Bill Campbell	1972	Michael Bonallack
1957	Mildred Zaharias	1973	Gene Littler
1958	Margaret Curtis	1974	Byron Nelson
1959	Findlay Douglas	1975	Jack Nicklaus
1960	Charles Evans, Jnr	1976	Ben Hogan
1961	Joe Carr	1977	Joseph C. Dey
1962	Horton Smith	1978	Bob Hope and Bing Crosby
1963	Patty Berg	1979	Tom Kite
1964	Charles Coe	1980	Charles Yates
1965	Glenna Vare	1981	Jo-Anne Carner
1966	Gary Player	1982	William Patton
1967	Richard Tufts	1983	Maureen Garrett
1968	Robert Dickson	1984	Fuzzy Zoeller
1969	Gerald Micklem	1985	Jeff Sweetser
1970	Roberto de Vicenzo		

Bob Hope Classics

The Bob Hope Classic in the US is unique among world professional tournaments because it is played over five rounds. Show business personalities and leading amateurs join the professionals, with each pro playing a different set of three amateurs/personalities on each of four different courses. The leading professionals at the end of four rounds then play-off on a fifth course.

The first Classic was held in 1960 and won by Arnold Palmer. Ironically, Palmer's last US Tour win, in 1973, was also the Bob Hope Classic.

Craig Stadler and former British Open winner Bill Rogers both enjoyed their first US Tour wins in the Classic, in 1980 and 1978 respectively, but one man who does not have such pleasant memories is former US Vice-president Spiro Agnew. In 1970 a wayward shot of his hit Doug Sanders on the head and the following year, he hit three spectators with his first two tee shots!

The Bob Hope Classic was introduced to Britain in 1980

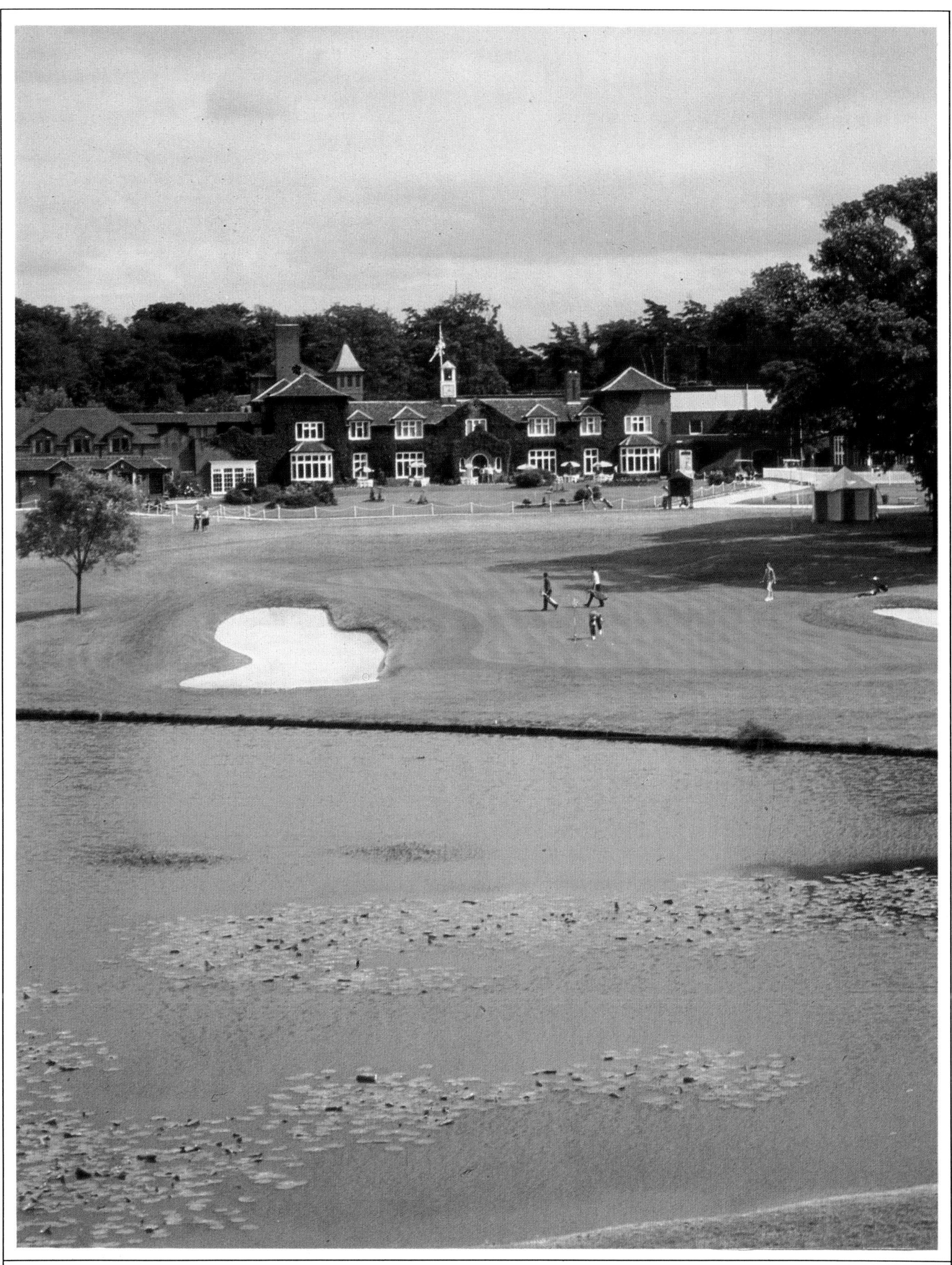

The beautiful setting of the Belfry, England's answer to the Augusta National.

when it was held at the RAC Club, Epsom, Surrey. Unlike its American counterpart it was only played over four rounds and the first winner was Spain's José-Maria Canizares, who also won the last event in 1983. One man largely responsible for the organization of the British Classic was the late entertainer Dickie Henderson.

Winners – US (since 1970)

1970	B. Devlin	339	1979	J. Mahaffey	343
1971	A. Palmer	342	1980	C. Stadler	343
1972	B. Rosburg	344	1981	B. Lietzke	335
1973	A. Palmer	343	1982	E. Fiori	335
1974	H. Green	341	1983	K. Fergus	335
1975	J. Miller	339	1984	J. Mahaffey	340
1976	J. Miller	344	1985	L. Wadkins	333
1977	R. Massengale	337	1986	D. Hammond	335
1978	B. Rogers	339			

Most wins
5 – Arnold Palmer (1960, 1962, 1968, 1971, 1973)

Lowest score (90 holes)
333 – L. Wadkins (1985)

Winners – Great Britain

1980	J-M. Canizares	RAC Club, Epsom	269
1981	B. Langer	Moor Park	200(a)
1982	G. Brand, Jnr	Moor Park	272
1983	J-M. Canizares	Moor Park	269

(a) over 54 holes

Most wins
2 – José-Maria Canizares (1980, 1983)

Lowest score (72 holes)
269 – José-Maria Canizares (1980, 1983)

Bogey

In Britain this is the number of strokes in which a good player is expected to complete a hole or a course. In the United States, however, it describes a hole which has been played one stroke over par.

In a bogey competition the participants play to the bogey of each hole and receive three-quarters of their handicap. They receive plus one point if they complete a hole under par, no points for a par and minus one point if a hole is played over par. The player with the most points at the end of the round is the winner.

Bonallack, Michael

Michael Bonallack was elected president of the English Golf Union in 1982 and appointed secretary of the Royal and Ancient Club the following year. Both appointments were just rewards for a man who had been one of the best British amateur players of the present day.

He won the English Amateur title a record five times and the Amateur Championship five times, including three in succession. Bonallack was selected for every Great Britain Walker Cup team between 1957 and 1973, and was captain in 1969 and 1971. He also represented England in every Home International championship between 1957 and 1974. He was awarded the OBE in 1971.

Although he did not possess a text-book swing, he made up for that with an excellent short game. Alan Thirwell felt the full force of this during the 1963 English Amateur Championship at Burnham and Berrow. The match lasted 33 holes and Bonallack was down in two from the edge of the green no less than 22 times.

Bonallack is not the only member of his family to play golf. His sister Sally was a Curtis Cup player, winning the English Women's Championship in 1968, the same year in which Michael gained the men's title. Michael's wife Angela was twice English Women's champion and her sister, Shirley Ward, was English Girls' champion. Michael's brother Tony played county golf for Essex.

Career highlights
English Amateur 1962, 1963, 1965, 1967, 1968
Amateur Championship 1961, 1965, 1968, 1969, 1970
Walker Cup 1957, 1959, 1961, 1963, 1965, 1967, 1969 (capt), 1971 (capt), 1973

Books

The first golf book published was *The Golfers' Manual* in 1857. Many of the points made by its author, H. B. Farnie, who wrote under the pseudonym A. Keen Hand, are still relevant to the game as it is played today.

The first book to be published in the United States was *Golf in America, a Practical Manual* by James P. Lee. It was published in 1895.

Boros, Julius

In 1963 Julius Boros beat Arnold Palmer and Jacky Cupit in a play-off to win his second US Open. In doing so he became, at 43, the oldest American holder of the title. Five years later he became the oldest winner of the US PGA title.

This maturity is hardly surprising since Boros did not turn professional until the age of 30 after abandoning his career in accountancy. He had to wait less than three years before he won his first major title, the 1952 US Open. That year he was top money winner in the United States—a feat he repeated in 1955.

Boros had the perfect temperament for golf and the ability to relax at crucial moments. His swing was wristy but, nevertheless, very effective.

In 1977, 27 years after collecting his first golf winnings, Boros became the 14th man to win over $1 million from the sport.

Career highlights
US Open 1952, 1963
US PGA 1968
Ryder Cup 1959, 1963, 1965, 1967
British Open (best) 15th – 1966

Brabazon Trophy

The award presented to the winner of the English Open Amateur Stroke-Play Championship. The championship was first contested as the English Golf Union International Brabazon Trophy, in 1947 and changed to its current name in 1957.

Winners (since 1965)

Year	Name	Venue	Score
1965	C. A. Clark / D. J. Millensted / M. J. Burgess (tie)	Formby	289
1966	P. M. Townsend	Hunstanton	282
1967	R. D. B. M. Shade	Saunton	299
1968	M. F. Bonallack	Walton Heath	210 (*)
1969	R. Foster / M. F. Bonallack (tie)	Moortown	290
1970	R. Foster	Little Aston	287
1971	M. F. Bonallack	Hillside	294
1972	P. H. Moody	Hoylake	296
1973	R. Revell	Hunstanton	294
1974	N. Sundelson	Moortown	291
1975	A. W. Lyle	Hollinwell	298
1976	P. Hedges	Saunton	294
1977	A. W. Lyle	Hoylake	293
1978	G. Brand	Woodhall Spa	289
1979	D. Long	Little Aston	291
1980	R. Rafferty / P. McEvoy (tie)	Hunstanton	293
1981	P. Way	Hillside	292
1982	P. Downes	Woburn	299
1983	C. Banks	Hollinwell	294
1984	M. Davis	Cinque Ports	286
1985	R. Roper / P. Baker (tie)	Seaton Carew	296
1986	R. Kaplan	Sunningdale	286

(*) played over 54 holes

Most wins
4 – M. F. Bonallack (including one shared)

Lowest score (72 holes)
282 – P. M. Townsend (Hunstanton, 1966)

Braid, James

At the beginning of the 20th century James Braid, together with Harry Vardon and John Taylor, did more than anyone else to popularize golf in Britain. The three of them became known as the 'Great Triumvirate'.

Braid was born in Fife, Scotland, in 1870. A joiner by trade, he was tempted to London in 1893 to become a club-maker for the Army and Navy Stores. He turned professional that year and appeared in the first British Open outside Scotland, at Sandwich, in 1894.

The glory years for Braid were between 1901 and 1910. In that period he won the British Open five times and was runner-up on three occasions. His score of 291 at Prestwick in 1908 was an Open record that stood until beaten by Bobby Jones in 1927.

Braid was a powerful golfer and greatly respected by fellow professionals. One of the founder members of the Professional Golfers Association, he was the professional at Walton Heath for 45 years. In later life he was much sought after as a course designer and in 1950 was made an honorary member of the Royal and Ancient Club. He died in 1950.

See also Great Triumvirate.

Career highlights
British Open 1901, 1905, 1906, 1908, 1910
British Professional Match-Play 1903, 1905, 1907, 1911
French Open 1910

Braid Taylor Memorial Medal

Named after two members of the 'Great Triumvirate', James Braid and John Taylor, the award is made to the PGA member born in the United Kingdom or Republic of Ireland, or has one or both parents born in the United Kingdom or Republic of Ireland, who finishes highest in the British Open. The award was first made in 1966.

Winners

Year	Name	Position
1966	Dave Thomas	jt 2nd
1967	Clive Clark	jt 3rd
1968	Maurice Bembridge	5th
1969	Tony Jacklin	1st
1970	Tony Jacklin	5th
1971	Tony Jacklin	3rd
1972	Tony Jacklin	3rd
1973	Neil Coles	jt 2nd
1974	Peter Oosterhuis	2nd
1975	Peter Oosterhuis	jt 7th
	Neil Coles	jt 7th
1976	Tommy Horton	jt 5th
	Mark James	jt 5th
	Christy O'Connor, Jnr	jt 5th
1977	Tommy Horton	jt 9th
1978	Peter Oosterhuis	6th
1979	Mark James	4th
1980	Carl Mason	jt 4th
1981	Mark James	jt 3rd
1982	Peter Oosterhuis	jt 2nd
1983	Denis Durnian	jt 8th
	Nick Faldo	jt 8th
	Christy O'Connor, Jnr	jt 8th
1984	Nick Faldo	jt 6th
1985	Sandy Lyle	1st

Most wins
4 – Tony Jacklin
4 – Peter Oosterhuis

Brassie

Brassie (or brassey) is the old name for a No 2 wood. It was so called because it had a brass sole plate. Like the No 2 wood it was slightly lofted and was used for playing long shots from the fairway.

British Boys' Amateur Championship

A match-play competition open to boys under the age of 18. Established in 1921, it was the idea of Donald Mathieson, owner of *Golf Monthly*, and Lt Col Thomas South of Sutton Coldfield. It has been organized by the Royal and Ancient Club since 1949.

Winners (since 1965)

1965	G. R. Milne	1976	M. Mouland
1966	A. Phillips	1977	I. Ford
1967	L. P. Tupling	1978	S. Keppler
1968	S. C. Evans	1979	R. Rafferty
1969	M. Foster	1980	D. Muscroft
1970	I. D. Gradwell	1981	J. Lopez
1971	H. Clark	1982	M. Grieve
1972	G. Harvey	1983	J-M. Olazabal
1973	D. M. Robertson	1984	L. Vannett
1974	T. R. Shannon	1985	J. Cook
1975	B. Marchbank		

Most wins

2 – A. D. D. Mathieson (1921, 1923)
2 – R. W. Peattie (1924, 1925)
2 – J. Lindsay (1929, 1930)
2 – P. M. Townsend (1962, 1964)

Biggest winning margin (final)

A. Phillips beat A. Muller 12 & 11 (Moortown, 1966)

British Ladies' Open Amateur Championship

The Ladies' Golf Union was founded in 1893 and that same year held its first championship. The venue was St Annes, where women golfers had their own course, and the first winner was Lady Margaret Scott, who went on to win the next two championships before retiring.

The roll of honour for the championship contains many famous names. Joyce Wethered, perhaps the greatest woman golfer of all time, won the title four times. Cecilia Leitch also won the title four times and each victory was achieved in a different country—at Hunstanton (England), Newcastle, County Down (Northern Ireland), Turnberry (Scotland) and Harlech (Wales). Two great all-round sportswomen also won the title—Lottie Dod and Mildred Zaharias.

Winners (since 1965)

Year	Name	Venue	Score
1965	Miss B. Varangot (France)	St Andrews	4 & 3
1966	Miss E. Chadwick	Ganton	3 & 2
1967	Miss E. Chadwick	Harlech	1 hole
1968	Miss B. Varangot (France)	Walton Heath	20th hole
1969	Miss C. Lacoste (France)	Portrush	1 hole
1970	Miss D. Oxley	Gullane	1 hole
1971	Miss M. Walker	Alwoodley	3 & 1
1972	Miss M. Walker	Hunstanton	2 holes
1973	Miss A. Irvin	Carnoustie	3 & 2
1974	Miss C. Semple (US)	Porthcawl	2 & 1
1975	Mrs N. Syms (US)	St Andrews	3 & 2
1976	Miss C. Panton	Silloth	1 hole
1977	Mrs A. Uzielli	Hillside	6 & 5
1978	Miss E. Kennedy (Australia)	Notts	1 hole
1979	Miss M. Madill	Nairn	2 & 1
1980	Mrs A. Sander (US)	Woodhall Spa	3 & 1
1981	Mrs I. C. Robertson	Conway	20th hole
1982	Miss K. Douglas	Walton Heath	4 & 2
1983	Mrs J. Thornhill	Silloth	4 & 2
1984	Miss J. Rosenthal (US)	Troon	4 & 3
1985	Miss L. Behan	Ganton	1 hole
1986	Miss M. McGuire (NZ)	West Sussex	2 & 1

Most wins

4 – Cecilia Leitch (1914, 1920, 1921, 1926)
4 – Joyce Wethered (1922, 1924, 1925, 1929)

Biggest winning margin (final)

Joyce Wethered beat Cecilia Leitch 9 & 7 (Prince's, Sandwich, 1922)

First overseas winner

Miss Thion de la Chaume (France) 1927

British Open

The first championship of its kind, to play in the British Open remains the ultimate dream of every golfer. No matter how many of the other major titles he may win no professional golfer can regard his career as complete without winning the British Open.

Played over some of the finest seaside links in the world, it is not the prize money that attracts world stars to British shores every July to contest the Open, but the fact that it is part of golfing tradition—just as Wimbledon remains Lawn Tennis's supreme prize.

The first Open was organized by members of the Prestwick Club, and on 17 October 1860 Musselburgh's Willie Park beat a field of eight players with a 36-hole total of 174—two better than Old Tom Morris. The 36 holes were played in one day, and over three rounds of Prestwick's 12-hole course.

Prestwick was to play host to the championship a record 24 times between then and 1925. It was not until 1873 that the championship first moved to another venue: St Andrews. Before it moved, Prestwick had been fortunate enough to see the first of the great champions, Tom Morris, Jnr, who won the title four times in succession. His third successive win, in 1870, meant he could keep the Championship Belt that the Prestwick Club had provided for the winner. With no trophy in 1871 the Open was not held but the Prestwick Club persuaded the Royal and Ancient Club and the Honourable Company of Edinburgh Golfers to share with them the cost of a new trophy: a magnificent silver claret jug. The Open with the new trophy was contested in 1872 and is still the most cherished prize in world golf.

The 1894 Open was very significant: it was played at Sandwich, the first time it had been taken out of Scotland. The winner was J. H. Taylor—the first English professional to win the title. It was further significant as it marked the start of the domination of the championship by the Great Triumvirate of Taylor, James Braid and Harry Vardon.

Between 1894 and 1914, they won 16 championships

Arnold Palmer receives the Eisenhower Trophy after winning the Bob Hope Desert Classic at Palm Springs. Left to right: Dwight Eisenhower, Bob Hope, Ronald Reagan and Arnold Palmer.

Henry Cotton (right) and Horton Smith during the 1937 British Open at Carnoustie, which Cotton won.

between them. And in the five they did not win during that period, at least one of them finished second on each occasion.

One winner during the Triumvirate's reign was Frenchman Arnaud Massy who won in 1907 to take the title to Europe for the first time.

After the First World War, the Open had become too big for individual clubs to organize so in 1919 the Royal and Ancient agreed to take over the running of the championship.

The inter-war years saw British golfers lose their grip on the championship—and it was never to return. Jock Hutchison, in 1920, became the first American to win the title, and between then and the outbreak of the Second World War, American golfers won 12 times. The two most outstanding were Walter Hagen, who won on four occasions—three of them on English courses, and Bobby Jones, the last amateur to win the title. He won in 1926, 1927 and 1930, but his 1930 success was part of one of golf's greatest 'Grand Slams'. Not only did he win the British Open title, but also the US Open *and* the amateur titles of both countries.

Henry Cotton's win at Sandwich in 1934 brought some encouragement to the British fans as he ended a run of ten successive American victories. It was the start of a mini British revival, as all winners up to the war were British, including a second title for Cotton at Carnoustie in 1937.

The United States, thanks to Sam Snead, won the first

The large gallery watch Peter Thomson play an iron shot at the 17th hole during the 1956 Open at Hoylake. The Australian went on to win the championship for a third successive year.

Gary Player during the 1959 Open. Despite a disastrous first round he clawed his way back to win.

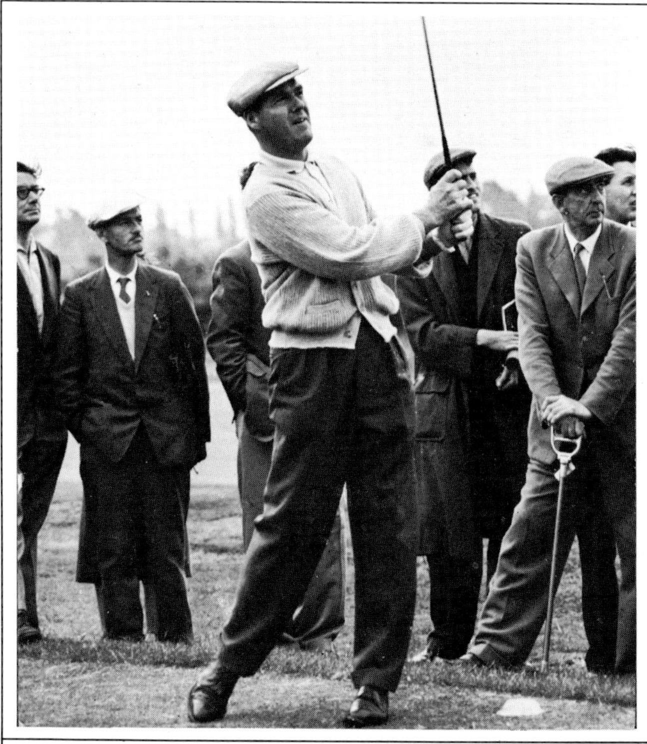

Kel Nagle, the winner of the Centenary Open in 1960, seen here during the first round at St Andrews.

Caddie Jimmy Dickinson watching apprehensively as Jack Nicklaus successfully gets out of a bunker in front of the 11th green during the 1966 Open at Muirfield.

'It's all mine' seems to be the expression on Tony Jacklin's face as he holds aloft the British Open trophy after winning at Royal Lytham in 1969.

post-war Open, but that was to be their last win until Ben Hogan in 1953 and Arnold Palmer in 1961. In the meantime the Commonwealth enjoyed a successful spell.

Cotton won his third title in 1948 but up to, and including, the centenary championship in 1960, South Africa and Australia shared ten wins between them. Bobby Locke, with four wins, and Gary Player with one, were the South African winners. While Peter Thomson (four) and Kel Nagle, the centenary winner, were the Australian champions.

Thomson won a fifth title in 1965 to become the first man to win twice at Birkdale, but the interim years had seen the arrival of one of golf's greats—Arnold Palmer.

Towards the late 1950s, many Americans were no longer making the trip across the Atlantic. Palmer was instrumental in getting many of them to return. His winning the title twice reminded them how important the championship was. Had Palmer not arrived, the championship could well have lost its standing as the world's greatest tournament.

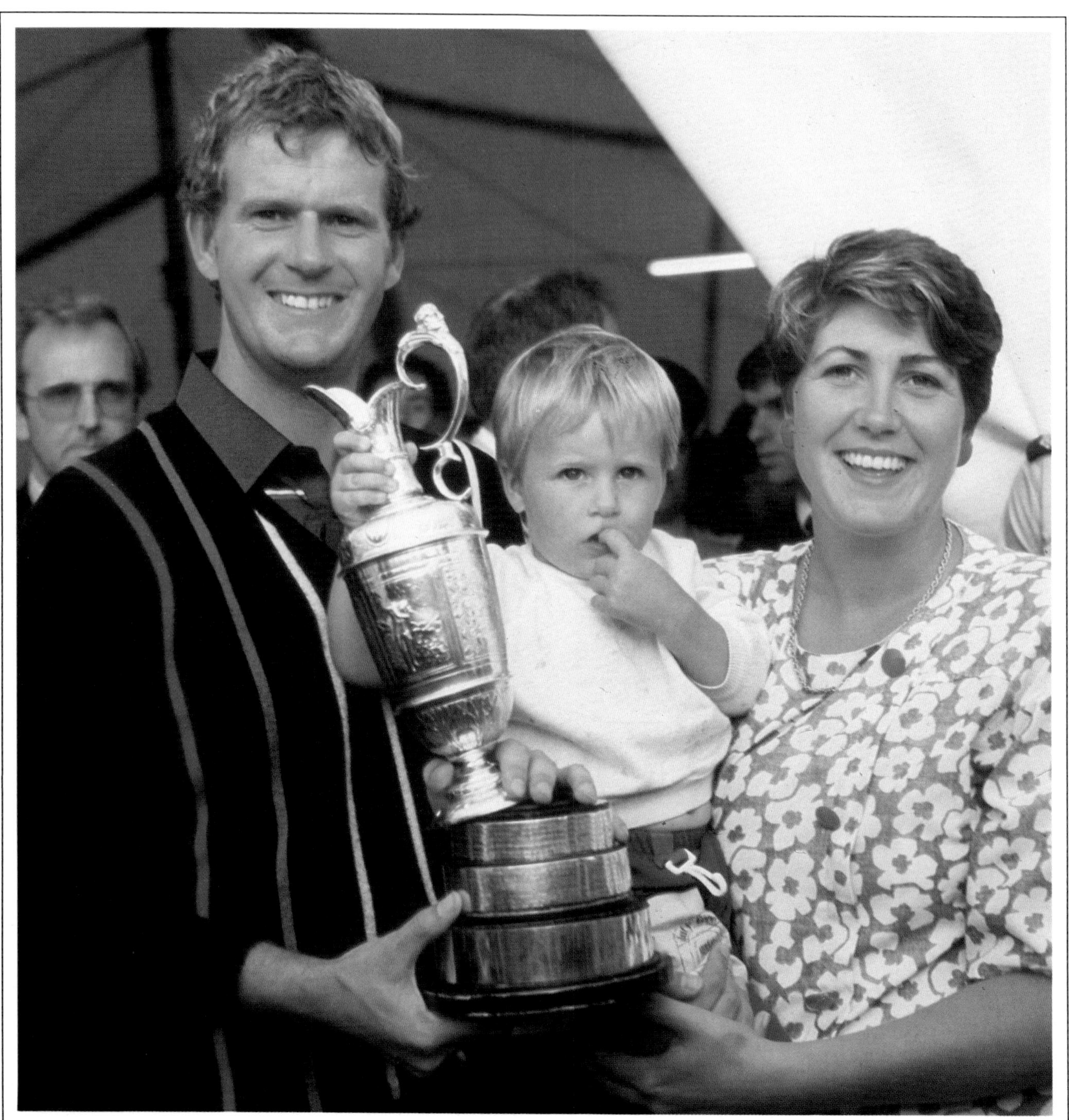

A delighted Lyle family. Sandy, with son Stuart and wife Christine, celebrates becoming the first Briton since Tony Jacklin to win the British Open.

Severiano Ballesteros after he won his first British Open, at Royal Lytham, in 1979.

The 1960s saw the arrival of the next in the long line of golfing greats to win the British Open—Jack Nicklaus. He first won the title at Muirfield in 1966 and went on to win it twice at St Andrews, in 1970 and 1978.

Nicklaus was just one of the new breed of American golfer ready to step up and take golf's supreme prize. There was also Tom Weiskopf, Johnny Miller and five times winner Tom Watson. But amidst all the American success came one lone British win, in 1969. At Royal Lytham, Tony Jacklin emerged from the crowds on the 18th as champion, the first Briton since Max Faulkner, in 1951, to win the title. Jacklin's win was to be the last by a British golfer until 1985 when Sandy Lyle won the title at Sandwich. However, the American stranglehold had been broken by Spain's Severiano Ballesteros who won the title in 1979 and again in 1984.

Prize money now exceeds £500,000 with the winner picking up more than £60,000. But the winning of the British Open carries much more in prestige; the gold medal presented to the winner, which he may keep, is one of golf's most cherished prizes.

Winners

Year	Name	Venue	Score
1860	W. Park (Snr)	Prestwick	174 (a)
1861	T. Morris (Snr)	Prestwick	163 (a)
1862	T. Morris (Snr)	Prestwick	163 (a)
1863	W. Park (Snr)	Prestwick	168 (a)
1864	T. Morris (Snr)	Prestwick	167 (a)
1865	A. Strath	Prestwick	162 (a)
1866	W. Park (Snr)	Prestwick	169 (a)
1867	T. Morris (Snr)	Prestwick	170 (a)
1868	T. Morris (Jnr)	Prestwick	157 (a)
1869	T. Morris (Jnr)	Prestwick	154 (a)
1870	T. Morris (Jnr)	Prestwick	149 (a)
1871	Not held		
1872	T. Morris (Jnr)	Prestwick	166 (a)
1873	T. Kidd	St Andrews	179 (a)
1874	M. Park	Musselburgh	159 (a)
1875	W. Park (Snr)	Prestwick	166 (a)
1876	B. Martin	St Andrews	176 (a)
1877	J. Anderson	Musselburgh	166 (a)
1878	J. Anderson	Prestwick	157 (a)
1879	J. Anderson	St Andrews	169 (a)
1880	B. Ferguson	Musselburgh	162 (a)
1881	B. Ferguson	Prestwick	170 (a)
1882	B. Ferguson	St Andrews	171 (a)
1883	W. Fernie	Musselburgh	159 (a)
1884	J. Simpson	Prestwick	160 (a)
1885	B. Martin	St Andrews	171 (a)
1886	D. Brown	Musselburgh	157 (a)
1887	W. Park (Jnr)	Prestwick	161 (a)
1888	J. Burns	St Andrews	171 (a)
1889	W. Park (Jnr)	Musselburgh	155 (a)
1890	J. Ball (*)	Prestwick	164 (a)
1891	H. Kirkaldy	St Andrews	166 (a)
1892	H. H. Hilton (*)	Muirfield	305
1893	W. Auchterlone	Prestwick	322
1894	J. H. Taylor	Sandwich	326
1895	J. H. Taylor	St Andrews	322
1896	H. Vardon	Muirfield	316
1897	H. H. Hilton (*)	Hoylake	314
1898	H. Vardon	Prestwick	307
1899	H. Vardon	Sandwich	310
1900	J. H. Taylor	St Andrews	309
1901	J. Braid	Muirfield	309
1902	A. Herd	Hoylake	307
1903	H. Vardon	Prestwick	300
1904	J. White	Sandwich	296
1905	J. Braid	St Andrews	318
1906	J. Braid	Muirfield	300
1907	A. Massy	Hoylake	312
1908	J. Braid	Prestwick	291
1909	J. H. Taylor	Deal	295
1910	J. Braid	St Andrews	299
1911	H. Vardon	Sandwich	303
1912	E. Ray	Muirfield	295
1913	J. H. Taylor	Hoylake	304
1914	H. Vardon	Prestwick	306
1915–19	Not held		
1920	G. Duncan	Deal	303
1921	J. Hutchison	St Andrews	296
1922	W. Hagen	Sandwich	300
1923	A. G. Havers	Troon	295
1924	W. Hagen	Hoylake	301
1925	J. Barnes	Prestwick	300
1926	R. T. Jones (*)	Lytham	291
1927	R. T. Jones (*)	St Andrews	285
1928	W. Hagen	Sandwich	292
1929	W. Hagen	Muirfield	292
1930	R. T. Jones (*)	Hoylake	291
1931	T. D. Armour	Carnoustie	296
1932	G. Sarazen	Prince's	283
1933	D. Shute	St Andrews	292
1934	T. H. Cotton	Sandwich	283
1935	A. Perry	Muirfield	283
1936	A. H. Padgham	Hoylake	287
1937	T. H. Cotton	Carnoustie	290
1938	R. A. Whitcombe	Sandwich	295
1939	R. Burton	St Andrews	290
1940–45	Not held		
1946	S. Snead	St Andrews	290
1947	F. Daly	Hoylake	293
1948	T. H. Cotton	Muirfield	284
1949	A. D. Locke	Sandwich	283
1950	A. D. Locke	Troon	279
1951	M. Faulkner	Portrush	285
1952	A. D. Locke	Lytham	287
1953	B. Hogan	Carnoustie	282
1954	P. W. Thomson	Birkdale	283
1955	P. W. Thomson	St Andrews	281
1956	P. W. Thomson	Hoylake	286
1957	A. D. Locke	St Andrews	279
1958	P. W. Thomson	Lytham	278
1959	G. Player	Muirfield	284
1960	K. D. Nagle	St Andrews	278
1961	A. D. Palmer	Birkdale	284
1962	A. D. Palmer	Troon	276
1963	R. J. Charles	Lytham	277
1964	A. Lema	St Andrews	279
1965	P. W. Thomson	Birkdale	285
1966	J. W. Nicklaus	Muirfield	282
1967	R. de Vicenzo	Hoylake	278
1968	G. Player	Carnoustie	289
1969	A. Jacklin	Lytham	280
1970	J. W. Nicklaus	St Andrews	283
1971	L. Trevino	Birkdale	278
1972	L. Trevino	Muirfield	278
1973	T. Weiskopf	Troon	276
1974	G. Player	Lytham	282
1975	T. Watson	Carnoustie	279
1976	J. Miller	Birkdale	279
1977	T. Watson	Turnberry	268
1978	J. Nicklaus	St Andrews	281
1979	S. Ballesteros	Lytham	283
1980	T. Watson	Muirfield	271
1981	B. Rogers	Sandwich	276
1982	T. Watson	Troon	284
1983	T. Watson	Birkdale	275
1984	S. Ballesteros	St Andrews	276
1985	A. W. Lyle	Sandwich	282

(a) Played over 36 holes
(*) Denotes amateur

British Open Records

Most wins (two or more)

6 – Harry Vardon (1896, 1898, 1899, 1903, 1911, 1914)
5 – James Braid (1901, 1905, 1906, 1908, 1910)
5 – J. H. Taylor (1894, 1895, 1900, 1909, 1913)
5 – Peter Thomson (1954, 1955, 1956, 1958, 1965)
5 – Tom Watson (1975, 1977, 1980, 1982, 1983)
4 – Tom Morris, Snr (1861, 1862, 1864, 1867)
4 – Tom Morris, Jnr (1868, 1869, 1870, 1872)
4 – Willie Park, Snr (1860, 1863, 1866, 1875)
4 – Walter Hagen (1922, 1924, 1928, 1929)
4 – Bobby Locke (1949, 1950, 1952, 1957)
3 – Jamie Anderson (1877, 1878, 1879)
3 – Bob Ferguson (1880, 1881, 1882)
3 – Bobby Jones (1926, 1927, 1930)
3 – Henry Cotton (1934, 1937, 1948)
3 – Gary Player (1959, 1968, 1974)
3 – Jack Nicklaus (1966, 1970, 1978)
2 – Bob Martin (1876, 1885)
2 – Harold Hilton (1892, 1897)
2 – Willie Park, Jnr (1887, 1889)
2 – Arnold Palmer (1961, 1962)
2 – Lee Trevino (1971, 1972)
2 – Severiano Ballesteros (1979, 1984)

Oldest winner

46 yrs 99 days – Tom Morris, Snr (1867)

Youngest winner

17 yrs 161 days – Tom Morris, Jnr (1868)

Progressive records (72 holes)

305 – Harold Hilton (1892)
300 – Harry Vardon (1903)
296 – Jack White (1904)
291 – James Braid (1908)
291 – Bobby Jones (1926)
285 – Bobby Jones (1927)
283 – Gene Sarazen (1932)
283 – Henry Cotton (1934)
283 – Alf Perry (1935)
283 – Bobby Locke (1949)
279 – Bobby Locke (1950)
279 – Bobby Locke (1957)
278 – Peter Thomson (1958)
278 – Kel Nagle (1960)
276 – Arnold Palmer (1961)
276 – Tom Weiskopf (1973)
268 – Tom Watson (1977)

Lowest 18 holes

63 – Mark Hayes (1977)
63 – Isao Aoki (1980)

British Open courses

Number of Times Used	Course	Year First Used	First Winner	Year Last Used
24	Prestwick	1860	W. Park, Snr	1925
23	St Andrews	1873	T. Kidd	1984
12	Muirfield	1892	H. H. Hilton	1980
11	Sandwich	1894	J. H. Taylor	1985
10	Hoylake	1897	H. H. Hilton	1967
7	Lytham	1926	R. T. Jones	1979
6	Musselburgh	1874	M. Park	1889
6	Birkdale	1954	P. W. Thomson	1983
5	Troon	1923	A. G. Havers	1982
5	Carnoustie	1931	T. D. Armour	1975
2	Deal	1909	J. H. Taylor	1920
1	Prince's	1932	G. Sarazen	1932
1	Portrush	1951	M. Faulkner	1951
1	Turnberry	1977	T. Watson	1977

Tom Watson holds the record for winning the Open at *five* different courses—Carnoustie, Turnberry, Muirfield, Troon, and Birkdale.

J. H. Taylor, Bobby Locke, and Peter Thomson all won the championship on four different courses.

British Open Milestones

1860 First championship held at Prestwick.
1865 Official scorecards were introduced.
1868 Young Tom Morris performed the first hole-in-one at the Open.
1885 The number of entrants for the competition passed 50 for the first time.
1890 John Ball became the first English, and first amateur, winner.
1892 Championship extended from 36 to 72 holes.
1894 First championship held in England, at Sandwich.
1907 Qualifying rounds first introduced.
1907 Arnaud Massy, from France, became the first overseas winner.
1914 First newsreel film made of the championship.
1919 The Royal and Ancient Club took over the management of the Open.
1921 Jock Hutchison, a Scot living in America, took the trophy out of Britain for the first time.
1922 Walter Hagen became the first American-born winner of the championship.
1934 Henry Cotton's round of 65 at Sandwich was to remain unbeaten until 1977.
1955 The first £1,000 first prize was at stake.
1955 BBC television covered the championship live for the first time.
1960 Kel Nagle of Australia won the Centenary Championship.
1963 New Zealand's Bob Charles became the first left-hander to win a major championship.
1966 Jack Nicklaus won the first Open scheduled to have been finished on a Saturday. Previously two rounds were played on the Friday to complete the championship.
1971 Lee Trevino won the 100th Open.
1974 The larger ball was made compulsory.
1977 Tom Watson won the first £10,000 first prize, as total prize money topped £100,000 for the first time.
1980 Play started on a Thursday and finished on a Sunday for the first time.
1984 Severiano Ballesteros won the first £50,000 first prize.

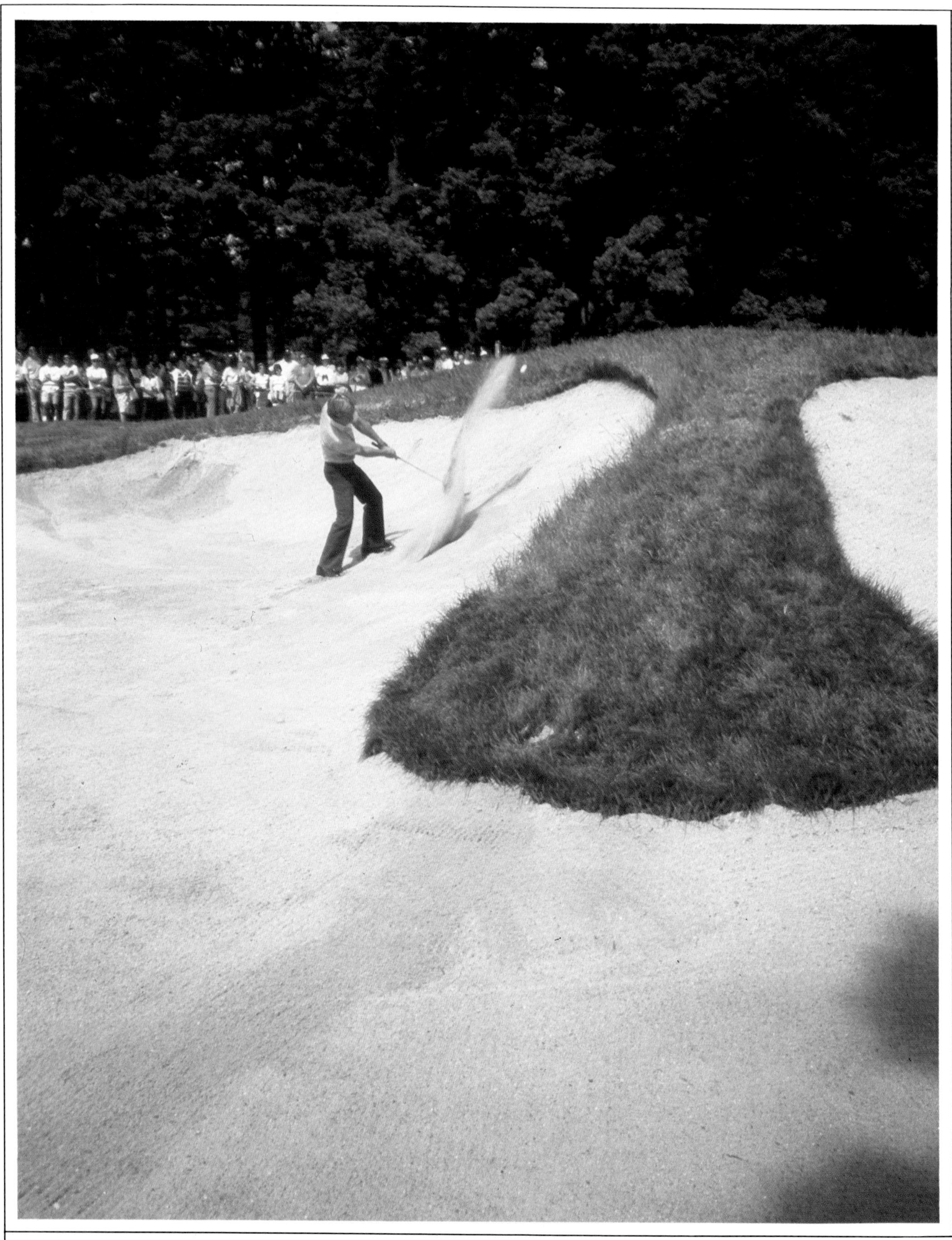

Ben Crenshaw successfully getting out of one of the larger bunkers on the Winged Foot course during the 1984 US Open.

Bunker
A bunker, or trap as it is called in the United States, is a crater in the ground filled with sand. Initially bunkers were natural hazards found on links courses but today most courses have strategically placed artificial bunkers. A player must not ground his club when setting up to play out of a bunker.

The biggest bunker in the world is on the 7th hole at the Pine Valley course, New Jersey. Appropriately it is called Hell's Half Acre.

Burma Road
The nickname applied to the West course at the Wentworth Club in Surrey. Because of its severity it is named after the route taken through the Burma jungle during the Second World War.

C

Caddie
A person who carries the clubs of a golfer. The experienced caddie, however, plays a more important role than that. Leading professionals rely upon their caddie to assist them in reading the game, and most caddies are good golfers in their own right.

At one time caddies were a familiar sight at most clubs, but today they are rarely seen except in leading tournaments. Many professionals employ the full-time services of a caddie who will travel the world with them.

The word 'caddie' is derived from the French word *cadet*. Mary Queen of Scots, a great golf fan, is thought to have introduced the word into the sport. The first person to use the services of a caddie is believed to have been the Marquis of Montrose, in the early 17th century.

Calamity Jane
The putter used by the leading amateur, Bobby Jones, throughout his career. It was given to him by an exiled Scot, and Jones was so successful with it that he named it after the legendary Wild West figure, Calamity Jane, who, like the putter, was supposed to sort out people's problems.

Copies of the putter were reproduced and sold by the thousand. Unfortunately for most purchasers they did not have the same result as for Jones.

Cambuta
Cambuta (or cambuca) was a form of golf in which the ball was hit with a crooked stick. It was played in England from the 14th century onwards.

Canada Cup
See World Cup

Canadian Open
Although golf came to Canada in 1873, some 15 years before it arrived in the United States, the Canadian Open was a late starter. It was not inaugurated until 1904 when J. H. Oke of Ottawa won over 36 holes at the Royal Montreal Club. In 1907 the stroke-play competition was extended to 72 holes and has remained unaltered since. The Canadian Open ranks high behind the British and US as one of the world's leading opens. Its home since 1977 (with the exception of 1980) has been the Glen Abbey Club at Oakville, Ontario.

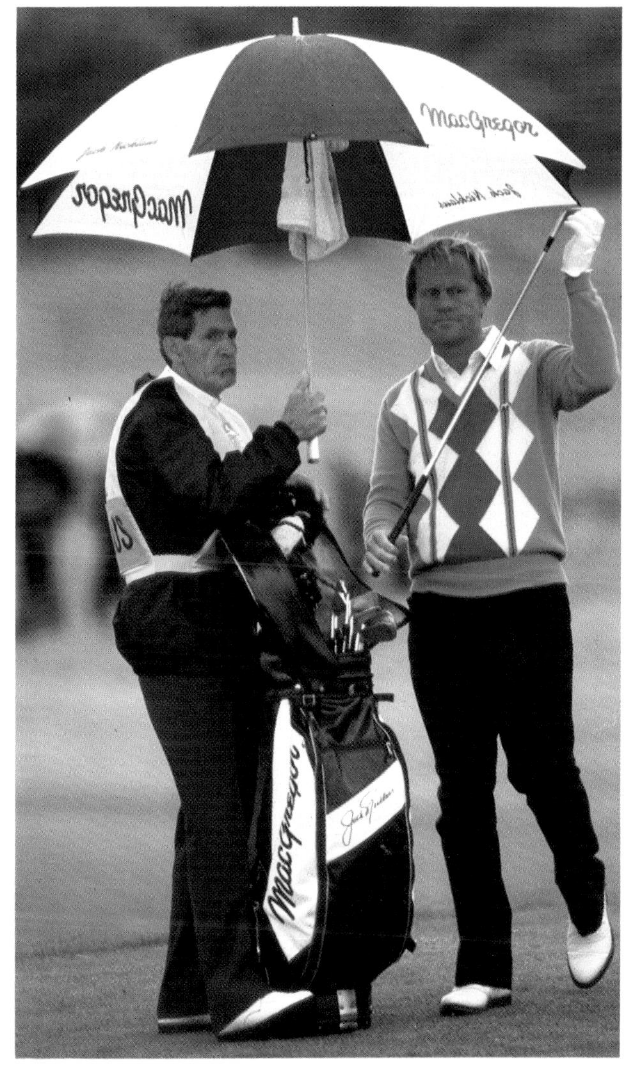

Jack Nicklaus with his caddie who has a more important role to play than just holding the umbrella!

Lee Trevino has gained the title on three occasions and his 1971 success was part of a remarkable treble that saw him win the opens of the United States, Great Britain and Canada within 21 days. The 1981 triumph of Peter Oosterhuis ended his seven-year spell on the US circuit without a win.

Canadian Open

Winners

Year	Name	Venue	Score
1904	J. H. Oke	Montreal	156(a)
1905	G. Cumming	Toronto	148(a)
1906	C. R. Murray	Ottawa	170(a)
1907	P. Barrett	Toronto	306
1908	A. Murray	Montreal	300
1909	K. Keffer	Toronto	309
1910	D. Kenny	Toronto	303
1911	C. R. Murray	Ottawa	314
1912	G. Sargeant	Toronto	299
1913	A. Murray	Montreal	295
1914	K. Keffer	Toronto	300
1915–18	Not held		
1919	J. D. Edgar	Hamilton	278
1920	J. D. Edgar	Ottawa	298
1921	W. Trovinger	Toronto	293
1922	A. Watrous	Montreal	303
1923	C. Hackney	Toronto	295
1924	L. Diegel	Montreal	285
1925	L. Diegel	Toronto	295
1926	M. Smith	Montreal	283
1927	T. Armour	Toronto	288
1928	L. Diegel	Toronto	282
1929	L. Diegel	Montreal	274
1930	T. Armour	Hamilton	277
1931	W. Hagen	Toronto	292
1932	H. Cooper	Ottawa	290
1933	J. Kirkwood	Toronto	282
1934	T. Armour	Toronto	287
1935	G. Kunes	Montreal	280
1936	W. Lawson Little	Toronto	271
1937	H. Cooper	Toronto	285
1938	S. Snead	Toronto	277
1939	H. McSpaden	St John's, New Brunswick	282
1940	S. Snead	Toronto	281
1941	S. Snead	Toronto	274
1942	C. Wood	Toronto	275
1943–44	Not held		
1945	B. Nelson	Toronto	280
1946	G. Fazio	Montreal	278
1947	A. D. Locke	Toronto	268
1948	C. Congdon	Vancouver	280
1949	E. J. Harrison	Toronto	271
1950	J. Ferrier	Montreal	271
1951	J. Ferrier	Toronto	273
1952	J. Palmer	Winnipeg	263
1953	D. Douglas	Toronto	273
1954	P. Fletcher	Vancouver	280
1955	A. Palmer	Toronto	265
1956	D. Sanders (*)	Quebec	273
1957	G. Bayer	Kitchener	271
1958	W. Ellis, Jnr	Edmonton	267
1959	D. Ford	Montreal	276
1960	A. Wall	Toronto	269
1961	J. Cupit	Winnipeg	270
1962	E. Kroll	Montreal	278
1963	D. Ford	Toronto	280
1964	K. D. Nagle	Montreal	277
1965	G. Littler	Toronto	273
1966	D. Massengale	Vancouver	280
1967	W. Casper	Montreal	279
1968	R. J. Charles	Toronto	274
1969	T. Aaron	Montreal	275
1970	K. Zarley	Oakville	279
1971	L. Trevino	Montreal	275
1972	G. Brewer	Oakville	275
1973	T. Weiskopf	Quebec	278
1974	B. Nichols	Toronto	270
1975	T. Weiskopf	Montreal	274
1976	J. Pate	Windsor	267
1977	L. Trevino	Oakville	280
1978	B. Lietzke	Oakville	283
1979	L. Trevino	Oakville	281
1980	B. Gilder	Montreal	274
1981	P. Oosterhuis	Oakville	280
1982	B. Lietzke	Oakville	277
1983	J. Cook	Oakville	277
1984	G. Norman	Oakville	278
1985	C. Strange	Oakville	279

(*) indicates amateur
(a) play over 36 holes

Most wins
4 – Leo Diegel (1924, 1925, 1928, 1929)

Lowest winning score (72 holes)
263 – John Palmer (St Charles GC, Winnipeg, 1952)

Captains

Appointed each year, the captain of the golf club is normally made from a list of long-standing members who have contributed a great deal towards the running of the club; becoming captain is considered to be a great honour. A player's handicap is irrelevant as high playing ability is not the sole factor in deciding the choice of captain.

The captain's reign of office normally lasts one year and starts with him hitting the first ball of the new season in a ceremony known as 'Driving In'. During his term of office the captain represents his club at functions at other golf clubs, and leads his club in inter-club matches.

Carnoustie

One of the longest courses in Britain, the public Carnoustie links can be stretched to more than 7200 yd (6584 m). When used for the 1968 British Open, its 7252-yd (6631-m) length made it the longest Open in history.

The famous Angus club dates back to 1842 but, surprisingly enough, it was not added to the British Open rota until 1931. Since then it has been used four more times and one of the greatest occasions in the long history of the course was in 1953 when Ben Hogan won the Open to complete his grand slam. Carnoustie was also the scene of Tom Watson's first British Open win, in 1975, when he beat Jack Newton of Australia in the play-off. The Car-

noustie club has also provided the world with many fine golfers including the 1884 British Open winner, Jack Simpson, and the US Open champions, Alex and Willie Smith. The championship course is a true test of skill, with many natural hazards, including wind, to overcome. The last three holes are the most daunting closing holes in British golf.
See also Longest Courses.

Championship course
Length 6809 yd (6226 m)
Par 74
Course record 65 – Jack Newton (British Open, 1975)

Carry
The distance travelled by a golf ball from the point where it is struck to the spot at which it first hits the ground. The term is also used to define a stroke that successfully overcomes a hazard.

Many carries in excess of 300 yd (275 m) have been recorded in non-competitive circumstances. But the record in tournament play is 305 yd (279 m) by Francisco Abreau (Spain) in the 1972 Algarve Open at Penina. He carried the ball over a ditch at the 18th hole.
See also Drive.

Casper, Billy
Billy Casper's victory in the 1966 US Open must rank as one of the great golf recoveries. He was trailing Arnold Palmer by seven shots, with nine holes to play, yet managed to force a play-off. At the turn of the play-off he was still behind but turned that deficit into a four-stroke victory. This was Casper's second US Open win, the first being seven years earlier.

A professional from 1954, he scored over 50 victories on the US circuit and one of them, the 1970 Los Angeles Open, took his career earnings to over $1 million. He was the second man, after Arnold Palmer, to achieve this feat.

In the 1960s Casper was one of the most consistent golfers and one of the world's best putters, but had to live in the shadow of Nicklaus, Palmer and Player.

A family man, Casper has 11 children and in 1966 he converted to the Mormon faith. In recent years his golf has been restricted to seniors' events.

Career highlights
US Open 1959, 1966
US Masters 1970
Canadian Open 1967
British Open (best) 4th – 1968
Ryder Cup 1961, 1963, 1965, 1967, 1969, 1971, 1973

Casual Water
A temporary accumulation of water on the course visible before or after the player takes his stance. Water hazards are not regarded as casual water, but snow and ice are. A player may lift and drop his ball from casual water without incurring a penalty.

Centre-shafted Putter
A putter with the shaft joined to the centre of the head, as opposed to the end or heel. Most early putters were end-shafted. The first centre-shafted putter was seen in Britain in 1904 when Walter Travis used his Schenectady putter (qv) in winning the British Amateur Championship at Sandwich. The legality of this kind of putter was challenged and it was subsequently banned in Britain. The ban was not lifted until 1949, but since then centre-shafted putters have become the most popular type.

Billy Casper in 1961, when he finished fourth on the US money list with $37,766.

Championship Belt
When the first British Open championship was held in 1860 the winner, Willie Park, received an ornate Moroccan leather and silver belt that had been presented by the Earl of Eglinton. The winner held the belt for one year

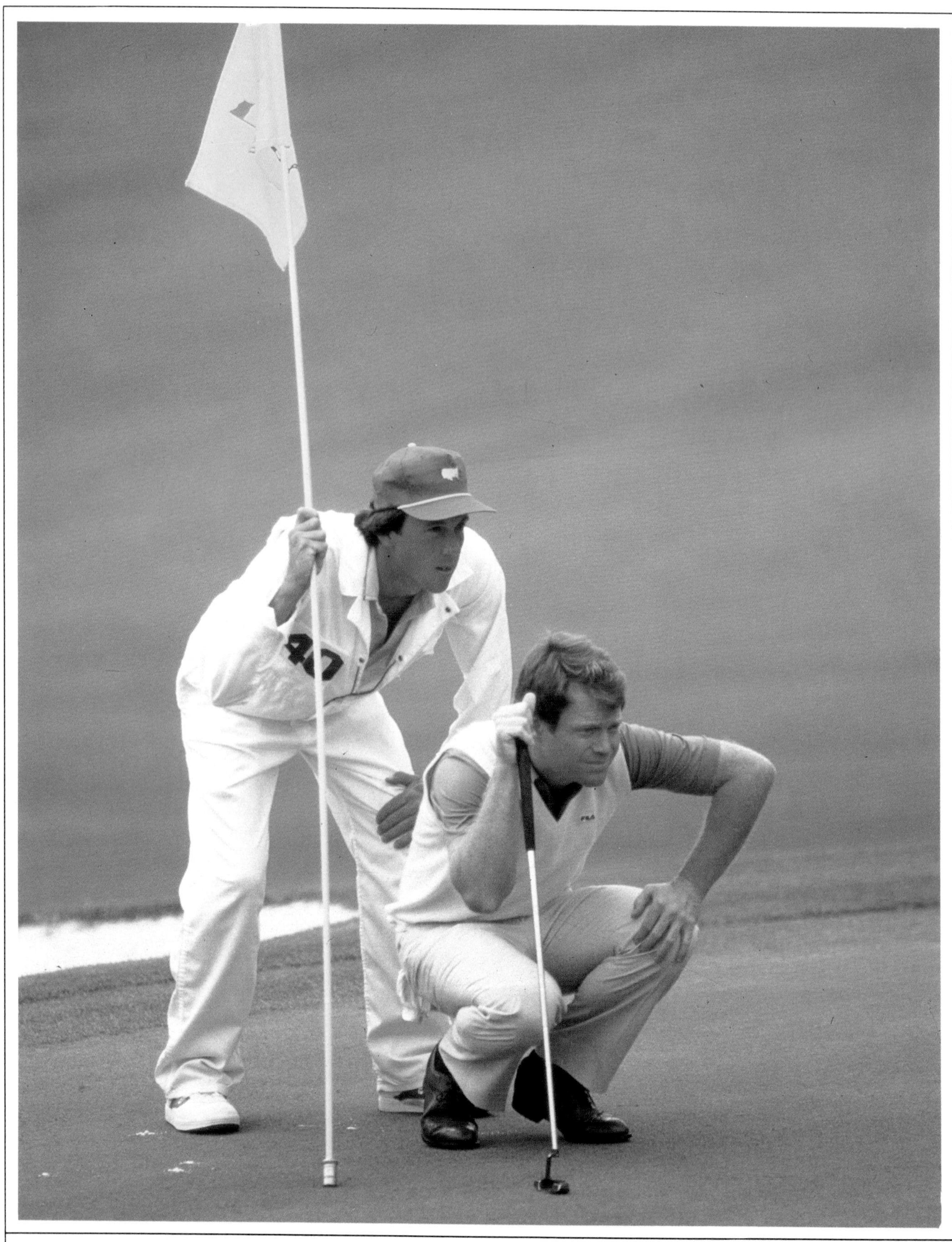

Tom Watson, seen here during the 1985 US Masters, won the first of his five British Open titles at Carnoustie in 1975.

but, in the event of one man's winning it three years in succession, he was allowed to keep it. Tom Morris Jnr accomplished this feat in 1868, 1869 and 1870 and thus made the belt his own property. There was no British Open the following year and, when it resumed in 1872, the current championship trophy was acquired to replace the belt. The cash value of the belt was in the region of £30, and it was given by the Morris family to the Royal and Ancient Club, where it remains today.

Charles, Bob

When Bob Charles won the 1963 British Open at Lytham he became the first New Zealander to gain the title and also the first left-handed golfer to win one of the world's major tournaments. Undoubtedly the greatest left-handed player the sport has seen, he was also one of the best putters of his era. Born in 1936, he was New Zealand Open champion, as an amateur, at the age of 18 and turned professional in 1960. His best days were in the 1960s when, apart from his Open success, he won the Piccadilly World Match-Play title, and the Canadian Open, and in 1968 and 1969 was runner-up in the British Open. He also enjoyed a successful spell on the US circuit, winning five tournaments.

He has continued to compete at the highest level and reached the last round of the 1985 British Open. Only illness prevented him completing four rounds.

Career highlights
British Open 1963
Canadian Open 1968
World Match-Play 1969

By far the world's most outstanding left-handed golfer, New Zealand's Bob Charles.

Cherry Hills

What do Cherry Hills and Royal Birkdale have in common? Answer—they both have plaques to commemorate great performances by Arnold Palmer.

At Cherry Hills the plaque commemorates his comeback in the final round of the 1960 US Open when he

The British Open championship belt that became the permanent property of Young Tom Morris after he won the title for the third year in succession in 1870.

made up seven strokes on the third-round leader, Mike Souchak, to win his first and only title. The eventual runner-up to Palmer that day was a young amateur called Jack Nicklaus.

The course, situated a mile above sea level in Denver, Colorado, has been used as the venue for the US Open three times. The first occasion was in 1938 when Ralph Guldahl won the title for the second successive year. It was next used in 1960 and then in 1978 when Andy North won.

The 14th hole, a long dogleg par-4 bordered by a creek on the left, is regarded as one of the finest of its kind in the United States.

Length 7089 yd (6482 m)
Par 71
Course record 64 – Doug Tewell (US PGA, 1985)

Chip

A lofted shot usually made when the player is approaching the green and the ball needs to be lifted over a hazard before running on to the green.

Chole

A game resembling golf played in France at least 100 years before golf first made its appearance in Scotland in the mid-15th century. It was a cross-country game in which the participants used a ball and stick.

Cleek

A Scottish term for a narrow-faced, hickory-shafted club that had a loft similar to a present-day No 2 iron. The cleek is now obsolete.

Closed Stance

The position adopted by a player who, when addressing the ball, has the left foot slightly forward of the right one. If the ball is struck correctly, it will travel to the right of its intended target.
See also Open Stance, Stance.

Coles, Neil

Neil Coles was one of the most consistent British golfers in the 1960s yet, despite winning most titles in Britain, he never won the supreme prize—the British Open.

Dunlop Masters champion in 1966, he was three times winner of the British Match-Play title and runner-up to Arnold Palmer in the inaugural World Match-Play championship at Wentworth in 1964. But his best British Open was in 1973 when he tied for second place with Johnny Miller, three strokes behind the winner, Tom Weiskopf.

Coles turned professional in 1950 and joined the European circuit in 1955, picking up just £115 in winnings. He won his first tournament, the Gor-Ray, the following year and in 1979 he became the first European to win £200,000 in prize money. That figure would have been much higher had not his fear of flying prevented him from taking part in many big tournaments.

A much respected member of the professional golf world, in 1982 he was honoured with the MBE for his services to the sport. His son Gary has been following in his footsteps. In 1985 he gained the Assistant's Championship, the title won by his father 29 years earlier.

Career highlights

British Match-Play 1964, 1965, 1973
Dunlop Masters 1966
World Match-Play runner-up 1964
German Open 1971
Spanish Open 1973
Ryder Cup 1961, 1963, 1965, 1967, 1969, 1971, 1973, 1977
British Open (best) jt 2nd – 1973

Cotton, Henry

When Henry Cotton beat Sidney Brews to win the 1934 British Open at Sandwich it ended the ten-year monopoly of the title by the United States. At the time Cotton was rated the best British golfer since the days of Harry Vardon, and he justified this opinion by winning the title for a second time at Carnoustie in 1937. Eleven years later, at the age of 41, he won his third British Open and, in 1956, while in his 50th year, finished joint sixth, just two strokes behind the 20-year-old Gary Player.

Born at Holmes Chapel, Cheshire, in 1907, Cotton turned professional at the age of 17 and enjoyed a successful 40-year playing career during which he won the Open titles of France, Belgium, Germany, Czechoslovakia and Italy. He competed in four Ryder Cup matches, and was twice captain of the Great Britain team. Captain of the Royal and Ancient Club between 1934 and 1948, he is now an honorary member.

Much in demand for his coaching skills, he also became a golf-course architect when his playing days were over. A testimony to his ability in this area is the magnificent Penina Club in Portugal, Henry's adopted 'home'. In 1946 he was awarded the MBE for his services to golf.

Career highlights

British Open 1934, 1937, 1948
Ryder Cup 1929, 1937, 1947 (capt), 1953 (non-playing capt)
French Open 1946, 1947
Belgian Open 1930, 1934, 1938
Italian Open 1936
German Open 1937, 1938, 1939
Czechoslovak Open 1937, 1938

Crans-sur-Sierre

The Crans-sur-Sierre golf club at Valais, about 5000 ft (1500 m) above the Rhone Valley and overlooked by the Matterhorn, is Switzerland's leading club and the home of the Swiss Open since 1939.

The original course was laid out in 1915 but remained closed during the First World War. The current courses (18 holes and nine holes) were opened in 1927. Both are tight courses but the rarefied atmosphere gives players an advantage with their drives.

Crans has, in recent years, been the scene of some record-breaking scores. José-Maria Canizares established the European nine-hole record of 27 strokes during the 1978 Swiss Open and Baldovino Dassu earlier established the 18-hole record of 60 strokes during the 1971 Open. In the same competition Peter Townsend scored a 61. In 1984 Jerry Anderson shot a four-round 261, which was just one stroke off the European record.

Length 6811 yd (6230 m)
Par 72
Course record 60 – Baldovino Dassu (Swiss Open, 1971)

Crenshaw, Ben

Ben Crenshaw had an outstanding amateur career and, when he turned professional in 1973, was talked about as a 'boy wonder'. After he won his first professional tournament, the San Antonio Open, it looked as if the predictions were going to prove accurate. But, unfortunately, that tag was too much for Crenshaw to carry and he never really got among the big winners.

Born in Texas in 1952, Crenshaw was Rookie of the Year in 1974 but his career was one of near misses after that. He was runner-up in the 1976 US Masters when beaten in a play-off by Australia's David Graham. He was second in the British Opens of 1978 and 1979, when he was also runner-up in the US PGA championship. In 1983 he was runner-up in the Masters for the second time, but the next year it all came good for him at Augusta when he beat Tom Watson by two strokes to win his first major title.

Career highlights
US Masters 1984
Ryder Cup 1981, 1983
British Open (best) jt 2nd – 1978, 1979

Crosby, Bing

Not only was Bing Crosby an outstandingly successful popular singer and the star of numerous films, but he was also a welcome sight on any golf course the world over. A gifted player, he could possibly, had the bright lights of show business not attracted him, have made a living from the sport he loved.

At one time he got his handicap as low as two and in 1950 competed in the British Amateur Championship at St Andrews. His appearance attracted large galleries reminiscent of those who used to watch Ben Hogan.

In 1936 he had become the first entertainment personality to sponsor his own golf tournament, the Bing Crosby Pro-Am, which eventually became a part of the US professional circuit.

He died suddenly after playing a round of golf at Madrid on 14 October 1977, but the Crosby golfing tradition was carried on by his son, Nathaniel, who won the US Amateur title in 1981.
See also Bing Crosby Pro-Am.

Curtis Cup

This is a women's team competition played every two years between Great Britain and Northern Ireland and the United States. First held at Wentworth in 1932, it was named after two American sisters, Margaret and Harriot Curtis, of Boston. They were both prominent golfers at

Bing Crosby with three fellow entertainers – in their younger days. From left to right: Bing (with pipe and champagne!), Donald Peers, Bob Hope and Ted Ray, taken at the Temple Golf Course, Maidenhead, in 1952.

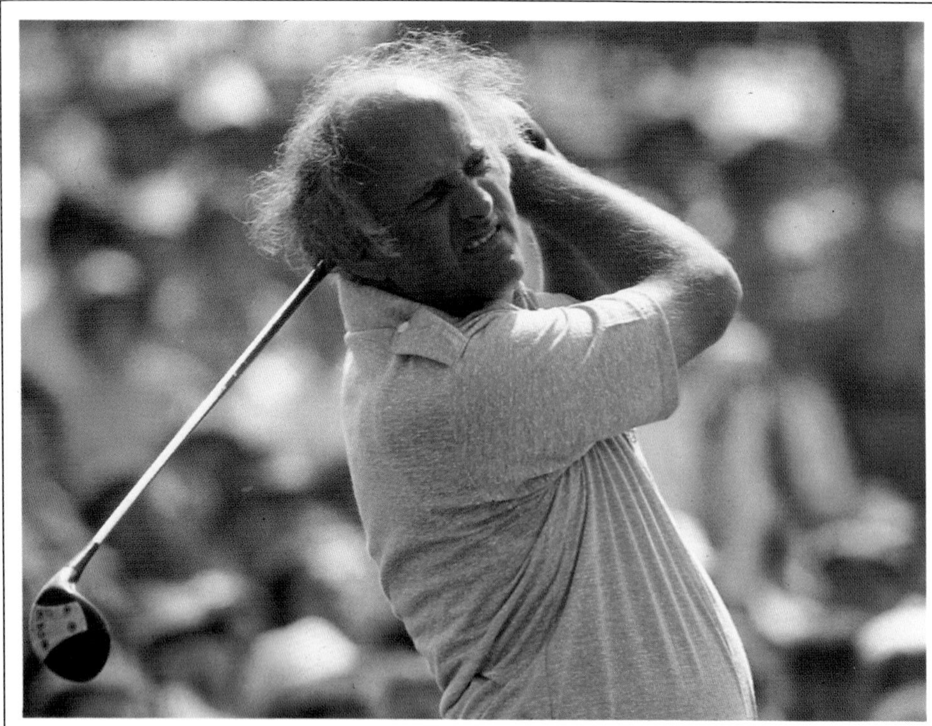

Neil Coles (MBE) will be celebrating 30 years as a tournament player in 1986.

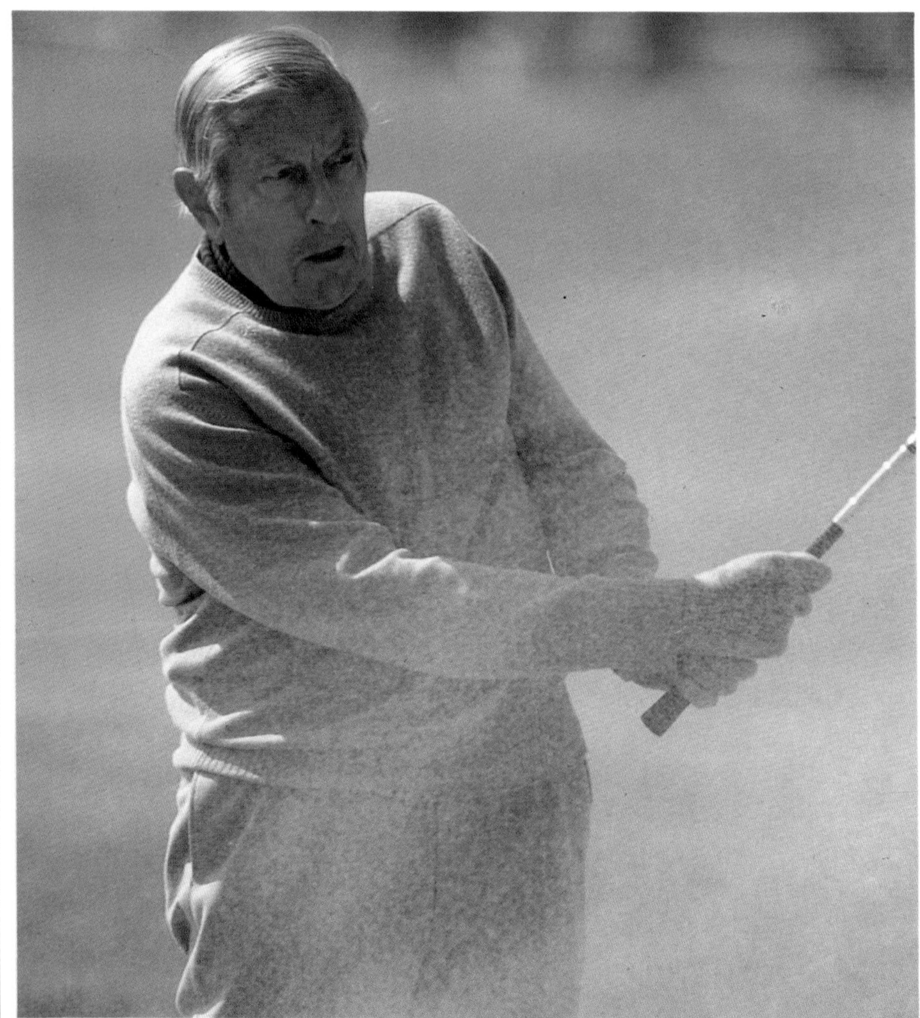

Well into his seventies, Henry Cotton still supported the British Open. This picture shows him in action at Troon in 1982.

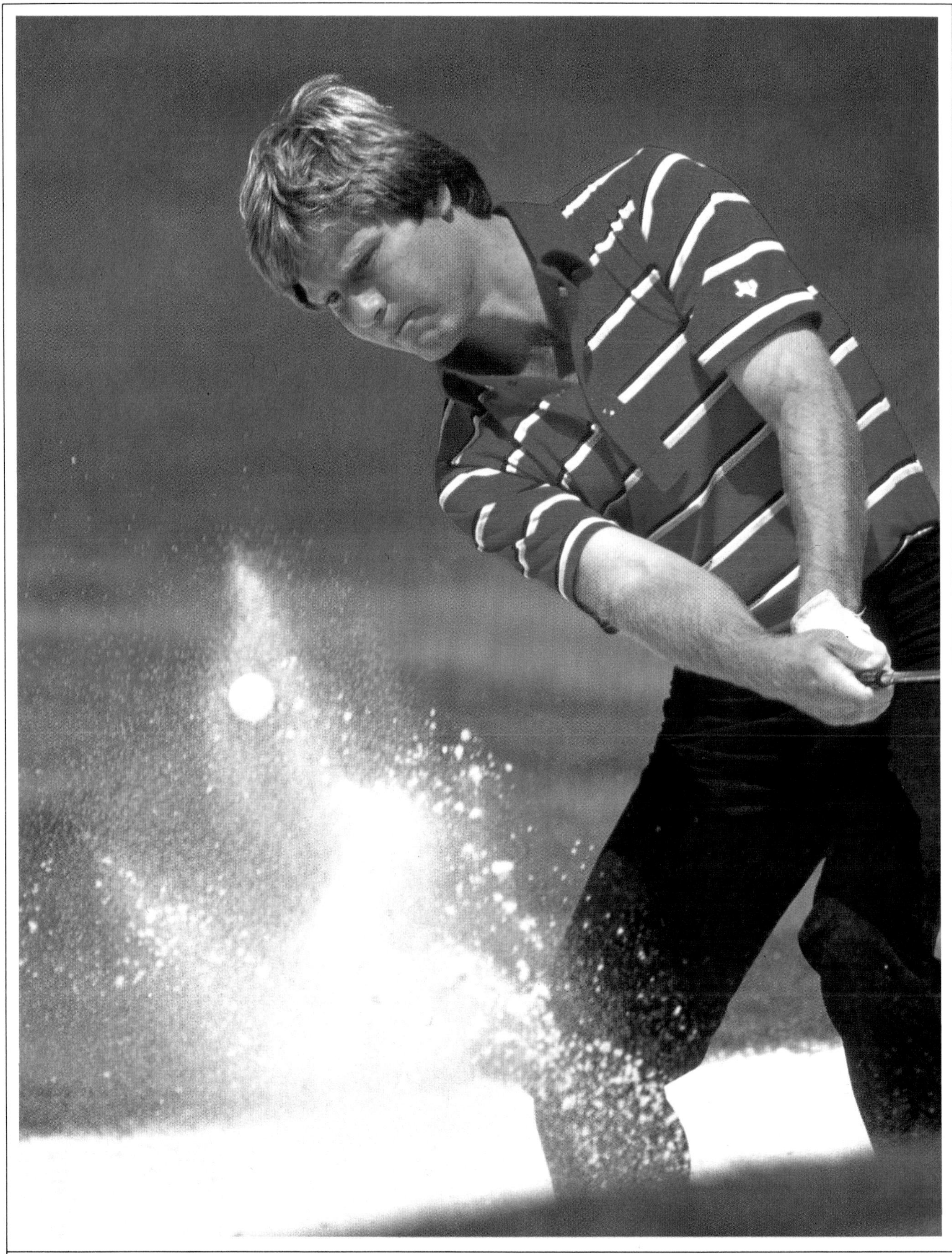

Ben Crenshaw, the 1984 US Masters Champion.

the turn of the century and their inspiration for an international team competition came after they had played in a match between American and British women at Royal Cromer in 1905. They had, however, to wait 27 years before their dreams were eventually fulfilled.

The United States has, as in the Ryder Cup, dominated the event, and British women have won the trophy only twice, although they have tied on two occasions.

Teams consist of not more than eight members and play is held over two days, with three foursomes and six singles, of 18 holes, on each day. Before 1964 matches were played over 36 holes.

Curtis Cup

Results

Year	Venue	Great Britain	United States
1932	Wentworth, England	3½	5½
1934	Chevy Chase, Maryland, US	2½	6½
1936	Gleneagles, Scotland	4½	4½
1938	Essex CC, Massachusetts, US	3½	5½
1940–46 not held			
1948	Royal Birkdale, England	2½	6½
1950	Buffalo CC, New York, US	1½	7½
1952	Muirfield, Scotland	5	4
1954	Merion, Pennsylvania, US	3	6
1956	Prince's, Sandwich, England	5	4
1958	Brae Burn, Massachusetts, US	4½	4½
1960	Lindrick, England	2½	6½
1962	Broadmoor, Colorado Springs, US	1	8
1964	Royal Porthcawl, Wales	7½	10½
1966	Hot Springs, Virginia, US	5	13
1968	Royal County Down, Newcastle, N. Ireland	7½	10½
1970	Brae Burn, Massachusetts, US	6½	11½
1972	Western Gailes, Scotland	8	10
1974	San Francisco GC, California, US	5	13
1976	Royal Lytham and St Annes, England	6½	11½
1978	Apawamis, New York, US	6	12
1980	St Pierre, Chepstow, England	5	13
1982	Denver, Colorado, US	3½	14½
1984	Muirfield, Scotland	8½	9½

Wins

19 – United States
2 – Great Britain and Northern Ireland
2 – tied

Biggest winning margin—team

United States 14½ Great Britain 3½ (1982)

Biggest winning margin—foursomes

Before 1964 (36 holes)
8 & 7 – Jean Ashley and Ann Casey Johnstone (US) beat Diane Frearson and Ruth Porter—1962

Since 1964 (18 holes)
8 & 6 – Carol Sorenson and Barbara Fay White (US) beat Bridget Jackson and Susan Armitage—1964

Biggest winning margin—singles

Before 1964 (36 holes)
9 & 8 – Polly Riley (US) beat Elizabeth Price—1954
9 & 8 – Margaret Smith (US) beat Philomena Garvey—1956

Since 1964 (18 holes)
7 & 6 – Mary Everard (GB) beat Noreen Uihlein—1978
7 & 6 – Kathy Baker (US) beat Isabella Robertson—1982
7 & 6 – Julie Inkster (US) beat Kitrina Douglas—1982

Most appearances

7 – Jessie Valentine (née Anderson)—GB 1936–58

Cut

(1) Another word for a slice (*see* slice).

(2) The division of the players in a tournament at which some are eliminated. Tournaments have different points at which the cut in the field is made. For example, the two cuts in the 1985 British Open were made as follows. At the end of the second round (36 holes) the 86 lowest-scoring players, from an original field of 153, qualified for the third round. They all had 36-hole scores of less than 150. At the end of the next round the 61 players whose scores were under 221 qualified for the final round.

Cypress Point

Cypress Point was laid out in the 1920s on the Monterey Peninsula at Pebble Beach and contains a large variety of fairways and greens. It is not a long course, but is certainly a testing one. Because of its length it has not been used for any major championships.

The short 16th hole at Cypress Point is one of golf's great disaster areas. It is also one of the most photographed. Because of the severity of this one hole, the course has been described as 'the best 17-hole course in the world.'

The drive at the 16th requires a carry of about 200 yd across the Pacific Ocean to a narrow green on a virtual island high above the rocks and ocean below. Two men have managed to hole-in-one at this notorious spot. One of them was Bing Crosby who took his Pro-Am tournament to the Californian course after the Second World War. The hole has also been the scene of many fiascos—Hans Merrell took a 19 at it during the 1959 Bing Crosby event!

Length 6464 yd (5911 m)
Par 72
Course record 65 – D. Hill (Crosby Pro-Am, 1976)

D

Daniel, Beth

Beth Daniel came to the fore in American women's golf in 1975 when, as a 19-year-old, she beat Donna Horton to win the US amateur championship. Two years later she beat Cathy Sherk to gain the title a second time.

After two Curtis Cup appearances she turned professional towards the end of the 1978 season and it was not long before she was achieving the same success in the professional game. She won the Rookie of the Year award in 1979 and was also the winner of that year's World Ladies' Championship of Golf in Japan. She won over $100,000 in her first full year as a professional and in 1980 became the first woman to win over $200,000 on the US circuit. Naturally she was also voted that year's US LPGA Player of the Year.

Although she has had some setbacks recently Beth Daniel is never too far away from the prize money.

Career highlights

US Women's Amateur 1975, 1977
Curtis Cup 1976, 1978
US LPGA Player of Year 1980

de Vicenzo, Roberto

The Argentine player, Roberto de Vicenzo, appeared in his first British Open in 1948 and finished third. During the next 18 years he finished third on three more occasions and was runner-up once. That, in the opinion of many, was the best the likeable and friendly South American was going to achieve in the championship. However, at Hoylake in 1967, he beat off a strong challenge from Jack Nicklaus to become, at 44 years 93 days, the oldest winner of the title this century.

The following year he came close to winning his second major event, the US Masters, but a simple error cost him dear. He inadvertently signed his scorecard, which his partner had completed crediting de Vicenzo with a four, instead of a three, on the 71st hole. The four had to stand and he eventually lost to Bob Goalby by just one stroke.

Altogether he won over 200 tournaments, including 40 national championships in 15 countries. He took part in the World Cup competition 19 times, including four times for Mexico, and was a member (with Tony Cerda) of the Argentina team that won the first title in 1953. He won the individual title on two occasions.

The sportsmanship and talents of de Vicenzo were given due recognition by the Royal and Ancient Club, which made him an honorary member in 1976.

Career highlights

British Open 1967
World Cup (team) 1953
World Cup (individual) 1962, 1970
World Seniors 1974

Divot

A piece of turf cut out of the ground by the club after striking the ball. Occasionally leading golfers will deliberately take a divot with the shot in order to impart the maximum amount of backspin to the ball. As a matter of etiquette all divots must be replaced so as to avoid damage to the course.

Dod, Charlotte 'Lottie'

Charlotte 'Lottie' Dod was one of the great all-round British sportswomen. Not only was she a leading hockey player, archer, billiards player and skater, but she was Wimbledon Ladies' Singles Champion five times. Her first win came when she was only 15 years old, and she still remains the youngest person to have won a Wimbledon title.

Having fulfilled her tennis ambitions, she turned her attention to golf and once again became a champion. She

Lottie Dod was not only a superb golfer, but she won the Wimbledon ladies' title five times between 1887 and 1893.

Captain Phyllis Preuss holds aloft the Curtis Cup after the United States had chalked up their 13th consecutive victory, at Muirfield in 1984.

One of golf's great, and most daunting, holes – the 16th at Cypress Point.

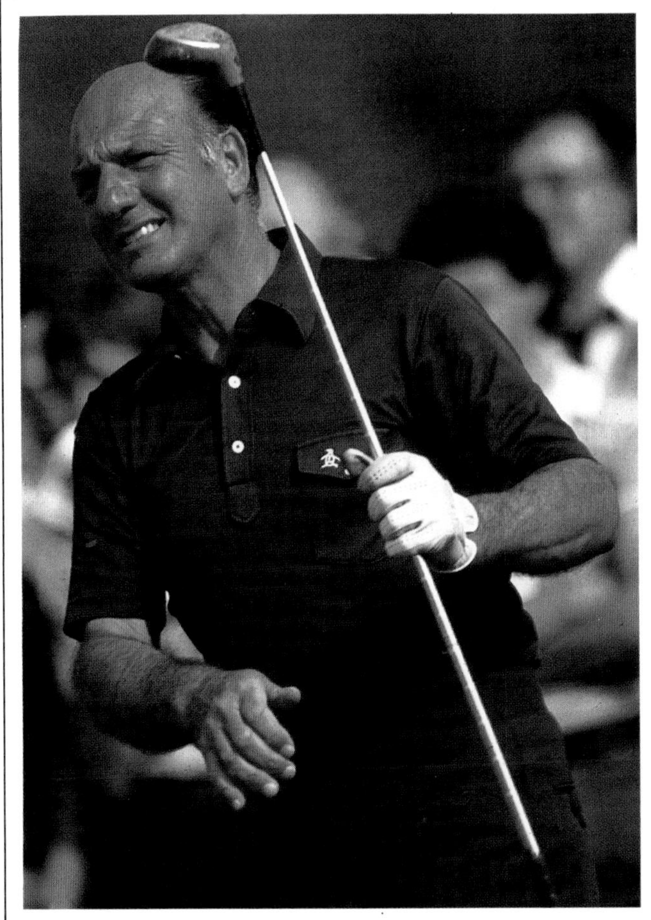

Argentine's Roberto de Vicenzo, the oldest man this century to win the British Open.

beat May Hezlet in the final to win the 1904 British Ladies Championship at Troon. By then Lottie Dod was 32 but went on to represent England at international level, as she had done in hockey some years earlier.

Career highlights
- Golf: Ladies' British Open 1904
- Tennis: Wimbledon Ladies Singles 1887, 1888, 1891, 1892, 1893
- Archery: Olympic Games (silver medal) 1908

Dogleg

A golf hole that has an angled fairway. The dogleg may turn to the left or to the right and, at the angle where the fairway changes, there is quite often a hazard to be found, thus leaving the golfer in two minds whether to attempt to play over the hazard or to play short and safe.

Doral Eastern Open

Unlike the Western Open, which has been in existence since 1899, the Eastern Open is a relative newcomer to the US calendar. Played in February over the Blue Monster Course at the Doral Country Club, a multi-course complex built on marshland near Miami airport, it was first contested in 1962. The first tournament was won by Billy Casper, who won it again two years later.

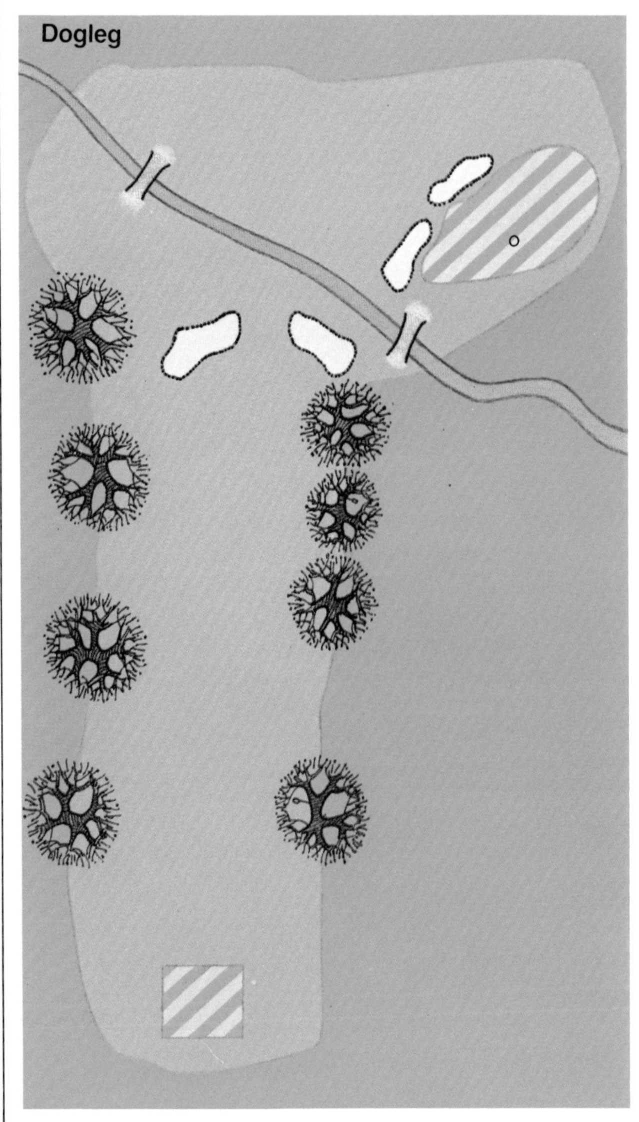

Winners (since 1970)

Year	Name	Score	Year	Name	Score
1970	M. Hill	279	1979	M. McCumber	279
1971	J. C. Snead	275	1980	R. Floyd	279
1972	J. Nicklaus	276	1981	R. Floyd	273
1973	L. Trevino	276	1982	A. Bean	278
1974	B. Allin	272	1983	G. Koch	271
1975	J. Nicklaus	276	1984	T. Kite	272
1976	H. Green	270	1985	M. McCumber	284
1977	A. Bean	277	1986	A. Bean	276
1978	T. Weiskopf	272			

Most wins
3 – Andy Bean (1977, 1982, 1986)
2 – Billy Casper (1962, 1964)
2 – Doug Sanders (1965, 1967)
2 – Jack Nicklaus (1972, 1975)
2 – Ray Floyd (1980, 1981)
2 – Mark McCumber (1979, 1985)

Lowest score (72 holes)
270 – Hubert Green (1976)

One man who enjoys playing the Eastern Open is Mark McCumber who hails from nearby Jacksonville. He won his first US Tour event when winning the title in 1979; when he won the title again in 1985, it was only his fourth Tour win.

Dormie
A player is said to be dormie when leading by as many holes as there are left to play. This situation can only occur in match-play conditions and does not apply if extra holes are required to settle the outcome of the match.

Double Bogey
The American term for a hole played in two strokes over par.
See also Bogey.

Double Eagle
The American term for an albatross.

Draw
(1) The order in which players or teams play each other in a competition.
(2) A controlled shot created by playing the ball from an in-to-out position (*see* in and out). The effect is similar to a hook shot, with the ball travelling to the right but, unlike the hook, it returns towards the line required. It can also be made to take a straight line to begin with and then curve to the left towards the end of its flight. The South African, Bobby Locke, was a master at playing the controlled draw.

Drive
A shot made from the tee, usually with a driver. Professionals can drive between 300 and 350 yd (275 and 320 m), depending on conditions, while the club golfer can concede anything up to 100 yd (91 m) on those figures. The record drive, under normal golf conditions, is credited to Tommie Campbell who drove 392 yd (358 m) at Dun Laoghaire Golf Club, Republic of Ireland, in July 1964. Michael Austin drove 515 yd (470 m) during the 1974 US Seniors' Championship at Las Vegas. Aided by a 35-mph tailwind, he drove 65 yd (59 m) past the 450 yd (411 m) par-4 5th hole.

The longest drive in the British Open is believed to have been an estimated 430 yd (393 m) by Craig Wood in the play-off to decide the 1933 championship at St Andrews. His drive, which landed in the bunker short of the 5th green, was aided by a following wind and extremely dry ground conditions.

Driver
A wooden-headed club with a nearly straight face used for driving from a tee. The driver, also known as the No 1 wood, is the most powerful club in a golfer's bag. The club first acquired its name in the mid 19th century.

Driving Ranges
An American innovation, driving ranges were first seen in Britain in 1963. Within five years another 20 were in operation, mostly carrying the 'Arnold Palmer Driving Range' name.

Driving areas normally consist of covered bays from which the golfer can practise his driving after hiring a supply of balls. The driving areas are generally marked out with distance posts to aid the golfer. Many ranges also have putting and pitch-and-putt courses for further practice, and some provide social amenities.

There are over 50 ranges in Britain, most of which are floodlit, but some of the biggest in the world are in Japan. Here several large tiered arenas have been built, enabling as many as 1000 golfers to hit balls into the driving area at one time.

Dropping the Ball
Unless the rules state otherwise, a player drops the ball when he is unable to play his stroke. The ball must be held at shoulder-height and at arm's length, and dropped. It must land as near as possible to its previous position, but not nearer to the hole.

The rules relating to dropping the ball have caused a great deal of confusion. At one time a player had to get his opponent to drop the ball for him. There was even a time when the ball had to be dropped by a caddy. The rules, over the years, have stated which part of the body the ball has to be dropped over and which way the person dropping the ball has to face.
See also Rules of Golf.

Dunhill Cup
The first World Team Championship for the Dunhill Cup was played at St Andrews in 1985. Its prize money of $1.2 million (at the time of the announcement of the competition it was worth just over £1 million after the currency conversion) made it the richest-ever sporting event sponsored by a British company. The prize money was double that for the 1985 British Open.

The idea for the tournament came from promoter Mark McCormack who saw it as a rival to the World Cup but, because of the cash incentives, would attract a better field . . . he was right.

Sixteen nations took part in a straight knockout competition. Teams consisted of three players, and each player took part in one 18-hole round against a member of the opposing team, the winning player gaining one point for his team.

The Australian trio of David Graham, Graham Marsh and Greg Norman beat the American team of Curtis Strange, Mark O'Meara and Ray Floyd by three matches to nil in the final. Each member of the winning team picked up around £70,000.

Dunlop Masters
When Dunlop sponsored their last Masters in 1982, after 36 years, British Golf lost one of its most prestigious tournaments. Although Silk Cut stepped in for one year, the Masters disappeared off the European PGA calendar completely after 1983.

The first Dunlop Masters was restricted to invited players, and winners of major championships and professional events. It was held at Stoneham, Southampton in 1946, and resulted in a tie between South African Bobby Locke and Jim Adams from Troon.

Five ex-British Open champions, Locke, Faulkner, Jacklin, Thomson and Charles all won the Masters, and

As space is at such a premium in Japan, they build three-tier driving ranges where over 1000 golfers can practise.

Dunlop Masters

Winners

Year	Name	Venue	Score
1946	A. D. Locke	Stoneham	286
	J. Adams		286
1947	A. Lees	Little Aston	286
1948	N. von Nida	Sunningdale	272
1949	C. H. Ward	St Andrews	290
1950	D. J. Rees	Hoylake	281
1951	M. Faulkner	Wentworth	281
1952	H. Weetman	Mere	281
1953	H. Bradshaw	Sunningdale	272
1954	A. D. Locke	Prince's	291
1955	H. Bradshaw	Little Aston	277
1956	C. O'Connor	Prestwick	277
1957	E. C. Brown	Hollinwell	275
1958	H. Weetman	Little Aston	276
1959	C. O'Connor	Portmarnock	276
1960	J. Hitchcock	Sunningdale	275
1961	P. W. Thomson	Porthcawl	284
1962	D. J. Rees	Wentworth	278
1963	B. J. Hunt	Little Aston	282
1964	C. Legrange	Birkdale	288
1965	B. J. Hunt	Portmarnock	283
1966	N. C. Coles	Lindrick	278
1967	A. Jacklin	St George's	274
1968	P. W. Thomson	Sunningdale	274
1969	C. Legrange	Little Aston	281
1970	B. Huggett	Lytham	293
1971	M. Bembridge	St Pierre	273

Year	Name	Venue	Score
1972	R. J. Charles	Northumberland	277
1973	A. Jacklin	St Pierre	272
1974	B. Gallacher	St Pierre	282
1975	B. Gallacher	Ganton	289
1976	B. Dassu	St Pierre	271
1977	G. Hunt	Lindrick	291
1978	T. A. Horton	St Pierre	279
1979	G. Marsh	Woburn	283
1980	B. Langer	St Pierre	270
1981	G. Norman	Woburn	273
1982	G. Norman	St Pierre	267

Most wins

2 – Bobby Locke (1946, 1954)
2 – Dai Rees (1950, 1962)
2 – Harry Weetman (1952, 1958)
2 – Harry Bradshaw (1953, 1955)
2 – Christy O'Connor (1956, 1959)
2 – Peter Thomson (1961, 1968)
2 – Bernard Hunt (1963, 1965)
2 – Cobie Legrange (1964, 1969)
2 – Tony Jacklin (1967, 1973)
2 – Bernard Gallacher (1974, 1975)
2 – Greg Norman (1981, 1982)

Lowest score (72 holes)

267 – Greg Norman (1982)

See also Silk Cut Masters

all the leading British professionals of the 1950s and 1960s won the title: Dai Rees, Christy O'Connor, Harry Bradshaw, Harry Weetman, Eric Brown, Bernard Hunt and Neil Coles. During its final years, overseas players sought the title and the last two Dunlop Masters went to Australia, via Greg Norman.

Dutch Open

The Dutch Open championship, inaugurated in 1919, was, appropriately, held at the Haagsche Golf Club at The Hague. The Netherlands' first club, it had been opened in 1893. The venue for the event, now sponsored by the airline KLM, varies each year.

The championship was held over 36 holes until 1934, when it became a 72-hole event. There have been two exceptions, in 1974 and 1977, when 54 holes were played.

A remarkable round was played by Bernhard Langer at Rosendaelsche (used for the championship for the first time in 1984) when he put together one eagle and eight birdies in his first round of 64. And one of Europe's favourite sons, Severiano Ballesteros, had his first win on the European circuit when he won the 1976 Dutch Open.

Winners

Year	Name	Venue	Score
1919	D. Oosterveer	The Hague	158
1920	H. Burrows	Haarlem	155
1921	H. Burrows	Domburg	151
1922	G. Pannell	Noordwijk	160
1923	H. Burrows	Hilversum	153
1924	A. Boomer	The Hague	138
1925	A. Boomer	The Hague	144
1926	A. Boomer	The Hague	151
1927	P. Boomer	The Hague	147
1928	E. R. Whitcombe	The Hague	141
1929	J. J. Taylor	Hilversum	153
1930	J. Oosterveer	The Hague	152
1931	F. Dyer	Haarlem	145
1932	A. Boyer	The Hague	137
1933	M. Dallemagne	Zandvoort	143
1934	S. F. Brews	Utrecht	286
1935	S. F. Brews	Zandvoort	275
1936	F. van Donck	Hilversum	285
1937	F. van Donck	Utrecht	286
1938	A. H. Padgham	The Hague	281
1939	A. D. Locke	Zandvoort	281
1940–47	Not held		
1948	C. Denny	Hilversum	290
1949	J. Adams	The Hague	294
1950	R. de Vicenzo	Breda	269
1951	F. van Donck	Kennemer	281
1952	C. Denny	Hilversum	284
1953	F. van Donck	Eindhoven	286
1954	U. Grappasonni	The Hague	295
1955	A. Angelini	Zandvoort	280
1956	A. Cerda	Eindhoven	277
1957	J. Jacobs	Hilversum	284
1958	D. Thomas	Zandvoort	277
1959	S. Sewgolum	The Hague	283
1960	S. Sewgolum	Eindhoven	280
1961	B. B. S. Wilkes	Zandvoort	279
1962	B. G. Huggett	Hilversum	274
1963	R. Waltman	Wassenaar	279
1964	S. Sewgolum	Eindhoven	275
1965	A. Miguel	Breda	278
1966	R. Sota	Zandvoort	276
1967	P. Townsend	The Hague	282
1968	J. Cockin	Hilversum	292
1969	G. Wolstenholme	Utrecht	277
1970	V. Fernandez	Eindhoven	279
1971	R. Sota	Zandvoort	277
1972	J. Newton	The Hague	277
1973	D. McClelland	The Hague	279
1974	B. Barnes	Hilversum	211(a)
1975	H. Baiocchi	Hilversum	279
1976	S. Ballesteros	Kennemer	275
1977	R. Byman	Kennemer	214(a)
1978	R. Byman	Noordwijk	285
1979	G. Marsh	Noordwijk	285
1980	S. Ballesteros	Hilversum	280
1981	H. Henning	The Hague	280
1982	P. Way	Utrecht	276
1983	K. Brown	Kennemer	274
1984	B. Langer	Rosendaelsche	275
1985	G. Marsh	Noordwijk	282

(a) play over 54 holes

Most wins

4 – Flory van Donck (1936, 1937, 1951, 1953)

Lowest score (72 holes)

269 – Roberto de Vicenzo (Breda, 1950)

Eagle

A hole played in two strokes under par. Like birdie, the word is of American origin and was first used in the early 1920s. The greatest number of consecutive eagles recorded is three, a feat achieved by Wilf Jones at the first, second and third holes at Moor Hall Golf Club, Sutton Coldfield, in 1968.

Eclectic Competition

A competition consisting of two or more rounds, in which a player's best score at each hole during the course of the entire competition counts towards his eventual 18-hole total. This form of competition is not suitable for match-play.

Australian Greg Norman won the last two of the Dunlop-sponsored Masters, 1981 and 1982.

Eisenhower, Dwight D.

Dwight D. Eisenhower was president of the United States between 1953 and 1961. Such was his popularity during his term of office that his love of golf encouraged Americans to take up the sport in large numbers. Hitherto it had been regarded as a game for the very rich.

A keen, all-round sportsman, Eisenhower played steady golf, regularly scoring in the mid-80s. A knee injury he had received playing football in his younger days handicapped his swing slightly and prevented him from getting into the single-figure handicap bracket.

Eisenhower Trophy

The trophy given by Dwight D. Eisenhower (see previous entry) and played for by four-man teams in the World Amateur Team Championship. Held every two years, the Championship first took place at St Andrews in 1958. The trophy bears the inscription: 'To foster friendship and sportsmanship among the Peoples of the World.'

See also World Amateur Team Championship

English Amateur Championship

The youngest of the national championships of the four home countries, it was not introduced until 1925. Like the Amateur Championship it was the brain-child of the Royal Liverpool club, who hosted the first meeting. The match-play event is open to British subjects born in England, the Channel Islands or the Isle of Man, or with one English-born parent, and to players who have not competed in the national championships of any of the other home countries.

The 1957 winner was the South African, Arthur Walker, who had one English-born parent.

Winners (since 1965)

Year	Name	Venue	Score
1965	M. F. Bonallack	Berkshire	3 & 2
1966	M. S. R. Lunt	Lytham	3 & 2
1967	M. F. Bonallack	Woodhall Spa	4 & 2
1968	M. F. Bonallack	Ganton	12 & 11
1969	J. H. Cook	Sandwich	6 & 4
1970	Dr D. Marsh	Birkdale	6 & 4
1971	W. Humphreys	Burnham and Berrow	9 & 8
1972	H. Ashby	Northumberland	5 & 4
1973	H. Ashby	Formby	5 & 4
1974	M. James	Woodhall Spa	6 & 5
1975	N. Faldo	Lytham	6 & 4
1976	P. Deeble	Ganton	3 & 1
1977	T. R. Shingler	Walton Heath	4 & 3
1978	P. Downes	Birkdale	1 hole
1979	R. Chapman	Sandwich	6 & 5
1980	P. Deeble	Moortown	4 & 3
1981	D. Blakeman	Burnham and Berrow	3 & 1
1982	A. Oldcorn	Hoylake	4 & 3
1983	G. Laurence	Wentworth	7 & 6
1984	D. Gilford	Woodhall Spa	4 & 3
1985	R. Winchester	Little Aston	1 hole

Most wins
5 – Michael Bonallack (1962, 1963, 1965, 1967, 1968)

Biggest win (final)
12 & 11 – Michael Bonallack beat P. D. Kelley (Ganton, 1968)

English Open Amateur Stroke Play Championship

See Brabazon Trophy

Estoril Golf Club

Although it has given way to Quinta do Lago and Penina as the leading championship course in Portugal, Estoril, the popular seaside course near Lisbon, is still regarded by many as the home of Portuguese golf. Between 1936 and 1961 every Portuguese amateur championship was held at Estoril, as was every Portuguese Open from 1953 until 1972. The Open last took place there in 1974 when the South African, Dale Hayes, broke the course record with a round of 62.

Length 5698 yd (5210 m)
Par 68
Course record 62 – Dale Hayes (Portuguese Open, 1974)

Etiquette

Golfers at all times are required to adhere to a code of etiquette as laid down by the rules of golf.

Much of the etiquette on a golf course is common courtesy, but players are reminded in the rules to give consideration to other players and to take care of the course. Typical examples of etiquette are as follows:

A player should replace divots on the fairway and repair ball marks and damage caused by spikes on the green.

After leaving a bunker a player should fill and level out all holes made by him.

No player should talk or stand close to or directly behind the ball or hole when another player is addressing the ball.

No player should play his shot until all players in front of him are out of range.

Players searching for a lost ball should, when it is apparent that the ball is not going to be found easily, signal for following players to pass through and continue their game.

Two-ball matches should be allowed to play through three- or four-ball matches, unless local rules dictate otherwise.

A player on his own must give way to all other matches.

European Masters

In 1983 Gaston Barras, president of the Swiss Open organizing committee, stole a march on other European countries and added the title European Masters to the Ebel-sponsored Swiss Open. To improve the event's status and popularity he increased the prize money by £70,000 and recruited the services of Jack Nicklaus as a special consultant.

For results and records see Swiss Open.

European Open

Now established at Sunningdale in Berkshire, the European Open was first held in 1978 when Walton Heath was the competition's home. The event has been sponsored by the Japanese electrical giant, Panasonic, since 1983, the year in which, appropriately, Isao Aoki won the title.

Winners

Year	Name	Venue	Score
1978	B. Wadkins	Walton Heath	283
1979	A. W. Lyle	Turnberry	275
1980	T. Kite	Walton Heath	284
1981	G. Marsh	Hoylake	275
1982	M. Pinero	Sunningdale	266
1983	I. Aoki	Sunningdale	274
1984	G. Brand, Jnr	Sunningdale	270
1985	B. Langer	Sunningdale	269

Most wins
No man has won more than one title

Lowest score (72 holes)
266 – Manuel Pinero (Sunningdale, 1982)

European PGA Tour

The European PGA Tour was born in 1977 after the Tournament Players' Division, who had separated themselves from the PGA in 1975, merged with the Continental Tournament Players' Association. They became known as the European Players' Division.

Prior to the merger there had been a British Tour and a European Tour, and both Tours had been in existence for many years.

Prize money totalled just over £1 million in 1977, but in 1985 a total of over £4 million was at stake.

Prior to the 1985 season, each tournament on the Tour had an 18-hole pre-qualifying event on the Monday before starting on the Thursday. This meant many golfers travelling across Europe to play 18 holes and then being eliminated. In 1985, however, the European Tour followed the line taken by their American counterparts two years earlier by making all events 'All Exempt'. The PGA drew up 13 categories of exempt players who were eligible for tournaments under their auspices. Regular full-field European PGA Tour competitions carry maximum starting fields of 144.

At the end of each season, since 1976, a European PGA Tour Qualifying school has been held in which the leading 50 qualifiers become part of the All-Exempt Ranking system for the following season.

European PGA Tour records

Most wins in career
31 – Neil Coles (1956–82)

Most official wins in one year
7 – Norman Von Nida (Australia), 1947
7 – Flory van Donck (Belgium), 1953

Most consecutive victories
4 – Alf Padgham (1935–36)

Lowest score (72 holes)
260 – Kel Nagle (Irish Hospitals Tournament, 1961)
260 – Mike Clayton (Timex Open, 1984)

Lowest score (54 holes)
193 – Mike Clayton (Timex Open, 1984)
193 – Peter Teravainen (Timex Open, 1984)

Lowest score (36 holes)
125 – Sam Torrance (Monte Carlo Open, 1985)

Lowest score (18 holes)
60 – Baldovino Dassu (Swiss Open, 1971)

Lowest score (9 holes)
27 – José-Maria Canizares (Swiss Open, 1978)

Oldest winner
58 years – Sandy Herd (News of the World Match-Play, 1926)

Youngest winner
19 years 4 months – Severiano Ballesteros (Dutch Open, 1976)

Leading money-winners (since 1968)

		£
1968	Gay Brewer	23,107
1969	Billy Casper	23,483
1970	Christy O'Connor	31,532
1971	Gary Player	11,281
1972	Bob Charles	18,538
1973	Tony Jacklin	24,839
1974	Peter Oosterhuis	32,127
1975	Dale Hayes	20,507
1976	Severiano Ballesteros	39,504
1977	Severiano Ballesteros	46,436
1978	Severiano Ballesteros	54,348
1979	Sandy Lyle	49,233
1980	Greg Norman	74,829
1981	Bernhard Langer	95,991
1982	Sandy Lyle	86,141
1983	Nick Faldo	140,761
1984	Bernhard Langer	160,883
1985	Sandy Lyle	162,553

Most times leading money-winner
3 – Severiano Ballesteros (1976, 1977, 1978)
3 – Sandy Lyle (1979, 1982, 1985)

The events that made up the 1985 European Tour were:
Tunisian Open
Cespa Madrid Open
Italian Open
Car Care Plan International
GSI Open
Whyte & Mackay PGA Championship
Four Stars National Pro-Celebrity
Dunhill British Masters
Jersey Open
Carrolls Irish Open
Johnnie Walker Monte Carlo Open
Peugeot French Open
Lawrence Batley International
British Open
KLM Dutch Open
Scandinavian Enterprise Open
Glasgow Open
Benson & Hedges International Open
Lufthansa German Open
Panasonic European Open
Ebel European Masters-Swiss Open
Sanyo Open
Suntory World Match-Play
Lancôme Trophy
Compaigne de Chauffe Cannes Open
Dunhill Cup
Benson & Hedges Spanish Open
Quinta do Lago Portuguese Open

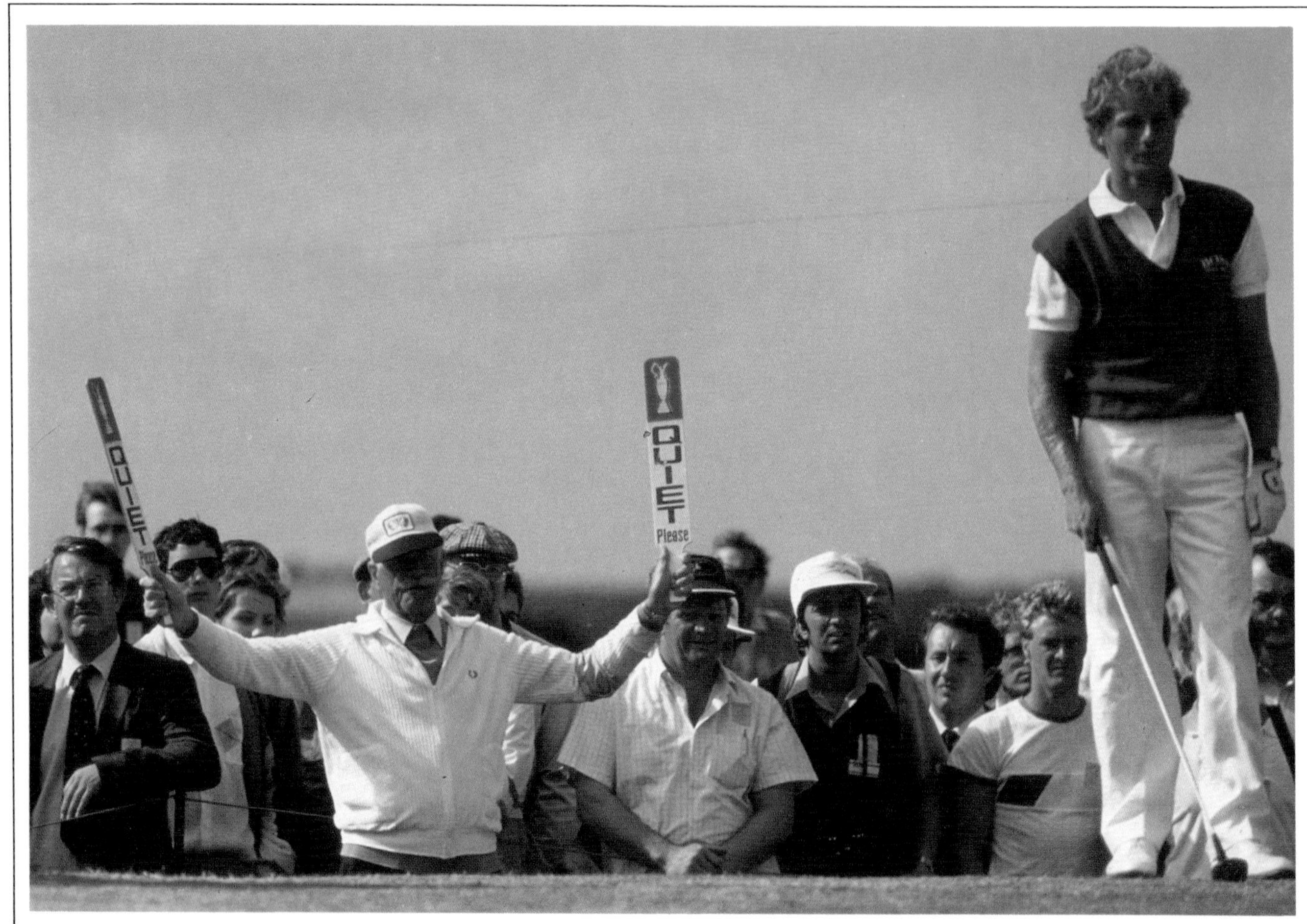

Extreme quiet on the putting green is one of the most important rules of etiquette. This steward ensures that Bernhard Langer has the maximum amount of silence during the 1985 British Open.

Extra Holes

Extra holes are played to decide the winner of a match if the scores are level at the end of a predetermined number of rounds. The extra holes can be in the form of a sudden death play-off or simply an agreed number of holes.

The most extra holes required to determine the winner of a major match-play competition is 12. That was the number Fred Daly needed to beat Alan Poulton in the British Professional Match-Play event at Walton Heath in 1952.

The most extra holes in any one match in a match-play competition is 13. This has happened twice and, by coincidence, was in the same competition, although in different years. Bill Collins (US) beat W. J. Branch at the 31st hole during their match in the News of the World Tournament at Turnberry in 1960 and Harold Henning beat Peter Alliss, also at the 31st hole, at Walton Heath in the following year.

See also Play-Off, Sudden Death, Longest Matches.

F

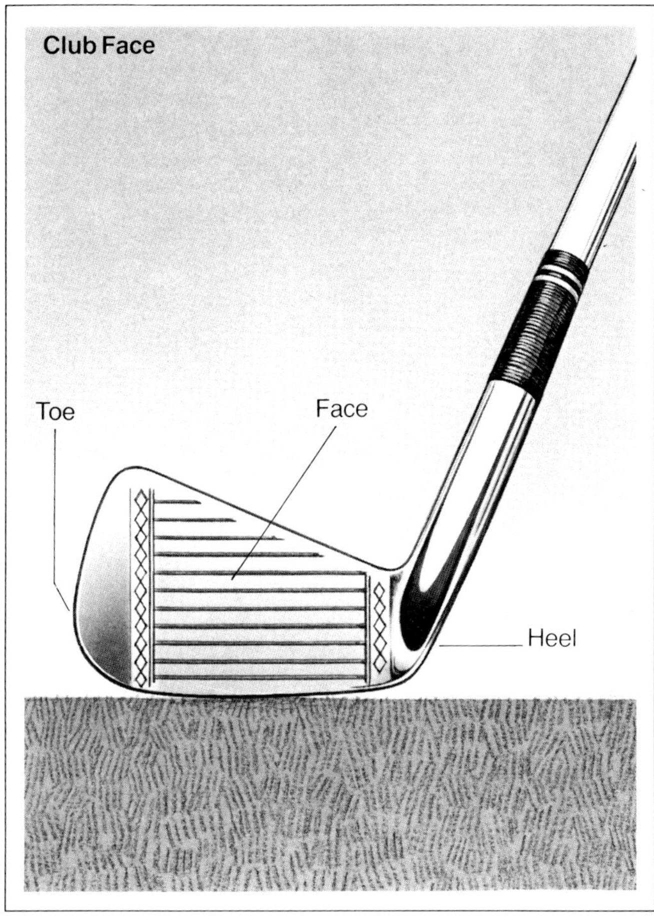

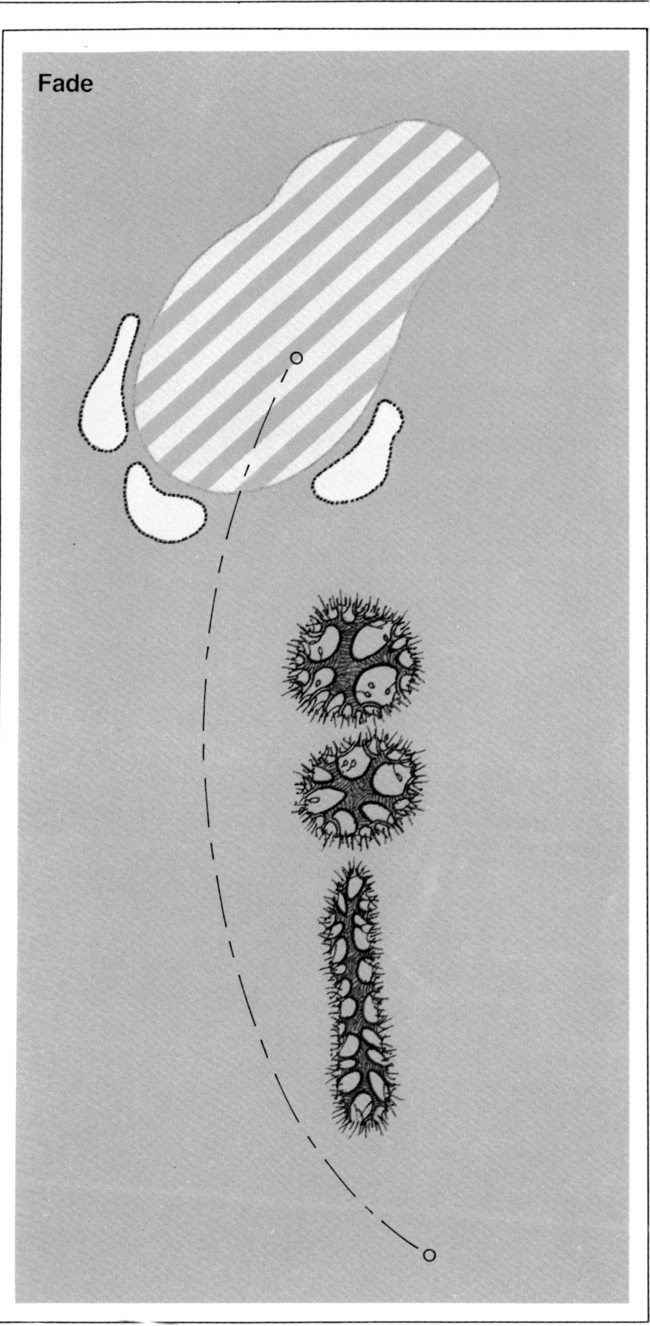

Face

(1) That part of the surface of the club head which is designed for hitting the ball. The rules of golf dealing with the specifications of the club face lay down strict guidelines about the design and size of grooves and the markings on them.
(2) The front part of a bunker where the sand rises sharply.

Fade

A controlled shot in which the ball travels from left to right towards its target. It is the opposite of a **draw**. To achieve a controlled fade the club face must be moving across the ball from right to left at the moment of impact.

Fairway

Nearly all golf holes have five distinct features: the teeing area, the rough, hazards, the green and the fairway. The fairway is the cut area of the course between the tee and the green, but not cut as close as the green itself. It is to the fairway on par-4 and -5 holes that the golfer tries to drive from the tee. The fairway does not necessarily have to extend the full distance between the tee and green. Quite often a road, lake, stream or rough can interrupt it.

Faldo, Nick

Nick Faldo has been around the British professional circuit for a long time, yet he is still under 30. The youngest-ever winner of the English Amateur Championship, in 1975, he turned professional the following year. In 1977 he was selected for the Great Britain Ryder Cup team and, at the age of 20, he became the youngest-ever competitor.

Faldo was Rookie of the Year in 1977, his first full year as a professional, and the following year won his first tournament on the European circuit—the Colgate PGA at

The emergence of Nick Faldo in the 1970s gave British golf new hope for the future.

Royal Birkdale. He won the same event again in 1980 and 1981.

Although his best British Open placing is 4th, his greatest performance was at Royal Birkdale in 1983 when he went into the final round two strokes behind the leader, Tom Watson. However, he could not keep up the challenge and fell away towards the end of the round. The following year, at St Andrews, he had two rounds of 68 and one of 69 but a disastrous fourth round of 76 let him down.

He joined the US circuit in 1981 and became the first Briton since Tony Jacklin to win in the United States, when he triumphed in the 1984 Sea Pines-Heritage Classic. His skills have earned him over £500,000 and he was the leading money winner on the European Tour in 1983.

Career highlights
French Open 1983
Swiss Open 1983
Ryder Cup 1977, 1979, 1981, 1983, 1985
English Amateur 1975
British Open (best) jt 4th – 1982

Families

Golf has, over the years, established more than its fair share of famous golfing families, some of which have included:

Old Tom and Young Tom **Morris**, perhaps the most famous of all golfing relatives. Father and son, they won the British Open eight times between them. Old Tom won it in 1861, 1862, 1864, and 1867 and Young Tom in 1868, 1869, 1870 and 1872.

During the same era there existed another famous father and son pair, who also both won the British Open. Willie **Park** senior was the first winner of the Open in 1860, and went on to win it on three more occasions. His son, Willie junior, won it in 1889.

In the Ryder Cup, Percy **Alliss** and his son Peter stand unique as the only father and son combination to play in the competition.

American father and son Clayton and Vance **Heafner** played Walker Cup and Ryder Cup golf respectively.

Perhaps the best known British golfing brothers were the **Whitcombe**s, Charles, Ernest and Reg. All three played in the Ryder Cup at Ridgewood, New Jersey in 1933.

Brothers Bernard and Geoffrey **Hunt** also appeared in the same Great Britain Ryder Cup team—in 1963 in Atlanta. Jay and Lionel **Hebert** both represented the United States in the 1957 Ryder Cup. Both of them also won the US PGA title.

Willie **Smith** won the US Open title in 1899. His brother Alex won the title in 1910. Another brother, Macdonald, was involved in a three-way play-off.

Any sport would have to go a long way to beat the golfing feats of Vitale **Turnesa**'s sons. He had seven of them, six of whom became professional golfers. Joe and Jim both played in the Ryder Cup, while Jim also won the US PGA title. Willie was twice the US Amateur Champion and, in 1948, the British Amateur Champion. He represented the United States in the Walker Cup.

Spain has produced two famous pairs of golfing brothers over the years. Firstly there was Angel and

Sebastian **Miguel**. But they have been succeeded in recent years by Manuel and Severiano **Ballesteros**. Ramon Sota, one of Spain's top players in the 1960s, is an uncle of Seve and Manuel.

Of other current brothers on the professional circuits perhaps the best known are the American pair of Bobby and Lanny **Wadkins**.

Gary **Player** has been followed into the world of professional golf by his son Wayne. When they both played in the 1979 British Open, they became the first pair of father and son to play in the Open since Ernest and Eddie Whitcombe.

Perhaps one of the most unusual finishes to a tournament was in the 1956 Tasmanian Open. The winner was Peter **Toogood**. His father Alfred was second, and brother, John, was third!

Father and son Antoine and André **Barras** contested the final of the 1952 Swiss Amateur Championship.

Harry and Arnold **Bentley** are the only brothers to have won the English Amateur title. They won in 1936 and 1939 respectively. Both also played Walker Cup golf.

Stanley **Lunt** and his son Michael stand unique as they both won the English Amateur title; Stanley in 1934, Michael in 1966.

Two famous pairs of British brothers and sisters were the **Wethered**s and the **Bonallack**s. Roger and Joyce Wethered were both national amateur champions and both played Walker Cup and Curtis Cup golf respectively. Michael and Sally Bonallack can both claim the

Baldovino Ballesteros is seen caddying for his famous brother, Severiano, at Wentworth.

Five times English amateur champion, Michael Bonallack is seen here after his first success in 1961. With him is his wife Angela who won the Ladies title twice.

same distinctions. Michael Bonallack's wife, Angela, was also twice English Women's Champion and her sister, Shirley Ward, was the 1964 English Girls' Champion. Michael's brother, Tony, made up this remarkable golf-playing family—he represented Essex at county level.

Baldovino **Dassu** of Italy set the record for the lowest 18-hole score on the European PGA Tour in 1971. His sister, Federica, established a Women's PGA 54-hole record in 1985.

One of the best known mother and daughter golfing combinations was Rene and Catherine **Lacoste** who both won the British Women's Championship.

And a famous father and daughter pair in recent times have been the **Panton**s. John topped the PGA Order of Merit in 1953 and daughter Cathy topped the Ladies PGA Order of Merit in 1979.

Despite the above list of famous sporting relatives, which includes many famous names, any sporting family would have to go a long way to beat that of the **Duncan**s. John Duncan was Welsh Amateur champion in 1905 and 1909. His wife Blanche was Welsh Ladies' champion five times—both won their respective titles in 1909. That same year John's brother, Hugh, reached the semi-final. John's son, Tony, was Welsh champion on four occasions and another son, George, was a Welsh Championship semi-finalist and international golfer. Two other sons, John and Derek, were both low-handicap players.

Some famous sportsmen from other fields with playing relatives include tennis player Buster Mottram and cricketers Glenn Turner and Rodney Marsh. Pip **Elson**, who holed-in-one during the 1979 European Open at Turnberry, is Mottram's cousin.

Greg **Turner**, the brother of leading New Zealand Test cricketer Glenn, won the 1985 New Zealand PGA Championship. It was only his third professional tournament.

Rodney and Graham **Marsh** have both proved to be outstanding performers in their two sports: Rodney as Australia's leading wicket-keeper in Test cricket, and Graham as one of the country's leading golfers.

Scotland's Sam Torrance shows perfect style, highlighting the follow-through.

Faulkner, Max

Max Faulkner is the only Briton to have won three of the most prestigious tournaments in the United Kingdom—the Open, the PGA Match-Play Championship and the Dunlop Masters, although the Australian, Peter Thomson, has also achieved this feat.

Faulkner's Open win was at Portrush in 1951 (the only time the Open has been held on the Irish course), and he had the good fortune to be in the clubhouse on 285 when bad weather came. Despite efforts by Charles Ward and Antonio Cerda he held on to win the title and the accompanying cheque for £325. A testimony to the magnitude of the triumph is the fact that no other Briton won the trophy for 18 years.

A tall man, Faulkner was a powerful hitter and also had a good swing. On and off the course he was a colourful and entertaining character and his flamboyance was displayed in the bright, casual clothes he always wore—notably his plus-fours.

He was still playing actively in the late 1960s and early 1970s and gained a second British Seniors title in 1970, two years after winning his first. He also won the 1968 Portuguese Open at the age of 52.

Career highlights
British Open 1951
Spanish Open 1952, 1953, 1957
British Seniors 1968, 1970
Ryder Cup 1947, 1949, 1951, 1953, 1957

Flight

The line the ball takes through the air. It varies according to the loft on the club used for the shot. Experienced players can deliberately play a ball with a low or high flight according to the needs of the shot.
See diagram on page 75.

Floyd, Ray

Ray Floyd turned professional as a 19-year-old in 1961. Two years later he joined the US Tour and in his first ten tournaments failed to make the 54-hole cut. In the 11th, the St Petersburg Open, he collected his first prize money when he won the $3,500 first prize. In 1977 Floyd won his tenth US tournament, at Pleasant Valley, and took his career earnings past the $1 million mark.

One Masters and two US PGA titles boosted his winnings considerably. His first major was the 1969 PGA title and in 1976 he won the Masters, completely dominating his opponents. He led from start to finish, beat Ben Crenshaw by eight strokes, set Masters records for 36 and 54 holes and equalled Jack Nicklaus's 72-hole record.

In 1982, in his 40th year, Floyd won the PGA title for the second time. This strong, long-hitter has remained a constant threat to younger players. And in 1986 he surprised many people by winning his first US open title at the age of 43, the oldest winner of the title.

Career highlights
US Open, 1986
US PGA 1969, 1982
US Masters 1976
Ryder Cup 1969, 1975, 1977, 1981, 1983, 1985
British Open (best) jt 2nd – 1978

Follow-through

The completion of the swing after the club has made contact with the ball. Although the follow-through has no bearing on the ball's flight, all golfers are taught to continue their swing after striking the ball.

The 1984 British Open at St Andrews drew record crowds, and took record gate receipts for the championship.

Max Faulkner sinks an 11-ft putt on the final green to win the British Professional Match-Play championship at Ganton in 1953. Dai Rees, the beaten finalist looks on.

Fore!
An interjection used by golfers to warn people that a ball is heading in their direction. It is believed to be derived from the military command 'Beware before!' used to warn soldiers to fall to the ground so as to enable gunfire to pass over them. The expression was reputedly first used by the Scottish reformer, John Knox, in the 16th century.

Four-ball
A match involving four players, usually one pair against another. The better ball of each pair can decide a hole, or, alternatively, the aggregate scores at the end of the round can decide the winning team. Although more popular than foursomes, a four-ball match takes considerably longer to complete. It is suitable for either match-play or stroke-play conditions.

Foursomes
A match involving four players, with two on each side. Each team plays alternate strokes at the same ball but, irrespective of who played the last stroke at the previous hole, they must take alternate turns at driving. Like the four-ball type of competition, the foursome is included in the Ryder Cup programme, with four matches being played on each of the first two days. Although foursomes is one of the oldest forms of golf it is little played outside Britain nowadays except in major international team tournaments.

French Open
The oldest of the continental Open championships, it was first played at La Boulie in 1906 and won by Arnaud Massy—the first and only French winner of the British Open.

Many famous golfers have won the French Open. Two members of the Great Triumvirate, Braid and Taylor, were successful before the First World War. Walter Hagen won once during the inter-war period and Henry Cotton and Byron Nelson were post-war winners. In recent times Ballesteros, Langer, Lyle and Norman have all gained the title.

One of the most popular men on the European circuit in the early 1970s was Lu Liang Huan, who delighted the Biarritz crowd in 1971 when he won the French title with a four-round total of 262, just two strokes outside the European record.

Fulford
This attractive course just outside York, one of England's finest cities, is well known for being, since 1971, the home of the Benson and Hedges International Open, a firmly established tournament on the European PGA circuit. Fulford opened in 1909 but had to wait until 1967 for the first major tournament to be held there. On that occasion Malcolm Gregson and Brian Huggett shared the first prize in the Martini International tournament. The 1976 Ladies' British Open Amateur Stroke-Play championship was also played at the course, as was the last PGA Match-Play tournament in 1979.

Length 6787 yd (6206 m)
Par 72
Course record 62 – Doug Sanders (Benson and Hedges International, 1975)
62 – Ian Woosnam (Benson and Hedges International, 1985)

French Open

Winners

Year	Name	Venue	Score
1906	A. Massy	La Boulie	292
1907	A. Massy	La Boulie	298
1908	J. H. Taylor	La Boulie	300
1909	J. H. Taylor	La Boulie	293
1910	J. Braid	La Boulie	298
1911	A. Massy	La Boulie	284
1912	J. Gassiat	La Boulie	289
1913	G. Duncan	Chantilly	304
1914	J. D. Edgar	Le Touquet	288
1915–19 Not held			
1920	W. Hagen	La Boulie	298
1921	A. Boomer	Le Touquet	284
1922	A. Boomer	La Boulie	286
1923	J. Ockenden	Dieppe	288
1924	C. J. H. Tolley (*)	La Boulie	290
1925	A. Massy	Chantilly	291
1926	A. Boomer	Saint-Cloud	280
1927	G. Duncan	Saint-Germain	299
1928	C. J. H. Tolley (*)	La Boulie	283
1929	A. Boomer	Fourqueux	283
1930	E. R. Whitcombe	Dieppe	282
1931	A. Boomer	Deauville	291
1932	A. J. Lacey	Saint-Cloud	295
1933	B. Gadd	Chantilly	283
1934	S. F. Brews	Dieppe	284
1935	S. F. Brews	Le Touquet	293
1936	M. Dallemagne	Saint-Germain	277
1937	M. Dallemagne	Saint-Cloud	278
1938	M. Dallemagne	Fourqueux	282
1939	M. Pose	Le Touquet	285
1940–45 Not held			
1946	T. H. Cotton	Saint-Cloud	269
1947	T. H. Cotton	Chantilly	285
1948	F. Cavalo	Saint-Cloud	287
1949	U. Grappasonni	Saint-Germain	275
1950	R. de Vicenzo	Chantilly	279
1951	H. Hassanein	Saint-Cloud	278
1952	A. D. Locke	Saint-Germain	268
1953	A. D. Locke	La Boulie	276
1954	F. van Donck	Saint-Cloud	275
1955	B. Nelson	La Boulie	271
1956	A. Miguel	Deauville	277
1957	F. van Donck	Saint-Cloud	266
1958	F. van Donck	Saint-Germain	276
1959	D. C. Thomas	La Boulie	276
1960	R. de Vicenzo	Saint-Cloud	275
1961	K. D. Nagle	La Boulie	271
1962	A. Murray	Saint-Germain	274
1963	B. Devlin	Saint-Cloud	273
1964	R. de Vicenzo	Chantilly	272
1965	R. Sota	Saint-Nom-La-Breteche	268
1966	D. J. Hutchinson	La Boulie	274
1967	B. J. Hunt	Saint-Germain	271
1968	P. J. Butler	Saint-Cloud	272
1969	J. Garaialde	Saint-Nom-La-Breteche	277
1970	D. Graham	Chantaco	268
1971	Lu Liang Huan	Biarritz	262
1972	B. Jaeckel	Biarritz and La Nivelle	265
1973	P. Oosterhuis	La Boulie	280
1974	P. Oosterhuis	Chantilly	284
1975	B. Barnes	La Boulie	281
1976	V. Tshabalala	Le Touquet	272
1977	S. Ballesteros	Le Touquet	282
1978	D. Hayes	La Baule	269
1979	B. Gallacher	Lyons	284
1980	G. Norman	Saint-Cloud	268
1981	A. W. Lyle	Saint-Germain	270
1982	S. Ballesteros	Saint-Nom-La-Breteche	278
1983	N. Faldo	La Boulie	277
1984	B. Langer	Saint-Cloud	270
1985	S. Ballesteros	Saint-Germain	263

(*) denotes amateur

Most wins
5 – Aubrey Boomer (1921, 1922, 1926, 1929, 1931)

Lowest score (72 holes)
262 – Lu Liang Huan (Biarritz, 1971)

Gate Money

Gate money has been charged in Britain since the beginning of the century. The leading professionals, who used to play exhibition money matches, would make spectators pay a fee in order to watch the game. The first British Open at which spectators had to pay was at Royal Lytham and St Annes in 1926. The first prize amounted to just £100 and members of the public paid a total £1,365 7s 6d to watch the championship. In 1985 the first prize was £65,000 and a crowd of nearly 200,000 paid over £1 million for the privilege of watching the world's top golfers.

The first time the gate money from the British Open exceeded £1 million was at St Andrews in 1984.

The record paying attendance for the British Open was 193,126 at the 1984 championship, and the record for one day was 34,897 on the first day of the same championship.

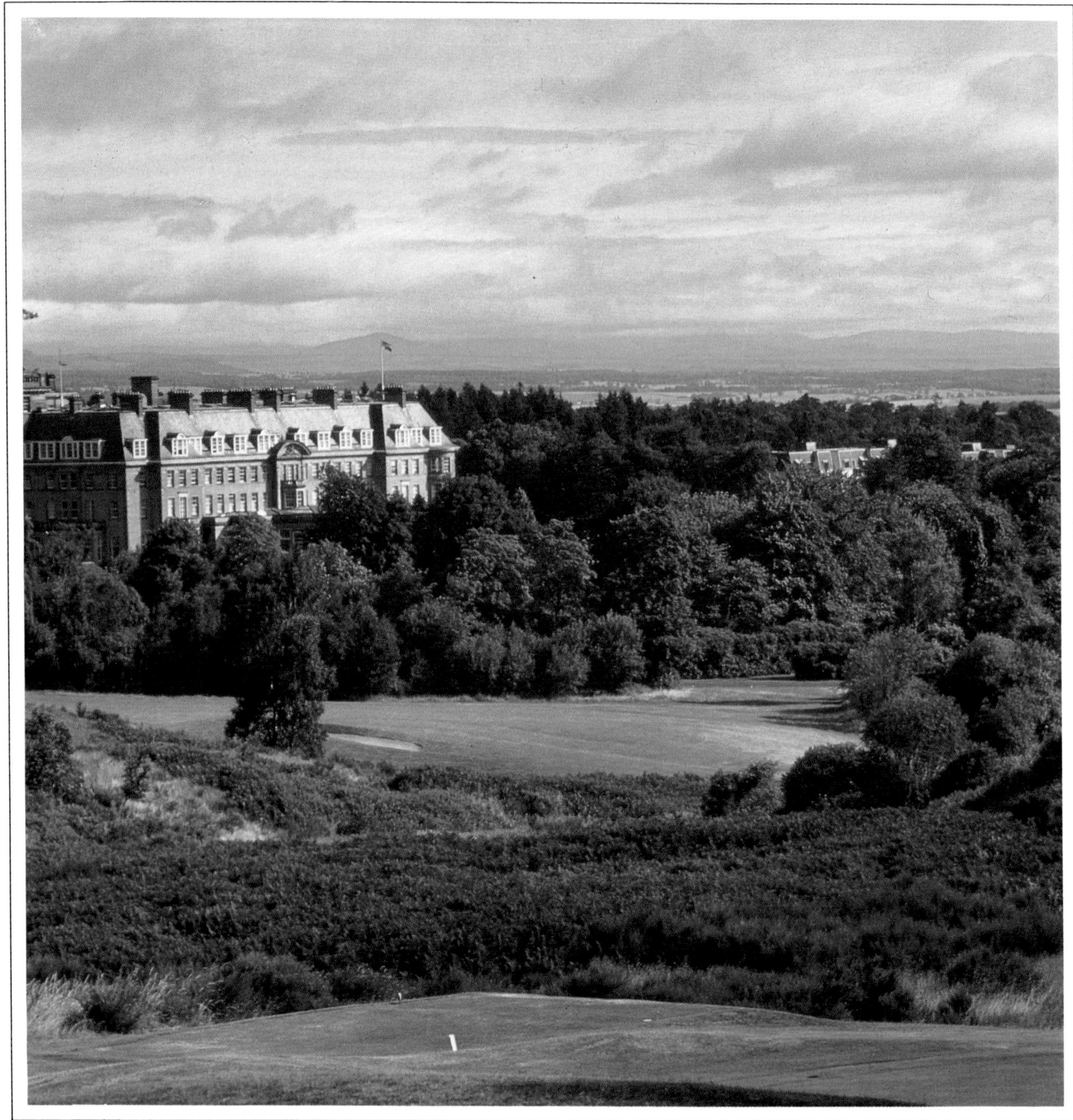

A view across the 6th hole at Gleneagles which highlights the beauty of one of Scotland's most famous courses.

The first time the British Open attendance topped the 100,000 mark was also at St Andrews, in 1978, when 125,271 people watched the event.

The first time admission was charged for the US Open was in 1922 at Skokie Country Club, Illinois.

German Open

The first German Open was held at the Baden–Baden course in 1912 and won by the great John Taylor. The president of the Baden–Baden club at the time was William Roosevelt, a nephew of the former US President, Theodore Roosevelt. After Taylor's victory the championship was suspended until 1926 when the winner was Percy Alliss, father of Peter. Percy also went on to win the title in each of the next three years.

The West German, Bernhard Langer, won the Open for the third time in five years in 1985, but the event, held at Bremen, was reduced to a 54-hole event because of bad weather. Also, as a result of the weather the South African-based Mark McNulty (the 1980 winner) was

Winners

Year	Name	Venue	Score
1912	J. H. Taylor	Baden–Baden	277
1913–25 Not held			
1926	P. Alliss	Berlin	284
1927	P. Alliss	Berlin	288
1928	P. Alliss	Berlin	280
1929	P. Alliss	Berlin	285
1930	A. Boyer	Baden–Baden	266
1931	R. Golias	Berlin	298
1932	A. Boyer	Bad Ems	282
1933	P. Alliss	Bad Ems	284
1934	A. H. Padgham	Bad Ems	285
1935	A. Boyer	Bad Ems	280
1936	A. Boyer	Berlin	291
1937	T. H. Cotton	Bad Ems	274
1938	T. H. Cotton	Frankfurt	285
1939	T. H. Cotton	Bad Ems	280
1940–50 Not held			
1951	A. Cerda	Hamburg	286
1952	A. Cerda	Hamburg	283
1953	F. van Donck	Frankfurt	271
1954	A. D. Locke	Krefeld	279
1955	K. Bousfield	Hamburg	279
1956	F. van Donck	Frankfurt	277
1957	H. Weetman	Cologne	279
1958	F. de Luca	Krefeld	275
1959	K. Bousfield	Hamburg	271
1960	P. W. Thomson	Cologne	281
1961	B. J. Hunt	Krefeld	272
1962	R. Verwey	Hamburg	276
1963	B. G. Huggett	Cologne	278
1964	R. de Vicenzo	Krefeld	275
1965	H. R. Henning	Hamburg	274
1966	R. Stanton	Frankfurt	274
1967	D. Swaelens	Krefeld	273
1968	B. Franklin	Cologne	285
1969	J. Garaialde	Frankfurt	272
1970	J. Garaialde	Krefeld	276
1971	N. C. Coles	Bremen	279
1972	G. Marsh	Frankfurt	271
1973	F. Abreu	Hubbelrath	276
1974	S. Owen	Krefeld	276
1975	M. Bembridge	Bremen	285
1976	S. Hobday	Frankfurt	266
1977	T. Britz	Düsseldorf	275
1978	S. Ballesteros	Cologne	268
1979	A. Jacklin	Frankfurt	277
1980	M. McNulty	Berlin	280
1981	B. Langer	Hamburg	272
1982	B. Langer	Stuttgart	279
1983	C. Pavin	Cologne	275
1984	W. Grady	Frankfurt	268
1985	B. Langer	Bremen	183(a)

(a) played over 54 holes

Most wins
5 – Percy Alliss (1926, 1927, 1928, 1929, 1933)
Lowest score (72 holes)
266 – Auguste Boyer (1930)
266 – Simon Hobday (1976)

deprived of a European record. His first round of 59 was the first below 60 on the European tour but, as the course had been reduced from par-74 to par-66, it was not ratified as a record.

Gimmie

An American term, a contraction of 'give me', used when the ball is so close to the hole that it cannot be missed and will be conceded by the player's opponent.

Gleneagles

Adjacent to the luxurious Gleneagles Hotel are four courses, the King's, Queen's, Prince's and Glendavon courses. The last two have been added within the last ten

Australia's most consistent player of the 1970s and 1980s, David Graham has enjoyed a successful career in the United States since 1971.

years but the King's and Queen's have been in existence since 1919, five years before the hotel itself opened. They were designed by James Braid and initially the Queen's course was only a nine-hole one.

Situated at Auchterarder in Perthshire and overlooking the Grampians and Ochils, Gleneagles enjoys a scenic beauty which is hard to better on any British golf course.

Since it is not a links course Gleneagles has never staged the British Open. Although it has been the setting for major events, it is nowadays used more by visiting golfers, being particularly popular with Americans. The first important event to be held at Gleneagles was the match between British and US professionals in 1921—the forerunner of the Ryder Cup. Percy Alliss won the first major individual competition at Gleneagles, the 1935 Penfold Tournament. Fred Daly won it on the other occasion it was held at Gleneagles, in 1948. The club has also staged the British Ladies' Open Amateur Championship, the Scottish Ladies' Championship and the Double Diamond World of Golf Classic three times during its short life.

King's course
Length 6705 yd (6131 m)
Par 72
Course record 63 – Brian Barnes (Double Diamond World of Golf Classic, 1977)

Gloves
Golf gloves were first worn by women golfers, usually on both hands. Some male golfers started wearing special gloves with no backs or fingers at the turn of the century, but players like Vardon and Taylor did not use them. It was just before the Second World War that leading golfers began to wear gloves and their popularity spread after the war.

Present-day gloves are made of leather and improve the grip on the club. Right-handed players wear the glove on their left hand and vice versa.

Golf Development Council
This was formed in 1965 with the aim of providing better facilities for golf and for raising the standards of golfing generally, in liaison with local authorities and Sports Councils. Several bodies connected with the game were founder members, including the Royal and Ancient Club.

Golf Foundation
Instituted in 1952, the Golf Foundation aims to develop and promote the game among youngsters. It has its own coaching scheme and players like Brian Barnes, Bernard Gallacher and Peter Oosterhuis have all benefited from this. Financial support for the Foundation is provided by companies and organizations within the game. Its headquarters are at 78, Third Avenue, Bush Hill Park, Enfield, EN1 1BX.

Golf Writers' Trophy
An annual award made by the British Association of Golf Writers to the person, or team, who they feel has done most for golf during the year. Inaugurated in 1951, it was first won by Max Faulkner. Tony Jacklin, Peter Oosterhuis and Severiano Ballesteros are the only players to have won two individual awards.

Winners (unless stated, all are players)

1951	Max Faulkner
1952	Elizabeth Price
1953	Joe Carr
1954	Frances Smith (née Stephens)
1955	Ladies' Golf Union's Touring Team
1956	John Beharrell
1957	Dai Rees
1958	Harry Bradshaw
1959	Eric Brown
1960	Sir Stuart Goodwin (sponsor)
1961	Commander R. C. Roe (ex-hon. secretary Royal and Ancient)
1962	Marley Spearman
1963	Michael Lunt
1964	Great Britain and Ireland Eisenhower Trophy Team
1965	Gerald Micklem (President, English Golf Union)
1966	Ronnie Shade
1967	John Panton
1968	Michael Bonallack
1969	Tony Jacklin
1970	Tony Jacklin
1971	British Walker Cup Team
1972	Michelle Walker
1973	Peter Oosterhuis
1974	Peter Oosterhuis
1975	The Golf Foundation
1976	Great Britain and Ireland Eisenhower Trophy Team
1977	Christy O'Connor
1978	Peter McEvoy
1979	Severiano Ballesteros
1980	Sandy Lyle
1981	Bernhard Langer
1982	Gordon Brand, Jnr
1983	Nick Faldo
1984	Severiano Ballesteros
1985	Europe's Ryder Cup Team

Goose-Necked Putter
A putter in which the shaft is joined to the end of the head but has a curve in it to give the impression, when looking down the shaft, that it is joined near the centre. Before the introduction of the centre-shafted putter the goose-necked (or wry-necked) putter was very popular. See diagram.

Graham, David
David Graham, the friendly Australian, is now firmly established on the US PGA circuit which he first joined in 1971. A professional since the age of 16, he switched from left- to right-handed play and went on to win major honours in more than ten different countries.

His first big success was with Bruce Devlin when, representing Australia, they won the 1970 World Cup. The following year Graham pulled off his first big individual event, the Japan Open, and in 1976 he deprived Hale Irwin of a hat trick of World Match-Play

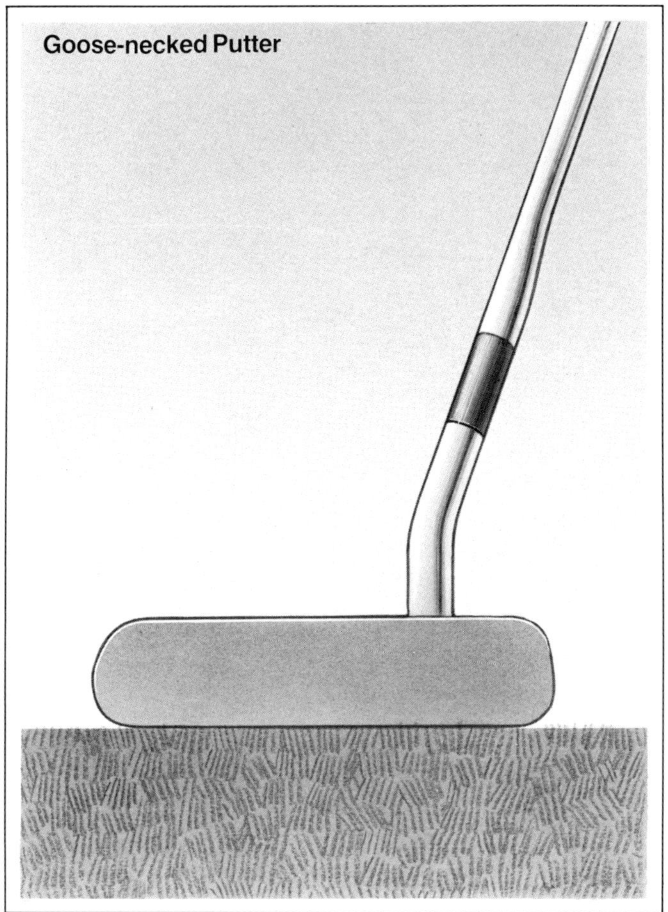
Goose-necked Putter

championship wins when he beat the American at the second extra hole at Wentworth.

He won the 1979 US PGA title and was voted sportsman of the year in his own country. However, he nearly let that first big title slip away from him. Going into the 72nd hole, he needed a four to win the title by two strokes: there was near disaster when he took a six. He had to play off with Ben Crenshaw but found his form again to win at the third extra hole.

His second major followed in 1981 when he won the US Open after coming from behind to clinch his victory.

Career highlights
US Open 1981
US PGA 1979
World Match-Play 1976
World Cup (team) 1970
British Open (best) jt 3rd – 1985

Grand Slam
The winning of the world's four major golf titles: the British Open, the US Open, the US Masters and the US Professional Golfers' Association Championship in the same year. No golfer has yet achieved this remarkable feat and the nearest any man came to it was in 1953 when Ben Hogan won them all except the US PGA. He is one of only four men to have taken the four major titles in different years. The others are Jack Nicklaus, Gary Player and Gene Sarazen.

Bobby Jones pulled off a remarkable 'tour de force' within the space of four months in 1930 when he won the British Amateur Championship, the British Open, the US Open and the US Amateur Championship.

Greater Greensboro Open
Held at Forest Oaks, Greensboro, North Carolina, the Greater Greensboro Open holds a special place in the hearts of two of the world's most outstanding golfers, Sam Snead and Severiano Ballesteros.

Seve won his first US Tour event here in 1978, while in 1965 Sam Snead won his 84th, and last, US Tour event at the age of 52. Snead was, ironically, the event's first winner back in 1938. He won it eight times, a US record for one man winning the same tournament.

Winners (since 1970)

Year	Name	Score
1970	G. Player	271
1971	B. Allin	275
1972	G. Archer	272
1973	J. Rodriguez	267
1974	B. Charles	270
1975	T. Weiskopf	275
1976	A. Geiberger	268
1977	D. Edwards	276
1978	S. Ballesteros	282
1979	R. Floyd	282
1980	C. Stadler	275
1981	L. Nelson	281
1982	D. Edwards	285
1983	L. Wadkins	275
1984	A. Bean	280
1985	J. Sindelar	285
1986	A. W. Lyle	276

Most wins
8 – Sam Snead (1938, 1946, 1949, 1950, 1955, 1956, 1960, 1965)

Lowest score (72 holes)
267 – George Archer (1967)
267 – Billy Casper (1968)
267 – Juan Rodriguez (1973)

Great Triumvirate, The
At the turn of the 20th century, three men dominated golf so much they became known as the Great Triumvirate.

They were James Braid from Scotland, John Henry Taylor from Devon, and Channel Islander Harry Vardon.

Between 1894 and 1914 they won 16 of the 21 British Opens. In the five years they did not win, one or other of them finished runner-up. They also raided America, but only won the US Open on one occasion. That was in 1900 when Vardon beat Taylor by two strokes.

They were named after the Triumvirate of Pompey, Caesar and Crassus who governed the Roman Empire in 60 BC.

For biographies of the three players see their individual entries.

A

C

B

This miniature of the Augusta Nationals
Club House serves as the permanent Masters
Tournament Trophy. Designed by a firm of
silversmiths in Chicago and built by hand in
England, this trophy is comprised of 900
separate pieces of silver. On the band around the
base of the trophy are the names of the past winners.
A small replica of this trophy will be presented
each year to the winner of the Masters.

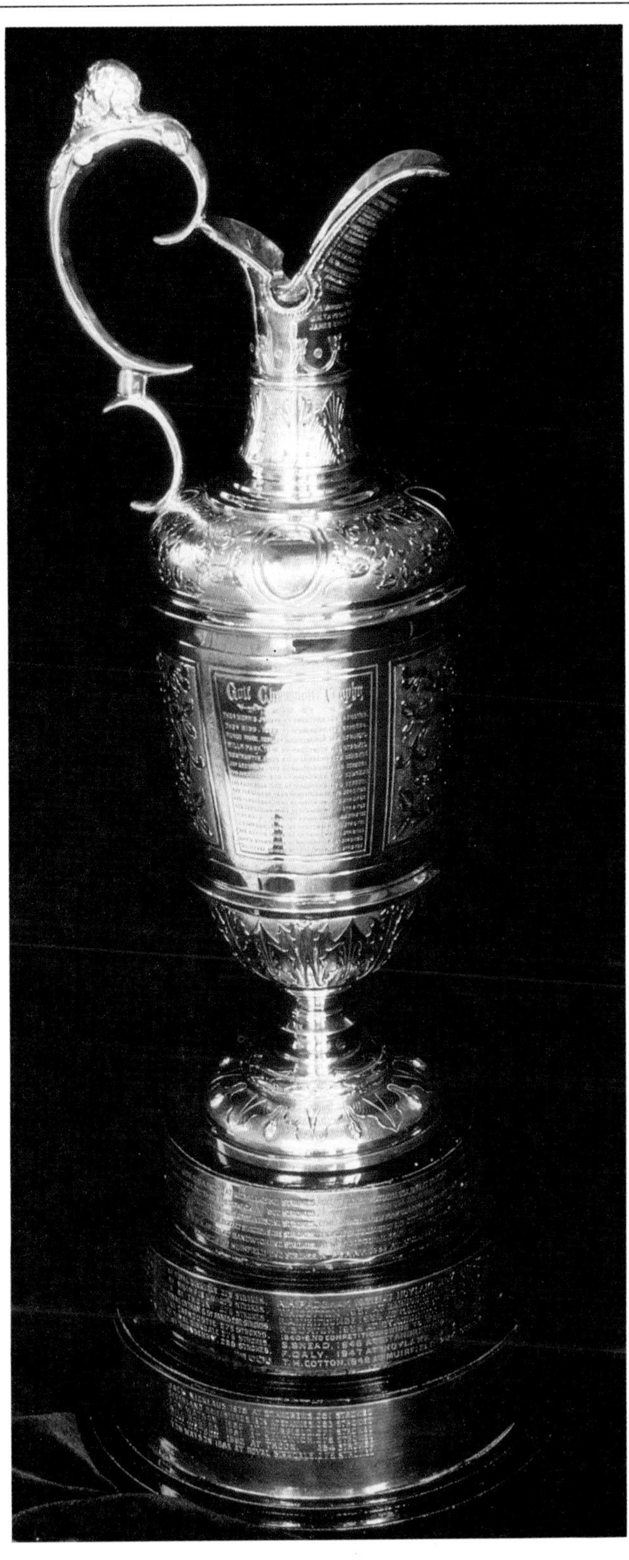

D

Golf's four most cherished prizes, the four Grand Slam trophies. They are (A) The US Open trophy, (B) the magnificent US Masters trophy which is a replica of the Augusta National clubhouse, (C) the US PGA trophy and (D) perhaps the most cherished of them all, the British Open's silver claret jug.

Green

The smooth stretch of grass at the end of a fairway specially prepared for putting and containing the hole into which the ball must be played. Originally the word was used to describe the whole area of a course upon which a round was played.

Greens come in different shapes and the rules of golf do not specify any minimum or maximum size of putting area. The world's biggest putting green is believed to be the 5th at the International Golf Club, Boston, Massachusetts, with an area in excess of 28,000 sq ft. If square it would measure approximately 170 ft by 170 ft (52×52 m).

Green Fee

The fee payable by a visitor to play a round of golf at a private club or on a municipal course. The amount of the fee varies considerably, as do the terms upon which a visitor can play at some clubs. The *Golfer's Handbook 1985* shows the fees at the public Blackpool Park, Lancashire, as being just £3. At the nearby Royal Lytham and St Annes Club it would cost £11 for a round but, before the visitor can play there, a letter of recommendation from the secretary of his own club is required.

Green, Hubert

One of Hubert Green's major qualities is his competitiveness and that was most evident during the final round of the 1977 US Open. With a death threat from a would-be assassin hanging over his head, he remained calm and went on to win the title, his first major success.

A professional since 1970, the lad from Birmingham, Alabama, was Rookie of the Year in 1971. In 1976 he won three successive US PGA tournaments, the Doral-Eastern Open, the Greater Jacksonville Open and the Heritage Classic. Those wins, together with his 1977 Open success, earned him Ryder Cup selection. He played in the Cup again in 1979 and became the first person to defeat Britain's Peter Oosterhuis in the competition. In between his two international appearances he missed the chance of a second major title when he threw away a seven-stroke lead he held over Gary Player, going into the final round of the 1978 US Masters to lose by one stroke.

With over $2 million in winnings and 20 US Tour victories to his credit, Green has remained a tough competitor. In 1985 he won his second major success when he beat Lee Trevino by two strokes at Cherry Hills to take the US PGA title.

Career highlights
US Open 1977
US PGA 1985
Ryder Cup 1977, 1979, 1985
British Open (best) 3rd – 1977

Grip

(1) That part of the shaft of a club designed to be held by the player. Any material may be added to it for extra purchase but it must not be moulded for any part of the hands.
(2) The way in which the player's hands grasp the club. This is one of the most important of golfing techniques,

The Great Triumvirate; (left to right) J. H. Taylor, James Braid and Harry Vardon.

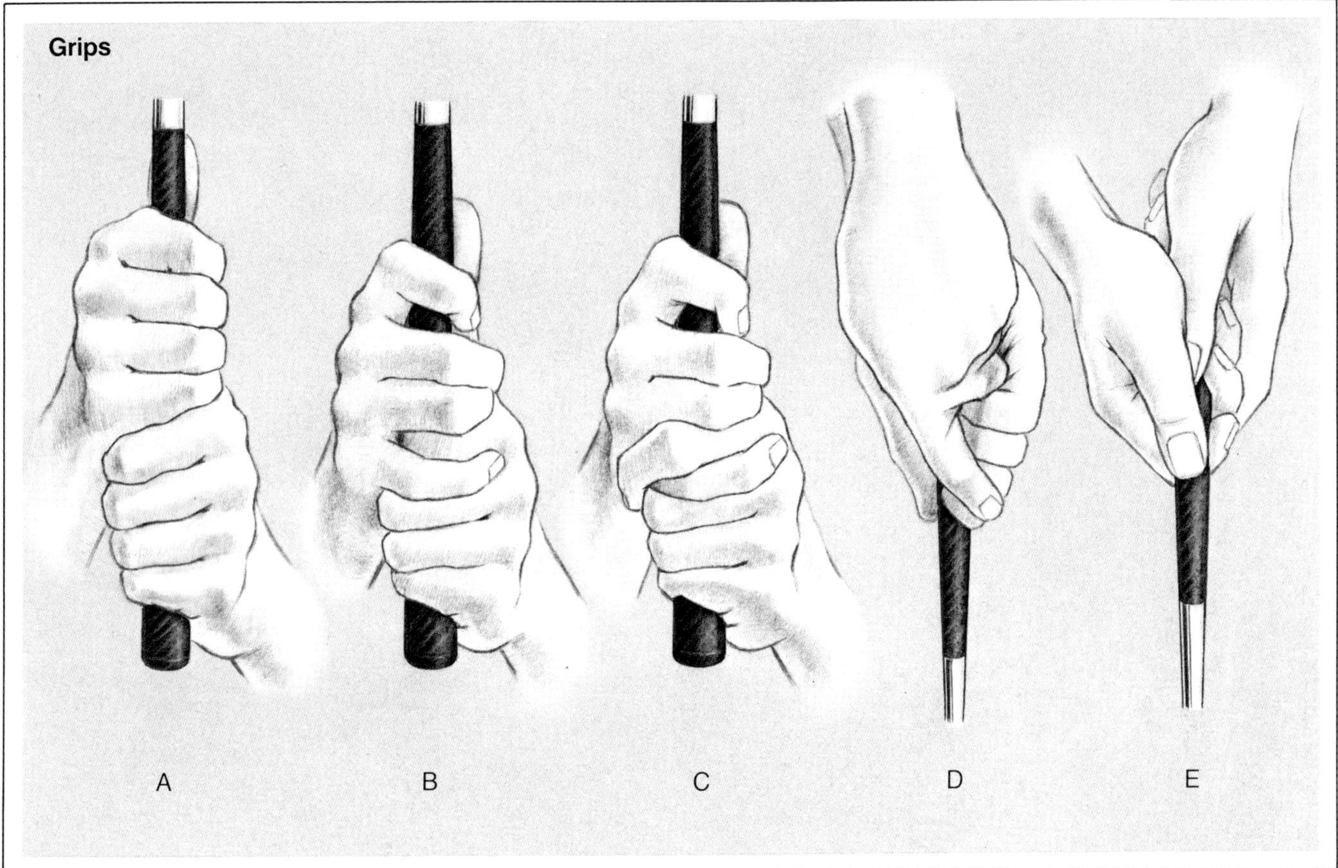

The illustration shows various grips: (**A**) *the double-handed grip;* (**B**) *the Vardon overlapping grip;* (**C**) *the interlocking grip;* (**D**) *and* (**E**) *are popular forms of grips used for putting.*

since the position of the club head at the moment of impact with the ball is determined by the hold the player has on the club.

There are many ways of gripping the club but the most popular are: the Vardon overlapping grip (named after Harry Vardon); the interlocking grip; and the two-handed grip. A different grip is normally adopted for putting. Each individual must decide which grip suits him or her, but most teachers of the game will agree that a player without a good grip will never make a good golfer. See diagrams.

Gross Score
A player's score before his or her handicap is deducted; it then becomes the net score. A 12-handicap player who completes a round in 86 strokes has a gross-86, net-74 score.

Ground the Club
To place the club head on the ground behind the ball before making a stroke. It may touch the surface lightly and must not be pressed into the ground. The club must not be grounded in a bunker.

Ground Under Repair
An area of a golf course being re-seeded, re-turfed or otherwise restored. It is designated 'ground under repair' by the club committee and clearly marked as such. Any player whose ball lands in the area may remove it without penalty.

H

Hagen, Walter
A former caddie, Walter Hagen went on to become one of the great golfers in the inter-war era. He won 11 major titles, making him second only to Jack Nicklaus. However, it was not only his collection of silverware that put him among the all-time greats. His flamboyant clothes and brash showmanship did much to popularize the sport in the 1920s.

Hagen was a great crowd puller and his exhibition matches were as popular as his tournament matches. It was in 1920 that he first entertained the British crowds with his exhibition play.

By that time he had twice won the US Open, in 1914 and 1919. The first occasion was just 12 months after his first appearance in the championship when, as an unknown, he finished joint 4th.

Underneath the extrovert exterior was a man with nerves of steel and a dynamic putting style, which won him five US PGA titles (including four in succession) and four British Open titles, starting in 1922 when he became the first US-born holder of the title.

Hagen was also responsible for getting the US team together to play Great Britain in an international at Wentworth in 1926. The following year he captained the US team in the first official Ryder Cup match, something he was to do on five more occasions.

He was accorded honorary membership of the Royal and Ancient Club in 1969. Two years later the first of the showmen-golfers died at the age of 76.

Career highlights
British Open 1922, 1924, 1928, 1929
US Open 1914, 1919
US PGA 1921, 1924, 1925, 1926, 1927
Ryder Cup 1927 (capt), 1929 (capt), 1931 (capt), 1933 (capt), 1935 (capt), 1937 (non-playing capt)

Halford Hewitt Cup

A team competition contested annually by old boys of public schools. It is said to be the world's largest golf tournament, with over 600 participants taking part as ten-man teams. The event is named after Halford Hewitt, himself a former golf-playing public schoolboy, and it

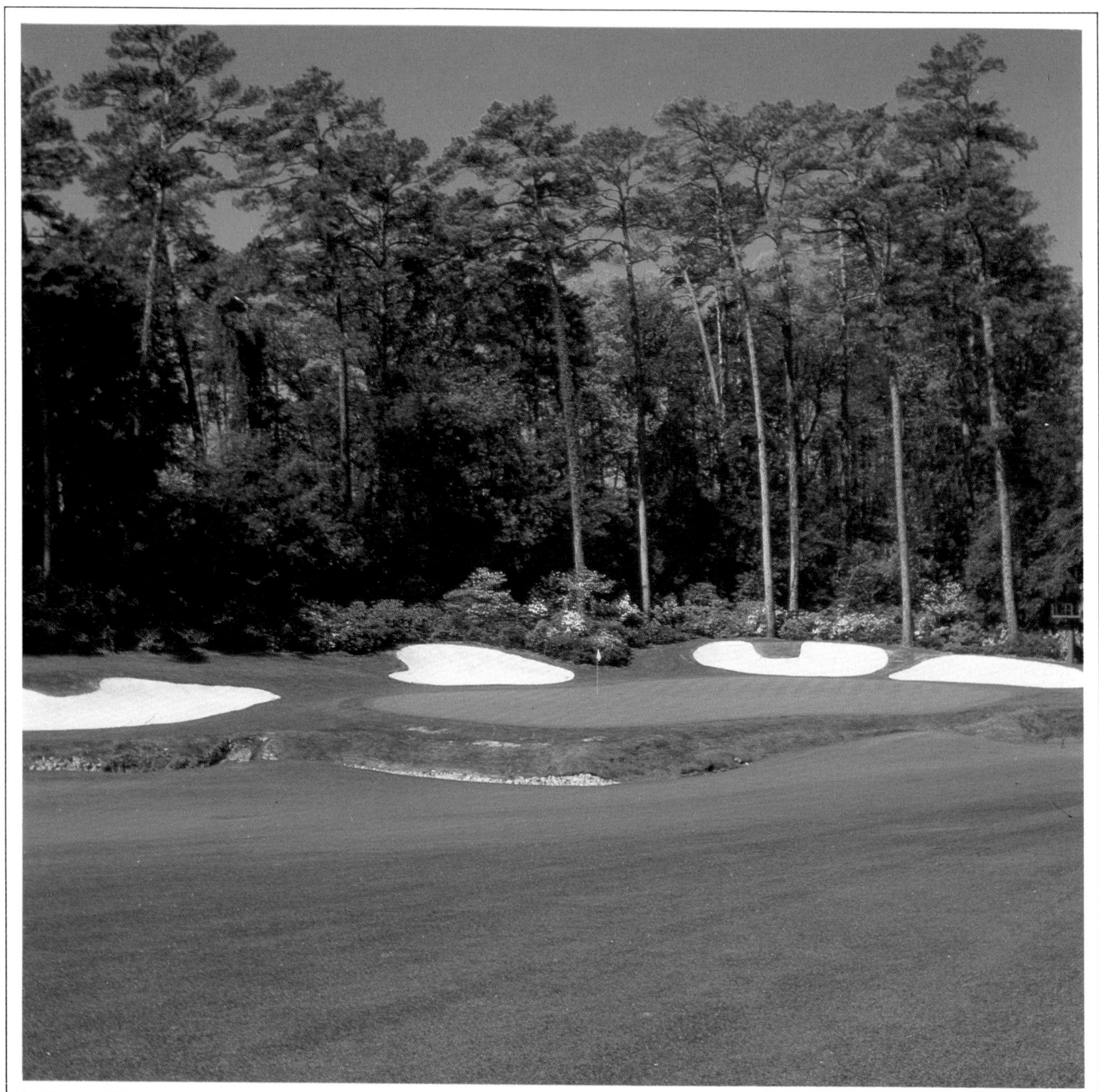

The 13th Green at the Augusta National in Georgia. Like many holes at Augusta, the green is surrounded by bunkers, a water hazard, and is bordered by beautiful flowers.

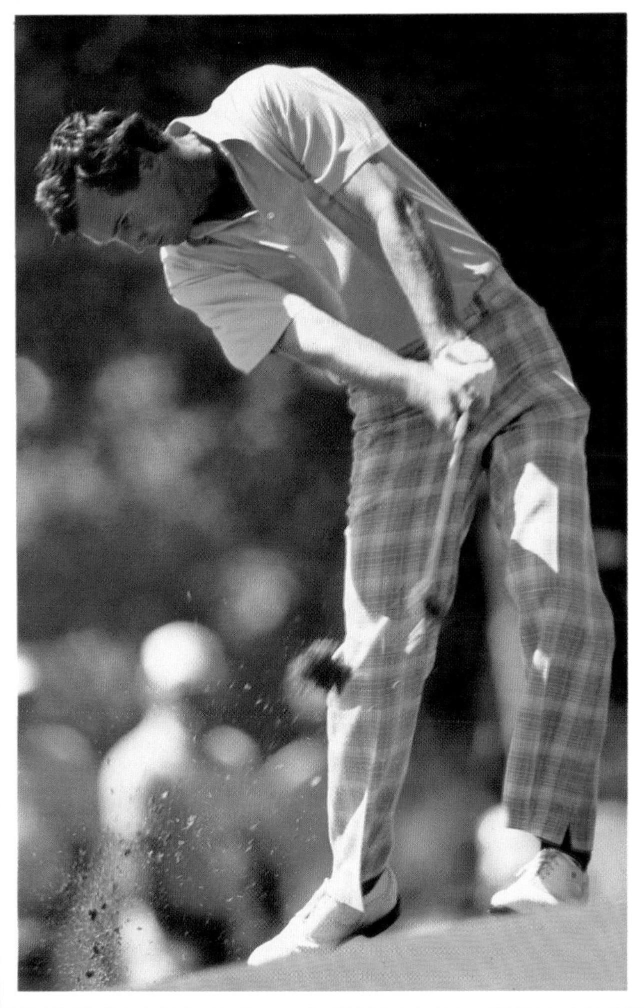

Hubert Green, 1977 US Open winner.

takes place each spring at Royal St George's, Sandwich, and Royal Cinque Ports, Deal.

The competition, which was instituted in 1924, is a knockout one, and all matches are foursomes.

Winners (since 1965)

1965	Rugby	1977	George Watson's
1966	Charterhouse	1978	Harrow
1967	Eton	1979	Stowe
1968	Eton	1980	Shrewsbury
1969	Eton	1981	George Watson's
1970	Merchiston Castle	1982	Charterhouse
1971	Charterhouse	1983	Charterhouse
1972	Marlborough	1984	Charterhouse
1973	Rossall	1985	Harrow
1974	Charterhouse	1986	Repton
1975	Harrow	**Most wins**	
1976	Merchiston Castle	14 – Charterhouse (1930–84)	

Halve, to
To play a hole in the same number of strokes as one's opponent. A match is said to be halved when the scores at the end are level.

Handicapping
Golf is one of the few sports whereby two people of different ability can play each other and theoretically both have an equal chance of winning. Such a situation exists because of the Standard Scratch Score and Handicapping Scheme introduced in Great Britain and Northern Ireland in 1926.

The rules of golf do not legislate for the allocation and adjustment of handicaps. That is the responsibility of clubs affiliated to each National Golf Union.

There are four categories of handicaps.
Category 1 is for handicaps of 5 or less.
Category 2 is for handicaps of 6–12 inclusive.
Category 3 is for handicaps of 13–20 inclusive.
Category 4 is for handicaps of 21–28 inclusive.

To obtain a handicap a player must submit three cards to the committee of his club. They will then allocate the player a handicap, subject to a maximum of 28.

Professional players have no handicap, in other words they are expected to play to the Standard Scratch Score (qv) of any course. Club players have their handicaps reviewed from time to time based on their performances in club competitions. Players returning cards of, say, 85, 94 and 91 against an SSS course of 70, would most probably be allotted an handicap of 16. That same player would then, in stroke-play (or medal) competitions, be allowed to deduct his handicap from his gross scores.

In match-play and Stableford competitions the use of the handicap is different. In a match-play event, the player with the higher handicap receives three quarters of the difference between the two players. Those strokes are then taken at the holes indicated on the stroke index.

For an explanation of how the handicap system affects Stableford competitions refer to the appropriate section within this encyclopedia.

The above is just a simple explanation as to how the handicap system works. It is far more complicated and precise details of the system can be obtained from The Council of National Golf Unions. Their Secretary is Alan Thirlwell, Formby Golf Club, Liverpool L37 1LQ.

Hazards
Obstructions, either natural or man-made, in the way of a golf shot. The rules of golf define a hazard as a 'bunker' or 'water hazard'. Roads and paths across a golf course are not described as hazards. A ball that lands in a hazard may be played but often this is not possible. The player must therefore remove the ball, drop it and incur a penalty.
See also Water Hazard, Lateral Water Hazard.

Head
That part of the club which strikes the ball and to which the shaft is joined. It is commonly known as the club head.
See diagram on page 51.

Heel
That part of the head of the club which is nearest to the shaft.
See diagram on page 51.

Walter Hagen, a very popular golfer, being watched by his usual vast gallery.

Heritage Classic

The Sea Pines Heritage Classic, played at the Harbour Town golf links, Hilton Head Island, South Carolina, has been part of the US PGA tour since 1969.

Winners (since 1970)

Year	Name	Score	Year	Name	Score
1970	B. Goalby	280	1979	T. Watson	270
1971	H. Irwin	279	1980	D. Tewell	280
1972	J. Miller	281	1981	B. Rogers	278
1973	H. Irwin	272	1982	T. Watson	280
1974	J. Miller	276	1983	F. Zoeller	275
1975	J. Nicklaus	271	1984	N. Faldo	270
1976	H. Green	274	1985	B. Langer	273
1977	G. Marsh	273	1986	F. Zoeller	276
1978	H. Green	277			

Most wins

2 – Hale Irwin (1971, 1973)
2 – Johnny Miller (1972, 1974)
2 – Hubert Green (1976, 1978)
2 – Tom Watson (1979, 1982)
2 – Fuzzy Zoeller (1983, 1986)

Lowest score (72 holes)

270 – Tom Watson (1979)
270 – Nick Faldo (1984)

Arnold Palmer was the first winner and in 1971 Hale Irwin won the Classic to register his first win on the professional tour. In 1984 Britain's Nick Faldo won the event to become the first Briton to win in the United States since Tony Jacklin in 1972. And the 1985 winner, Bernhard Langer of West Germany, became the first European to win two consecutive tournaments on the US Tour—the previous week he won the Masters title.

Hickory

A North American wood of the walnut family used for the manufacture of golf shafts prior to the legalization of the steel shaft in 1929. Hickory-shafted clubs are, with the exception of some putters, no longer made but there is nothing to prevent their use. They do, however, have qualities that a modern golfer would find unacceptable. For example, they twist and bend when swung. Even after the steel shaft was made legal, the legendary Bobby Jones continued using hickory-shafted clubs and won his four titles with them in 1930.

Highest Courses

The highest golf course in the world is at the Tuctu Club, Morococha, Peru. It is 14,335 ft (4369 m) above sea-level.

Bolivia has two high courses. The La Paz club in the country's capital (the highest capital city in the world) is situated 13,500 ft (4115 m) above sea-level, and the Oruro club, 120 miles south of La Paz, is 12,000 ft (3660 m) above sea-level.

The highest course in Britain is the nine-hole one at Leadhills, Lanarkshire, which is 1500 ft (460 m) above sea-level. The highest in England is at Church Stretton, Shropshire, and is 1250 ft (381 m) above sea-level.

Hilton, Harold

A legendary figure of the amateur game in Britain, Harold Horsfall Hilton remains one of only two men to win the amateur titles of Britain and the United States and the British Open title. The other was the great American player, Bobby Jones.

Hilton was born at West Kirby, Cheshire, in 1869. By coincidence the Royal Liverpool club at nearby Hoylake was formed the same year. Hilton was to become a member at Hoylake and it was appropriate that he should be the winner of the first British Open to be held on the course in 1897. Five years earlier he had won the first Open to be held at Muirfield.

He took the British amateur title four times, having previously lost in three finals, and the last of his wins was at the age of 44. He completed the British/US amateur championship double in 1911.

Hilton was a keen student of the game and his study of the science of golf led to his becoming a notable teacher and writer of books on the sport. He was for many years the editor of *Golf Illustrated*, before being appointed the first editor of *Golf Monthly*.

Career highlights
British Open 1892, 1897
British Amateur 1900, 1901, 1911, 1913
US Amateur 1911

Hogan, Ben

An act of bravery by Ben Hogan possibly saved the life of his wife Valerie in 1949. Seeing a bus coming towards their car he protected her, but took the full force of the impact himself. He was left for dead by the roadside and, when he eventually reached hospital some five hours later, was told he would most probably not walk again, let alone play golf. Just 11 months later Hogan was fighting out the play-off in the Los Angeles Open with Sam Snead, his courage having proved more than equal to any physical pain he had suffered.

A professional since the age of 17, he had found the road to the top a long, hard one, and it was not until 1938 that he won his first professional tournament. However, in the post-war years he developed into one of the all-time greats.

He won 13 tournaments on the US circuit in 1946, including his first major success, the PGA title. Two years later he won another 11 tournaments, including a second PGA title and the US Open. He took the Open again in 1950 and 1951, and in the latter year also won the Masters. But his greatest year was 1953 when he won the Masters, the US Open and the British Open to become the first man to capture three of the four majors in one year. The British Open win, at Carnoustie, was his last success in a major tournament. Two years later he was deprived of a fifth US Open title when he lost a play-off to the unknown Jack Fleck.

At his peak Hogan was one of the most popular men in the United States and was portrayed by Glenn Ford in the film *Follow the Sun*, the first full-length feature film about a golfer. A perfectionist, he enjoyed practising and his efforts reaped their reward. He won 62 tournaments on the US circuit and was the leading money winner five times. In 1965 US golf writers named him the 'greatest professional of all time'.

The stance and follow-through of one of the greatest golfers of the modern era, Ben Hogan, seen here during the 1956 World Cup at Wentworth.

Career highlights
US Open 1948, 1950, 1951, 1953
US PGA 1946, 1948
US Masters 1951, 1953
British Open 1953
Ryder Cup 1947 (capt), 1949 (capt), 1951, 1967 (non-playing capt)
World Cup (team) 1956
World Cup (individual) 1956

Hole
(1) The playing area between the tee and the green.
(2) The target at which the golfer aims on each green. The hole, which can be placed anywhere on the green, is 4.25 in (10.79 cm) in diameter and has a drop of at least 4 in (10.16 cm). If a lining is used it must be sunk at least 1 in (2.5 cm) below the surface of the putting green. The flagstick indicates the position of the hole on each green.

Holing Out
The act of hitting the ball into the hole.

Hole-in-one
A shot from the tee that finishes in the hole on the green. Some notable hole-in-one achievements are as follows:

The first recorded hole-in-one was by Tom Morris, Jnr, when he holed out at the 8th hole at Prestwick in 1868 on his way to winning the British Open.

The most holes-in-one achieved by a professional golfer were by the American, Art Wall, who is credited with 42 between 1936 and 1979. The British record is 31, held by Charles Chevalier of the Heaton Moor Club, Stockport.

The longest hole-in-one is believed to be 447 yd (409 m). Bob Mitera accomplished this feat at the downhill 10th hole at the Miracle Hill golf course, Omaha, Nebraska, in 1965 . . . he was aided by a tail wind. The longest in Britain was recorded by Peter Parkinson at The West Lancashire golf course, Liverpool, when he holed his tee shot at the 393-yd (359-m) 7th hole in 1972.

The only instance of successive holes-in-one in a major tournament was in the 1971 Martini International at Norwich when John Hudson from Hendon holed the 11th and 12th holes during the second round.

The US golfer, Joseph Boydstone, is credited with the most holes-in-one in a single year—11 in 1962. The British record is six by John Putt (appropriately named) of Frilford Heath Golf Club, Berkshire, in 1970.

The oldest person to have registered a hole-in-one was the 93-year-old Canadian Charles Youngman at Toronto in 1971.

The oldest person to hole-in-one during a major tournament was Gene Sarazen who was 71 when he holed out at Troon's 8th hole during the 1973 British Open. By coincidence an amateur, David Russell, also holed-in-one at the same hole during the championship. He was the youngest competitor while Sarazen was the oldest.

The youngest person to achieve a hole-in-one was Coby Orr of Colorado. He was just five years old when he holed out at the Riverside golf course, San Antonio, Texas in 1975.

The biggest prize for holing-in-one went to Japan's Isao Aoki for achieving the feat at the 2nd hole during the 1979 Suntory World Match-Play Championship at Wentworth.

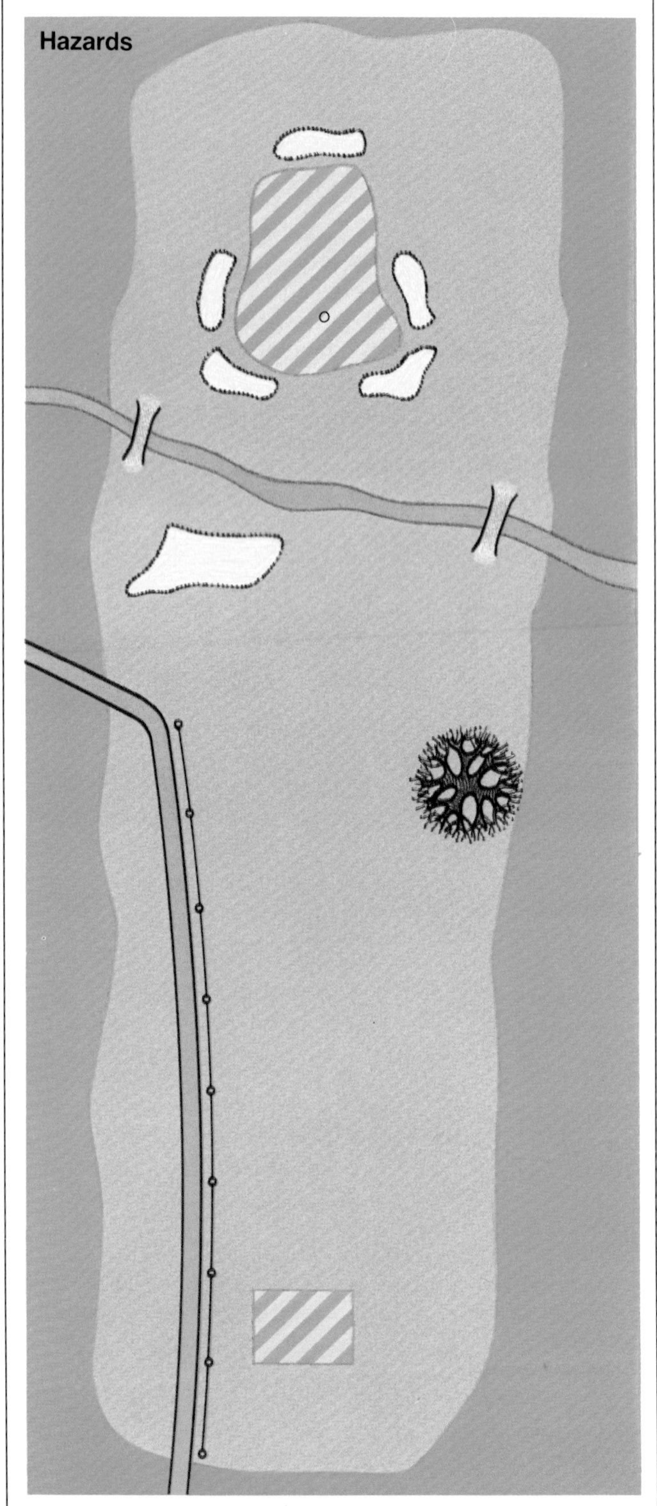

Many hazards can be encountered on a golf course: on the left is a lateral water hazard, a normal water hazard crosses the fairway in front of the green while bunkers surround the putting surface.

The first televised hole-in-one in Britain was by Tony Jacklin during the final round of the 1967 Dunlop Masters at Royal St George's, Sandwich, when his tee shot at the 16th entered the hole.

The first televised hole-in-one at the British Open was by Lionel Platts who holed the 212-yd (194-m) 4th at Royal Birkdale in 1971.

During the 1933 Irish Open Amateur championship at Royal County Down, Eric Fiddian holed-in-one during his morning round and again in the afternoon, but still lost the match 3 & 2 to Jack McLean.

In 1948 Charles Ward became the first person to hole-in-one twice in the British Open. He did so at St Andrews in 1946 and at Muirfield two years later.

When he holed-in-one at the 206-yd (188-m) 4th hole at Royal Birkdale in 1976 Peter Dawson became the first left-handed golfer to perform this feat in the British Open.

First holes-in-one in major championships

British Open 1868 – Tom Morris, Jnr (Prestwick – 8th hole)
US Open 1956 – Bob Kuntz (Oak Hill CC)
US Masters 1934 – Ross Somerville (16th hole)
Ryder Cup 1973 – Peter Butler – GB (Muirfield – 16th hole)

Home Internationals

The first amateur international was played at the Royal Liverpool Golf Club, Hoylake, in 1902. It was a match between England and Scotland. The teams consisted of ten players each and the visitors won by 32 holes to 25.

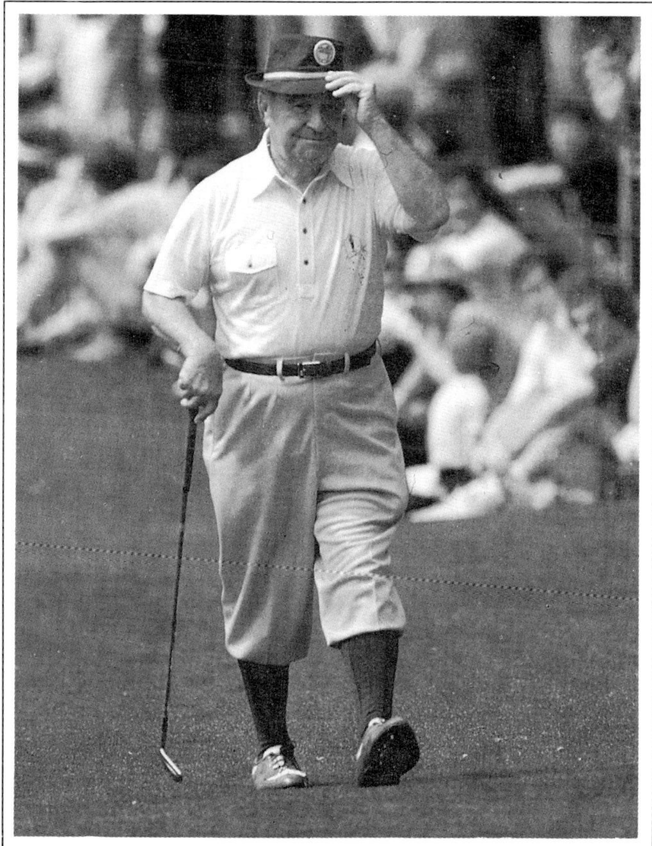

Gene Sarazen holed-in-one at the 1973 British Open, the oldest person to do so in a major tournament.

Home Internationals

Winners

Men

Year	Winner	Year	Winner
1932	Scotland	1963	Ireland
1933	Scotland	1964	England
1934	Scotland	1965	England
1935	England	1966	England
1936	Scotland	1967	Scotland
1937	Scotland	1968	England
1938	England	1969	England
1939–46	Not held	1970	Scotland
1971	Scotland	1971	Scotland
1947	England	1972	Scotland
1948	England	1973	England
1949	England	1974	England
1950	Ireland	1975	Scotland
1951	Scotland	1976	Scotland
1952	Scotland	1977	England
1953	Scotland	1978	England
1954	England	1979	Not held
1955	Ireland	1980	England
1956	Scotland	1981	Scotland
1957	England	1982	Scotland
1958	England	1983	Ireland
1959	England	1984	England
1960	England	1985	England
1961	Scotland		
1962	England		

Wins

23 – England
18 – Scotland
4 – Ireland

Winners

Women

Year	Winner	Year	Winner
1948	England	1968	England and Scotland (shared)
1949	England		
1950	Scotland	1969	Scotland
1951	Scotland	1970	England
1952	Scotland	1971	England
1953	England	1972	England
1954	England	1973	England
1955	Scotland	1974	Scotland
1956	Scotland	1975	England
1957	Scotland	1976	England
1958	England	1977	England
1959	England	1978	England
1960	England	1979	Scotland
1961	Scotland	1980	Ireland
1962	Scotland	1981	Scotland
1963	England	1982	England
1964	England	1983	Abandoned
1965	England	1984	England
1966	England	1985	England
1967	England		

Wins

24 – England
13 – Scotland
1 – Ireland

England and Scotland continued to meet each year and in 1932, at Troon, Wales and Ireland joined them to make up the current four-nation tournament known as the Home Internationals.

In 1952 Raymond Oppenheimer, a former England Rugby Union international, presented the Raymond Trophy which is awarded to the winning team in the series each year.

Women began their Home International series in 1948 at Royal Lytham, and a Girls' Home International series was introduced at Ilkley in 1969.

Hong Kong Open

Inaugurated in 1959, it was the first event on what has now become known as the Asian Circuit. It is an early season event, normally held in late February at the Royal Hong Kong course at Fanling.

The popular Lu Liang Huan was the first winner when just 22 years of age. The British Open winners, Peter Thomson and Kel Nagle, have both taken the championship, and Nagle set a championship best round of 62 on his way to the 1961 title. During the 1974 championship four golfers actually holed-in-one.

Winners (since 1970)

Year	Name	Venue	Score
1970	I. Katsumata	Fanling	274
1971	O. Moody	Fanling	266
1972	W. Godfrey	Fanling	272
1973	F. Phillips	Fanling	278
1974	Lu Liang Huan	Fanling	280
1975	Yo Hsieh Yung	Fanling	288
1976	Ho Ming Chung	Fanling	279
1977	Nan Hsieh Min	Fanling	280
1978	Yo Hsieh Yung	Fanling	275
1979	G. Norman	Fanling	273
1980	Kuo Chi Hsiung	Fanling	274
1981	Chen Tse Ming	Fanling	279
1982	K. Cox	Fanling	276
1983	G. Norman	Fanling	134(a)
1984	B. Brask	Fanling	268
1985	M. Aebli	Fanling	270
1986	S. Kanai	Fanling	285

(a) over 36 holes

Most wins
4 – Yo Hsieh Yung (1963, 1964, 1975, 1978)

Lowest score (72 holes)
261 – Kel Nagle (1961)

Honour

The right to play first from the teeing area. At the beginning of a game the honour is either mutually agreed or else decided by lot. After that the person or team winning each hole is entitled to the honour, which must not be declined. If the hole is halved then the person who had the honour at the previous hole retains it.

Honourable Company of Edinburgh Golfers

The society of the Gentleman Golfers of Edinburgh was formed at a meeting on 1 May 1744 when enthusiastic golfers, under their president Duncan Forbes of Culloden, gathered to play on the links at Leith. The Provost of Edinburgh donated a silver club which was to become an annual challenge trophy. The Gentlemen Golfers drew up their own set of rules (the first ever to be formulated for golf), which were adopted by the Royal and Ancient Club on its formation in 1754.

In 1795 the Gentlemen Golfers were granted permission by the council and magistrates of Edinburgh to adopt the title of Honourable Company of Edinburgh Golfers. In 1831 the company wound up its affairs and was homeless for five years until it moved to Musselburgh in 1836. It established its present home at Muirfield in 1891.

Hook

A shot that veers to the left of its intended target. Unlike the draw it is not deliberate but is the result of an error on the player's part, normally the consequence of an incorrect swing.

See also Draw, Slice.

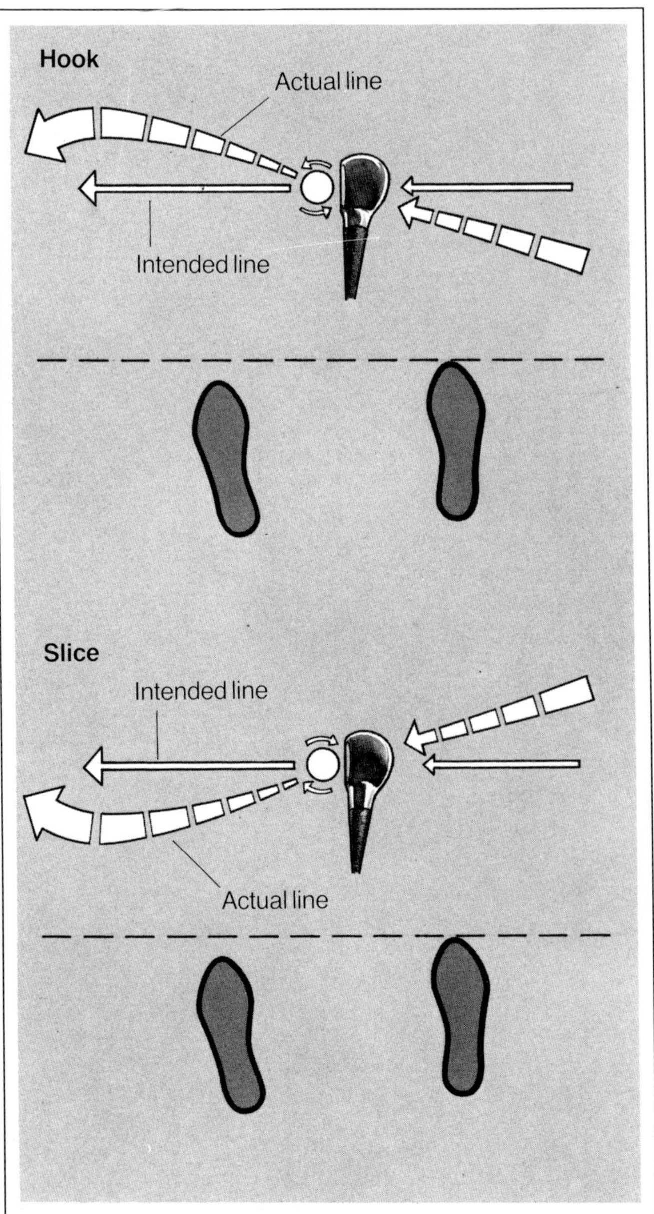

I

Important Dates

1457 Golf was first mentioned in a Scottish Act of Parliament which discouraged the playing of the sport because of the need for archery practice.

1744 The first golf club came into existence when the Gentlemen Golfers of Edinburgh (later the Honourable Company of Edinburgh Golfers) was formed. They drew up the first set of rules for the game.

1744 The first recorded golf tournament took place at Leith, Scotland, on 2 April, and was won by John Rattray.

1754 The Royal and Ancient Club was established as the Society of St Andrews Golfers.

1759 Stroke-play first mentioned. Previously all golf had consisted of matches.

1779 Golf is believed to have been first played in the United States, near New York.

1811 The first women's golf tournament was organized at Musselburgh on 9 January for the town's 'fishwives'.

1818 The Edinburgh Burgess Golfing Society met the Bruntsfield Links Club at Bruntsfield on 4 June in the first inter-club match.

1829 The first golf club outside Britain was founded at Calcutta, India. It later became the Royal Calcutta Club.

1833 Perth became the first golf club to attain 'royal' status, when the title was bestowed upon it by William IV.

1834 The Royal and Ancient Club was granted its name.

1848 The gutta-percha (gutty) ball was introduced.

1856 The first European course outside Britain opened at Pau, France.

1857 H. B. Farnie published *The Golfer's Manual*, the first golfing handbook.

1860 Willie Park won the first British Open, at Prestwick.

1867 The first women's golf club was founded at St Andrews.

1878 The first Oxford–Cambridge match was held at Wimbledon.

1885 Allan MacFie won the first British Amateur Championship, at Hoylake.

1893 The Ladies' Golf Union was formed. The first Ladies' Amateur Championship, at Lytham, was won by Lady Margaret Scott.

1894 John Taylor won the first British Open to be held in England, at Sandwich.

1894 The United States Golf Association was formed.

1895 The first US Open was won by Horace Rawlins at Newport, Rhode Island.

1895 The first US Amateur Championship, also held at Newport, Rhode Island, was won by Charles Blair Macdonald.

1898 The rubber-cored ball was invented by Coburn Haskell at Cleveland, Ohio.

1899 George F. Grant of Boston, Massachusetts, patented the golf tee.

1901 The Professional Golfers' Association (PGA) of Britain was founded in London.

1902 The first international match between England and Scotland took place at Hoylake.

1910 Arthur F. Knight of Schenectady, New York, patented the steel-shafted club.

1916 The Professional Golfers' Association of America (the US PGA) was founded in New York.

1916 An Englishman, Jim Barnes, won the first US PGA title at Siwanoy, New York.

1919 Control of the British Open and British Amateur championships was taken over by the Royal and Ancient Club.

1921 The first restrictions on the size of the golf ball were introduced.

1922 The United States won the first Walker Cup, at Long Island, New York.

1927 The United States won the first official Ryder Cup match, at Worcester, Massachusetts.

1932 The United States won the first Curtis Cup match, at Wentworth, England.

1934 Horton Smith won the first US Masters at Augusta, Georgia.

1937 The European Golf Association was formed in Luxembourg.

1938 On 15 July BBC television covered its first golf match at Roehampton in South-west London.

1953 Argentina won the first Canada Cup (later World Cup).

1958 The first World Amateur Team Championship for the Eisenhower Trophy was held at St Andrews and won by Australia, which beat the United States in a play-off.

1959 The Asian Circuit began in Hong Kong.

1960 The larger American ball was used in a British tournament (at Wentworth) for the first time.

1964 The Women's World Amateur Team Championship for the Espirito Santo Trophy was inaugurated, in Paris, and won by the host nation.

1974 The use of the larger ball was made compulsory in the British Open for the first time.

1975 The Tournament Players' Division of the British PGA was formed.

1979 European golfers were allowed to take part in the Ryder Cup for the first time.

In

(1) The last nine holes on a golf course.

(2) A movement in which the club head is taken back inside the line of flight of the ball so that, at impact, it is facing to the right of the intended target. On completion of its swing it ends up outside the line of flight. Thus it has travelled from 'in' to 'out'.

In Play

A ball is in play from the moment it is struck from the teeing area. It remains in play until it is holed, goes out of bounds, is lifted or lost, or is replaced by another ball in accordance with the rules.

Indian Open

Although the first Indian Amateur Championship was contested in 1892, the first Indian Open was not held until 1964. India's golf patron, the Australian, Peter Thomson, encouraged the Indian Golf Union to stage such an event and, ironically, Thomson was the first winner, at Delhi. It was officially included in the Asian Circuit in 1970 and the 1972 winner, the 21-year-old Brian Jones from Australia, was taking part in his first major professional event.

Hazards are a common feature on all golf courses but an unusual one encountered by the competitors in the 1973 Indian Open was bees. In order to get rid of them the organizers created another hazard by lighting fires around the course.

Indian Open

Winners

Year	Name	Venue	Score
1964	P. W. Thomson	Delhi	292
1965	P. G. Sethi(*)	Calcutta	282
1966	P. W. Thomson	Delhi	284
1967	Not held		
1968	K. Hosoishi	Delhi	285
1969	B. Arda	Calcutta	291
1970	Chen C. Chung	Calcutta	279
1971	G. Marsh	Delhi	275
1972	B. Jones	Calcutta	282
1973	G. Marsh	Delhi	280
1974	Kuo Chie Hsiung	Calcutta	287
1975	T. Ball	Delhi	282
1976	P. W. Thomson	Calcutta	288
1977	B. Jones	Delhi	284
1978	B. Brask	Calcutta	284
1979	G. Burrows	Delhi	284
1980	K. Cox	Tollygunge	286
1981	P. Stewart	Delhi	284
1982	San Hsu Sheng	Calcutta	277
1983	J. Takahashi	Delhi	285
1984	R. Alarcon	Calcutta	279
1985	T. Grimes	Delhi	279

(*) denotes amateur

Most wins

3 – Peter Thomson (1964, 1966, 1976)

Lowest score (72 holes)

275 – Graham Marsh (Delhi, 1971)

Inverness

One of the oldest clubs in the United States, the Inverness Club is situated in Toledo, Ohio. When it first opened in 1903 the members wrote to Scotland's Inverness Club asking permission to use its name. The Highland club readily agreed and a long association between the two bodies began.

The club originally consisted of two nine-hole courses but in 1919 Donald Ross, an exiled Scot, turned it into a splendid 18-hole course. His efforts were rewarded in the following year when Inverness was used as the venue for

Christy O'Connor (Snr), four times winner of the Carroll's International Tournament.

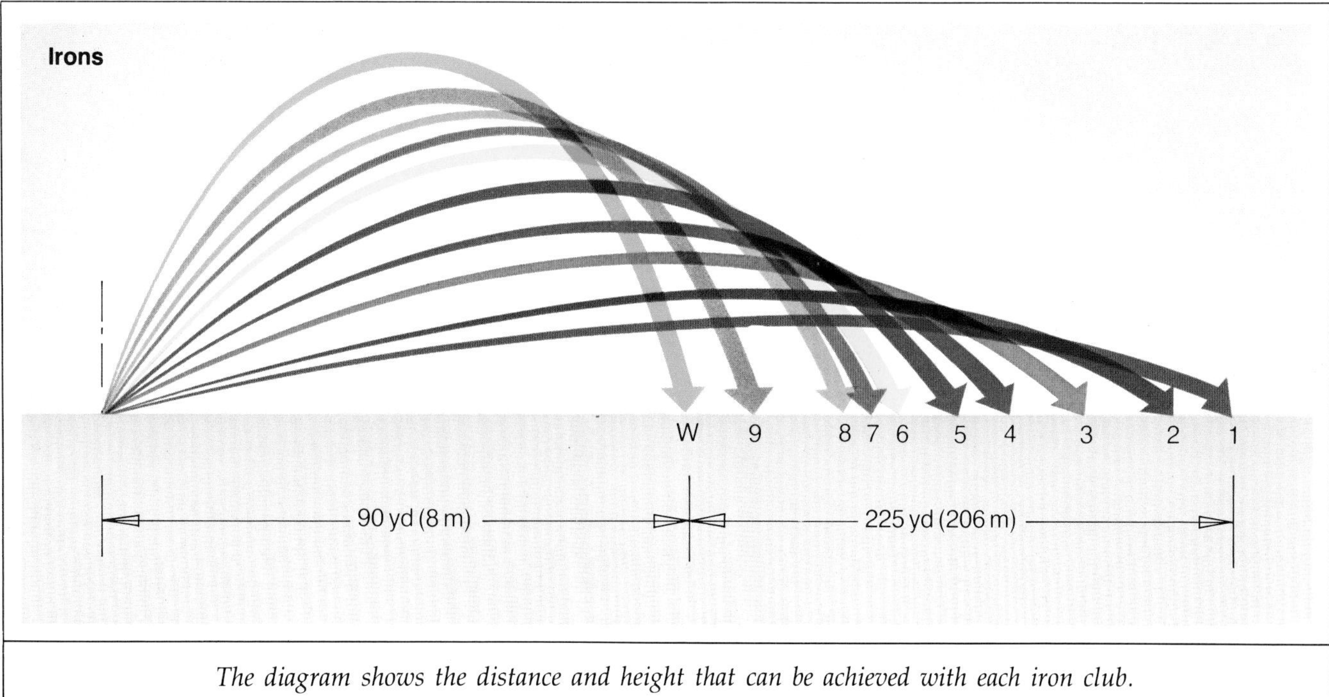

The diagram shows the distance and height that can be achieved with each iron club.

the US Open, which was won by an Englishman, Ted Ray.

Inverness set a precedent at that championship by opening its doors to professional players. For the first time at a major championship they were allowed to change in the locker rooms. Walter Hagen showed his appreciation by arranging a collection among the professional players and presented a clock to the club.

The US Open has since been played on the Ohio course three times—in 1931, 1957 and 1979.

Irish Open

First held in 1927, the Irish Open led a precarious existence in the period following the Second World War and in 1953 was held for the last time for over 20 years. In 1975, however, the tobacco firm of Carrolls announced that, from that year, their previously successful Carrolls International would be called the Carrolls Irish Open. This has been held every year since and has attracted a truly international field, recent winners being the Europeans, Severiano Ballesteros and Bernhard Langer, and the American pair, Ben Crenshaw and Hubert Green.

One of the best-known trios of golfing brothers, the Whitcombes (Charles, Ernest and Reggie), all won the Irish Open between 1928 and 1936.

Irons

Clubs with heads made of iron or some other metal. Ever since the early days of golf such clubs have been used. Formerly they had names like niblick, cleek, mashie, etc., but today they are graded according to the loft of the club face and numbered—the higher the number the greater the loft. For example, the No 1 iron has a loft of approximately 17–18 degrees and an average player could hit a good shot a distance of between 180 and 200 yd (164–182 m) with this iron. The No 9 iron, however, has a loft

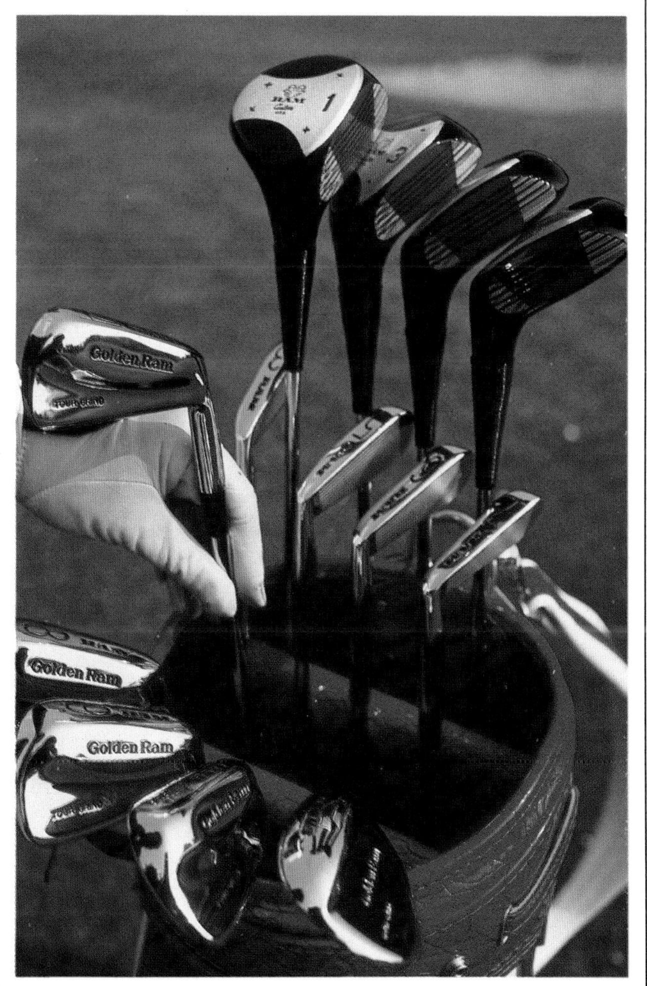

A golf bag containing a near-full set of clubs.

Irish Open

Winners

Year	Name	Venue	Score
1927	G. Duncan	Portmarnock	312
1928	E. R. Whitcombe	Newcastle	288
1929	A. Mitchell	Portmarnock	309
1930	C. A. Whitcombe	Portrush	289
1931	E. W. Kenyon	Dollymount	291
1932	A. H. Padgham	Cork	283
1933	E. W. Kenyon	Malone	286
1934	S. Easterbrook	Portmarnock	284
1935	E. R. Whitcombe	Newcastle	292
1936	R. A. Whitcombe	Dollymount	281
1937	B. Gadd	Portrush	284
1938	A. D. Locke	Portmarnock	292
1939	A. Lees	Newcastle	287
1940–45	Not held		
1946	F. Daly	Portmarnock	288
1947	H. Bradshaw	Portrush	290
1948	D. J. Rees	Portmarnock	295
1949	H. Bradshaw	Belvoir Park	286
1950	H. O. Pickworth	Dollymount	287
1951–52	Not held		
1953	E. C. Brown	Belvoir Park	272
1954–74	Not held		
1975	C. O'Connor, Jnr	Woodbrook	275
1976	B. Crenshaw	Portmarnock	284
1977	H. Green	Portmarnock	283
1978	K. Brown	Portmarnock	281
1979	M. James	Portmarnock	282
1980	M. James	Portmarnock	284
1981	S. Torrance	Portmarnock	276
1982	J. O'Leary	Portmarnock	287
1983	S. Ballesteros	Dublin	271
1984	B. Langer	Dublin	267
1985	S. Ballesteros	Dublin	278

Most wins

2 – Ernest Whitcombe (1928, 1935)
2 – E. W. Kenyon (1931, 1933)
2 – Harry Bradshaw (1947, 1949)
2 – Mark James (1979, 1980)
2 – Severiano Ballesteros (1983, 1985)

Lowest score (72 holes)

267 – Bernhard Langer (Dublin, 1984)

of around 47 degrees, which would enable an average player to hit a good shot around 100–120 yd (91–109 m). The pitching wedge and sand wedge (*see* wedge) are the two most lofted irons.

Each iron has its purpose, whether it be for playing the long fairway shot (No 1 iron), the chip (No 9 iron or pitching wedge) or bunker shot (sand-wedge). For a guide to the distance and loft of irons see the illustration on page 75.

The present-day equivalent of the old iron clubs are as follows:

cleek	No 2 iron
jigger	No 4 iron
mashie	No 5 iron
mashie-niblick	No 7 iron
niblick	No 8/9 iron

Irwin, Hale

Although not the most spectacular of players, Hale Irwin is certainly one of the most solidly competent. He turned professional at the age of 23 in 1968, when he competed in his first tournament, the Cleveland Open. On that occasion he collected just over $400 but has since gone on to win more than $2 million.

His first major success was in the 1971 Heritage Classic and then, in 1974, he surprised many people by winning the US Open at Winged Foot by two strokes from another up and coming youngster, Fuzzy Zoeller. Irwin went to Wentworth for the World Match-Play championship in 1974 and won the first of his two titles. Only David Graham, at the second extra hole in 1976, deprived him of a hat-trick.

If 1974 was Irwin's first big year then his second was 1979. He won his second US Open, at Inverness (despite a disastrous final round of 75), played in his third Ryder Cup, was a member of the US team that took the World Cup, and gained the individual title. He also led in the British Open, going into the final round, but fell away to finish sixth.

A graduate from Colorado University, he was a useful footballer in his college days and could well have achieved similar success in that sport.

Career highlights

US Open 1974, 1979
World Match-Play 1974, 1975
World Cup (team) 1979
(individual) 1979
Ryder Cup 1975, 1977, 1979, 1981
British Open (best) jt 2nd – 1983

Italian Open

One of the younger of the national European Open championships, the Italian Open was first held at Stresa in 1925. Over the years it has been the scene of some outstanding rounds. Percy Alliss won the 1935 title with a four-round total of 262 to establish a record for any national championship. This record stood for over 30 years. Alliss' feat was performed at the San Remo course where, 12 years later, Flory van Donck completed the four rounds in 263. During the 1985 event at Milan Severiano Ballesteros equalled the world record of eight consecutive birdies in one round.

Italian Open

Winners

Year	Name	Venue	Score
1925	F. Pasquali	Stresa	154(*)
1926	A. Boyer	Stresa	147(*)
1927	Percy Alliss	Stresa	145(*)
1928	A. Boyer	Villa d'Este	145(*)
1929	R. Golias	Villa d'Este	143(*)
1930	A. Boyer	Villa d'Este	140(*)
1931	A. Boyer	Villa d'Este	141(*)
1932	A. Boomer	Villa d'Este	143(*)
1933	Not held		
1934	N. Nutley	San Remo	132(*)
1935	Percy Alliss	San Remo	262
1936	T. H. Cotton	Setriere	268
1937	M. Dallemagne	San Remo	276
1938	F. van Donck	Villa d'Este	276
1939–46	Not held		
1947	F. van Donck	San Remo	263
1948	A. Casera	San Remo	267
1949	H. Hassanein	Villa d'Este	263
1950	U. Grappasonni	Rome	281
1951	J. Adams	Milan	289
1952	E. Brown	Milan	273
1953	F. van Donck	Villa d'Este	267
1954	U. Grappasonni	Villa d'Este	272
1955	F. van Donck	Venice	287
1956	A. Cerda	Milan	284
1957	H. Henning	Villa d'Este	273
1958	Peter Alliss	Varese	282
1959	P. W. Thomson	Villa d'Este	269
1960	B. Wilkes	Venice	285
1961–70	Not held		
1971	R. Sota	Garlenda	282
1972	N. Wood	Villa d'Este	271
1973	A. Jacklin	Rome	284
1974	P. Oosterhuis	Venice	249(†)
1975	W. Casper	Monticello	286
1976	B. Dassu	Is Molas	280
1977	A. Gallardo	Monticello	286
1978	D. Hayes	Pevero	293
1979	B. Barnes	Monticello	281
1980	M. Mannelli	Rome	276
1981	J.-M. Canizares	Milan	280
1982	M. James	Is Molas	280
1983	B. Langer	Ugolino	271
1984	A. W. Lyle	Milan	277
1985	M. Pinero	Milan	267
1986	D. Feherty	Albarella	270

(*) over 36 holes (†) play curtailed to 63 holes

Most wins
4 – Auguste Boyer (1926, 1928, 1930, 1931)
4 – Flory van Donck (1938, 1947, 1953, 1955)

Lowest score (72 holes)
262 – Percy Alliss (San Remo, 1935)

J

Jacklin, Tony

Tony Jacklin has enjoyed three great personal successes during his quarter-century professional career. The first was in 1969 when, by winning the British Open, he did for British golf what England's triumph in the World Cup in 1966 has done for British soccer. Less than a year later he became the first Briton since Ted Ray in 1920 to win the US Open title. However, both those achievements were overshadowed, in terms of prestige, in 1985 when Jacklin led the European team to victory over the United States in the Ryder Cup to inflict the first defeat upon the Americans since 1957.

The son of a Scunthorpe steelworker, Jacklin took up his first golfing post at the age of 17 when he became assistant to Bill Shankland, the famous Potters Bar professional, in 1961. He turned professional the following year, and was Rookie of the Year in 1963. Dunlop Masters champion in 1967, he was selected for the Ryder Cup that year. After having made his US debut at Pleasant Valley in 1965 he won his first US Tour event, the Jacksonville Open, in 1968. Then followed the five most successful playing years of his career. In addition to gaining the British and US Opens, he won the Jacksonville Open for a second time, the Dunlop Masters—also for a second time—and the Italian Open.

More recently titles have been few and far between and, since 1980, he has won only the Jersey Open and Sun Alliance PGA title. Nevertheless, he has remained one of Britain's most popular golfers and can always guarantee a good following whenever he plays. Jacklin is an honorary life-president of the Royal and Ancient Club, and has received the OBE in recognition of his services to golf.

Career highlights
British Open 1969
US Open 1970
Dunlop Masters 1967, 1973
Ryder Cup 1967, 1969, 1971, 1973, 1975, 1977, 1979, 1983 (non-playing capt), 1985 (non-playing capt)

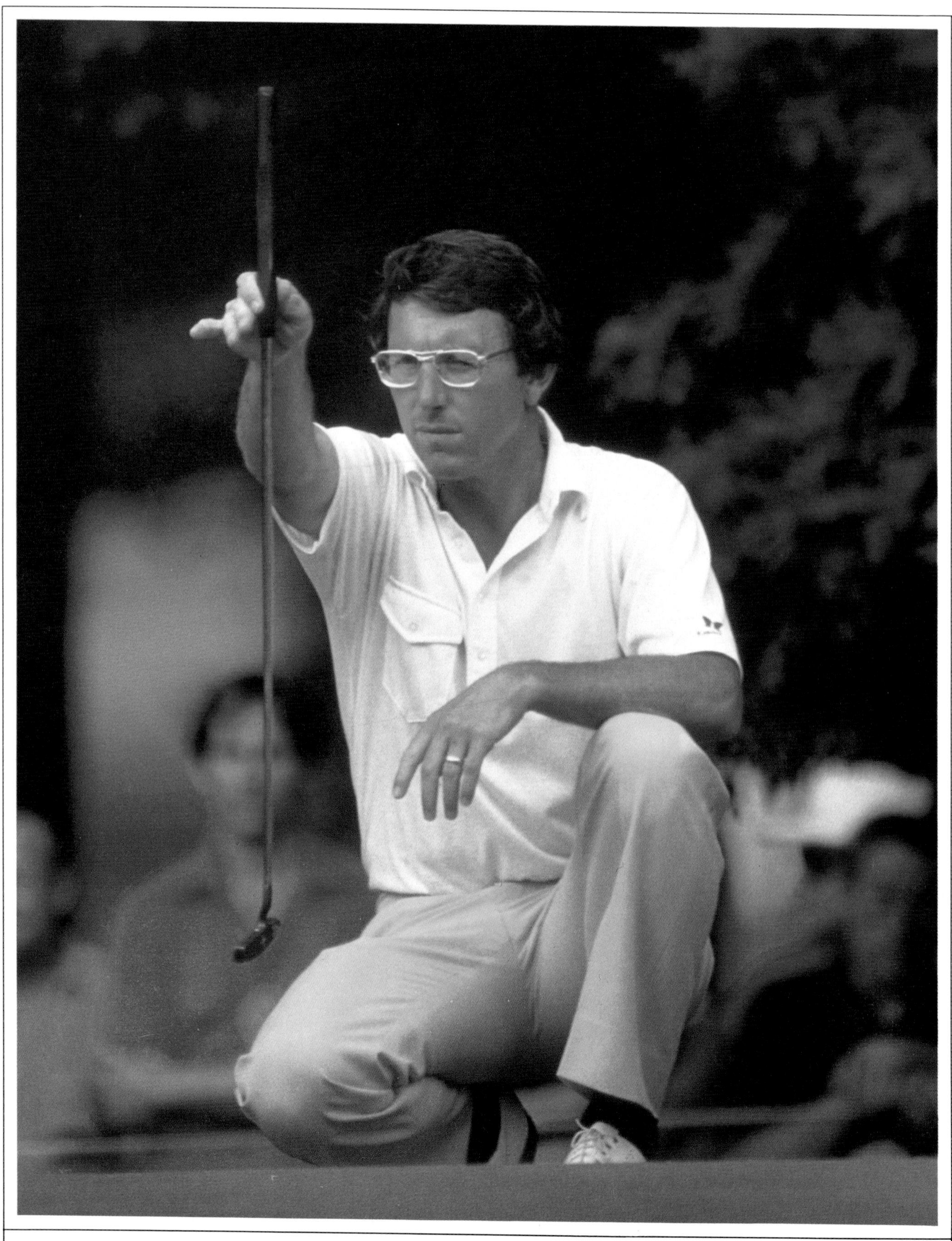

Hale Irwin, twice winner of the US Open, lines up a putt during the 1984 Championship at Winged Foot.

Japan Open

Japan's first golf course was built in 1901. Twenty-three years later the Japan Golf Association was formed and then, in 1927, held its first Open championship, at Hodogoya. The winner was Rokuro Akaboshi, the only amateur to gain the title. His four-round total was 309!

Still not regarded as a fully international event, the Japan Open has, however, been gradually winning acceptance, since Severiano Ballesteros, in 1977, became the first non-Asian holder of the title.

Winners (since 1965)

Year	Name	Venue	Score
1965	T. Kitta	Miyoshi	284
1966	S. Sato	Sodegaura	285
1967	T. Kitta	Hirono	282
1968	T. Kono	Sobu	284
1969	H. Sugimoto	Onu	284
1970	M. Kitta	Musashi	282
1971	Y. Fujji	Aichi	282
1972	H. Chang-Sang	Iwai City	278
1973	B. Arda	Osaka	278
1974	M. Ozaki	Central	279
1975	T. Murakami	Kasugai	278
1976	K. Shimada	Central	288
1977	S. Ballesteros	Narashino	284
1978	S. Ballesteros	Yokohama	281
1979	Kuo Chie-Hsiung	Kyoto	285
1980	S. Kikuchi	Sagamihara	296
1981	Y. Hagawa	Nippon Rhine	280
1982	T. Nakajima	Ina	276
1983	I. Aoki	Osaka	281
1984	K. Uehara	Saitama	283
1985	T. Nakajima	Aichi	285

Most wins
6 – Tomekichi Miyamoto (1929, 1930, 1932, 1935, 1936, 1940)

Lowest score (72 holes)
276 – Tsuneyuki Nakajimi (1982)

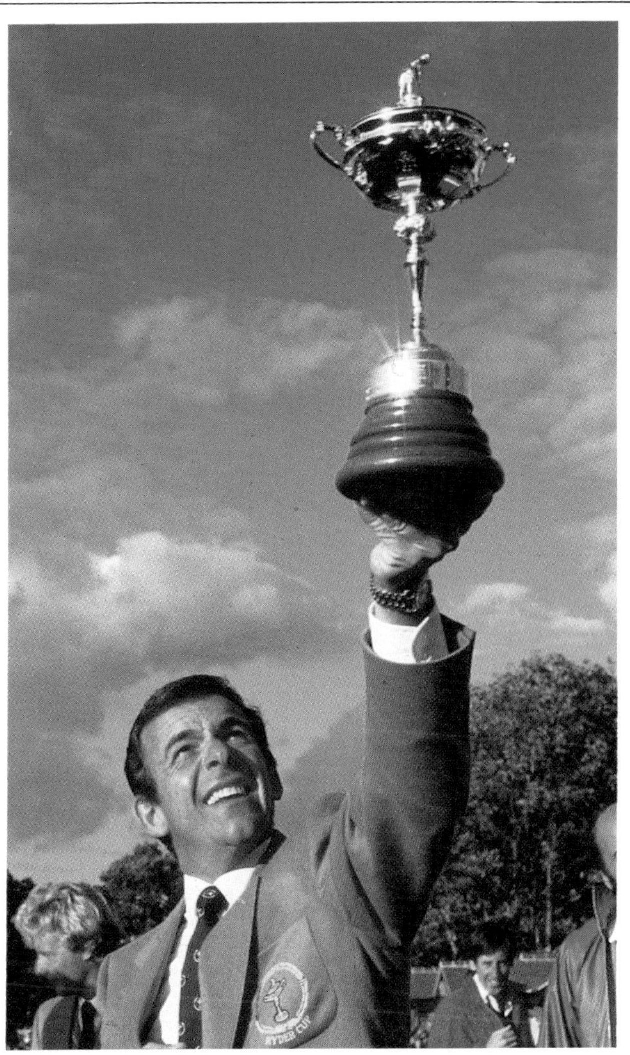

Leading Great Britain and Europe to Ryder Cup triumph over the United States in 1985 was one of Tony Jacklin's proudest moments in golf. He is seen here holding aloft the famous trophy.

Jersey Open

Despite its size and the fact that it only possesses two 18-hole golf courses, La Moye and Royal Jersey, the small Channel Island of Jersey has a long-standing association with the game. Both Harry Vardon and Ted Ray were born at Grouville, not far from St Helier. It is La Moye which has housed all Jersey Opens since their inception in 1978, as it is 500 yd (457 m) longer than the Royal Jersey course. It was at La Moye, in 1981, that Tony Jacklin, then resident on the island, won the last of his Open titles.

Jersey Open

Winners

Year	Name	Score
1978	B. G. Huggett	271
1979	A. W. Lyle	271
1980	J.-M. Canizares	281
1981	A. Jacklin	279
1982	B. Gallacher	273
1983	J. Hall	278
1984	B. Gallacher	274
1985	H. Clark	279
1986	J. Morgan	275

Most wins
2 – Bernard Gallacher (1982, 1984)

Lowest score (72 holes)
271 – Brian Huggett (1978)
271 – Sandy Lyle (1979)

Jigger

A popular iron club used in days gone by. Very useful for playing out of the rough, it was the equivalent of a present-day No 4 iron.

Jones, Bobby

Without doubt Robert Tyre Jones, Jnr, was the greatest amateur golfer of all times. To win the US and British Amateur titles in one season is a rare enough feat, but to add the US and British Opens to those titles all in one season is nothing short of miraculous. Bobby Jones won all four titles in 1930. However, his remarkable success among amateurs and professionals extended over a number of years. He was US Open champion four times, runner-up on another four occasions and won the British Open three times. On the amateur front he gained the British title just once, but won the US championship five times and was runner-up on two more occasions.

Jones' record, unparalleled in the world of golf, is made even more remarkable by the fact that he played his last competitive tournament in 1930 at the age of 28.

A graduate of the Atlanta School of Technology and of Harvard, he was one of the most highly educated men to have played golf at the top level; he had degrees in law, engineering and literature.

After his retirement from playing he wrote many articles on the sport he loved, made instructional films and was also responsible for instituting the US Masters at the Augusta National. In 1958 he was made a freeman of the Burgh of St Andrews in a touching ceremony before the start of the inaugural World Amateur Team Championship for the Eisenhower Trophy. By then Jones, crippled with a muscular disease, was just a shadow of his former self. Resigned to his illness, he died in 1971 at the age of 69. Golf had lost a friend and a great champion.

Career highlights

US Open 1923, 1926, 1929, 1930
British Open 1926, 1927, 1930
British Amateur 1930
US Amateur 1924, 1925, 1927, 1928, 1930
Walker Cup 1922, 1924, 1926, 1928 (capt), 1930 (capt)

K

Kenya Open

The Australian golfer, Peter Thomson, was the driving force behind the establishment of the Kenya Open, just as he had been with other events in Africa and the Far East. The Kenya Open, now part of the Safari Tour, was first contested at the Muthaiga Club in 1967 and all subsequent championships since 1970 have been played on the course 5500 ft (1676 m) above sea-level, just three miles from Nairobi.

Winners

Year	Name	Venue	Score
1967	G. Wolstenholme	Muthaiga	279
1968	M. Bembridge	Karen	279
1969	M. Bembridge	Nairobi	279
1970	J. Dorrestein	Muthaiga	273
1971	E. Jones	Muthaiga	283
1972	D. Llewellyn	Muthaiga	279
1973	J. Dorrestein	Muthaiga	276
1974	D. Jagger	Muthaiga	274
1975	G. Smith	Muthaiga	276
1976	Not held		
1977	L. Higgins	Muthaiga	283
1978	S. Ballesteros	Muthaiga	274
1979	M. Bembridge	Muthaiga	271
1980	B. Waites	Muthaiga	271
1981	B. Barnes	Muthaiga	274
1982	E. Darcy	Muthaiga	274
1983	K. Brown	Muthaiga	274
1984	J.-M. Canizares	Muthaiga	277
1985	B. Harvey	Muthaiga	278
1986	I. Woosnam	Muthaiga	273

Most wins

3 – Maurice Bembridge (1968, 1969, 1979)

Lowest score (72 holes)

271 – Maurice Bembridge (Muthaiga, 1979)
271 – Brian Waites (Muthaiga, 1980)

L

Ladies Golf

Ladies have been playing golf as long as men, and one of the first known female golfers was Mary Queen of Scots who played in the mid-16th century.

The first known ladies' golf club was the St Andrews Ladies' Club which was formed in 1867. In the following year the Westward Ho! Ladies' Club was formed in Devon. It is, however, reported that ladies played at Musselburgh long before the formation of the St Andrews club.

The Ladies' Golf Union was formed in 1893 and the first winner of the Ladies' Championship that year was Lady Margaret Scott.

Working closely with the Royal and Ancient Club, the LGU is recognized as the governing body of ladies golf in most parts of the world. Apart from being responsible for organizing national championships, they maintain, regulate, and enforce their own system of handicapping.

A United States women's amateur championship has been in existence since 1895 and the premier team event, the Curtis Cup (qv) was first contested in 1932.

La Moye

One of only two 18-hole courses on the Channel Island of Jersey, La Moye was established in 1902 by a local headmaster, George Boomer, whose son Aubrey was to win 11 European Open titles.

La Moye is the permanent home of the Jersey Open, and has been since the event was introduced in 1978. The first big professional event to be staged at La Moye, however, was the Rediffusion Tournament between 1963 and 1966.

One of the most spectacular rounds of golf seen at the course was during the 1983 Jersey Open when the Argentinian, Vicente Fernandez, shot ten birdies during his second round of 62.

A popular course with holidaymakers, La Moye is well designed—a fine blend of the old course and new holes. The beauty of the course, which overlooks the English Channel, reflects that of the island of Jersey itself.

Length 6686 yd (6114 m)
Par 72
Course record 62 – Vicente Fernandez (Jersey Open, 1983) and Gordon Brand, Jnr (Jersey Open, 1986)

Lancôme Trophy

Held over the St Nom-La-Breteche course near Versailles each October, the 30-strong field in the Lancôme Trophy is made up of champions from the previous twelve months from the European, American, Australian and Asian circuits. The tournament came from an idea conceived by Mark McCormack and a French amateur golfer, Gatean Mourgue d'Algue, who both saw it as being a European 'Champion of Champions' event.

All Lancôme trophies, since the first one in 1970, have been held at St Nom-La-Breteche.

Winners

Year	Name	Score
1970	A. Jacklin	206(a)
1971	A. Palmer	202(a)
1972	T. Aaron	279
1973	J. Miller	277
1974	W. Casper	283
1975	G. Player	278
1976	S. Ballesteros	283
1977	G. Marsh	273
1978	L. Trevino	272
1979	J. Miller	281
1980	L. Trevino	280
1981	D. Graham	280
1982	D. Graham	276
1983	S. Ballesteros	269
1984	A. W. Lyle	278
1985	N. Price	275

(a) over 54 holes

Most wins
2 – Johnny Miller (1973, 1979)
2 – Lee Trevino (1978, 1980)
2 – David Graham (1981, 1982)
2 – Severiano Ballesteros (1976, 1983)

Lowest score (72 holes)
269 – Severiano Ballesteros (1983)

Langer, Bernhard

Although Bernhard Langer has only been part of the European PGA tour since the early 1980s, he is already a household name.

Recognition in Britain first came in 1980 when he won the Dunlop Masters at St Pierre, Chepstow. The previous year the young European had won the German Open, Cacharel Under-25 tournament, and was the leading money winner in South America – a feat he emulated in Europe in 1981.

He was Europe's leading money winner for the second time in 1984 but, in between, he had suffered some near-misses. He finished second to Bill Rogers in the 1981 British Open at Sandwich. At St Andrews in 1984, after leading at one stage on the final day, and looking like taking the title, he finished runner-up once more, this time to fellow European Severiano Ballesteros.

It was Ballesteros who forced Langer to be 'bridesmaid' once more in that year's World Match-Play final at Wentworth as the German suffered a 2 & 1 defeat.

The pair of them renewed their rivalry at Wentworth 12 months later and once more it was Seve who came out on top – but more convincingly that time.

Bernhard had, however, in the meantime 'broken his duck' by winning his first major, the 1985 US Masters at Augusta. If 1985 started with that Masters win, it also ended with success as Bernhard was a member of the all-conquering European Ryder Cup team at the Belfry.

Still in his twenties, Germany's most outstanding golfer has many years of top-level golf ahead of him, and it should not be long before he is adding to his list of major successes.

Career highlights
US Masters 1985
British Open (best) 2nd – 1981, jt 2nd – 1984
Dunlop Masters 1980
Ryder Cup 1981, 1983, 1985

Lateral Water Hazard

A water hazard, or part of a water hazard, that runs parallel to the fairway thus making it impracticable to drop the ball behind the hazard and keep to the spot where the ball last crossed it. Lateral water hazards should be marked with red marker posts or lines.

A player may, if he wishes, play a ball in a lateral water hazard. However, generally he will opt to drop the ball within two club-lengths of the spot where the ball crossed the margin of the water, but not nearer the hole, and incur a one-stroke penalty.
See diagram under Hazards.

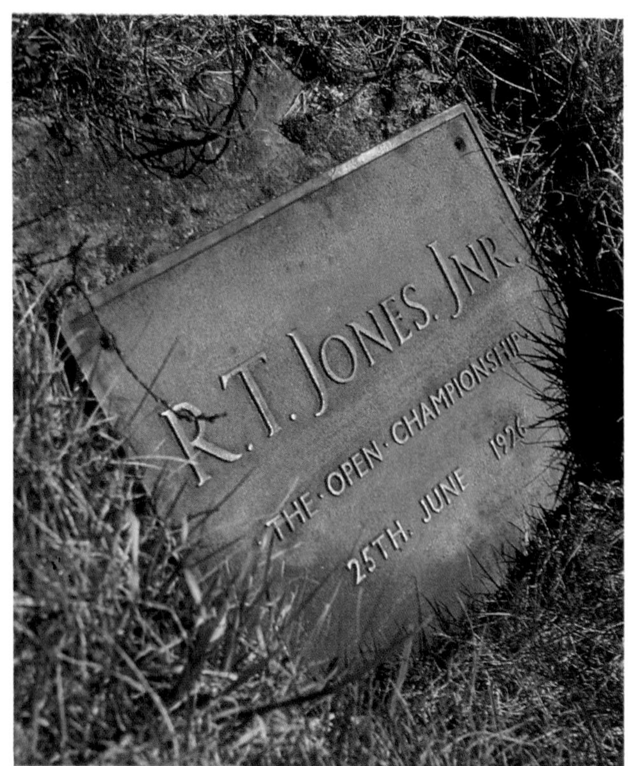

This plaque at the 17th hole at Royal Lytham and St Annes commemorates a great shot by Bobby Jones during the 1926 British Open, which he won.

Lema, Tony

People who have been playing the St Andrews course for years have still to master it. Tony Lema arrived there in 1964 for the Open and, after little more than 24 hours practice on the course, proceeded to win the title by five strokes from Jack Nicklaus, who stormed through the last two rounds with a 66 and 68. Not only was it Lema's first British Open, it was also his first golf in Europe.

The previous year, in his first US Masters, he had finished second to Nicklaus, losing by just one stroke. Everything was, at last, turning out well for Lema who had been on the US Tour since 1958. He had a graceful swing and was destined to win many honours in the game. He represented the United States in two Ryder Cup matches and once in the World Cup. In 1964 he returned to Britain to defend his British Open title at Birkdale and finished fifth. In the following year he reached the semi-final of the World Match-Play championship at Wentworth. He went down in one of the great matches of that tournament when he lost at the 37th to Gary Player after being seven up at the 20th hole.

He was nicknamed 'Champagne Tony' because of his high life style, but the true potential of the man who once served as a marine in the Korean War was never known. In 1966, when only 32, he was tragically killed in an aircraft crash in Illinois.

Career highlights
British Open 1964
Ryder Cup 1963, 1965

Lie

(1) The position in which the ball comes to rest after a shot. It must be played from where it has fallen unless this is impossible, or local rules permit it to be moved. Occasionally in the winter months preferred lies are permitted in order to protect the fairway.
(2) The angle between the horizontal and the club shaft when the club is held ready for striking.

Lightning

Lightning is always a potential hazard but on a golf course the risk is increased. Trees, umbrellas, golf clubs and flag sticks are all lightning conductors and extremely dangerous. Consequently, the rules of golf permit a player to discontinue play in a competition during a thunderstorm without incurring a penalty.

There have been fatalities as a result of lightning on a golf course. The worst instance was at Scranton, Pennsylvania, in 1957 when three golfers were struck and killed. In Britain, possibly the best-known incident involved the Tottenham Hotspur and Scotland footballer, John White, who was killed on the Crews Hill course at Enfield in 1964.

Lee Trevino, Bobby Nichols and Jerry Heard were more fortunate. All three were struck by lightning during the 1975 Western Open but later recovered in hospital. Britain's Mark James was struck in the course of the 1977 Swiss Open and in the same year Severiano Ballesteros was hit during the Scandinavian Open.

Links

Although still used to describe an area upon which golf is played, a links is, properly, a seaside golf course. The British Open is held only on links courses.

Lip

The edge of the hole. A ball that skirts the hole without dropping into it is said to be 'on the lip'.

Local Rules

Rules relating to a particular golf course which would not be generally applicable to other courses. For example, at the Beverley, Humberside, course the player is allowed, because of the cattle that graze over it, to drop his ball, without penalty, should it land in cow dung.

Perhaps the most unusual of all local rules are at a Ugandan club which permits the player to move the ball without penalty if it comes to rest within dangerous proximity to a crocodile.

The 6th hole at Koolan Island Golf Club, Australia, is part of the airstrip of a local airport. The local rule states that aircraft and vehicular traffic have right of way at all times!

Locke, Bobby

In the 1950s the rivalry between the South African, Bobby Locke, and the Australian, Peter Thomson, was reminiscent of the days of the Great Triumvirate. Between 1949 and 1958 the pair of them won eight of the ten British Opens and Locke, with his fourth win in 1957, became the first man since the days of Braid, Taylor and Vardon to capture four titles.

Born in the Transvaal in 1917, Arthur D'Arcy Locke

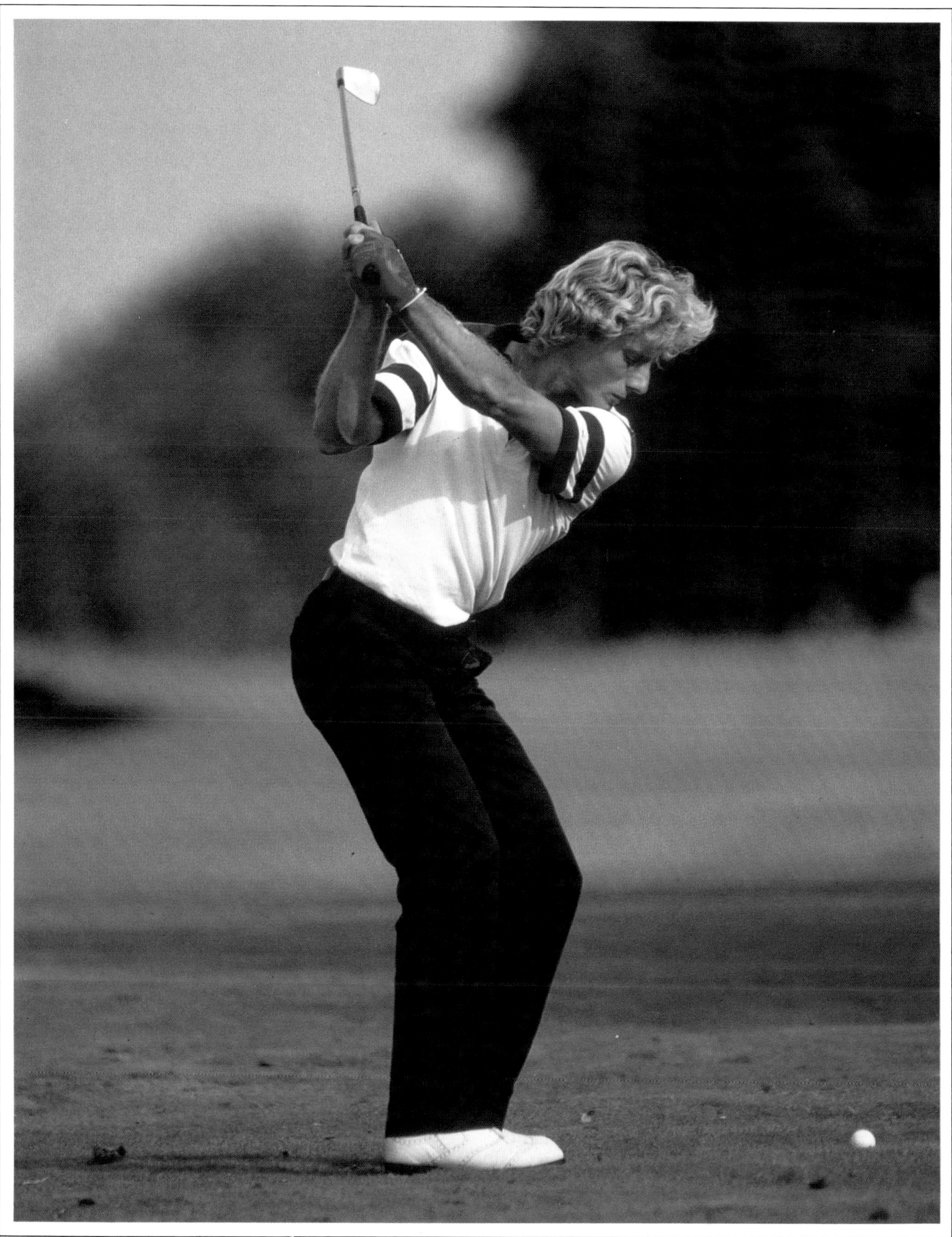

Bernhard Langer shows characteristic determination in the 1983 Benson and Hedges International at Fulford.

won the South African Boys' title at the age of 14. He subsequently took two amateur titles, nine Open titles (two as an amateur) and six professional titles in his homeland. He also went on to win the Open titles of the following countries: Britain, New Zealand, France, Canada, Switzerland, West Germany, France and Egypt.

He turned professional in 1938 but his career was interrupted by the war years, during which he served as a bomber pilot with the South African Air Force. However, after the war the sparkle was still there. The man with the looping swing, devastating putting skills and distinctive plus-fours started on a ten-year journey to the top of the golfing ladder.

His first British Open win was at Sandwich in 1949 when he beat Harry Bradshaw after a play-off. The following year he lowered the Open record aggregate to 279 when he won at Troon. These two triumphs came on top of a successful three-year spell in the United States when he won ten tournaments. If he had liked the country more and applied himself better, he could well have won the Masters and the US Open.

The fourth of Locke's British Open wins was at St Andrews in 1957 when he beat Peter Thomson by three strokes. He was then in his 40th year and that was to be his last win of any note. He was still competing in the British Open in the 1970s but a car accident a few years earlier had virtually ended his competitive career.

Career highlights

British Open 1949, 1950, 1952, 1957
South African Open 1935, 1937, 1938, 1939, 1940, 1946, 1950, 1951, 1955

Loft

The degree of slope on the face of a club which ultimately determines the length and trajectory of the shot (see diagram). To 'loft' the ball means to play a high shot over a hazard, normally to the green.

Longest Courses

If we discount the 3397-mile course followed by Floyd Rood when he played across the United States in 1963–4 in 114,737 strokes, the world's longest course is Dub's Dread at Piper, Kansas. It measures 8101 yd (7408 m) and has a par of 78. The International Golf Club at Bolton, Massachusetts, can be extended to 8325 yd (7612 m)—par 77.

The longest course to be used for a major championship was Carnoustie when it was extended to 7252 yd (6631 m), par 72, for the 1968 British Open. The longest course to be used for the US Open was at the Bellerive Country Club, St Louis, in 1955. It measured 7191 yd (6575 m).

Longest Drives

See Drive.

Longest Holes

The longest recorded golf holes have been as follows:
860 yd (786 m), par 7—6th hole at Koolan Island Golf Club, Western Australia
838 yd (766 m), par 6—6th hole at Prescott Country Club, Arkansas, United States

Bobby Locke, four times winner of the British Open, during the 1958 Dunlop Tournament at Wentworth.

831 yd (760 m), par 7—7th hole at Sano Course, Satsuki golf club, Japan

The longest hole to be used for a major championship was the 614 yd—(561 m), par-5 16th hole at the Olympic Country Club, San Francisco. The longest hole ever seen in the British Open was the 577-yd (528-m) 6th hole at Troon in 1973.

Longest Matches

With so many circumstances dictating the length of golf matches, it would be unfair to compare them in terms of time spent. The following is a list of the longest matches, in terms of holes played, in 36-hole championship *finals*.

42 Holes
1962 Irish Amateur Championship (Baltray)
M. Edwards beat J. Harrington.

41 Holes
1952 Irish Amateur Championship (Hollywood, Belfast)
T. W. Egan beat J. C. Brown.
1960 English Amateur Championship (Hunstanton)
D. N. Sewell beat M. J. Christmas.
1966 American Ladies' Amateur Championship (Pittsburgh)
Mrs D. Garner beat Mrs J. D. Streit.

The longest match in a major professional championship was in the 1932 US PGA championship when Johnny Golden beat Walter Hagen at the 43rd hole.

In terms of time the longest duration of a major championship final is 29 hours 15 minutes. The 1954 US Women's Amateur Championship final between Barbara Romack and Mickey Wright began on a Saturday morning but violent thunderstorms halted the second 18-holes in the afternoon. It was resumed the following day.

The longest tournament ever staged was the World Open at Pinehurst, North Carolina. First held in 1973, it was a two-week event over 144 holes.

The 1931 US Open at Inverness actually lasted eight rounds. Billy Burke and George von Elm tied after 72 holes. They were still level after 36 extra holes and then played another 36 before Burke won by one stroke.
See also Extra Holes.

Longhurst, Henry

After a long career in newspapers and radio, Henry Longhurst became the best-known and best-loved television commentator golf has ever known. His voice and great knowledge were tailor-made for the sport and, when he died at the age of 69 in 1978, a golfing institution died with him.

Born in Bedfordshire in 1909, he captained the Cambridge University golf team and, after completing his studies went into journalism, specializing in his first love, golf. He wrote a regular weekly article for the *Sunday Times* which was read by fanatics and casual golfers alike.

Henry Longhurst, the much-loved 'voice of golf', at work at St Andrews in 1952.

He was a good amateur player, good enough in fact to win the 1936 German Amateur Open title and finish runner-up in the French championship the following year.

Longhurst's wide-ranging interests took him into politics during the Second World War, when he served as MP for Acton in Middlesex. Awarded the CBE for his services to golf, he was one of a few golfers to be accorded honorary membership to the Royal and Ancient Club.

Lopez, Nancy

Nancy Lopez slipped as low as 14th in the US LPGA money list after two bad seasons in 1983 and 1984 and she entered the 1985 season believing she had lost the ability to win. But how wrong she was. She went on to top the

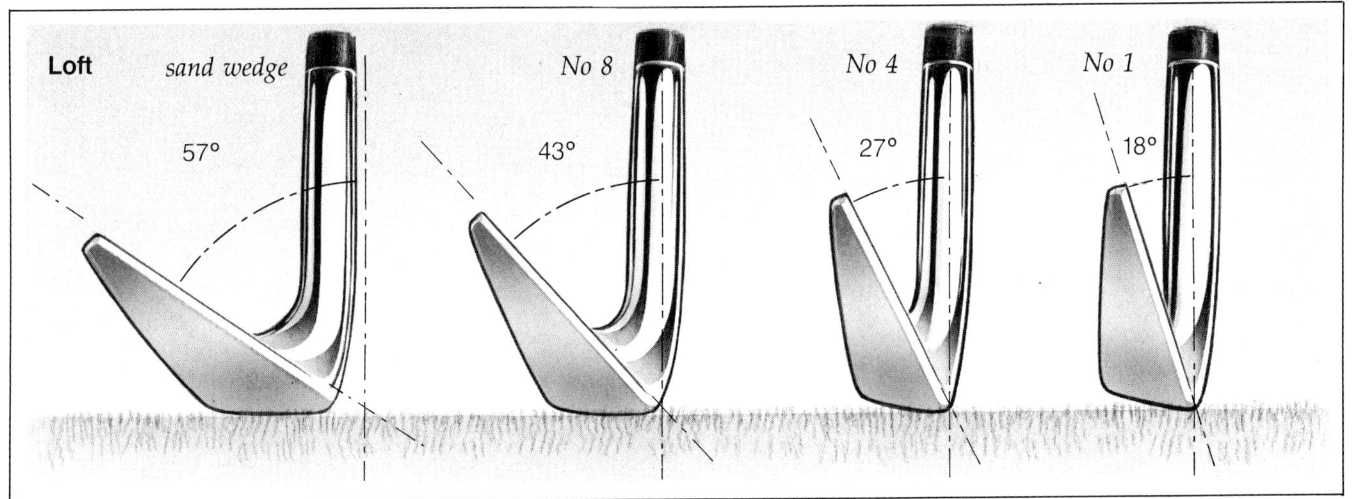

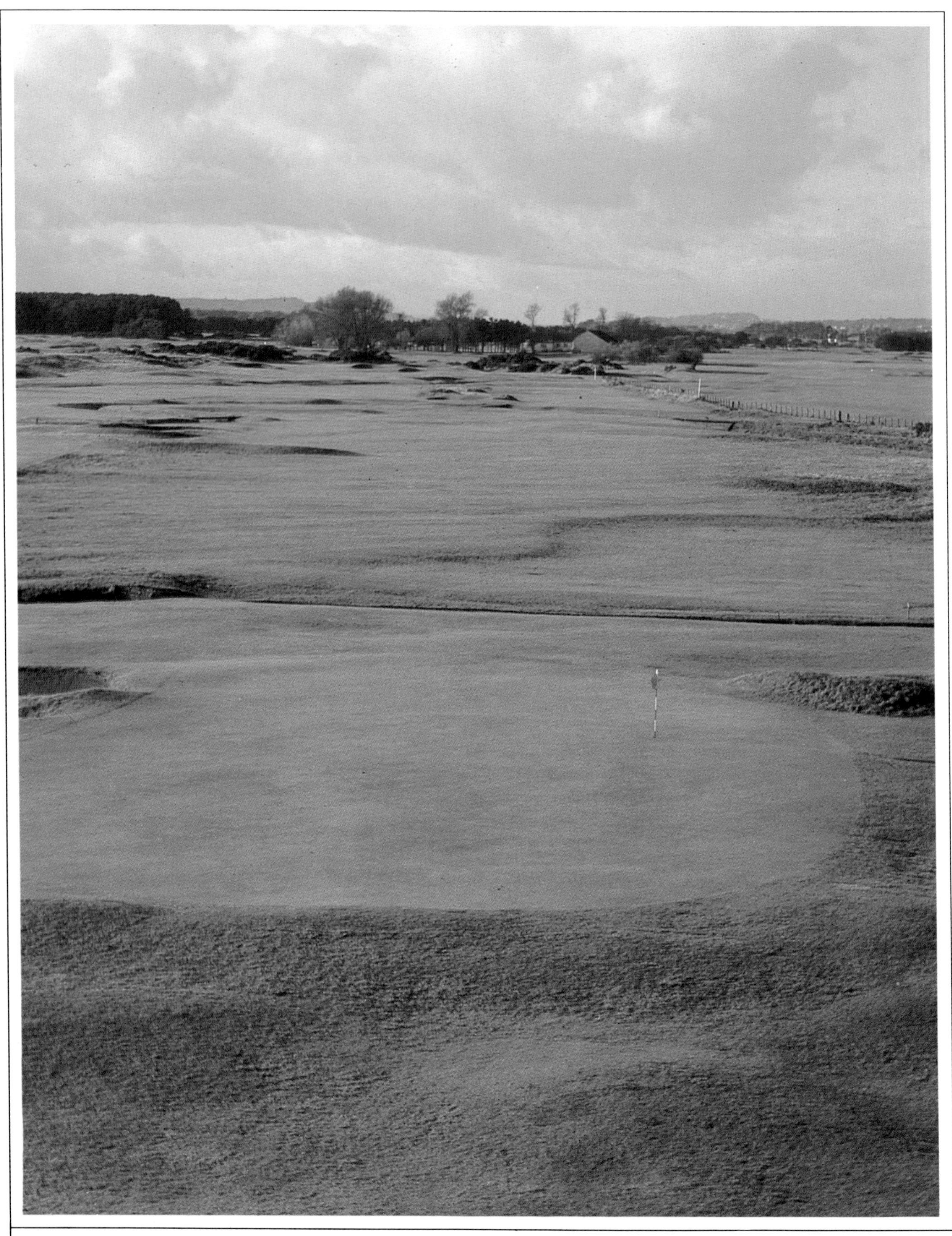

Carnoustie has been the longest course to have been used for the British Open. When the 1968 championship was held there the course measured 7252 yd (6631 m).

money list with over $400,000—a new record. She gives a lot of the credit to her second husband, the New York Met's baseball star, Ray Knight, who has been her inspiration.

Nancy, from Roswell, New Mexico, took the professional game by storm when she turned pro in 1977. Her first tournament was the US Women's Open when she finished second to Hollis Stacy at Hazeltine, the scene of Tony Jacklin's US Open win in 1970. In her first 12 months on the US LPGA circuit she won over $161,000 to create a record for someone in their first year as a professional. Her first full year saw her win nine tournaments, including five in succession. In 1979 she was victorious in eight more tournaments and won a record amount of nearly $200,000 in prize money.

In her first three years as a professional Nancy Lopez took a total of over $350,000 (the legendary Mickey Walker needed 23 years to win that much) but the US Women's Open title has so far eluded her.

Career highlights
Curtis Cup 1976
Women's World Amateur Team Championship 1976
US LPGA Championship 1978

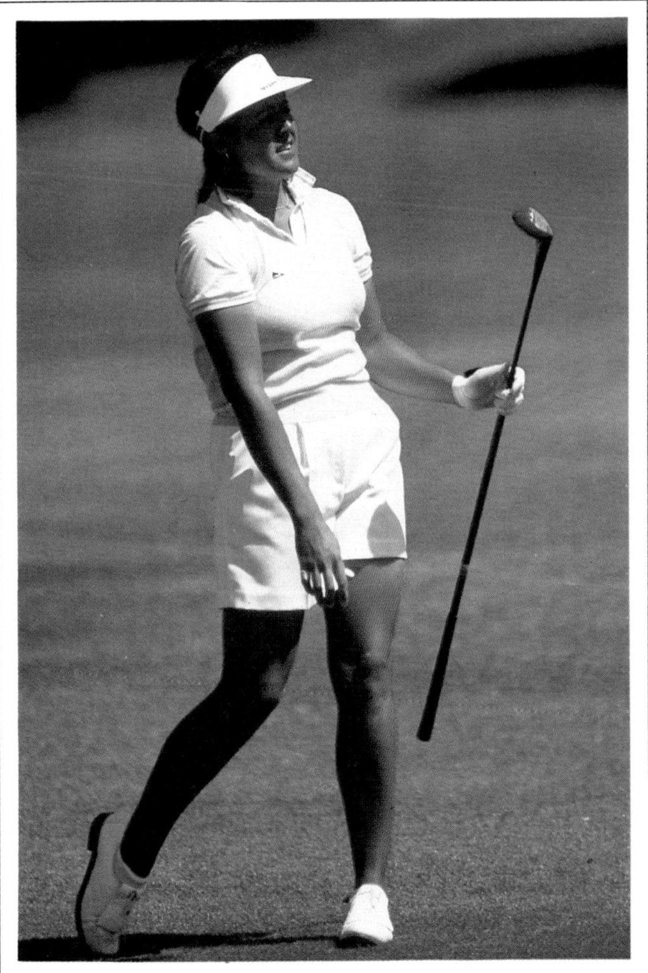

Nancy Lopez, the leading woman golfer of the 1980s.

Los Angeles Open

The Los Angeles Open has been contested since 1926, when Harry Cooper won the title. Excluding the major tournaments, it is the third oldest continuous tournament in the United States after the Western Open and Texas Open.

An early-season event, it offers top prize money in excess of $70,000. Singer Glen Campbell followed the lead taken by other show business personalities, by sponsoring the Open for a while, but his name has not been lent to it since 1983. The event is held at the Riviera Country Club, Los Angeles.

Winners (Since 1970)

Year	Name	Score
1970	W. Casper	276
1971	B. Lunn	274
1972	G. Archer	270
1973	R. Funseth	276
1974	D. Stockton	276
1975	P. Fitzsimons	275
1976	H. Irwin	272
1977	T. Purtzer	273
1978	G. Morgan	278
1979	L. Wadkins	276
1980	T. Watson	276
1981	J. Miller	270
1982	T. Watson	271
1983	G. Morgan	270
1984	D. Edwards	279
1985	L. Wadkins	264
1986	D. Tervell	270

Most wins
4 – Mac Smith (1928, 1929, 1932, 1934)
4 – Lloyd Mangrum (1949, 1951, 1953, 1956)

Lowest score (72 holes)
264 – Lanny Wadkins (1985)

Lost Ball

A ball which, five minutes after the player or caddie have started to look for it, has not been found and identified. A player may, however, declare his ball lost any time within the five minutes and can, if he so wishes, declare it lost without attempting to look for it.

If the ball is not found, the player must, except in certain circumstances, play the shot again from a spot as near as possible to where the original shot was made, under a penalty of one stroke.

Low Scoring

The low-scoring records shown on page 88 are for major professional events. (For records in the British Open, United States Open, United States Masters and United States PGA see these entries.)

Lu Liang Huan

It is hard to imagine that anybody could upstage Lee Trevino at the British Open, but at Birkdale in 1971 Taiwan's Lu Liang Huan did just that.

It was the 100th playing of the Open and the friendly Asian, wearing, and regularly raising, a trilby hat became

Low Scoring

European PGA Tour

72 holes
260 – Kel Nagle (Australia)
Irish Hospitals Tournament, Woodbrook, 1961

54 holes
193 – Mike Clayton (Australia)
Timex Open, Biarritz, 1984
193 – Peter Teravainen (US)
Timex Open, Biarritz, 1984

36 holes
125 – Sam Torrance (Scotland)
Monte Carlo Open, Mont Agel, 1985

18 holes
60 – Baldovino Dassu (Italy)
Swiss Open, Crans-sur-Sierre, 1971

(Mark McNulty (South Africa) shot a 59 in the 1985 German Open at Bremen but the course was reduced to a par-66 because of the weather and the PGA never ratified the round as a record)

9 holes
28 – José-Maria Canizares (Spain)
Swiss Open, Crans-sur-Sierre, 1978

United States

72 holes
257 – Mike Souchak
Texas Open, 1955

54 holes
189 – Chandler Harper
Texas Open, 1954

36 holes
122 – Sam Snead
Greenbrier Open, 1959

18 holes
59 – Sam Snead
Greenbrier Open, 1957
59 – Al Geiberger
Danny Thomas Memphis Classic, 1977

Others

72 holes
255 – Peter Tupling (England)
Nigerian Open, Lagos, 1981

54 holes
193 – Peter Tupling (England)
Nigerian Open, Lagos, 1981

36 holes
124 – Sandy Lyle (England)
Nigerian Open, Lagos, 1978

18 holes
59 – Gary Player (South Africa)
Brazilian Open, Rio de Janeiro, 1974
59 – David Jagger (England)
Nigerian Open Pro-Am, 1973

9 holes
27 – Bill Brask (US)
New Zealand PGA, Taruanga, 1976

Women

18 holes
62 – Mickey Wright (US)
Tall City Open, Texas, 1954

affectionately known as 'Mr Lu'. His impact was the greatest ever by an Asian golfer on any British or US championship and he narrowly lost the title by just one stroke. Trevino shot a 69 in the opening round to Lu's 70. In each of the next three rounds they ended up level to give the Texan his one-stroke advantage.

A professional from 1955, Lu won his first major title, the Hong Kong Open, in 1959 and at 22 became the youngest winner on the Asian professional circuit. By the time he came to Birkdale in 1971 Lu was a member of the fast-growing Japanese professional circuit. The following year he enjoyed his best win when he and Hsieh Min Nan, representing Taiwan, won the World Cup in Melbourne, Australia.

Now approaching 50, Lu is rarely seen in Britain but is still part of the Far East golfing circuit.

Career highlights
World Cup (team) 1972
British Open (best) 2nd – 1971
French Open 1971

Lucifer Golfing Society

Formed in 1921 as the Match Society, it changed its name after discovering the existence of another association with the same name. The aims of the Lucifer Golfing Society are to serve the interests of golf and to strengthen golfing friendships. Membership is restricted to 100. The society's main event is the Lucifer Empire Meeting for overseas golfers held annually at Walton Heath. The South African, Bobby Locke, won the 1936 Empire Trophy as a 19-year-old.

Lyle, Sandy

Quite often outstanding youngsters in any sport fail to fulfil their early promise when they step up into the senior or professional category. That has certainly not been the case with the English-born 'Scotsman' Sandy Lyle.

Born in Shrewsbury, the son of a Scottish professional, Alex Lyle, Sandy made his international debut at the age of 14. In 1975, while just 17, he represented England at Boy's, Youth's and full international level. That same

Lu Liang Huan, affectionately know as 'Mr Lu', in action at the 1975 British Open at Carnoustie.

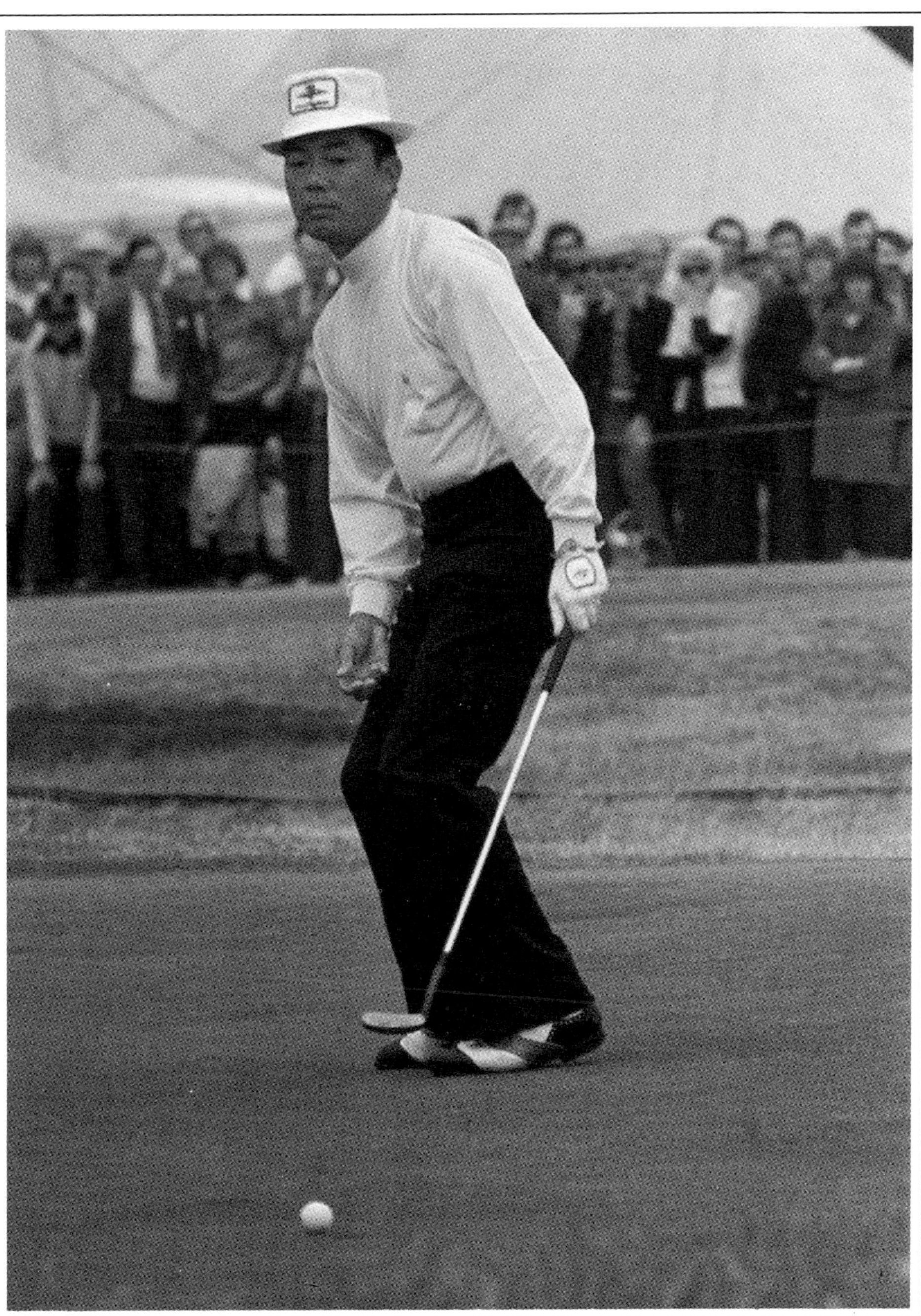

year he became the youngest-ever winner of the English Amateur Stroke Play championship.

Lyle turned professional in September 1977 and the following year won his first professional event, the Nigerian Open. His total for the first 36 holes was 124, the lowest ever recorded by a British golfer in a leading tournament.

He won his first European PGA tournament, the Jersey Open, in 1979 and that year added to his 1977 Walker Cup honours by gaining selection for the Ryder Cup team (only Mark James, two years earlier, had been selected for both teams within a two-year period).

In 1980 Lyle became the first Briton to win the individual title in the World Cup and that year lost to Greg Norman by one hole in the final of the World Match-Play Championship at Wentworth. Two years later he was runner-up once more when he lost at the first play-off hole to Severiano Ballesteros.

Lyle has remained a consistent and powerful performer since he turned professional. His playing career reached a peak in 1985 when he took the British Open and was a member of the Great Britain and Europe team that won the Ryder Cup for the first time in 28 years.

Career highlights

British Open 1985
World Cup (individual) 1980
Greater Greensboro Open 1986
Italian Open 1984
French Open 1981
Ryder Cup 1979, 1981, 1983, 1985
Walker Cup 1977

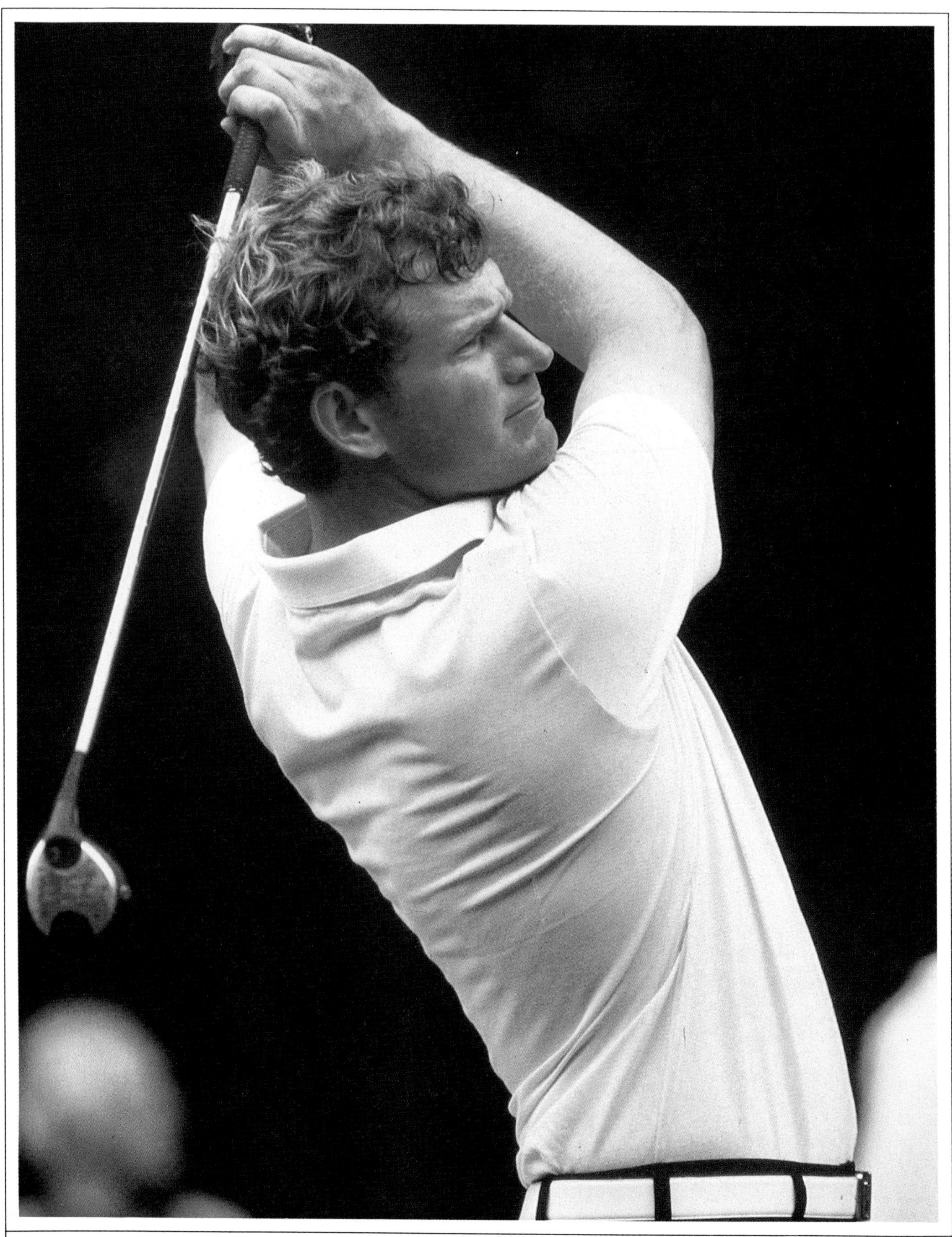

Sandy Lyle, the first winner of the British Open for 16 years when he won the title at Royal St George's, Sandwich in 1985.

M

McCormack, Mark

Mark McCormack has not only amassed a fortune from his business interests but has also brought great wealth to the sportsmen and sportswomen managed by him. Graduating from Princeton University in 1954 with a degree in law, McCormack was a keen, and good, golfer who played in the British and US Amateur Championships. He also took part in the US Open on one occasion.

He made his name in the early 1960s when he helped to build Arnold Palmer's vast financial empire. Palmer was, incidentally, a former member of the same golf team as McCormack at Wake Forest University.

During this period McCormack managed golf's 'big three'—Nicklaus, Player and Palmer—and through their television exposure did much to popularize golf on both sides of the Atlantic. His group helps to promote all kinds of personalities but concentrates its activities on golf and tennis players.

Mark McCormack, the man who has turned men from top golfers into sporting superstars.

McCormack is often heard behind the microphone providing expert comments on golf and he has given his well-known *Mark McCormack Golf Annual* to the sport.

Madrid Open

The Madrid Open, first held in 1968, was officially recognized by the British PGA in 1972. In recent years it has been the second event on the European PGA calendar. It is played in April at the Puerta de Hierro course near Madrid.

Spaniards have a good record in the event and two of them, José-Maria Canizares and Manuel Pinero, tied for first place in the 1985 Open before Pinero won the play-off to take the title for the third time—11 years after his first success. It was, however, an Italian, Francisco Abreu, who took the 1976 championship by storm when he beat Antonio Garrido by nine strokes to register one of the biggest winning margins on the European tour.

Winners

Year	Name	Venue	Score
1968	G. Garrido	Madrid	279
1969	R. Sota	Madrid	278
1970	M. Cabrera	Madrid	286
1971	V. Barrios	Puerta de Hierro	285
1972	J. Kinsella	Puerta de Hierro	283
1973	G. Garrido	Madrid	287
1974	M. Pinero	Puerta de Hierro	283
1975	R. Shearer	Lomas Bosque	135(a)
1976	F. Abreu	Puerta de Hierro	275
1977	A. Garrido	Hípica Espanola	278
1978	H. Clark	Puerta de Hierro	282
1979	S. Hobday	Puerta de Hierro	285
1980	S. Ballesteros	Puerta de Hierro	270
1981	M. Pinero	Puerta de Hierro	279
1982	S. Ballesteros	Puerta de Hierro	273
1983	A. W. Lyle	Puerta de Hierro	285
1984	H. Clark	Puerta de Hierro	274
1985	M. Pinero	Puerta de Hierro	278

(a) over 36 holes

Most wins
3 – Manuel Pinero (1974, 1981, 1985)

Lowest score (72 holes)
270 – Severiano Ballesteros (Puerta de Hierro, 1980)

Malaysian Open

The Malaysian Golf Association was formed in 1962 and the following year the first Malaysian Open was held at the association's headquarters at the Royal Selangor Golf Club in Kuala Lumpur. Most subsequent Opens have been held at the club and the event is firmly established as part of the Asian golf circuit. Japanese and Australian golfers have dominated the tournament.

Malaysian Open

Winners (since 1970)

Year	Name	Venue	Score
1970	B. Arda	Kuala Lumpur	273
1971	T. Kono	Kuala Lumpur	269
1972	T. Murakami	Kuala Lumpur	276
1973	H. Sugimoto	Kuala Lumpur	277
1974	G. Marsh	Ipoh	278
1975	G. Marsh	Kuala Lumpur	276
1976	San Hsu-Sheng	Kuala Lumpur	279
1977	S. Ginn	Kuala Lumpur	276
1978	B. Jones	Kuala Lumpur	276
1979	Lu Hsi-Chuen	Kuala Lumpur	277
1980	M. McNulty	Kuala Lumpur	270
1981	Lu Hsi-Chuen	Kuala Lumpur	276
1982	D. Hepler	Kuala Lumpur	208(a)
1983	T. Gale	Kelab, Kuala Lumpur	279
1984	L. Chien-Soon	Kuala Lumpur	275
1985	T. Gale	Kuala Lumpur	270
1986	S. Ginn	Kuala Lumpur	276

(a) played over 54 holes

Most wins

2 – Takaoki Kono (1969, 1971)
2 – Graham Marsh (1974, 1975)
2 – Lu Hsi-Chuen (1979, 1981)
2 – Terry Gale (1983, 1985)
2 – Stewart Ginn (1977, 1986)

Lowest score (72 holes)

269 – Takaoki Kono (Kuala Lumpur, 1971)

Marsh, Graham

The globetrotting Australian, Graham Marsh, has won tournaments in Britain, Europe, the United States, New Zealand, India, and his native Australia. A former schoolteacher, he gave up that career to turn professional upon the advice of another leading Australian, Peter Thomson. That advice proved sound and Marsh has never looked back since winning his first professional event, the New Zealand Watties tournament, in 1970.

His greatest achievement has been in beating Ray Floyd to win the 1977 World Match-Play title at Wentworth. That year he tried his hand on the American circuit and was their Rookie of the Year—at the age of 33! He won the Heritage Classic during his first American season.

Marsh enjoys playing in Britain and has captured some leading trophies. He has won the Dunlop Masters, the European Open, and the Benson and Hedges International twice. Always a consistent player in the British Open, he gave his best performance at Birkdale in 1983. He returned a blistering final round of 64 which put him in the running for the title for a while, but had to content himself with fourth place behind Tom Watson. Marsh's younger brother, Rodney, is a former Australian test cricketer.

Career highlights

World Match-Play 1977
Dunlop Masters 1976
British Open (best) 4th – 1983

Mashie

An obsolete iron club, equivalent to the present-day No 5 iron. Its name is probably derived from *massue*, the French for club.

Mashie Niblick

Like the mashie, the mashie niblick, sometimes known as the spade mashie, is an obsolete iron club. The loft of the club face was greater than that of the mashie and would have been the equivalent of the present-day No 7 iron.

Massy, Arnaud

The Frenchman, Arnaud Massy, the first continental golfer of international status, became, in 1907, the first foreign player to win the British Open when he beat off a challenge from the Great Triumvirate and Ted Ray to take the title at Hoylake. Severiano Ballesteros was the next continental player to win the title—72 years later.

Massy started his golf as a left-handed player simply because the set of clubs he was given were those of a left-handed player. When he came to Britain for the first time in 1902 he tried right-handed clubs and found that they improved his play.

Massy came close to a second British Open win in 1911 when he lost a play-off to Harry Vardon at Sandwich. After that he returned to his native France where he took up a professional post. He played competitively beyond the age of 50 and won the Spanish Open in 1928 while in his 51st year. He died in 1958 at the age of 81.

Career highlights

British Open 1907
French Open 1906, 1907, 1911, 1925
Spanish Open 1912, 1927, 1928

Match

A contest between two players or two sides. The sides may consist of two players each, or two may play against one. Either stroke-play or match-play conditions can be used to determine the results of a match.

Match-Play

A competition in which an individual or team attempts to win more holes than their opponents. The individual or team that completes a hole in the least number of strokes wins that hole. If both complete the hole in the same number of strokes then neither side wins the hole, which is 'halved'. Once one person, or team, leads by more holes than remain to be played then they win the match.

The scoring in match-play events often confuses people. Hopefully the following explanation will clear up any confusion:

Scores of, say, 7 & 6 and 7 & 5 are straightforward. They indicate that one player is leading by seven holes with six to play or seven holes with five to play. The other player cannot therefore win and the match comes to an end.

Sometimes a score of 3 & 1 is seen and this means that, going into the penultimate hole, one player was leading by two holes but then won the next. He was then three up, with just one to play. If he had halved that hole he would still have won the match but by 2 & 1, as he would have been leading by two with one hole remaining.

Scores of '1 hole' and '2 holes' are also seen. In the first of these instances this scoreline would arise if either both players were level going into the last hole, which one of them then won, or if one player led by one hole going into the last, which was then halved. He would still win the match by '1 hole'. If, in this second case, he won the last hole instead of halving, his victory would be recorded as '2 holes'.

A victory shown as '37th hole' or '38th hole' simply means the players were level at the end of the match and played extra sudden-death holes; the score indicates at which extra hole the match was resolved.

The biggest possible winning margin in a 18-hole match is 10 & 8, while in a 36-hole match it is 19 & 17.

Medal-Play

Another name for stroke-play. The expression is now more widely used in Britain to describe this type of competition.
See Stroke Play.

Medinah

The Medinah Golf Club near Chicago has twice been used to stage the US Open. On both occasions the winning scores have been high, 286 and 287 respectively.

The first time was in 1949 when Cary Middlecoff won by one stroke from Sam Snead and Clayton Heafner. Snead took three putts from the edge of the 17th green, which lost him the title. Lou Graham beat John Mahaffey in a play-off in 1975—the 25th occasion on which a play-off had been needed to decide the US Open winner.

The Medinah championship course, known as Old No 3, is difficult, but looks more so than it actually is. All fairways are bounded by woods which give the effect of narrowness. There are nine dogleg holes and the hardest hole is the 204-yd (186-m) par-3 17th hole—Snead's disaster hole. The drive is across part of Lake Kadijah and over a bunker at the front of the green, which is surrounded by sand.

Championship course (Old No 3)
Length 7032 yd (6430 m)
Par 71
Course record 63 – Harry Cooper (Medinah Open, 1930)

Merion

Merion, at Ardmore, Pennsylvania, holds the distinction of staging more US Golf Association events than any other American course except Augusta, which is the permanent home of the Masters. The long connection with Merion began in 1904 when the US Women's Amateur Championship was held there. In 1916 the Men's Amateur Championship was contested over the course.

The club started life in the mid-19th century as the Merion Cricket Club, and it was not until about 1897 that a golf course was laid out. This was replaced by a new one in 1912. A second course was constructed in 1914, the original one becoming known as the East course. Although the East course is short for a championship course, the fact that it has been used so often for major events is a testimony to the skills of its designer, Hugh Wilson. It is subtly laid out with well-bunkered small greens.

Merion has played host to the US Open three times. The first occasion was in 1934 when Olin Dutra won after making up an eight-stroke deficit over the last two rounds. In 1950 Ben Hogan had an emotional victory following a three-way play-off, to win his first Open after his horrifying car crash. In 1971 Lee Trevino beat Jack Nicklaus, also in a play-off.

Length 6544 yd (5984 m)
Par 70
Course record 64 – Lee Mackey (US Open, 1950)

Miller, Johnny

Johnny Miller took the golfing world by storm in the 1970s and seemed poised to stay at the top for many years to come. However, inconsistency in his play, devotion to his family and the Mormon faith led to a decline in his career.

An athletic six-footer, Miller was the US Junior champion in 1964. He turned professional in 1969 and, between 1971 and 1976, won 20 tournaments world wide, including 16 on the US Tour. His first major success was in the 1973 US Open when he shot a record 63 in his final round at Oakmont. Miller was joint second (with Neil Coles) behind Tom Watson in that year's British Open, and was a member of the winning American team, and individual winner, in the World Cup.

Further team and individual World Cup honours followed in 1975 as did his Ryder Cup debut. Then, in 1976, he won the British Open at Birkdale, played in the hottest conditions seen for many years. Miller beat Jack Nicklaus and Severiano Ballesteros by six strokes to take the title.

By 1978, however, the one-time top US money-winner, and former player of the year, had slipped to 111th in the money list. He showed signs of his old form in 1982 when he beat Severiano Ballesteros to win the Sun City Classic in South Africa and collect the sport's richest first prize—$500,000.

Career highlights
British Open 1976
US Open 1973
World Cup (team) 1973, 1975
(individual) 1973, 1975
Ryder Cup 1975, 1981

Mixed Foursome

The same as a foursome except each side must consist of a man and a woman. The most famous mixed foursomes tournament is the one held at the Worplesdon Golf Club, Surrey, which has taken place every year since 1921. Perhaps the best-known holders of the title were Michael and Angela Bonallack who in 1958 became the first married couple to win the event.

Money Winners

For leading United States and European Tour money winners see appropriate sections.
See also Ladies Golf and Prize Money.

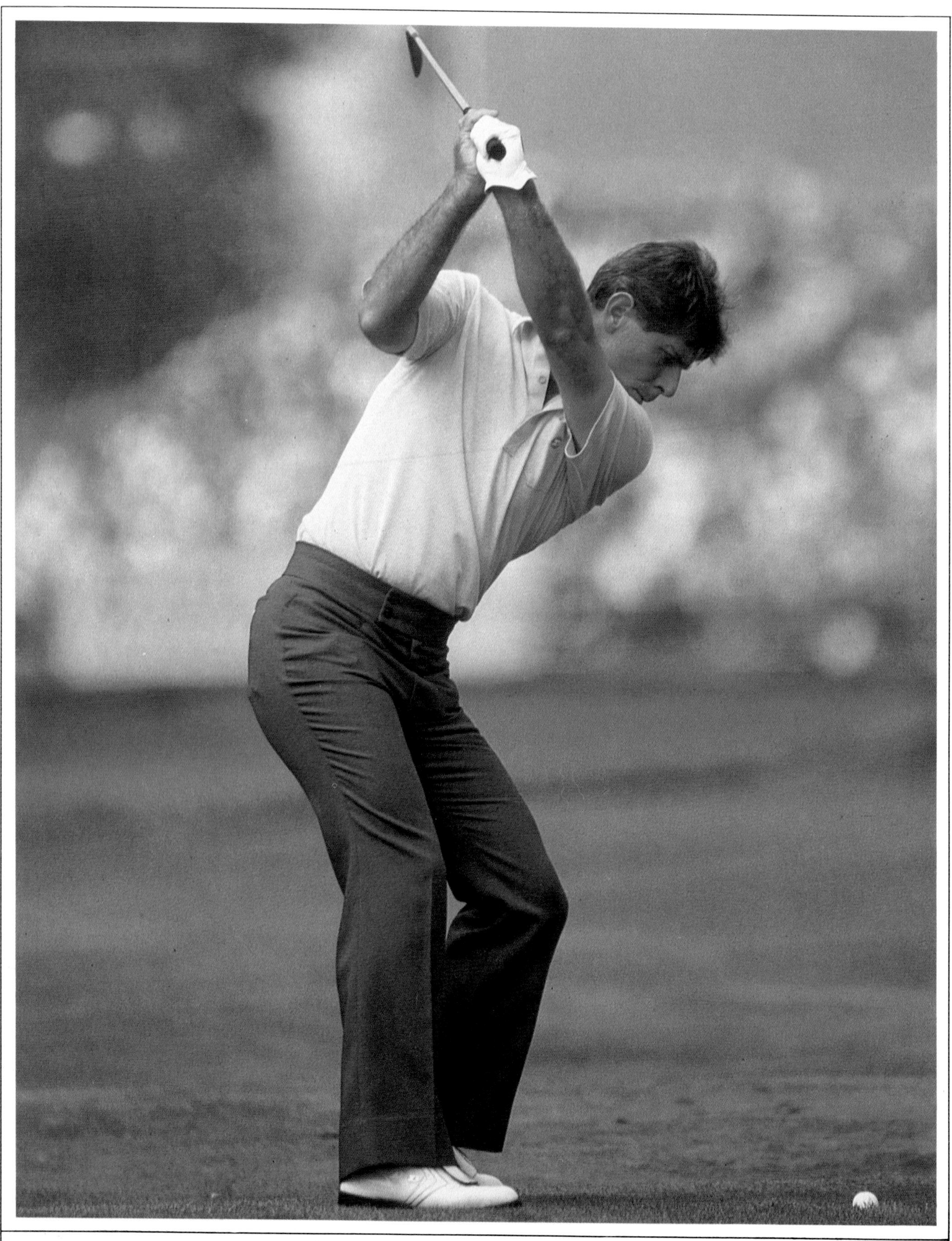

Graham Marsh, one half of Australia's most famous pair of sporting brothers of recent times. He is the brother of former Australian test cricketer Rodney Marsh.

Moortown

One of the many fine clubs around Leeds, Moortown is situated in a green-belt area just off the Leeds–Harrogate Road north of the city. Although not difficult, the course is demanding and calls for accurate driving. Woodland, heather and water play an important part of the course, which was designed by Alister Mackenzie. The first seven fairways are divided by water and, altogether, ten of the holes have water hazards on them.

Founded in 1909, Moortown has staged many championships, mostly amateur—Men's, Women's and Boys. Michael Bonallack won the first of his five English Amateur championships at Moortown in 1962.

However, the club's greatest moment had been in 1929 when it was the venue for the first Ryder Cup match to be played in Britain. The home side enjoyed one of its rare wins and the vast crowds saw the British team captain, George Duncan, beat his American counterpart, Walter Hagen, 10 and 8.

The hottest property in golf during the 1970s, American Johnny Miller.

The grave of Young Tom Morris who died at the age of 24. As a measure of his popularity, the gravestone was erected as a result of donations made from 60 golfing societies.

Length 6606 yd (6040 m)
Par 69
Course record 64 – Wayne Riley (Car Care Plan International, 1985)

Morris, Tom (Young)

Between 1868 and 1872 Young Tom Morris won the British Open four times. In fact he took the title on four consecutive occasions, since it was not held in 1871—and that was because of Morris. The rules stated that any man winning the title three years in succession should be allowed to keep the trophy—a championship belt. Morris won it for the third consecutive year in 1870. Since there was no trophy the following year, the event did not

Young Tom Morris wearing the first British Open trophy – a championship belt made of red Morocco leather and silver plates.

take place. When it was revived in 1872, Morris was the first winner of the new trophy—a claret jug.

No man came anywhere near to matching Morris's record until the late 1950s when the Australian, Peter Thomson, won the Open four times in five years.

Young Tom, born at St Andrews, took over the mantle of supremacy from his father, Old Tom, when he won his first British Open at the age of 17½ (he is still the youngest winner of the title). Father and son won eight British Open championships between them, but Young Tom was the better of the two.

Tom's young wife and their newborn child died in September 1875. He himself fell into a state of depression and died on Christmas Day of that year. A monument erected to him can be seen in the churchyard of St Andrew's church.

Career highlights
British Open 1868, 1869, 1870, 1872

Morris, Tom (Old)

Tom Morris, known as Old Tom in order to distinguish him from his son, was one of the pioneers of professional golf in Scotland. Runner-up to Willie Park in the first British Open in 1860, he played in every Open championship up to 1896, when he was 75 years of age.

Born at St Andrews he was an apprentice ball-maker to Allan Robertson and lived for some years at Prestwick before eventually returning to St Andrews as green keeper and as professional to the Royal and Ancient Club, posts he held for nearly 40 years.

Tom won the first of his four British Opens in 1861 and the last in 1867. The following year he was succeeded as champion by Young Tom, who went on to add four more titles to the family name. Old Tom had another son, John Ogilvie Fairlie, who was a useful professional golfer but not to the same standard as his brother, although he did finish third in the 1878 Open.

Old Tom lived to the age of 87 and is buried at St Andrews. The home green on St Andrews' Old Course is named after him.

Career highlights
British Open 1861, 1862, 1864, 1867

Muirfield

The Muirfield links can claim to house the oldest golf club in the world—the Honourable Company of Edinburgh Golfers who, as the Gentlemen Golfers of Edinburgh, came into existence in 1744. After playing at Leith and then Musselburgh, the Honourable Company eventually settled at Muirfield in 1891. The following year Harold Hilton won the first British Open to be held there.

That was the first of 12 occasions on which the British Open was staged at the East Lothian course on the shores of the Firth of Forth. Muirfield witnessed many historic

Old Tom Morris, a pioneer of golf in Scotland, won four British Opens between 1861 and 1867.

moments in golfing history and was also the scene of most of the leading amateur championships.

Henry Cotton gave an exhibition of brilliant driving there during the second round of the 1948 championship which was attended by King George VI. Gary Player won his first Open at Muirfield in 1959, despite taking a six at the last hole. Isao Aoki equalled the British Open record with a 63 during the 1980 championship, and there was the memorable sight of Jack Nicklaus beating the rough to win there in 1966.

The Ryder Cup came to Muirfield in 1973 when it was staged for the first and only time in Scotland.

Muirfield is a true championship course which leading golfers regard as the supreme test. It is difficult but fair, since all the hazards are clearly visible, except the wind. It is also an excellent course for spectators.

Length 6941 yd (6347 m)
Par 73
Course record 63 – Isao Aoki (British Open, 1980)

Municipal Courses

Golf courses run by local authorities on which members of the public are permitted to play upon payment of the appropriate green fee. Two of Scotland's great championship courses, St Andrews and Carnoustie, are municipal courses.

Although municipal courses are quite often not up to the standard of private ones, they do give ordinary people an opportunity to play golf at a moderate cost.

N

Nap

The surface or 'grain' of the grass on a putting green which goes in the direction in which it has been cut. A ball played 'with the nap' will travel faster than one played 'against the nap'. The nap is more obvious on coarser grass, found in drier climates, and hardly noticeable on British greens.

Nassau

A popular form of golf match in the United States. It is, in fact, three matches in one. The player winning the first nine holes is the first winner, the one who wins the last nine is the second winner, and the third winner is the player who is overall victor over 18 holes.

Nelson, Byron

Byron Nelson dominated American golf to such an extent in 1944 and 1945 that he became known as 'Mr Golf'. In those two years he became the leading money-winner, which was hardly surprising as he was victorious in 31 tournaments. In 1944 he won 13 of the 23 events he entered and in the following year he shattered all American records. He won a record 18 tournaments, including 11 consecutive ones, which beat his own previous record of three in a row. He had 19 consecutive rounds under 70 and a season stroke average of 68.33 per round, enabling him to complete one of the all-time great golfing records.

The former caddie from Fort Worth, Texas, turned professional in 1933 and went on to win 54 US tournaments including five 'majors'. His first major tournament win was the 1937 US Masters and then, in 1942, he beat Ben Hogan by one stroke in the first 18-hole play-off in the Masters to take the title a second time. Two years after his first Masters success he won a three-man play-off to gain his only US Open title. In 1946 he was to finish second to Lloyd Mangrum in another three-man play-off in the Open. But it was the US PGA tournament that he dominated. Between 1939 and 1945 he appeared in five finals, winning two.

Ill health forced Nelson to give up competitive golf but he managed a comeback to win the 1955 French Open at the age of 43. By that time he had become a respected golf teacher and broadcaster. He was honoured with the non-playing captaincy of the 1965 Ryder Cup team that beat Great Britain at Royal Birkdale.

Career highlights
US Open 1939
US Masters 1937, 1942
US PGA 1940, 1945
British Open (best) 5th – 1937
Ryder Cup 1937, 1947, 1965 (non-playing captain)

Net Score

A player's score after his handicap has been deducted. A 24-handicap player who completes a round in 96 strokes would have a net score of 72.
See also Gross Score.

Newton, Jack

On 24 July 1983 the playing career of the 33-year-old Australian, Jack Newton, was brought to an abrupt end when he was hit by the propeller of a Cessna aircraft. He suffered the loss of his right arm and an eye and fought for his life for several weeks.

Just two months earlier he had come close to winning what was to be his final tournament when he lost to Terry Gale in the play-off for the Western Australian Open.

In the final round of the 1975 British Open at Carnoustie Newton was in the lead, but dropped two strokes to Tom Watson, with a 74. They went into an 18-hole play-off and Watson won his first British Open by one stroke, with Newton yielding at the last hole. That was the nearest he ever came to winning a major title, although five years later he was joint second, with Gibby Gilbert, behind Severiano Ballesteros, in the US Masters.

A big hitter, Newton had turned professional in 1970 but was unlucky with injuries, first to his elbow and then to his foot. His first important victories came in 1972 when he won the Dutch Open, and the Benson and Hedges Festival at Fulford.

Newton has shown great courage since his accident

A splendid aerial view of Muirfield, home of the Honourable Company of Edinburgh Golfers.

and has started playing golf again—getting his handicap below 20 in no time at all.

Career highlights
Australian Open 1979
Dutch Open 1972
British Open (best) 2nd – 1975

Niblick

A small-faced iron club, the hickory-shafted niblick, now obsolete, would have been the equivalent of a No 8 or No 9 iron. It was used, as the wedge is today, for playing shots out of bunkers and for lofted shots over hazards.

Nicklaus, Jack

The achievements of Jack Nicklaus are the envy of all golfers. He won all the leading honours as an amateur before turning professional in 1962. Since then, his record has surpassed even that of such greats as Ben Hogan, Walter Hagen, Bobby Jones and Sam Snead.

Born in Columbus, Ohio, in 1940, Jack was the US Amateur Champion in 1959 and 1961. His first professional win was, amazingly, in the 1962 US Open at Oakmont, beating Arnold Palmer in a classic play-off. He has since won the US Open title on three more occasions, won the Masters five times, the US PGA title five times, and the British Open on three occasions.

His 70 US Tour wins is second only to Sam Snead's record of 84. But, in addition to 70 wins, Jack has finished second no fewer than 58 times. His career winnings of $4,686,280 are nearly $1 million more than his nearest rival, Tom Watson—who succeeded Nicklaus as the 'Golden Boy' of American golf in the 1970s.

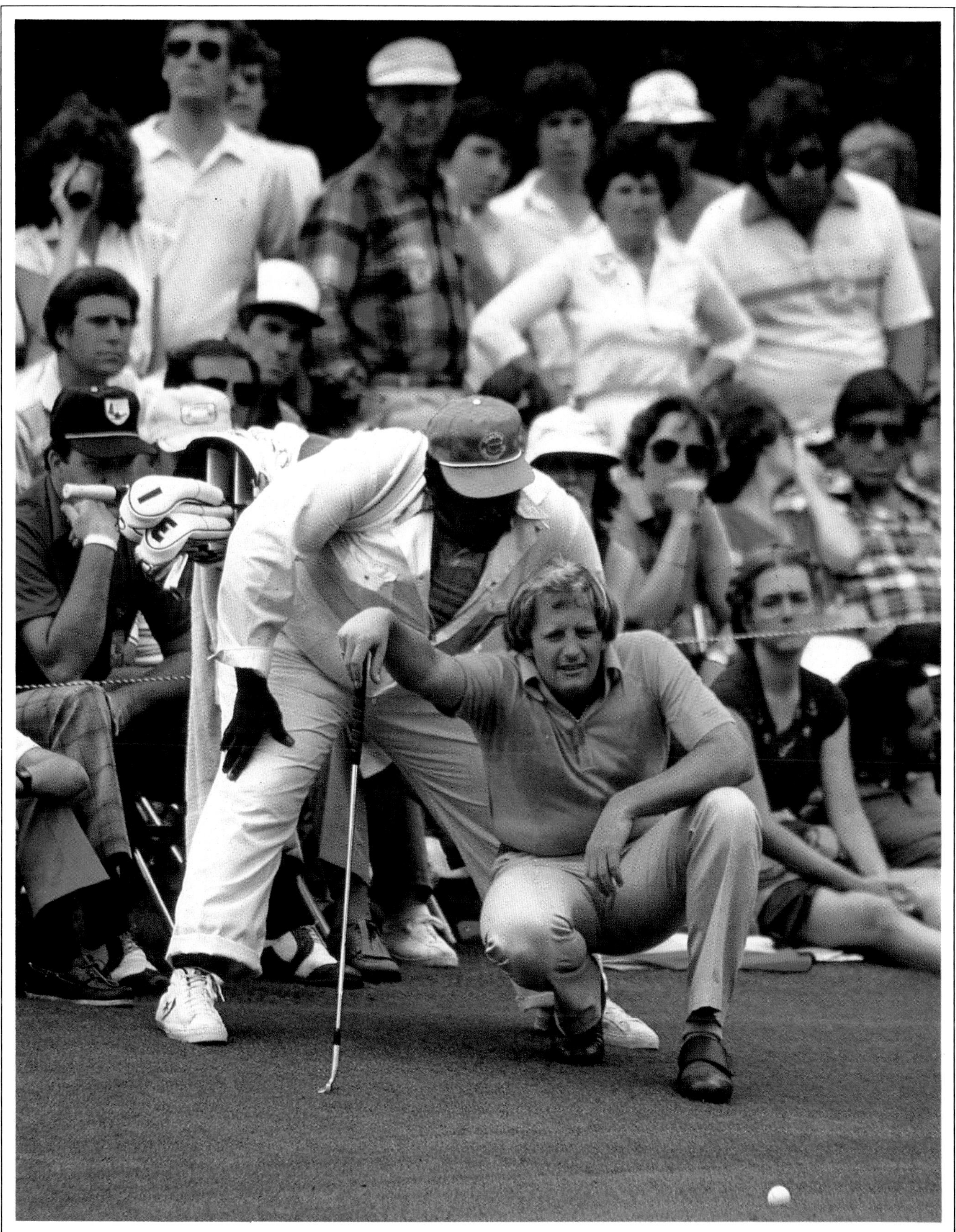

Jack Newton came very close to winning the British Open in 1975 when he lost the 18-hole play-off with Tom Watson by just one stroke.

Nicklaus won over $100,000 in a record 16 consecutive seasons and, every year between 1962 and 1978, he finished in the top five money-winners in the United States.

Popular the world over, Jack has a great affection for the British golf courses. And he has a remarkable record in the British Open since he first played at Troon in 1962 when he took a ten at the 11th in his first round total of 80. The following year he finished third. Altogether, in addition to his three wins he has finished either second or third a total of ten times.

British fans will never forget the generosity, and sportsmanship, of Nicklaus, when he gave Tony Jacklin a 'missable' four-foot put to halve the 1969 Ryder Cup match at Royal Birkdale.

And it was in the Ryder Cup that Nicklaus got one of his great personal satisfying moments from the game—of which there have been many. In 1983 he captained the United States team, for the first time, to a close victory over Europe in a memorable match at Palm Beach. He is to captain the side for a second time when the Cup is again played on American soil in 1987.

Jack Nicklaus has been all that is good in golf. And to be given the title of 'world's greatest golfer', after it had been bestowed upon such notable predecessors as Harry Vardon, Bobby Jones and Ben Hogan, is the ultimate in compliments. The 'Golden Bear' is certainly worthy of such a tag.

Career highlights

US Open 1962, 1967, 1972, 1980
US Masters 1963, 1965, 1966, 1972, 1975, 1986
US PGA 1963, 1971, 1973, 1975, 1980
British Open 1966, 1970, 1978
World Cup (team) 1963, 1964, 1966, 1967, 1971, 1973
(individual) 1963, 1964, 1971
World Match-Play 1970
Ryder Cup 1969, 1971, 1973, 1975, 1977, 1981, 1983 (non-playing capt)
Walker Cup 1959, 1961
US Amateur 1959, 1961

During an Australian tournament, *Jack Nicklaus shows how* not *to treat a No 5 iron.*

Nigerian Open

First held in 1969, the Nigerian Open is played on the Ikoyi course at Lagos, the country's oldest course. It was in the 1981 competition that Britain's Peter Tupling not only won his first event after 12 years as a professional, but also created a 72-hole world record score of 255. During the 1978 Open Sandy Lyle had successive rounds of 61 and 63 to register an African 36-hole record of 124.

Winners

Year	Name	Score
1969	M. C. Douglas	281
1970	J. Cook	276
1971	L. Elder	267
1972	Not held	
1973	T. Horton	267
1974	J. Newton	275
1975	D. Jagger	270
1976	W. Longmuir	209(a)
1977	D. Jagger	273
1978	A. W. Lyle	269
1979	J. Morgan	269
1980	W. Longmuir	264
1981	P. Tupling	255
1982	D. Jagger	274
1983	G. Brand	275
1984	E. Murray	271
1985	W. Longmuir	277
1986	G. Brand	272

(a) over 54 holes

Most wins
3 – David Jagger (1975, 1977, 1982)
3 – Bill Longmuir (1976, 1980, 1985)

Lowest score (72 holes)
255 – Peter Tupling (1981)

Nineteenth Hole

The name given to the first extra hole of a match undecided at the 18th. The expression is, however, more frequently used to describe the clubhouse bar!

Norman, Greg

The Australian, Greg Norman, won his first two tournaments on the US Tour in 1984—the Kemper Open and then the prestigious Canadian Open. These successes elevated him from 74th to 9th in the US money list, with winnings of $310,230. He also came closest to his first major victory when, in the play-off for the US Open, he lost to Fuzzy Zoeller.

Norman turned professional in 1976 and won his first event, the Australian West Lakes Classic, that same year. He ventured away from his homeland, amidst speculation that he was shaping up to become the best Australian since Peter Thomson. Joining the European circuit, after six years he did eventually, in 1982, finish the season as the No 1 player. Victories in that year's Benson and Hedges International and in the Dunlop Masters, which he retained after winning it in 1981, helped to move him into the top position. However, one 1982 tournament he would surely have liked to forget was the Martini International at Lindrick. At the par-4 17th hole during his final round Norman, the defending champion, took 14 strokes.

The two biggest wins of Norman's career to date were both in the World Match-Play championship at Wentworth. On each occasion he prevented a British victory—by Sandy Lyle in 1980 and by Nick Faldo in 1983.

Career highlights
World Match-Play 1980, 1983
Canadian Open 1984
Australian Open 1980
French Open 1980
British Open (best) jt 6th – 1984

Northerly Courses, most

The world's most northerly golf course is at Bjorkliden in northern Norway, just inside the Arctic Circle. The most northerly course in the British Isles is at Lerwick Gott, 3½ miles north of Lerwick in the Shetlands. The most northerly on mainland Britain is at Thurso, Caithness. England's most northerly course is the public one at Magdalene Fields, Berwick-upon-Tweed, Northumberland.

Nose

Another word for the toe of the golf club.

Oakland Hills

After winning the US Open at Oakland Hills in 1951 Ben Hogan said: 'I vowed I would bring this monster to its knees'. He was referring to the severity of the course which had been modernized by Robert Trent Jones, under the direction of the US Golf Association. This body was of the opinion that par was being achieved far too easily and wanted the 1951 Open to be one that called for a display of top skills. After three rounds not one of the competitors had broken par of 70. But in the final round Hogan, with one of his best ever scores (67), and the runner-up, Clayton Heafner (69), managed to perform this difficult feat.

Situated at Birmingham, near Detroit, Michigan, Oakland Hills is not an attractive course, but offers intriguing holes to the golfer. It was opened in 1918 and its original designer was the well-known course architect, Donald Ross. The club's first professional was Walter Hagen, although he only stayed 12 months. The US Open has been staged at Oakland Hills five times—in 1924, 1937, 1951, 1961 and 1985.

Length 7054 yd (6450 m)
Par 70
Course record 65 – Allen Tapie (US PGA, 1975)
65 – David Graham (US PGA, 1979)
65 – Tze-Chung Chen (US Open, 1985)
65 – Denis Watson (US Open, 1985)

Oakmont

Together with Baltusrol, the Oakmont Country Club, near Pittsburgh, Pennsylvania, has been used to stage the US Open championship a record six times. The first was in 1927 when Tommy Armour won and the last in 1983 when Larry Nelson just beat Tom Watson. It was during that 1983 Open that the record attendance for one day's play at the US Open was set up: 38,046 paid to see the third day's play. No doubt the Watson–Ballesteros confrontation drew many spectators to the course.

Oakmont, which was laid out by H. C. Fownes in 1903, is a severe test of skill and nerve for the golfer. The greens are regarded as the fastest in the United States and nearly 200 bunkers make it a difficult course. One of them, the 'Church Pews', is about 40 yd by 10 yd (36×9 m) and has nine smaller bunkers within the perimeter of one large one!

The first championship to be staged at Oakmont was the 1919 US Amateur, in which Bobby Jones was beaten in the final. When it was next held there, Jones won the title.

Length 6972 yd (6375 m)
Par 71
Course record 63 – Johnny Miller (US Open, 1973)

O'Connor, Christy (Senior)

The Irish player, Christy O'Connor, first visited Great Britain in 1954 when he reached the semi-final of the Penfold Tournament at Maesdu, Llandudno. The following year he paid his second visit in order to play in the same tournament, renamed the Swallow-Penfold, and won the title at Southport and Ainsdale. Significantly, he collected the first-ever £1000 winner's cheque in British golf. Fifteen years later he won the John Player Classic at Hollinwell, Notts, which netted him the then biggest first prize in Europe, £25,000.

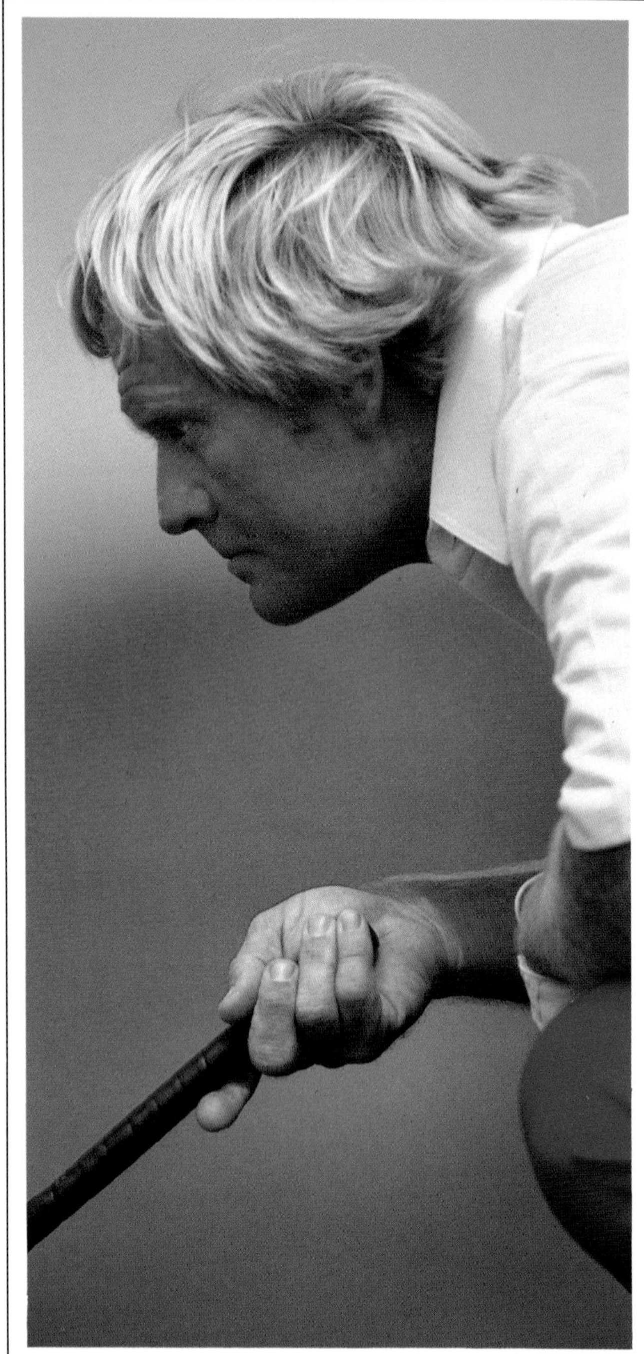

The greatest golfer of the modern era – Jack Nicklaus.

O'Connor was one of the most reliable British performers for over 25 years, and between 1955 and 1973 appeared in more Ryder Cup teams than any other man. That record still stands today.

He played in his first British Open in 1951 when it was held for the only time in Ireland, at Portrush. The closest he came to winning the title was in 1965 when he finished second to the Australian, Peter Thomson, at Birkdale. Four years earlier, at the same venue, he had finished joint third behind Arnold Palmer.

O'Connor still plays on the seniors circuit regularly. He has twice won the world title and six times the British one. His nephew, Christy O'Connor Junior, is a consistent performer on the European circuit.

Career highlights
World Cup 1958
Dunlop Masters 1956, 1959
World Seniors 1976, 1977
British Open (best) 2nd – 1965
Ryder Cup 1955, 1957, 1959, 1961, 1963, 1965, 1967, 1969, 1971, 1973

Oddities

The following is a selection of odd, unusual, and humorous golfing stories:

☆ Barrow-in-Furness crane driver Maurice Flitcroft fulfilled an ambition in 1976 when he took part in the British Open, well, the qualifying competition at least. Having only recently taken up the sport he thought he had a good chance of qualifying and thus entered. As a result of his application not being fully vetted he took part in the qualifying competition at Formby and shot a round of 121.

Consequently, the Royal and Ancient tightened up their vetting procedure. But Maurice still slipped through the net seven years later when he turned up at Pleasington for the qualifying tournament for the 1983 British Open. This time Maurice had assumed the name of Gerald Hoppy from Switzerland. After just nine holes his identity was revealed, or rather his playing gave his identity away—63 strokes for just nine holes. And that was the end of Mr Hoppy, alias Flitcroft . . . But, no doubt he will be back.

☆ During the second round of the 1968 British Open at Carnoustie, Britain's John Morgan, while addressing the ball on the 10th fairway, was bitten by a rat.

☆ The US Masters, at Augusta, Georgia, had traditionally employed the services of Black caddies. That tradition has been broken in recent years and Nick de Paul, when he caddied for Seve Ballesteros in 1980, was the first white caddie to carry the victor's clubs.

☆ And still with Ballesteros: two days after winning the 1984 British Open he beat Lee Trevino to win the Epson Trophy at St Andrews. It was a unique competition in which each player was allowed only *one* club. Both chose No 5 irons, and Ballesteros putted left-handed.

☆ John Schroeder, the leader after the first round of the 1977 British Open at Turnberry, was the son of Ted Schroeder the 1949 Men's Singles Champion at Wimbledon.

☆ The first British Open, at Prestwick in 1860, was played over just 36 holes. It was, however, not over two rounds of 18 holes but over three 12-hole rounds.

☆ Gordon Brand Junior, when he won the 1982 Coral Welsh Classic, became the first player to win a tournament on the PGA European Tour in his first season as a professional.

☆ Players at the Wimbledon Common Club have to wear either a red jacket, shirt or pullover so that the public walking on the course can distinguish which are the golfers!

☆ Francis Ouimet, the 1913 US Open champion, was elected Captain of the Royal and Ancient Club in

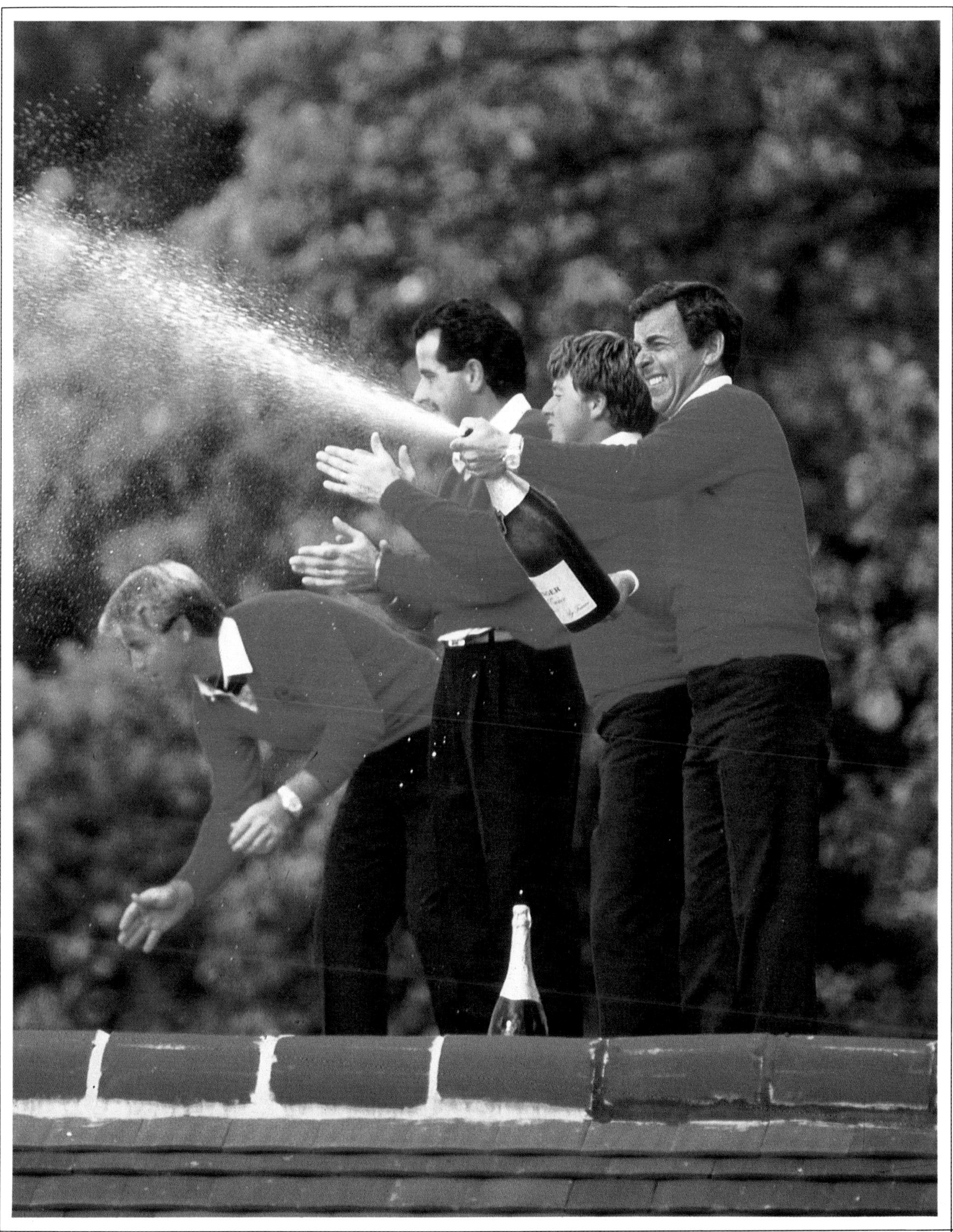

Tony Jacklin and members of his victorious 1985 Ryder Cup team celebrate on the roof of the 19th hole – the clubhouse – at the Belfry after their success.

1951—the first non-British subject to be elected to the post.

☆ During the 1978 US Open, Robert Impaglia had the unwanted distinction of becoming the first person to be penalized two strokes for slow play in the championship.

☆ Bobby Locke, four-times winner of the British Open, was fined £70 for attempted murder in 1979.

☆ During the 1985 British Open at St George's, Nick Faldo's playing partner, Phillip Parkin, received a leg injury. Faldo helped out by carrying him, piggy-back fashion, in between strokes.

☆ Who was the first Japanese golfer to win a major tournament in Britain? No, it wasn't Isao Aoki, but Chako Higuchi who won the European Women's Open in 1976.

☆ The week after winning the US Open in 1927 Tommy Armour took 23 shots at *one hole* during the Shawnee Open!

☆ The special prize for a hole-in-one at the 8th during the 1985 New South Wales Open at Canberra was either £5,000 or a pre-paid funeral with a monument . . . The prize was offered by a local PGA member, and funeral director, Paul Smith. It turned out that if a play-off was required, the 8th hole just happened to be one of the holes that would be used for the *sudden-death* play-off!

☆ David Canipe started the first two rounds of the 1984 US Open with scores of 69–69. His last two rounds were, by complete contrast, 81–83.

☆ Craig Stadler created a US Tour record in 1985 for the most money won in a year by a player failing to win a tournament. He won $297,926.

☆ Michael Meacher, a Member of Parliament, caddied for his son David on the first day of the annual President's Putter tournament at Rye, Sussex, in 1985 (see entry).

☆ During the 1985 South African Masters, Vaughan Tucker reprimanded his caddie for moving his ball without permission. The caddie then disappeared into the rough and returned with a snake which he brandished in Tucker's face.

☆ Tommy Armour lost an eye during the First World War, but still went on to win the US Open, US PGA and British Open titles.

☆ Another golfer who overcame physical disabilities to go on and become a champion was Ed Furgol. He shattered his left arm in a playground accident as a child which left it withered. Despite the handicap he was a leading professional for over 20 years and won the US Open in 1954. He also played in the Ryder Cup.

☆ American Billy Casper must rate as golf's leading 'stud!' . . . He has 11 children, ranging in ages from seven to 28. He also has six grandchildren—well, that was at the last count!

☆ Before taking up golf for a living, American Ray Floyd used to manage a topless all-girl band.

☆ The 1951 Great Britain Walker Cup captain, and great golf administrator, Raymond Oppenheimer, was a leading breeder of bull terriers.

☆ Dai Rees is the only golfer to have won the BBC Sports Personality of the Year Award. He won the title in 1957.

☆ In 1977 Tom Weiskopf forfeited his Ryder Cup place in order to follow his favourite pastime of hunting in Canada.

Oldest Champions

The following have been the oldest winners of major championships.

British Open
46 yr – Tom Morris, Snr (Prestwick, 1867)
44 yr – Roberto de Vicenzo (Hoylake, 1967)

US Open
43 yr 9 months – Ray Floyd (Shinnecock Hills, 1986)

US Masters
46 yr – Jack Nicklaus (Augusta, 1986)

US PGA
48 yr – Julius Boros (Pecan Valley, 1968)

British Amateur Championship
54 yr – Hon. Michael Scott (Hoylake, 1933)

English Amateur Championship
41 yr – Terry Shingler (Walton Heath, 1977)

US Amateur Championship
47 yr – Jack Westland (Seattle, 1952)

British Ladies' Amateur Championship
43 yr – Mrs Jessie Valentine (Hunstanton, 1955)

US Ladies' Amateur Championship
41 yr – Dorothy Campbell Hurd (Rhode Island, 1924)

The oldest competitor in the Ryder Cup was Ted Ray who was 50 when he represented Great Britain and Northern Ireland in 1927.

The Honourable Michael Scott was the oldest Walker Cup competitor when he represented Great Britain at the age of 56 in 1934.

The Belgian, Flory van Donck, was 67 when he represented his country in the 1979 World Cup competition in Athens.

Dai Rees was 60 when he finished joint second in the 1973 Martini International at Barnton.

Sam Snead was 52 when he won the 1965 Greensboro Open—the oldest winner on the US Tour. He was joint second in the 1974 Glen Campbell Open at the age of 61.

When he holed-in-one at the 8th hole during the 1973 British Open at Troon the American, Gene Sarazen, became, at 71, the oldest person to accomplish this feat in a major championship.

Sid Brews was 53 when he won the New Zealand Open in 1952.

Sandy Herd became the oldest winner of a tournament in Britain and Europe when he won the 1926 News of the World Match-Play Championship at the age of 58.

Oldest Clubs

The following is a list of oldest golf clubs in various countries:

England	Royal Blackheath	c 1766
Ireland	Royal Belfast	1881
Scotland	Honourable Company of Edinburgh Golfers	1744
Wales	Pontnewydd	1875
United States	St Andrews Club	1888
Europe	Pau GC (France)	1856
Asia	Royal Calcutta (India)	1829
Australasia	Royal Adelaide (Australia)	1870

Olympic Games

Although golf was contested at only two Olympics it still managed to produce its share of characters. At the first Olympic golf tournament, held in Paris in 1900, there was a 36-hole competition for men and a nine-hole event for women. The winner of the ladies' title was Margaret Abbott, who made history by becoming the first American woman to gain an Olympic gold medal in any sport. She maintained that she won the title only because her fellow competitors arrived unsuitably dressed in high-heeled shoes!

Golf was played at the St Louis Olympics four years later but there were only men's events—individual and team. A Canadian, George Lyon (the only non-American in the competition), won the individual title and, at 46, became one of the oldest-ever Olympic champions. He was a player very much in the style of Lee Trevino, laughing and joking his way around the course. Lyon was also an all-round sportsman. He won eight Canadian Amateur golf titles, and excelled at baseball, tennis, cricket and athletics (he once broke the Canadian pole vault record).

Because of a dispute and subsequent boycott there was no golf at the 1908 London Olympics, although it was scheduled to take place. Lyon, the only entrant, was offered a gold medal but refused to accept it. Golf has not been seen at the Olympic Games since.

Olympic Medallists

1900 Paris

Men

Gold	Charles Sands (US)
Silver	Walter Rutherford (GB)
Bronze	David Robertson (GB)

Women

Gold	Margaret Abbott (US)
Silver	Polly Whittier (Switzerland)
Bronze	Hager Pratt (US)

1904 St Louis

Men—Individual

Gold	George Lyon (Canada)
Silver	Chandler Egan (US)
Bronze	Burt McKinnie (US)

Men—Team

Gold	United States
Silver	United States
Bronze	United States

One-Armed Championships

Both Great Britain and the United States hold championships for disabled golfers who have the use of only one arm. The first British championship was held by the Burgess Golfing Society of Edinburgh in September 1933 and has taken place every year since except during 1941–5. Players are not permitted to use artificial aids.

Winners (since 1970)

1970	T. Atkinson
1971	A. Wilmott
1972	G. Kerr
1973	D. C. Fightmaster
1974	A. Wilmott
1975	D. C. Fightmaster
1976	D. R. Lawrie
1977	A. Wilmott
1978	A. Wilmott
1979	A. Robinson
1980	R. P. Reid
1981	A. Robinson
1982	M. J. O'Grady
1983	A. Robinson
1984	A. Robinson
1985	A. Robinson
1986	A. Robinson

Most wins

7 – Alex Wilmott (1958, 1962, 1967, 1971, 1974, 1977, 1978)

Oosterhuis, Peter

Twelve months after his first attempt to obtain a US professional circuit ticket, Peter Oosterhuis did, eventually, acquire one—in November 1974. Six and a half years later his dedication and hard work were rewarded when he became the first Briton since Tony Jacklin to achieve victory on the US Tour, winning the 1981 Canadian Open—a triumph which most American professionals warmed to. Oosterhuis had decided, after finishing third in the 1973 US Masters (the highest ever placing by a Briton), that he wanted to play in the United States.

He came very close that day, at Augusta, to winning the coveted Green Jacket. He led after three rounds but a final round of 74 put him on a triple tie for third place.

Outstanding as an amateur, Oosterhuis won nearly every honour available, except a national title. He was selected for the Great Britain Walker Cup team while still at his school, Dulwich College, in 1967. The following year he turned professional and his first victory came in the 1970 South African General Motors Open. As leader of the Order of Merit he was the Vardon Trophy winner between 1971 and 1974—the first, and so far the only, man to take the award four times. In 1974 he finished second to Gary Player in the British Open at Lytham, and in 1982 was second again, this time to Tom Watson, at Troon.

Oosterhuis is now settled in the United States and rarely returns to Britain. He continues to play in the US despite losing his 'ticket' at the end of the 1985 season.

Career highlights

Canadian Open 1981
French Open 1973, 1974
Walker Cup 1967
Ryder Cup 1971, 1973, 1977, 1979, 1981
British Open (best) 2nd – 1974, jt 2nd – 1982

Open Stance

The position adopted by a player who, when addressing the ball, draws the left foot back from the intended line of

Australia's Greg Norman has won tournaments both sides of the Atlantic, as well as on the Asian circuit and in his home country.

flight. If the ball is struck correctly it will fly to the left of its intended target before veering right.
See diagram under Stance.

Origins of Golf
Golf is one of the few sports that cannot pinpoint its exact beginnings. Over the years historians have tried but have still not reached a definite conclusion. Sir Walter Simpson, a 19th-century writer on golf, thought that it was probably first played by a shepherd who, with his upturned crook, hit a stone or pebble. That is quite likely but when all this took place must remain a matter for conjecture.

It is known, however, that golf, or gouf as it was called, was played in Scotland in the 15th century. An Act of Parliament by James I in 1457 banned the playing of the sport because it interfered with archery practice.

One hundred years earlier a stained-glass window was installed in Gloucester Cathedral depicting a man hitting a ball with a stick or club. Around that time there was also mention of a stick and ball game called chole (qv).

Amidst all the uncertainty there is another strong contender—a Dutch game called kolf or colf, which was played around 1300. Records have been found which describe it as a ball game played with an iron-headed stick. The ball was hit towards a target—a door, a tree or something similar.

Out
(1) Another name for the first nine holes on a golf course.
(2) A movement in which the club head is taken back outside the line of flight of the ball so that, at impact, it is facing to the left of the intended target. On completion of its swing it ends up inside the line of flight. Thus it has travelled from 'out' to 'in'.

Out of Bounds
A ball is out of bounds if it lands in an area where play is prohibited. The boundary fence of a golf course normally indicates an out-of-bounds area, but occasionally officials can create an artificial boundary to prevent wayward shots. The whole of the ball must be outside the boundary, whether this is a marking on the course or a fence or wall. However, a player may stand out of bounds to play a shot in bounds. Any ball that goes out of bounds must be replayed from the spot as near as possible to the position from where the original ball was played. In this instance a one-stroke penalty is incurred.

Oxford and Cambridge Golfing Society
The Oxford and Cambridge Golfing Society, for past and present golfers, was the idea of a former Cambridge golfer, John Low. The Society, as it is affectionately known, was formed on 23 March 1898 with Low as its first captain. A series of matches between members of the Society and various teams, international or otherwise, were arranged. A visit to the United States by the Society in 1903 is regarded as the forerunner to the Walker Cup. The highlight of the Society's calendar is the President's Putter, held at Rye, East Sussex, each January and first contested in 1920.
See also President's Putter.

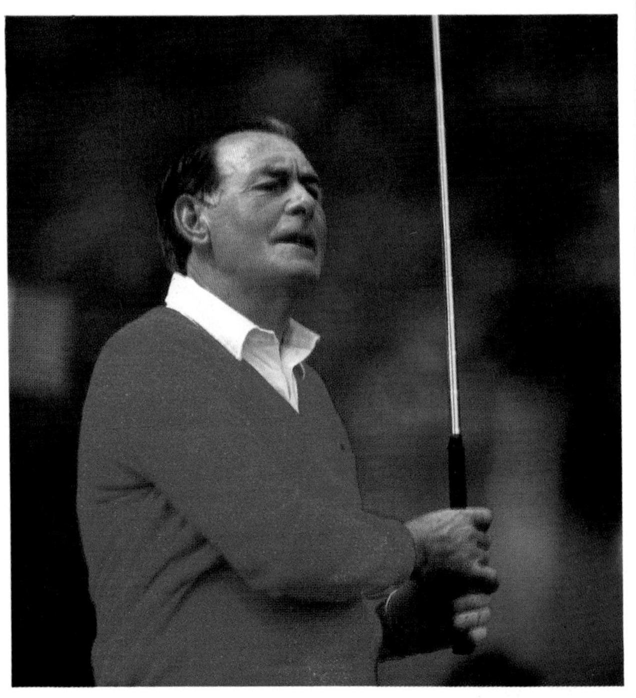

Ireland's best known, and best loved, golfer – Christy O'Connor, Snr.

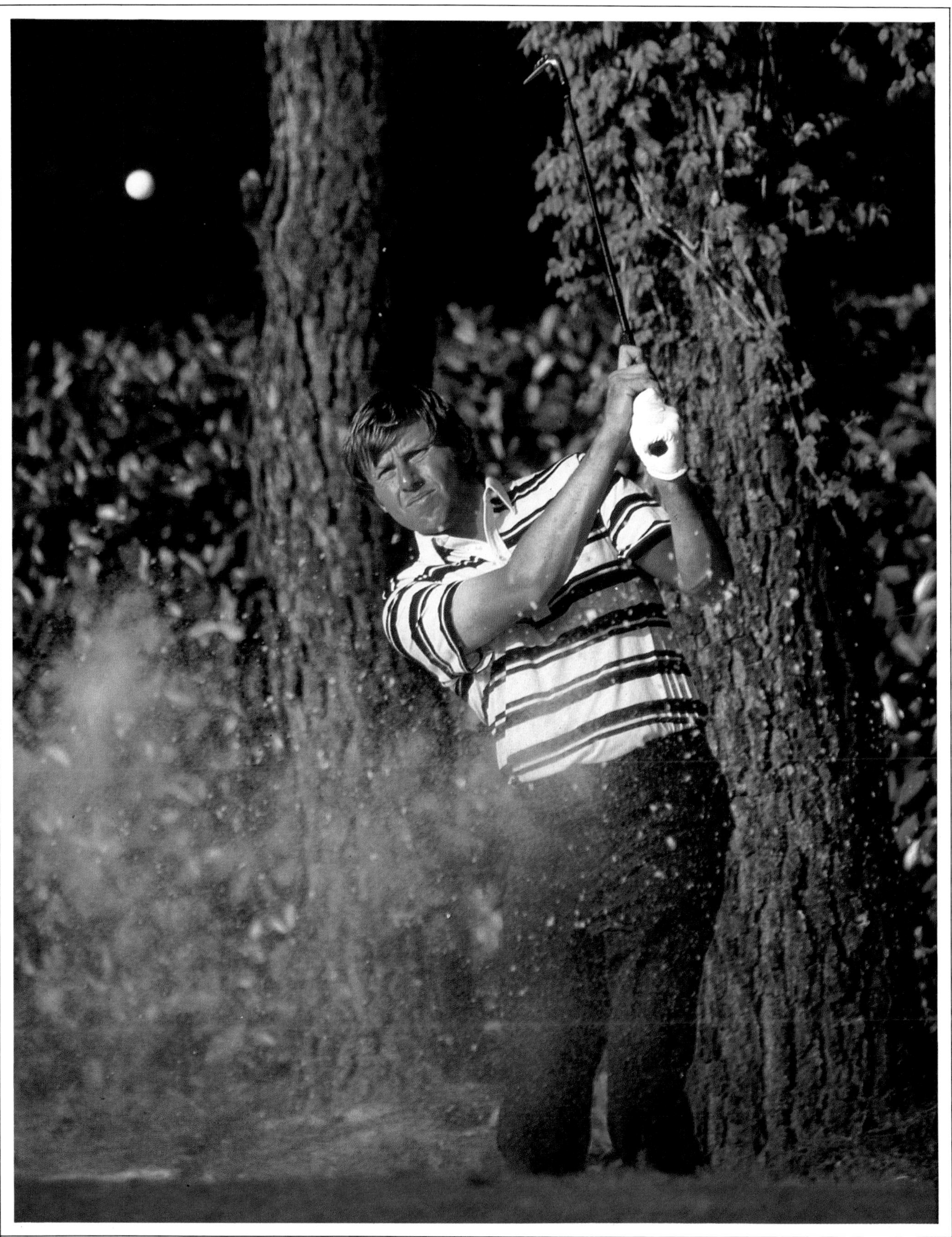

After six years on the United States Tour, Britain's Peter Oosterhuis eventually won a major event – the 1981 Canadian Open.

P

Palmer, Arnold

When Arnold Palmer returned to Royal Birkdale for the 1983 British Open, the scene was little different from what it was when he first played in the event 23 years earlier. His famous 'army' of fans still followed him around the 72 holes, willing him to produce that bit of Palmer magic.

It was at Birkdale in 1961 that Palmer won his first British Open by one stroke from Dai Rees. He took the title for a second time in the following year, which meant that in his first three British Opens, from 1960 to 1962, he had finished second, first and again first—a performance even Tom Morris Junior could not match.

Palmer won the US Amateur title in 1954, turned professional the following year and immediately went on to take the Canadian Open title. The first of his major triumphs was in 1958 when he won the US Masters on what was to be the first of four occasions. He added a second Masters title, and a first US Open, in 1960 and was becoming golf's hottest property. He teamed up with the promoter, Mark McCormack, who turned Palmer from an extraordinary golfer into an empire and an institution.

Because Palmer regarded the British Open highly among the major championships, he succeeded in getting many other leading Americans to follow him across the Atlantic and thus ensure that the event retained its status. This move by Palmer has provided an example for the world's top players to this day, and it is hardly surprising that the Royal and Ancient Club made him an honorary member in 1979.

Born in Latrobe, Pennsylvania, Palmer won more than 60 tournaments on the US Tour and was the leading prize money earner on four occasions. In 1963 he was the first man to win over $100,000 in a season. He was also, in 1968, the first man to pass the $1 million mark in career winnings. That milestone came 13 years after he had picked up his first cheque, $145, for finishing 25th in the 1955 Fort Wayne Open.

From those humble beginnings Palmer went on to capture most of the major honours: the US Open, the British Open twice, the US Masters four times, the World Match-Play title twice, the World Cup (team) six times and the individual once. But the one tournament that eluded him was the US PGA. He finished second on three occasions, but the nearest he came to success was at Pecan Valley in 1968 when he finished one stroke behind the 48-year-old winner, Julius Boros.

There are many memorable moments from Arnold Palmer's career but perhaps his greatest achievement was in winning his one and only US Open, at Cherry Hills, in 1960. He was lying 15th going into the final round and seven shots behind the leader, Mike Souchak. Palmer proceeded to birdie six of the first seven holes on his way to a round of 65 and a championship-winning total of 280, beating a young amateur called Nicklaus by two strokes.

Career highlights

US Amateur 1954
US Open 1960
British Open 1961, 1962
US Masters 1958, 1960, 1962, 1964
World Match-Play 1964, 1967
World Cup (team) 1960, 1962, 1963, 1964, 1966, 1967
World Cup (individual) 1967
Ryder Cup 1961, 1963, 1965, 1967, 1971, 1973, 1975 (non-playing captain)

Par

The score an expert golfer would expect to make at a given hole, allowing for normal playing conditions, no flukes and two strokes on the putting green. The par of each hole is decided by the length of the hole and not by its difficulty—that aspect is taken care of by the Standard Scratch Score (qv).

In Great Britain the following lengths of a hole determine its par:

250 yd (220 m) or under—par 3
251 yd (230 m) to 475 yd (434 m) inclusive—par 4
476 yd (435 m) and over—par 5

Park, Willie

It is impossible to talk about Willie Park Senior without reference to the remainder of this remarkable Musselburgh golfing family. While the distinction of winning the first British Open fell to Willie Senior, two other members of the family also took the title. His son, Willie Junior, won it in 1887 and 1889 and his brother Mungo in 1874. If Willie Senior's four wins are added to that total, between them they notched up seven British Open successes. Willie Junior's daughter, Doris, was also a well-known international and championship player.

Willie Senior was one of the finest putters of his day and a great money-match player, particularly with Old Tom Morris. He had a notice printed in *Bell's Life* for over 20 years which offered a challenge to any golfer in the world to play him for £100. Very few took up the offer.

Willie Junior became one of the leading golf course designers and constructors in Britain, the United States and Canada.

Career highlights: Willie Park Senior

British Open 1860, 1863, 1866, 1875

Pate, Jerry

In 1981 Jerry Pate was captured by the world's photographers diving fully clothed into a lake on the Cordova course, Tennessee, after winning the Danny Thomas-Memphis Classic. The reason for Pate's spontaneous action was that he had just won his first tournament on the US Tour for two years.

It is hardly surprising that Pate was glad to relieve himself of feelings of frustration and worry because things had started to turn sour on the man who made an enormous impact in his first year as a professional.

He won the US Amateur title in 1974 at the first attempt and turned professional at the end of 1975. During his first year he won the US Open at Duluth in his native Georgia. Two weeks later he took the Canadian Open to become the third man, after Tommy Armour (1927) and Lee Trevino (1971), to win both titles in the same year.

He was Rookie of the Year for 1976 and his winnings of $153,000 were at that time a record amount for a rookie. He later went on to become the youngest person to win $1 million.

Career highlights

US Open 1976
US Amateur 1974
British Open (best) jt 15th – 1977
Walker Cup 1975
Ryder Cup 1981

Pebble Beach

One of the three courses used for the Bing Crosby tournament, Pebble Beach is among the most beautiful, spectacular and exciting golf courses in the world.

Situated on the Monterey peninsula, some 120 miles south of San Francisco, it is laid out along the shoreline of the Pacific Ocean. The 7th hole is the most photographed golf hole in the world. The green juts out into the Pacific and players have waves lapping up behind them as they are putting—assuming that they reach the green! Only 100 yards long, it is the shortest hole in championship golf in the United States. The 8th hole requires a second shot that has to carry across a 100 ft (30 m) drop into the ocean, and the 18th, running along the rocky coastline, is, perhaps, the finest finishing hole in the United States.

Built in 1918, Pebble Beach was the first of several courses to spring up on the peninsula: Cypress Point, Monterey and Spyglass Hill were all added later.

Pebble Beach was ignored, until recently, for championship golf. It has twice been the setting for the US Open: in 1972 when Jack Nicklaus returned to the course 11 years after winning the US Amateur title there and in 1982 when Tom Watson won his first, and only, US Open.

Length 6832 yd (6247 m)
Par 72
Course record 62 – Tom Kite (Bing Crosby Pro-Am, 1983)

Penalty Stroke

A stroke (or strokes) added to a player's score for breach of certain rules. The penalty can be incurred for a variety of reasons but the most common are a lost ball, a ball out of bounds or an unplayable ball.

Pensacola Open

Although the Pensacola Open attracts one of the smallest prize funds on the US Tour it has a long association with the professional game in the United States. Despite surviving two lengthy periods of absence from the US calendar (1932–44 and 1947–55) it returned and has been contested every year since 1956.

The Pensacola Open has its home at the Perdido Bay Resort in Florida, and it was here in 1979 that Curtis Strange, won his first US Tour event.

The first Open was held in 1929 and won by Horton Smith, who took the first US Masters title five years later.

Winners (Since 1970)

Year	Name	Score	Year	Name	Score
1970	D. Lotz	275	1978	M. McLendon	272
1971	G. Littler	276	1979	C. Strange	271
1972	D. Hill	271	1980	D. Halldorson	265
1973	H. Blancas	277	1981	J. Pate	271
1974	L. Elder	274	1982	C. Peete	268
1975	J. McGee	274	1983	M. McCumber	266
1976	M. Hayes	275	1984	B. Kratzert	270
1977	L. Thompson	268	1985	D. Edwards	269

Most wins

2 – Arnold Palmer (1960, 1963)
2 – Doug Sanders (1962, 1965)
2 – Gay Brewer (1966, 1967)

Lowest score (72 holes)

262 – Gay Brewer (1967)

PGA Championship

The PGA Championship began life as the PGA Closed Championship in 1955 at Pannal and was won by Ken Bousfield. In 1967 Closed and Open PGA championships were held, but since 1969 it has been an Open event.

Winners (since 1965)

Year	Name	Venue	Score
1965	P. Alliss	Prince's	286
1966	G. Wolstenholme	Saunton	278
1967	B. C. Huggett	Thorndon Park	271 (closed)
1967	M. E. Gregson	Hunstanton	275 (open)
1968	P. M. Townsend	Mid-Surrey	275 (closed)
1968	D. Talbot	Dunbar	276 (open)
1969	B. Gallacher	Ashburnham	291
1970–71	Not held		
1972	A. Jacklin	Wentworth	279
1973	P. Oosterhuis	Wentworth	280
1974	M. Bembridge	Wentworth	278
1975	A. Palmer	Sandwich	285
1976	N. C. Coles	Sandwich	280
1977	M. Pinero	Sandwich	283
1978	N. Faldo	Birkdale	278
1979	V. Fernandez	St Andrews	288
1980	N. Faldo	Sandwich	283
1981	N. Faldo	Ganton	274
1982	A. Jacklin	Hillside	284
1983	S. Ballesteros	Sandwich	278
1984	H. Clark	Wentworth	204(a)
1985	P. Way	Wentworth	282
1986	R. Davis	Wentworth	281

(a) over 54 holes

Most wins

3 – Peter Alliss (1957, 1962, 1965)
3 – Nick Faldo (1978, 1980, 1981)

Lowest score (72 holes)

266 – B. J. Bamford (Mid-Surrey, 1961)

A study in concentration – the great Arnold Palmer prepares for a putt.

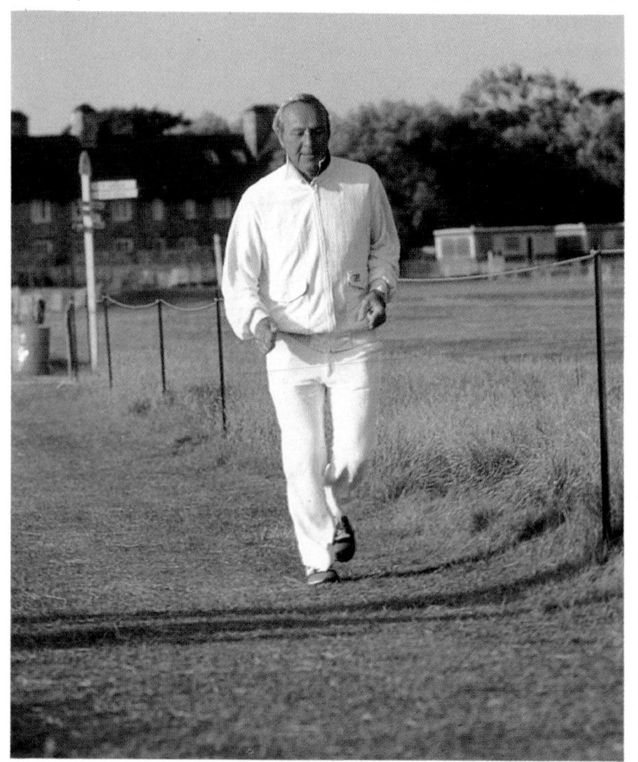

The loneliness of the long-distance golfer . . . Arnold Palmer keeping himself fit.

The 1975 event was won by Arnold Palmer, perhaps some consolation for the fact that he never captured the US PGA title. Tony Jacklin's last major championship win was in the PGA, at Hillside, Southport, in 1982.

Philippines Open

Now part of the Asian golf circuit, the Philippines Open was acknowledged as Asia's premier tournament when first held in 1935. Prize money now exceeds $100,000, and with the odd exception, the event has been played on the country's oldest course at Manila.

The 1979 winner was one of the Philippines' leading professionals, Ben Arda, who took the title 16 years after last winning it in 1963, at the age of 49!

Winners (since 1970)

Year	Name	Venue	Score
1970	Yo Hsieh Yung	Manila	282
1971	Chien Chung	Manila	282
1972	H. Sugimoto	Manila	286
1973	King-Seung Hack	Manila	289
1974	Lu Liang Huan	Manila	281
1975	Hsiong Kuo Chie	Manila	276
1976	Q. Mancao	Manila	281
1977	Yo Hsieh Yung	Manila	281
1978	Lu Liang Huan	Manila	278
1979	B. Arda	Manila	286
1980	Lu Hsi-Chuen	Manila	287
1981	T. Sieckmann	Manila	287
1982	Hsieh Min-Nan	Manila	292
1983	Lu Hsi-Chuen	Rizal	277
1984	R. Lavares	Manila	272
1985	Not held		

Most wins
Lu Liang Huan (1965, 1974, 1978)

Lowest score (72 holes)
272 – R. Lavares (1984)

Phoenix Open

An early-season event, the Phoenix Open has been contested since 1935, making it one of the oldest professional events in the United States.

Played at the Phoenix Country Club, Arizona, the first winner was Ky Laffoon. It was not held between 1936–8 but returned for two years in 1939. The war years then deprived Arizona of its biggest championship for another couple of years but it has been contested every year since 1944.

Arnold Palmer won the event three years in succession, 1961–3—one of the rare occasions any man has won a US Tour event in three consecutive years.

Winners (since 1970)

Year	Name	Score	Year	Name	Score
1970	D. Douglass	271	1979	B. Crenshaw	199(a)
1971	M. Barber	261	1980	J. Mitchell	272
1972	H. Blancas	273	1981	D. Graham	268
1973	B. Crampton	268	1982	L. Wadkins	263
1974	J. Miller	271	1983	B. Gilder	271
1975	J. Miller	260	1984	T. Purtzer	268
1976	B. Gilder	268	1985	C. Peete	270
1977	J. Pate	277	1986	H. Sutton	267
1978	M. Barber	272			

(a) played over 54 holes

Most wins
3 – Arnold Palmer (1961, 1962, 1963)
3 – Gene Littler (1955, 1959, 1969)

Lowest score (72 holes)
260 – Johnny Miller (1975)

Pick and Drop

A player may pick a ball from an unplayable lie—from a ditch, puddle, etc—and drop it in accordance with the rules, incurring the appropriate penalty if applicable.

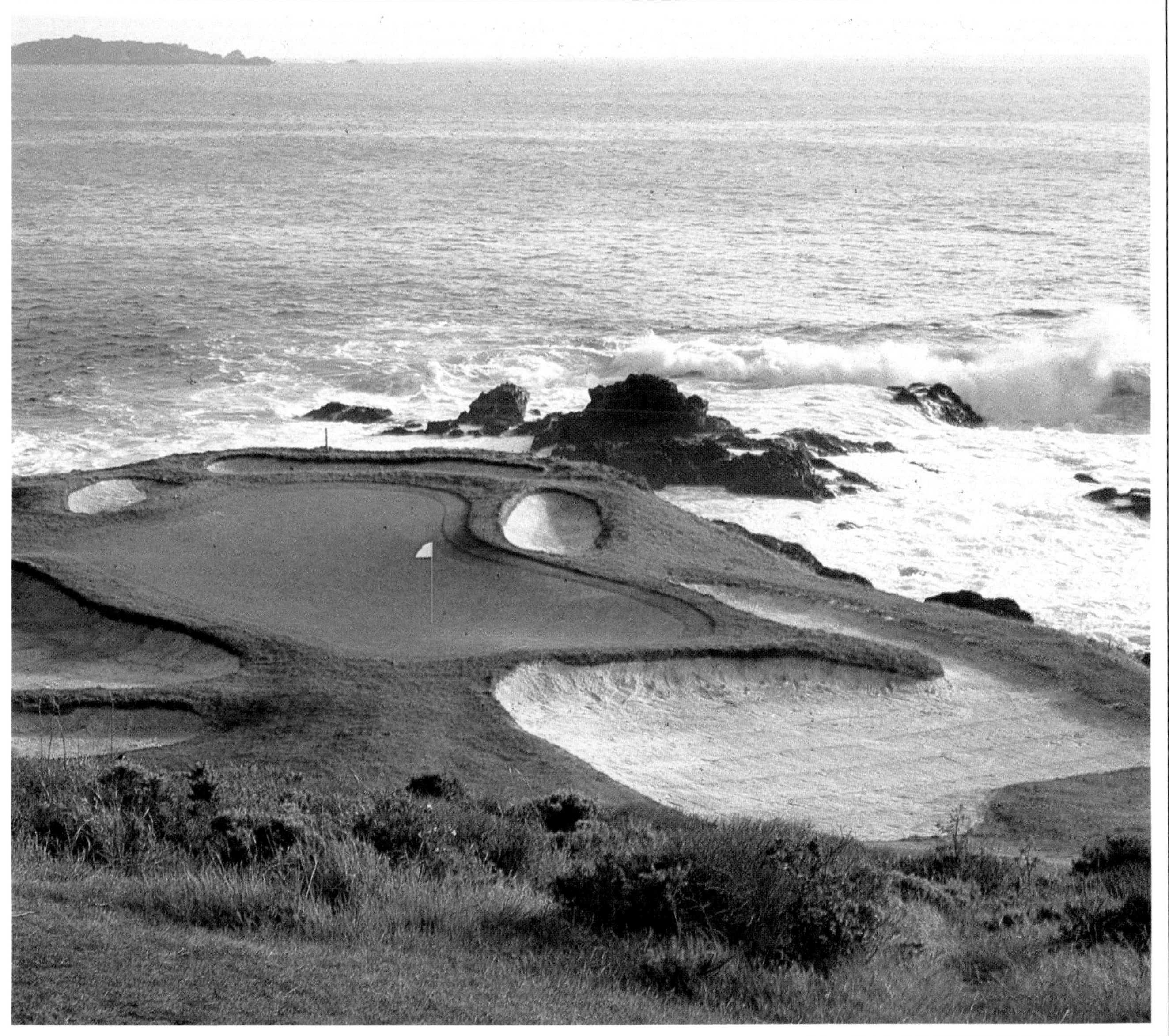

The most photographed golf hole in the world, the 120-yd (110-m) 7th at Pebble Beach.

Pinehurst

Of the five golf courses at Pinehurst, North Carolina, the Number 2 course is by far the best—and toughest. Set among heavily wooded undulating terrain it combines two rare features on American courses; scenic beauty and excellent golf. It is used little for championship golf because the course, in its rural surroundings, lacks the facilities big cities and populated areas can offer major championship events.

The first nine-hole course was laid in 1898 and the following year it was extended to 18 holes. Donald Ross arrived from Scotland in 1900 to take up his duties as golf coach but a large part of his time was spent planning and building the four other courses that were to be added.

The Number 2 course was completed in 1907, and Number 3 course three years later. In 1919 it became the first American club to offer four courses when the Number 4 opened. The fifth and final course was opened in the 1950s, shortly after Ross' death.

Pinehurst was used for the US PGA championship in 1936, but since the war the only major events to have been played there were the 1951 Ryder Cup and 1962 US Amateur Championship.

Number 2 course
Length 7028 yd (6426 m)
Par 71
Course record 62 – Gibby Gilbert (World Open, 1973)

Pin High

The ball is said to be pin high when it lands on the green level with the flag, but to the right or left of it.

Pitch

A short distance shot played with loft, normally to the green. Upon landing on the green, the ball will either stop immediately or run a short distance.

Pitch and Putt

Pitch and Putt courses are miniature golf courses with holes around 100 yd (91.5 m) in length. They are often to be found attached to driving ranges (qv), hotels or at seaside resorts.

Pitch and Run

A pitch shot played to the edge of the green. The ball then runs towards its intended target.

Pitch Mark

The depression made by the ball after it lands on the green, normally from a pitch shot. Under the etiquette rules of golf, a player should repair pitch marks so following golfers do not have to putt over them.

Player, Gary

Born in Johannesburg in 1935, Gary Player, by his good manners and sportsmanship, has done nothing but enhance the popularity of golf the world over. Underneath the good nature is a determination to win, and Player has plenty of trophies to stand testament to that desire.

He became a professional in 1953, and after a successful spell in Britain, set off for the US in 1957. He was to start a long and happy relationship with the United States, as he became the first overseas player to seriously

Gary Player with one third of his children . . .

assault the US circuit. It was, however, back in Britain in 1959 that he won his first major title, the British Open —the first of his three wins, in three decades.

Back in America Player, between 1961 and 1978, won the three major US titles a total of six times. And in 1965, after clinching the US Open, he became the third man, after Ben Hogan and Gene Sarazen, to win all four of the world's leading titles. He also became the first foreign golfer, since Britain's Ted Ray in 1920, to win the US title.

Perhaps Gary's greatest year was 1974. He won the British Open for the third time, the US Masters for the second time, won his 100th professional tournament and became the first person to shoot a sub-60 round in a National Open championship when he scored a 59 in the second round of the Brazilian Open.

Golf's second Great Triumvirate was born in the 1970s when 'The Big Three' of Nicklaus, Palmer and Player delighted crowds all over the world, and monopolized the leading events.

Gary has always maintained his roots in Johannesburg where he runs a horse farm, and lives with wife Vivienne and six children—one of them, Wayne, is following his father's footsteps in the world of professional golf.

Career highlights
British Open 1959, 1968, 1974
US Open 1965
US Masters 1961, 1974, 1978
US PGA 1962, 1972
World Match-Play 1965, 1966, 1968, 1971, 1973
World Cup (individual) 1965, 1977
(team) 1965
South African Open 13 wins (1956–81)

Play-Off
Unless the rules of a competition allow the first position to be shared, in the event of a tie, involving two or more players, the game must be continued.

In a match-play competition, play continues until one player wins a hole. This is called a sudden death play-off. Alternatively, the play-off can be over an agreed number of holes—normally another 18.

A total of 12 play-offs have been required in the British Open (although one of them never took place) and have either been over 36 or 18 holes. The first was to have been in 1876 but David Strath refused to play-off against Bob Martin. The last play-off in the Open was in 1975 when Jack Newton lost by one stroke over 18 holes to Tom Watson at Carnoustie.

Plugged Ball
A ball that remains in its own pitch mark. This can occur on the fairway, as a result of wet conditions, or in the face of a bunker. Unless local rules allow its removal without penalty, the ball must be played from where it lies.

Plus-fours
In the 1920s and 1930s, wide-bottomed trousers were the fashion. And because they often interfered with the golf swing many golfers turned to the knickerbocker type of trouser, known as 'plus-fours'.

They were so called because they were cut off four inches below the knee. Those extra four inches were gathered up and fastened, either with elastic, or buttons, just below the knee and were worn with long socks.

Tommy Armour was one of the leading professionals who used to wear plus-fours in the inter-war years, while in the post-war years South African Bobby Locke, and Britain's Max Faulkner were regularly seen sporting them. Very few golfers wear them these days.

Practice Swing
A swing, or swings, for the purpose of loosening up or practice. The player must not intend to hit or make contact with the ball. If the player intends to hit the ball, and misses, it is not a practice swing and must count as one stroke.

Preferred Lies
During the winter months, most clubs permit players to select the lie of their ball on the fairway. This is called a preferred lie. The idea of such a ruling is to preserve the fairway from damage. Preferred lies can also be allowed during the summer months in unusually adverse weather conditions, particularly after a great deal of rain has fallen on the course. When a player moves his ball to enjoy the benefit of a preferred lie it must be to a position as near as possible to where it originally came to rest.

President's Putter
Organized by the Oxford and Cambridge Golfing Society at Rye, Sussex, every January, the President's Putter is a match-play competition which was first held in 1920. At the end, the winner hangs the ball he used in the final on a putter which is displayed in a glass case at the Rye clubhouse—he also receives a silver medal.

One of the most famous winners in recent times has been England cricket captain Ted Dexter who, after many years of trying, eventually won the Putter in 1983. He won the title for a second time in 1985 and, at the age of 50, became the oldest winner of the event.

See also Oxford and Cambridge Golfing Society.

Winners (since 1970)

Year	Winner	Year	Winner
1970	D. M. A. Steel	1979	Cancelled
1971	G. T. Duncan	1980	S. Melville
1972	P. Moody	1981	A. W. J. Holmes
1973	A. D. Swanston	1982	D. M. A. Steel
1974	R. Biggs	1983	E. R. Dexter
1975	C. J. Weight	1984	A. Edmond
1976	K. J. Reece	1985	E. R. Dexter
1977	A. W. J. Holmes	1986	J. Catlan
1978	M. J. Reece		

Most wins
4 – Roger Wethered

Prestwick
Founded in 1851, Prestwick, in Ayrshire, was the home of the first British Open in 1860. It went on to stage the first 12 championships and was used a record 24 times for the Open, the last time being in 1925, when American Jim Barnes won. It was taken off the championship rota because it was felt to be too short, and because it could not accommodate the large galleries that were becoming

The face tells it all . . . it is determination that has won the likeable South African, Gary Player, so many titles the world over.

Former England test cricket captain Ted Dexter (left) has won President's Putter twice. The Oxford & Cambridge Golfing Society President, Neil Fisher, is seen holding the splendid trophy.

commonplace. The course has also been used for the British Amateur championship nine times.

Originally a 12-hole course when it opened in 1851 (the Open consisted of three rounds, comprising 36 holes) six more holes were added in 1883.

It was at Prestwick in 1869 that Young Tom Morris achieved the first hole-in-one in the British Open; Old Tom Morris was at one time the greenkeeper at the famous links. It is not a difficult course, but one hole that presents its problems is the par-5 third, on which there is the notorious Cardinal bunker.

Very much a male stronghold, the club did not have ladies' tees until 1978 when they had to be installed for the Scottish Ladies' Championship.

Length 6544 yd (5984 m)
Par 71
Course record 67 – Eric Brown (Dunlop Masters, 1956)
67 – Christy O'Connor, Snr (Dunlop Masters, 1956)

The leading money-winner of all time, Jack Nicklaus. His total career earnings exceed $4\frac{1}{2}$ million.

Prize Money

Commercialization and sponsorship has helped put golfers in the big money-winning league. First prizes in excess of £50,000 are commonplace and total prize money for major competitions is normally in excess of £500,000.

The following are some milestones in golf's prize money history:

First £1,000 first prize in Britain
1955 Swallow–Penfold tournament at Southport and Ainsdale.
Winner: Christy O'Connor

First £25,000 first prize in Britain
1970 John Player Golf Classic at Hollinwell, Nottinghamshire.
Winner: Christy O'Connor

First $100,000 first prize
1973 World Open at Pinehurst, North Carolina.
Winner: Miller Barber

First $500,000 first prize
1982 Million Dollar Sun City Challenge at Sun City, South Africa.
Winner: Johnny Miller
(This is the biggest first prize in the sport's history)

Professional

There are two types of professional golfer—the tournament professional who concentrates on playing competitions for money, and the club professional who, while he does play in competitions, gains his main source of income from giving lessons and from the sale of equipment at his club shop. Most golf clubs have a professional.

Professional Golfer's Association

The Professional Golfer's Association (PGA) was formed in London in 1901. One of the founders was a leading professional, J. H. Taylor, who wanted to protect professional players from being exploited. Taylor was the PGA's first chairman, and James Braid was the PGA's first captain.

The first championship organized by the PGA was the News of the World Match-Play tournament at Sunningdale in 1903. But for the first 30 years of its life, the PGA's role was primarily to look after the interests of club professionals—tournaments were few and far between. But that all changed when Charles Roe was appointed secretary in 1933—he was responsible for elevating the PGA to its current standing.

Most professionals are members of the PGA and the Tournament Player's Division controls all tournaments under their auspices. In 1971 the British PGA joined

British Open Milestones

First Prizes
First £500 – 1953: winner – Ben Hogan
First £1,000 – 1955: winner – Peter Thomson
First £5,000 – 1970: winner – Jack Nicklaus
First £10,000 – 1977: winner – Tom Watson
First £25,000 – 1980: winner – Tom Watson
First £50,000 – 1984: winner – Severiano Ballesteros
Record: £65,000 – Sandy Lyle (1985)

Total Prize Money
First £1,000 – 1946
First £10,000 – 1965
First £100,000 – 1977
First £500,000 – 1985
Record: £530,866 (1985)

US Open Milestones

First prizes
First $1,000 – 1929: winner – Bobby Jones (being an amateur, Jones did not collect the prize money, it went to 2nd placed Al Espinosa)
First $5,000 – 1953: winner – Ben Hogan
First $25,000 – 1965: winner – Gary Player
First $50,000 – 1979: winner – Hale Irwin
First $100,000 – 1985: winner – Andy North
(North received a record $130,000)

Total Prize Money
First $5,000 – 1936
First $20,000 – 1953
First $100,000 – 1965
First $250,000 – 1976
First $500,000 – 1984

Most Prize Money in Career

	$
1 Jack Nicklaus	4,686,280
2 Tom Watson	3,806,941
3 Lee Trevino	3,177,975
4 Ray Floyd	2,868,952
5 Hale Irwin	2,751,051
6 Tom Kite	2,525,327

(Correct as at end of 1985)
The first to win $1 million was Arnold Palmer, who reached the milestone in 1968.

Leading European Prize Money Winners in Career

	£
1 Severiano Ballesteros	747,724
2 Sandy Lyle	592,173
3 Bernhard Langer	554,475
4 Sam Torrance	477,051
5 Nick Faldo	474,211
6 Howard Clark	372,688

(Correct as at end of 1985)

Most Prize Money in One Season

PGA European Tour £162,552 – Sandy Lyle (1985)
US PGA Tour $542,321 – Curtis Strange (1985)

First to win $100,000 in Season on US PGA Tour

Arnold Palmer (1963)

First to win £100,000 on PGA European Tour

Nick Faldo (1983)

forces with the European Golf Association to form the PGA European Tour.

The PGA moved its headquarters to The Belfry, Sutton Coldfield, in 1977; the Women's PGA, a division of the PGA, also have their headquarters there.

Professional Golfer's Association of America

The Professional Golfer's Association of America (US PGA) was founded in New York in 1916, 15 years after its British counterpart. They now have their headquarters at Palm Beach Gardens, Florida, where they moved in 1965. Every year players wishing to join the US PGA Tour must undergo a course and golf test.

The aim of the US PGA is the same as the British PGA—to protect the interest of its members. In 1968 the Tournament Players' Division was formed.

Pull

Another name for slice.
See also Slice.

Push

Another name for hook.
See also Hook.

Putting

This is the final act on each hole, when the ball is played with a putter, normally on the putting green (qv) towards, and eventually into, the hole. The term is derived from the Dutch word *putten* which means to place in the hole.

Putting Green

Commonly called 'the green', it is the specially prepared part in which the hole is cut. The grass on the green is cut lower than on any other part of the course. Greens vary in size (there are no regulations governing them) and character. The art of maintaining greens to a high standard is the responsibility of the green-keeper.

R

Ray, Ted

Like his great contemporary Harry Vardon, Ted Ray was born on the island of Jersey. An unorthodox stylist, he was a very powerful and long hitter. His driving was, however, a bit erratic but he made up for this with excellent powers of recovery.

A great character, he could always be identified by his battered hat and pipe, which rarely left his mouth—even when he played a stroke.

Ray lived in the shadow of Vardon, Taylor and Braid, but gained recognition by winning the 1912 British Open at Muirfield, with Vardon and Braid in second and third places.

The following year he was involved in a three-way play-off for the US Open title at Brookline but finished third to Vardon and winner Francis Ouimet. In 1920, however, he won the US title and, at the age of 43, became the oldest winner. It was 50 years before another Briton, Tony Jacklin, won the US Open.

Ray was runner-up in the 1925 British Open, at the age of 48, and two years later he captained the first British Ryder Cup team.

Career highlights
British Open 1912
US Open 1920
Ryder Cup 1927 (captain)

Ted Ray was an unorthodox stylist as well as being identified by battered hat and pipe!

Records

While individual players', and tournament, records can be found elsewhere in this encyclopedia, it is perhaps worth looking at the composite records of all the great champions. The following table compares their records in major championships:

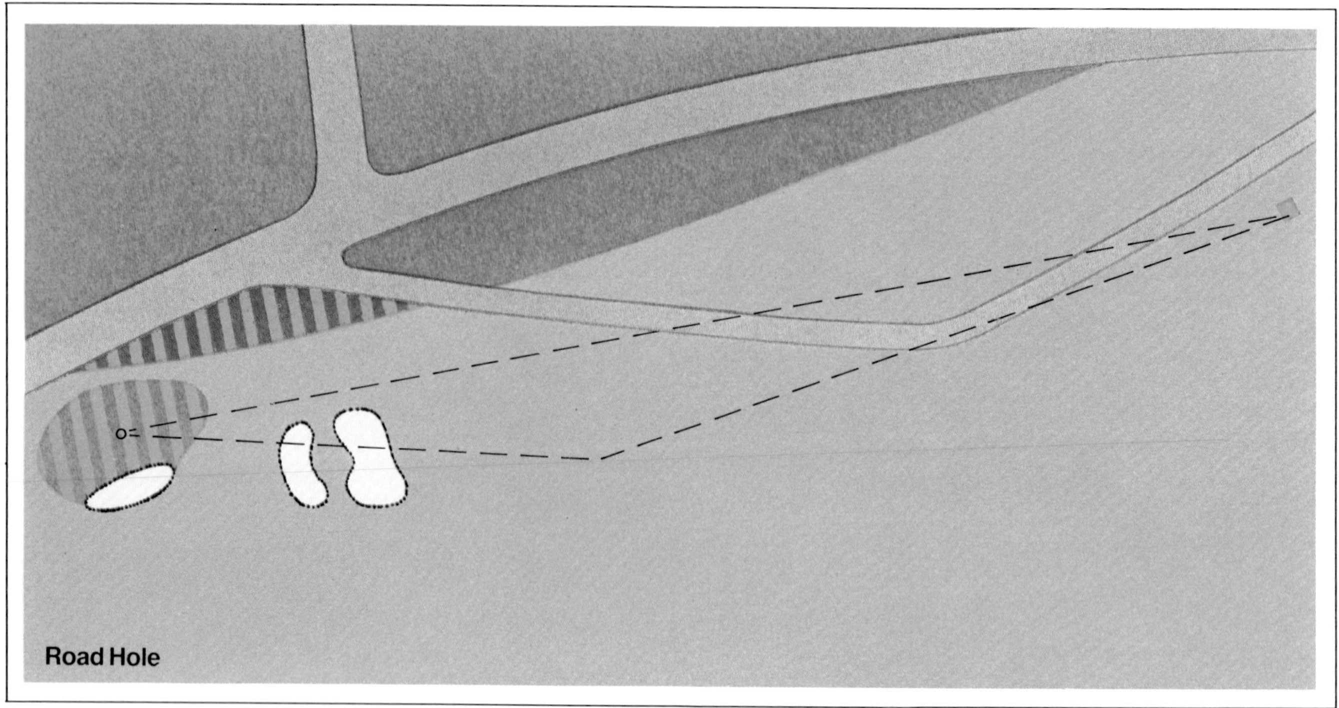

Major Wins	Name	Individual Record	
18	Jack Nicklaus	US Masters	6
		US PGA	5
		US Open	4
		British Open	3
11	Walter Hagen	US PGA	5
		British Open	4
		US Open	2
9	Ben Hogan	US Open	4
		US Masters	2
		US PGA	2
		British Open	1
9	Gary Player	British Open	3
		US Masters	3
		US PGA	2
		US Open	1
8	Tom Watson	British Open	5
		US Masters	2
		US Open	1
7	Harry Vardon	British Open	6
		US Open	1
7	Bobby Jones	US Open	4
		British Open	3
7	Gene Sarazen	US PGA	3
		US Open	2
		British Open	1
		US Masters	1
7	Sam Snead	US Masters	3
		US PGA	3
		British Open	1
7	Arnold Palmer	US Masters	4
		British Open	2
		US Open	1
6	Lee Trevino	British Open	2
		US Open	2
		US PGA	2

Rees, Dai

What Dai Rees lacked in physical attributes he made up for in enthusiasm and aggression. In a career spanning 50 years he won everything the British game could offer—except one. Four times winner of the PGA Match-Play title, and twice Dunlop Masters champion he could not, however, win golf's most cherished prize, the British Open.

By far the most outstanding British player of the 1950s and 1960s he was runner-up in the Open on three occasions. In 1953 he was joint second to Ben Hogan and the following year, at Royal Birkdale, was just one stroke away from the champion Peter Thomson. And in 1961 he gave his best performance in the championship when, at the age of 48, he finished second to Arnold Palmer, again at Birkdale.

It is perhaps as a Ryder Cup player that Rees is better known. He played in nine teams between 1937 and 1961 and was captain in 1957 at Lindrick when Great Britain won the cup—their only win between 1933 and 1985. Following that success Dai Rees was honoured with a CBE.

Rees was the professional at the South Herts club for 37 years and was playing golf shortly before his death in November 1983. In 1975 he became, at the age of 65, the South of England Professional champion—two years earlier he was runner-up to Maurice Bembridge in the Martini tournament at Barnton.

Career highlights

Dunlop Masters 1950, 1962
PGA Match-Play 1936, 1938, 1949, 1950
British Open (best) jt 2nd – 1953, jt 2nd – 1954, 2nd – 1961
Ryder Cup 1937, 1947, 1949, 1951, 1953, 1955 (capt) 1957 (capt), 1959 (capt), 1961 (capt), 1967 (non-playing capt)

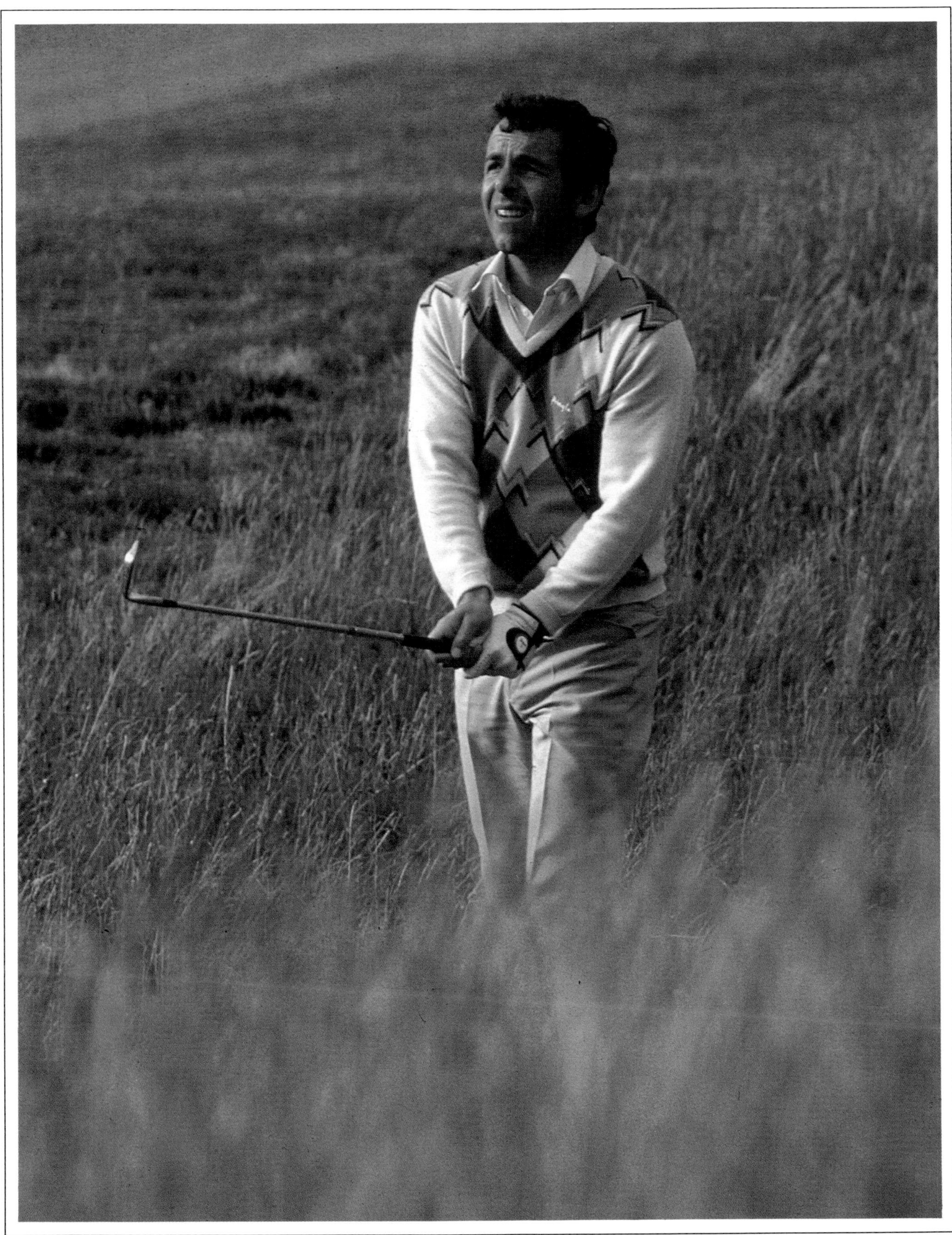

Tony Jacklin has obviously got his shot out of the rough, but he does not look too pleased with the outcome.

Dai Rees was captain of the last Ryder Cup team to beat the United States before Tony Jacklin in 1985. Rees is seen holding aloft the trophy after Great Britain's win at Lindrick in 1957.

Referee
The person put in charge of a golf match. He accompanies players on their round and resolves questions that may arise about the rules of the game.

Road Hole
The 17th hole on the Old Course at St Andrews, known as the 'Road Hole', is perhaps the most celebrated golf hole in the world.

Apart from a difficult undulating putting surface and a bunker to the left of the green, the driver has to decide whether to attempt to drive to the green across the dogleg or play safe, in which case the path to the putting surface is hindered by two bunkers. No matter what shot is played, there is then the added hazard of the road which runs along the right of the fairway and continues round the back of the green. The road is not out of bounds, and a player must play from it. It is easier to play off than it used to be for it was at one time a track as opposed to a smooth road surface.

Many golfers, thinking they were on their way to victory, have come to grief at the Road Hole with disastrous results. It is only 461 yd (421.5 m) in length, and a par 4, but most golfers, even the best in the world, are grateful just to make par, let alone contemplate birdies.

One golfer who will never forget the Road Hole is Japan's Tsuneyuki Nakajima. During the 1978 British Open he reached the green in two but then putted into the bunker. He took five shots to get out of the bunker, to register a nine for the hole. He was up with the leaders prior to that disaster.

Rogers, Bill
A professional since 1974, Texan Bill Rogers had a memorable year in 1981 that silenced even his harshest critics.

For several years he had been labelled as the man who could not win. This was not strictly true. He won his first US tournament—the Bob Hope Desert Classic—in 1978, and in 1979 beat defending champion Isao Aoki to win the World Match-Play title at Wentworth. But they were just a handful of wins among many near-misses. In 1981, however, he seemed to get it right at last.

He won seven tournaments worldwide, including three in the United States. He also won the Australian Open, and British Open at Sandwich when he beat Bernhard Langer by four strokes. The season was crowned with his first, and only, Ryder Cup appearance.

Rogers' winnings have exceeded $1.25 million but since 1981 he has slipped down the US money-winning chart fast. British fans did, however, have cause to remember Bill Rogers again in recent years when he registered a rare albatross during the 1983 British Open at Royal Birkdale.

Career highlights
British Open 1981
World Match-Play 1979
Ryder Cup 1981
Walker Cup 1973

Rookie

Player in his first year as a professional. Awards, known as Rookie of the Year, are made to first-year professionals in Great Britain and the United States.

The first British winner was Tommy Goodwin in 1960, while the first American winner, three years earlier, was Ken Venturi.

Notable British winners have included: Tony Jacklin (1963), Bernard Gallacher (1968), Peter Oosterhuis (1969) and Sam Torrance (1972).

In America, notable winners have included: Jack Nicklaus (1962), Lee Trevino (1967), Hubert Green (1971), Tom Kite (1973) and Ben Crenshaw (1974). Recent winners have been:

Great Britain	*United States*
1976 Mark James	1976 Jerry Pate
1977 Nick Faldo	1977 Graham Marsh
1978 Sandy Lyle	1978 Pat McGowan
1979 Mike Miller	1979 John Fought
1980 Paul Hoad	1980 Gary Hallberg
1981 Jeremy Bennett	1981 Mark O'Meara
1982 Gordon Brand, Jnr	1982 Hal Sutton
1983 Grant Turner	1983 Nick Price
1984 Philip Parkin	1984 Corey Pavin
1985 Paul Thomas	1985 Phil Blackmar

Rough

The long grass bordering the fairway is known as the 'rough'. It is the part of the course which is neither the tee, fairway, green nor a hazard. The rules of golf do not recognize the existence of rough.

Round

A round of golf consists of 18 holes, unless otherwise stated or authorized. The holes must be played in the correct numerical order.

Royal and Ancient Golf Club

Housed at St Andrews, the Royal and Ancient Golf Club (R & A) is the ruling body of the game in the eyes of most countries, except the United States. The US Golf Association does, however, work very closely with the R & A.

Golf was played on the St Andrews links in the 16th century, but it was on 14 May 1754 that 22 noblemen and 'others' met to play for a silver club. Those 22 formed themselves into the Society of St Andrews Golfers—the forerunner of the R & A.

They adopted the code of rules drawn up by the Honourable Company of Edinburgh Golfers 11 years earlier, and gradually amended the rules.

In 1834 King William IV granted permission for the club to change its name to the Royal and Ancient Golf Club.

The present clubhouse was opened in 1854, after previously holding meetings at the Black Bull Tavern, and Union Parlour. In 1860 they formed part of the committee that organized the inaugural British Open at Prestwick.

After being approached by several leading clubs of the day to act as the authoritative body on the rules of golf, the R & A agreed in 1897. Other countries gradually turned to the R & A for guidance, and consequently they became affiliated. Surprisingly, the Home Unions did not recognize the R & A as the ruling body in Great Britain until 1924.

Several committees sit at the R & A and one of the most important is the Rules Committee which meets to review the rules of golf from time to time.

The current secretary of the R & A is the former leading amateur player Michael Bonallack, OBE, and the current captain is Lancashire dental surgeon Hector Maclaine. The post of Captain of the Royal and Ancient is one of the most prestigious honours in golf.

Royal Birkdale

Royal Birkdale is one of the several fine golf courses situated along the Fylde coast between Southport and Formby.

The original nine-hole golf course was developed by eight enthusiasts in 1889, and was situated nearer to Southport town centre, using the Portland Hotel as their headquarters. In 1897 they were asked to vacate the land and developed the site on which now stands one of the most famous courses in England. The course was redesigned and the plush clubhouse erected in 1931.

Birkdale was granted royal patronage in 1951 and since then it has become one of the leading championship courses. Approaching 7000 yd (6408 m) it gives the appearance of being severe, but it would be more accurate to describe it as demanding, but fair.

Although it staged its first championship in 1909—the British Ladies' Championship—it is only since the 1950s that it has staged major events. The first British Open was in 1954, and since then five more Opens have been held at the links. Major international events—the Ryder Cup, Walker Cup and Curtis Cup have all been held at Birkdale.

One person for whom Royal Birkdale holds a special affection is Arnold Palmer. He won his first British Open there in 1961 and played one of golf's memorable shots from behind a bush at the 15th (now the 16th) to hit the green 140 yards away. A plaque can be found marking the spot from where the great shot was made.

Length 6968 yd (6372 m)
Par 71
Course record 64 – Craig Stadler (British Open, 1983)
64 – Graham Marsh (British Open, 1983)

Royal Blackheath

Blackheath is the oldest golf club in England. Its exact origins are not known but it is said that James VI of Scotland (James I of England) played golf at Blackheath when he came south in the early 17th century. There is

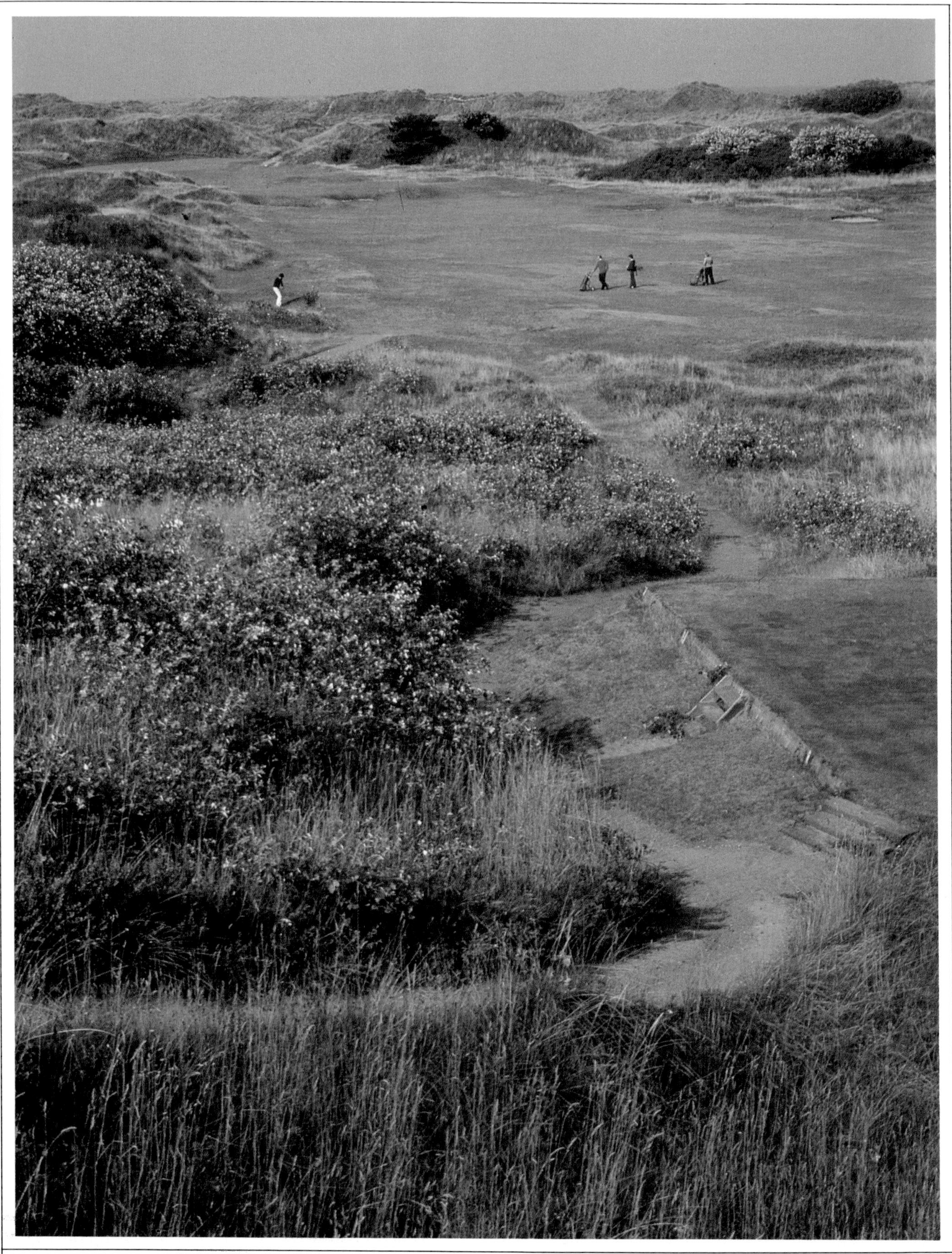

Wayward shots are to be avoided when playing the tough Royal Birkdale course.

definite evidence that a society existed at Blackheath in 1766 and that unquestionably makes it the oldest club in England.

Originally situated at Blackheath, they were forced to move to Eltham, near London, in 1923. The old Eltham Club had been established since 1891, and upon Blackheath moving there, the course was re-designed by James Braid. However, it is too small for major championships.

Length 6024 yd (5508 m)
Par 71
Course record 66 – W. C. Thomas
66 – D. M. Woolmer

Royal Burgess Golfing Society of Edinburgh

Any golfer who does not visit the Royal Burgess Golfing Society at Barnton, Edinburgh, is missing out on the chance to be part of golf's heritage.

The club was founded in 1735 and is regarded as the oldest in the world. It can certainly claim to be the longest continuously established society or club, even surpassing the Honourable Company of Edinburgh Golfers.

Originally known as the Edinburgh Golfing Society they assumed their present title in 1787 and in 1929 became one of the Royal golf clubs after the Duke of York played at the club regularly. When King Edward VIII acceded to the throne in 1936 he was the club captain —the first time in over 100 years a British club had the reigning monarch as its captain.

The first society shared Edinburgh's Brunsfield links, but in 1874 amalgamated with the Musselburgh club. Twenty years later they sought, and developed, their own course, at Barnton, five miles from Edinburgh. Tom Morris laid out the original course which was later altered by James Braid.

Length 6604 yd (6039 m)
Par 70
Course record 63 – Paul Lennard (Martini International, 1973)

Royal Calcutta

The Royal Calcutta club is the oldest golf club outside Britain, being founded in 1829. And since 1892, it has been the home of one of the oldest championships in the world, the Indian Amateur.

The original site was at Dum Dum, a suburb of Calcutta, but the club moved to the south of the city, to Tollygunge; the old site is now the home of Calcutta's international airport. Originally flat and paddy-like, great care has been taken over the years to build artificial mounds, and plant numerous trees. The 'Royal' status was bestowed upon the club in 1911 by King George V.

Length 7285 yd (6661 m)
Par 73
Course record 65 – Brian Jones (Indian Open, 1984)
65 – Rigoberto Velasquez (Indian Open, 1984)
65 – Jeff Lewis (Indian Open, 1984)

Royal Dublin

A 'Royal' golf club since 1891, the Dublin club is the oldest in the Republic of Ireland, and the second oldest in all of Ireland.

Founded by Scotsman John Lumsden in 1885, the course was taken over by the Army during the First World War. After the war it had to be completely re-designed, which was carried out by H. S. Colt. The clubhouse had to be rebuilt in 1953, after a fire destroyed the original one. To compensate for all their disasters and tragedies Ireland's favourite golfing son, Christy O'Connor, was appointed professional at the club in 1959.

The Carrolls Irish Open, the leading Irish tournament on the European PGA tour, has been staged at Royal Dublin since 1983 and it seems to be making its permanent home there.

Length 6810 yd (6227 m)
Par 71
Course record 63 – Bernhard Langer (Carrolls Irish Open, 1985)

'Royal' Golf Clubs

A golf club cannot assume the title 'Royal' unless bestowed upon it by the sovereign or a member of the Royal house. The title is normally granted along with the club receiving royal patronage.

The first club to receive the Royal designation was the Perth Golfing Society in 1833. The most recent was Troon in 1978. There are 36 Royal Golf Clubs in Great Britain, Ireland and the Channel Isles.

Royal Hong Kong

The Hong Kong golf club was born out of a poorly attended meeting in 1889 that was called with a view to establishing a golf club in Hong Kong. Despite its lack of numbers, the enthusiasm was such that the first club was formed and ground was found and developed at Happy Valley, Kowloon.

Queen Victoria granted Royal patronage to the club in 1897 and they immediately set about expanding. A new nine-hole course was opened at nearby Deep Water Bay and in 1911 a third course was laid out at Fanling, nearly 25 miles away. The war years saw all three courses devastated. After the Second World War, the process of rebuilding Fanling started. The club survived and today there exist three 18-hole courses, the New Course being the home of the Hong Kong Open.

New Course
Length 6684 yd (6112 m)
Par 70
Course record 62 – Kel Nagle (Hong Kong Open, 1961)

Royal Liverpool

The Royal Liverpool club at Hoylake is steeped in golfing history. Not only has it produced such legendary golfers as John Ball and Harold Hilton but it was responsible for inaugurating many of today's championships.

Hoylake housed the first Amateur Championship in 1885, the first English Amateur Championship in 1925, and was the scene of the first international matches between England and Scotland, and Great Britain and the United States. It was also the venue for the first Home International matches. Naturally, the famous links have been used to house the British Open as well.

The first Open at Hoylake was in 1897 when the club's own amateur, Harold Hilton, won the title. Between then and 1967 it played host to the Open on nine more occasions and such famous champions as Peter Thomson, Bobby Jones, John Taylor and Walter Hagen won the title on the Wirral links. The last winner, Roberto de Vicenzo, was the only one of the ten Hoylake champions to win the title with a sub-70 round . . . he recorded a third round 67.

The club was formed in 1869 by exiled Scottish businessmen in Liverpool, and the club's first professional was Jack Morris, nephew of Old Tom. It did not achieve its full complement of 18 holes until 1871, but the course has changed very little since then, and there are many out-of-bounds areas waiting to greet any wayward shots!

Length 6737 yd (6160 m)
Par 74
Course record 64 – Brian Waites (European Open, 1981)

Royal Lytham and St Annes

No matter what great golfing moments the future has in store for Royal Lytham, it is doubtful that they will better a glorious July day in 1969 when Tony Jacklin became the first British golfer since 1951 to win the Open.

Lytham has housed seven British Open championships, dating back to 1926 when Bobby Jones won the title—amazingly he is the only American to have won the title on the famous Lancashire links. The other winners, apart from Jacklin have been Bobby Locke (South Africa), Peter Thomson (Australia), Bob Charles (New Zealand), Gary Player (South Africa) and Severiano Ballesteros (Spain).

The original links were laid out in 1886, but ten years later the members moved to the present site. The club's first professional was George Lowe, and the 'Royal' tag was bestowed upon the club in 1926.

A popular course, it has staged championships since the latter part of the 19th century when, in 1893, Lady Margaret Scott won the British Ladies' Championship at the original course.

The atmosphere at the club is friendly, and the course is one that is enjoyed by both club players and professionals. It is a flat course, but like many links courses, one has to contend with wind that blows in from the Fylde estuary.

Length 6673 yd (6102 m)
Par 71
Course record 65 – Eric Brown (British Open, 1958)
65 – Leopoldo Ruiz (British Open, 1958)
65 – Christy O'Connor, Snr (British Open, 1969)
65 – Bill Longmuir (British Open, 1979)
65 – Severiano Ballesteros (British Open, 1979)

Royal Melbourne

The Royal Melbourne has the distinction of being the oldest continuous club in Australia. The Royal Adelaide club was founded in 1870, some 21 years before Melbourne, but was dissolved between 1876 and 1892.

When Melbourne opened, in July 1891, it had an official club costume of a scarlet coat with gold buttons, knickerbockers and a Tam o'Shanter . . .

The club moved premises in 1901 and a new course was laid out. It soon became popular and was regularly used for Australian championships. Its many deep bunkers make it a test of any golfer's skill. This course later became known as the West course because a second, the East course, was constructed in 1932 to give Royal Melbourne 36 first-class golf holes. A composite course from the two was designed for the World Cup competitions of 1959 and 1972.

Length (composite course) 6977 yd (6380 m)
Par 72
Course record 65 – Sam Snead (World Cup, 1959)

Royal Mid-Surrey

A parkland course set in Old Deer Park, Richmond, the Royal Mid-Surrey was founded in 1892 and designed by the famous J. H. Taylor. He was the club's professional for 47 years, and while at Mid-Surrey won the British Open three times. Henry Cotton, in 1948, also won the title while professional at the club.

The course is bounded by the River Thames, Kew Gardens and Richmond's Rugby Union ground, and is also beneath the flight-path into Heathrow airport. The Mid in the name is short for Middlesex, which lies on the other side of the river.

Royal patronage was bestowed upon the club in 1926, and that year the Prince of Wales accepted the club captaincy.

There are two courses at Mid-Surrey: the Outer course (for male members), and the Inner course (for the ladies). Generally regarded as a members club as opposed to a championship course it has staged several events including the English Amateur Championship and the British Boys Championship in 1962, which Peter Townsend won. He won the PGA title when last held at the course in 1968.

Outer course
Length 6331 yd (5789 m)
Par 69
Course record 64 – Bob Charles (Eccentric Club Pro-Am, 1979)
64 – Bernard Gallacher (Eccentric Club Pro-Am,1979)

Royal Montreal

The Montreal Golf Club is the oldest club in North America, being founded in 1873. It is also one of the oldest Royal golf clubs: Queen Victoria granted it its status just 11 years after its formation.

The club's present site at Ile Bizard, Quebec, is its third home. The first was in the centre of Montreal but an increase in membership forced it to move to Dorval, some ten miles away, in 1896. They moved to their present site in 1958. Although not used for many major professional tournaments these days, Royal Montreal has staged some important events over the years including the Canadian Open, and the inaugural Canada Cup (now World Cup) in 1953.

The course is long and has large raised greens which are heavily bunkered and have narrow entrances.

Length 6740 yd (6163 m)
Par 70
Course record 65 – Jack Nicklaus (Canadian Open, 1975)
65 – Tom Weiskopf (Canadian Open, 1975)

Royal Musselburgh

Situated at Prestonpans, East Lothian, the Royal Musselburgh club was founded in 1774, which makes it one of the oldest in the world. It was, between 1836 and 1891, the home of the Honourable Company of Edinburgh Golfers, before they moved on to Muirfield.

Royal Musselburgh is full of golfing history. Not only did it stage the British Open six times between 1874 and 1889, but it produced some great winners of the championship. The first winner in 1860, Willie Park, was a member of Musselburgh. Subsequent winners Mungo Park, Bob Ferguson, David Brown and Park's son, Willie Junior were also members of Musselburgh. After the Honourable Company of Edinburgh Golfers moved in 1891, Musselburgh was removed from the British Open rota.

The club joined the list of Royal clubs in 1876 when the Duke of Connaught became its president.

Musselburgh originally consisted of just seven holes. Gradually it developed into an eight-hole course, then nine, then 18. The club moved to its present surroundings at Prestonpans in 1924, and Prestongrange House provides one of the finest clubhouses to be seen in Britain.

Length 6207 yd (5676 m)
Par 70
Course record 67 – Eric Brown (1968)

Royal Portrush

Royal Portrush, on the most northerly point of Northern Ireland, has been staging championship golf since 1892 when the first Irish Open Amateur championship was held there. However, it was in 1951 that it experienced its finest hour.

Max Faulkner of England won the first, and only, British Open to be played on Irish soil. He was to be the last British winner until Tony Jacklin 18 years later. Portrush also staged the first professional tournament to be held in Ireland when, in 1895, the club's first professional, Sandy Herd, beat Harry Vardon in the final.

The original course, laid out in 1888, consisted of nine holes. Within a year there were 18. Today there are three courses: the Dunluce course, the Valley course, and a nine-hole course. The Duke of York was a patron of the club in the late 19th century, and in 1892 the club, then known as the Country Club, became the Royal Country Club. It became Royal Portrush in 1895.

Narrow fairways coupled with severe winds coming in off the sea make this a test of accuracy for any golfer. The 14th, 15th and 16th are three holes that call for pinpoint accuracy. Hardly surprising two of them are called Calamity Corner and Purgatory.

Dunluce Course
Length 6810 yd (6227 m)
Par 73
Course record 66 – Jack Hargreaves (British Open, 1951)

Royal St George's

The British Open returned to south-east England in 1981 after an absence of 32 years. Founded in 1887, St George's, Sandwich, had staged ten British Opens between 1894 (when it became the first English course to stage the championship) and 1949. But it had lost its place as a championship venue because of the inadequate facilities and amenities in nearby Sandwich. They were given another chance in 1981, and large crowds turned out to justify its return to the British Open rota. On that occasion the winner was American Bill Rogers. Four years later when next held at St George's the champion was Sandy Lyle—the first British Open winner for 16 years.

But St George's contains many more memories than just the British Open. John Ball won the Amateur Championship in 1892, and in 1967, during the Dunlop Masters, it was the scene of Tony Jacklin's memorable hole-in-one at the 16th, the first televised ace in Britain. The course has also housed many other important events, including the Walker Cup.

Like all links courses, the wind from the sea can play havoc with the best of shots. It is no different at St George's, but another 'hazard' is the many undulating bumps on the course. Quite often it would be helpful to have one leg six inches shorter than the other in order to get a good stance.

Length 6857 yd (6270 m)
Par 70
Course record 64 – Christy O'Connor, Jnr (British Open, 1985)

Royal Troon

The undulating fairways and savage rough make Troon one of the most testing championship golf courses in Britain.

Situated north of Ayr on Scotland's west coast, six of the greens run alongside the Firth of Clyde and the winds can be so severe that fish are reported to have been seen floating on greens.

Founded in 1878, the club was first used for the British Open in 1923. Archie Havers won the first title while Bobby Locke took the second in 1950.

One man who mastered Troon was Arnold Palmer on his way to winning the 1962 British Open. As all before him were falling (some scoring holes into double figures), Palmer went on to win by a staggering six shots from Kel Nagle, and 13 strokes from third place Brian Huggett.

Palmer was followed by Tom Weiskopf in 1973 who equalled Palmer's Open record of 276. Troon last played

Royal St George's, Sandwich, returned to the rota of British Open courses in 1981 after an absence of 32 years.

host to the Open in 1982 when Tom Watson beat Britain's Peter Oosterhuis by one stroke.

Strangely, the longest and shortest holes in the British Open have been at Troon. The 577-yd (528-m) 6th is the longest, while the notorious 8th, known as the Postage Stamp, is the shortest, at 126 yd (115 m). The latter was the scene of 71-year-old Gene Sarazen's televised hole-in-one during the 1973 Open. But don't mention the hole to German amateur Herman Tisses—he took 15 at the hole during the 1950 Open.

Troon was granted its Royal status in 1978, the club's centenary year. And in 1989, it will be holding the British Open for the sixth time.

Championship Course

Length 7067 yd (6462 m)
Par 72
Course record 65 – Jack Nicklaus (British Open, 1973)

Royalty

Three 15th-century Scottish Kings—James II, III and IV—banned the playing of golf (or 'gouf' as it was then known) because it interfered with archery practice. The tide turned in 1502 when James IV acquired a set of golf clubs and balls, and played at Perth. His son and daughter, James V and Mary Queen of Scots, both took up the sport, Mary soon becoming a fanatic. She was known to have played golf just two weeks after the death of her husband Lord Darnley, an act for which she was heavily criticized.

It was Mary's son, James VI of Scotland and James I of England, who brought the sport south of the border when he acceded to the English throne. He is reported to have played golf at Greenwich and Blackheath. Since then a succession of members of the Royal family have enjoyed the sport. Perhaps the best of the golf-playing 'Royals' were Edward VIII and George VI who both played actively when they were the Prince of Wales and Duke of York respectively.

Prince Leopold, upon becoming King Leopold III of Belgium, played in both the Belgian and French amateur championships—the only instance of a reigning monarch playing in national championships. In 1949 he reached the semi-final of the French championship.

The following members of the Royal family have been captains of the Royal and Ancient club:

1863 – Prince of Wales
1876 – Prince Leopold of Belgium
1922 – Prince of Wales (later Edward VIII)
1930 – Duke of York (later George VI)
1937 – Duke of Kent

Rules of Golf

Golfers in most countries play the game according to the rules as laid down by the Royal and Ancient Club at St Andrews. The United States Golf Association (USGA) have their own rules, but liaise very closely with the R & A on all matters connected with the rules.

The first set of rules were drawn up in 1744 by the Gentlemen Golfers of Edinburgh (later the Honourable Company of Edinburgh Golfers). Then there existed just 13 rules; today there are 34.

As other golfing societies were established each drew up its own set of rules, based on the Edinburgh Golfer's original 13. But the swing to the rules drawn up by the St Andrews Golfing Society was more prevalent towards the middle of the 19th century. By the end of the century, with golf becoming popular in many more countries, golfers turned to the Royal and Ancient for guidance. In 1897 the first Rules of Golf Committee was appointed by the R & A.

The R & A and the USGA became the world's two governing bodies but their rules started to drift. In 1951 they got together to try and unify the two sets of rules. The main differences between the two were resolved, and the following year a standard set of rules, with a couple of differences, were introduced for adoption by both bodies.

The current rules of golf are divided into three sections as follows:

Section I : Etiquette
Section II : Definitions
Section III: The Rules of Play

Section one is self explanatory, while section two covers 46 definitions, ranging from 'Addressing the Ball' to 'Wrong Ball'. The third section covers every contingency that may arise during a round of golf. The 34 rules are itemized under the following headings:

Rule 1: The Game
Rule 2: Match-Play
Rule 3: Stroke-Play
Rule 4: Clubs
Rule 5: The Ball
Rule 6: The Player
Rule 7: Practice
Rule 8: Advice
Rule 9: Information as to Strokes Taken
Rule 10: Order of Play
Rule 11: Teeing Ground
Rule 12: Searching for and Identifying Ball
Rule 13: Ball Played As It Lies: Lie, Area of Intended Swing and Line of Play; Stance
Rule 14: Striking the Ball
Rule 15: Playing a Wrong Ball
Rule 16: The Putting Green
Rule 17: The Flagstick
Rule 18: Ball at Rest Moved
Rule 19: Ball in Motion Deflected or Stopped
Rule 20: Lifting, Dropping and Placing: Playing from Wrong Place
Rule 21: Cleaning Ball
Rule 22: Ball Interfering with or Assisting Play
Rule 23: Loose Impediments
Rule 24: Obstructions
Rule 25: Abnormal Ground Conditions and Wrong Putting Green
Rule 26: Water Hazards (Including Lateral Water Hazards)
Rule 27: Ball Lost or Out of Bounds; Provisional Ball
Rule 28: Ball Unplayable
Rule 29: Threesomes and Foursomes
Rule 30: Three-Ball, Best-Ball and Four-Ball Match Play
Rule 31: Four-Ball Stroke Play
Rule 32: Bogey, Par and Stableford Competitions
Rule 33: The Committee
Rule 34: Disputes and Decisions

In addition there are three appendices covering the following points:

Appendix I : Local Rules and Conditions of the Competition
Appendix II : Design of Clubs
Appendix III: The Ball

Copies of the complete set of rules can be obtained from the Royal and Ancient Club at St Andrews, or can be found in the *Golfer's Handbook* (see Bibliography).

Run

The course the ball takes after it has finished bouncing. The run will vary according to ground undulations and weather conditions. Wet ground will cause very little run whereas hard ground will create a great deal.

Run-Up

A short shot, normally to the green, played with a straight-faced club. The ball travels either along the ground or just a short distance off it.

Ryder Cup

Great Britain's professionals first played their American counterparts at Gleneagles in 1921. A second match took place at Wentworth in 1926 and it was this tournament that inspired Samuel Ryder of St Albans to put up a trophy to be contested biennially by the two nations. In 1927, at Worcester, Massachusetts, the first Ryder Cup match was played.

Each side consists of 12 players and since 1979 the title of the Great Britain and Northern Ireland team has been changed to that of 'Europe', as a result of allowing non-British players into the team. This move was made in an effort to break the American stranglehold on the trophy. It paid off in 1985 when the Americans were defeated for the first time since 1957 when non-playing captain Tony Jacklin led his team to a memorable victory at the Belfry.

In the first Ryder Cup in 1927, Walter Hagen captained the American side and Ted Ray the British team. Ray was to be the first of many captains to feel the full force of American superiority. But those early days of the Cup gave no indication as to what lay in store for a succession of British teams over the years.

The first Ryder Cup match on English soil was at Moortown in 1929 and George Duncan levelled the score by leading his team to a 7–5 win. The United States won again on their home soil in 1931, and back in England two years later it was Britain's turn to win once more. So, after four competitions, it was two wins apiece. By the time the 1957 Ryder Cup at Lindrick came around, the United States had won the trophy nine times while Britain were stuck on two.

But at Lindrick all previous defeats were soon forgotten as Dai Rees led his gallant men to a three point victory. They came back after trailing 3–1 at the end of the foursomes to win six of the eight singles by convincing margins. Of the other two, one was halved while poor Peter Alliss was the only member of the British team to suffer defeat.

Sadly, Lindrick was not to be the turning point. Between that win and the 1985 success, Britain's best result was a 16–16 draw at Royal Birkdale in 1969 when Jack Nicklaus displayed great sportsmanship and generosity in giving Tony Jacklin a 'missable' putt to halve the match.

The format has changed over the years. For example the first Ryder Cup consisted of just eight players per side who played four foursomes and eight singles. The 1985 event consisted of four foursome and four-ball matches on the first and second days, and 12 singles on the third and final day. Between 1927 and 1959 all matches were played over 36 holes. Since 1961 they have been over 18 holes.

The first British Ryder Cup party at Waterloo Station on their way to Worcester, Massachusetts in 1927. From left to right: George Duncan (with hands in pocket), Archie Compston, Ted Ray (captain), Fred Robson, Samuel Ryder (who instigated the event), F. G. Gadd, Charles Whitcombe, Arthur Havers, Abe Mitchell and G. A. Philpott (Manager).

The successful Great Britain and Northern Ireland Ryder Cup team who beat the United States at Lindrick in 1957. Back row (left to right): Harry Bradshaw, Peter Mills, Peter Alliss, Bernard Hunt and Harry Weetman. Front row (left to right): Max Faulkner, Eric Brown, Dai Rees (Captain), Ken Bousfield and Christy O'Connor.

Results

1927 Worcester, Massachusetts

USA	9½	W. Hagen, capt
GB & NI	2½	E. Ray, capt

1929 Moortown, Leeds

GB & NI	7	G. Duncan, capt
USA	5	W. Hagen, capt

1931 Scioto, Columbus, Ohio

USA	9	W. Hagen, capt
GB & NI	3	C. A. Whitcombe, capt

1933 Southport and Ainsdale

GB & NI	6½	J. H. Taylor, capt(*)
USA	5½	W. Hagen, capt

1935 Ridgewood, New Jersey

USA	9	W. Hagen, capt
GB & NI	3	C. A. Whitcombe, capt

1937 Southport and Ainsdale

USA	8	W. Hagen, capt(*)
GB & NI	4	C. A. Whitcombe, capt

1939–45 Not held

1947 Portland, Oregon

USA	11	B. Hogan, capt
GB & NI	1	T. H. Cotton, capt

1949 Ganton, Scarborough

USA	7	B. Hogan, capt(*)
GB & NI	5	C. A. Whitcombe, capt(*)

1951 Pinehurst, North Carolina

USA	9½	S. Snead, capt
GB & NI	2½	A. J. Lacey, capt(*)

1953 Wentworth, Surrey

USA	6½	L. Mangrum, capt
GB & NI	5½	T. H. Cotton, capt(*)

1955 Palm Springs, California

USA	8	C. Harbert, capt
GB & NI	4	D. Rees, capt

1957 Lindrick, Sheffield

GB & NI	7½	D. Rees, capt
USA	4½	J. Burke, capt

1959 Palm Desert, California

USA	8½	S. Snead, capt
GB & NI	3½	D. Rees, capt

1961 Royal Lytham and St Annes

USA	14½	J. Barber, capt
GB & NI	9½	D. Rees, capt

Results (continued)

1963 Atlanta, Georgia
- USA 23 A. Palmer, capt
- GB & NI 9 J. Fallon, capt(*)

1965 Royal Birkdale, Southport
- USA 19½ B. Nelson, capt(*)
- GB & NI 12½ H. Weetman, capt(*)

1967 Houston, Texas
- USA 23½ B. Hogan, capt(*)
- GB & NI 8½ D. Rees, capt(*)

1969 Royal Birkdale, Southport
- USA 16 S. Snead, capt(*)
- GB & NI 16 E. C. Brown, capt(*)

1971 St Louis, Missouri
- USA 18½ J. Hebert, capt(*)
- GB & NI 13½ E. C. Brown, capt

1973 Muirfield, Scotland
- USA 19 J. Burke, capt(*)
- GB & NI 13 B. J. Hunt, capt(*)

1975 Laurel Valley, Pennsylvania
- USA 21 A. Palmer, capt(*)
- GB & NI 11 B. J. Hunt, capt(*)

1977 Royal Lytham and St Annes
- USA 12½ D. Finsterwald, capt(*)
- GB & NI 7½ B. Huggett, capt(*)

1979 Greenbrier, West Virginia
- USA 17 W. Casper, capt(*)
- Europe 11 J. Jacobs, capt(*)

1981 Walton Heath, Surrey
- USA 18½ D. Marr, capt(*)
- Europe 9½ J. Jacobs, capt(*)

1983 PGA National Golf Club, Palm Beach Gardens, Florida
- USA 14½ J. Nicklaus, capt(*)
- Europe 13½ A. W. Jacklin, capt(*)

1985 The Belfry, Sutton Coldfield
- Europe 16½ A. W. Jacklin, capt(*)
- USA 11½ L. Trevino, capt(*)

(*) indicates non-playing captain

Wins

United States – 21
Great Britain – 3
Europe – 1
Tied – 1

Records

36 hole matches

Biggest Winning Margins (Team)
- USA – 10: won 11–1 at Portland, Oregon, 1947
- GB & NI – 3: won 7½–4½ at Lindrick, 1957

Biggest Winning Margin (Foursomes)
- USA – 10 & 9: W. Hagen & D. Shute beat G. Duncan & G. Havers (1931)
  – 10 & 9: E. Oliver & L. Worsham beat T. H. Cotton & A. Lees (1947)
- GB & NI – 7 & 5: A. Boomer & C. A. Whitcombe beat L. Diegel & W. Mehlhorn (1927)

Biggest Winning Margin (Four-balls)
Not contested until 1963

Biggest Winning Margin (Singles)
- USA – 9 & 8: L. Diegel beat A. Mitchell (1929)
- GB & NI – 10 & 8: G. Duncan beat W. Hagen (1929)

18 hole matches

Biggest Winning Margins (Team)
- USA – 15: won 23½–8½ at Houston, Texas, 1967
- GB/Europe – 5: won 16½–11½ at The Belfry, 1985

Biggest Winning Margin (Foursomes)
- USA – 7 & 6: H. Irwin & T. Kite beat K. Brown & D. Smyth (1979)
- GB/Europe – 7 & 5: J.-M. Canizares & J. Rivero beat C. Peete & T. Kite (1985)

Biggest Winning Margin (Four-balls)
- USA – 7 & 5: L. Trevino & J. Pate beat N. Faldo & S. Torrance (1981)
- GB/Europe – 6 & 5: D. Smyth & J.-M. Canizares beat B. Rogers & B. Lietzke (1981)

Biggest Winning Margin (Singles)
- USA – 7 & 6: M. Barner beat M. Bembridge (1969)
  – 7 & 6: L. Trevino beat B. Huggett (1971)
- GB/Europe– 5 & 4: B. J. Hunt beat J. Barber (1961)
  – 5 & 4: C. O'Connor beat F. Beard (1969)
  – 5 & 4: P. Dawson beat D. January (1977)
  – 5 & 4: B. Langer beat H. Sutton (1985)

Most appearances
- USA 9 – Sam Snead (1937–59) (includes the two occasions he was chosen during war even though no competition was held)
- GB/Europe10 – Christy O'Connor (1955–73)

Youngest players
- USA – 21 yr 4 days – Horton Smith (1927)
- GB/Europe – 20 yr 58 days – Nick Faldo (1977)

Oldest players
- USA – 47 yr 300 days – Don January (1977)
- GB/Europe – 50 yr 65 days – Ted Ray (1927)

'Just try getting it back off us' seems to be the mood of the European team after their 1985 Ryder Cup triumph which ended 26 years of United States domination.

S

Safari Tour

The Safari Tour, so called because it involves tournaments played in Central Africa, has been in existence since the early 1970s, and comes under the auspices of the PGA European Tour.

Just five tournaments constitute the tour in 1986: The Nigerian Open, Ivory Coast Open, Kenya Open, Zambia Open, and the Zimbabwe Open. The Kenya Open is the oldest of the five, first being played in 1967. It was followed two years later by the Nigerian Open. The most recent is the Zimbabwe Open which was first added to the programme in 1985.

The Tour only lasts just over a month in February and March, and is popular with many British professionals preparing for the European season.

British professionals have dominated prize money on the Safari Tour in recent years, and the past six years winners have been:

1981 Brian Barnes	£15,539
1982 David Jagger	£21,393
1983 Gordon Brand	£24,438
1984 Ewen Murray	£22,816
1985 Bill Longmuir	£25,717
1986 Gordon Brand	£31,539

Safari Tour records

Lowest 18 Holes
59 – David Jagger (Nigerian Open, 1973)

Lowest 36 Holes
124 – Sandy Lyle (Nigerian Open, 1978)

Lowest 54 Holes
193 – Peter Tupling (Nigerian Open, 1981)

Lowest 72 Holes
255 – Peter Tupling (Nigerian Open, 1981)

St Andrews (Scotland)

Without doubt St Andrews is the 'home of golf'. Situated at the seaside town of St Andrews, Fife, on Scotland's east coast, and just 13 miles south of Dundee, St Andrews may not be the oldest club in Scotland, but it is the most famous.

St Andrews houses four courses: the Old, New, Eden and Jubilee. All four are municipal courses. It is the Old course that has staged all the great golfing tournaments, including the British Open on 23 occasions, just one short of Prestwick's record. St Andrews is also the home of the Royal and Ancient Club, the sport's ruling body.

Part of the character of the Old course is that it retains some of the features of the original course which dates back to the 16th century. Originally it was an 11-hole course and a round consisted of 22 holes each played twice in opposite directions. The large double greens, which still exist, are evidence of this. One notable feature of the Old course are the many bunkers, most of which have names. Golf was free on the St Andrews links for over 400 years, but as the sport became more popular in the 20th century, an Act of Parliament was passed legalizing a modest playing fee which was introduced in 1913.

Golf was played at St Andrews in the mid-16th century, and one of the patrons was Mary Queen of Scots. But it was not until 1754 that the St Andrews Club was formed when 22 noblemen, and others, of Fife held an open competition for a silver club.

The 17th hole on the Old course, known as the 'Road Hole' (qv), is perhaps the most celebrated golf hole in the world. And the 18th must be the finest stage on which to end a championship.

Tom Kidd, from St Andrews, won the first British Open to be played on the Old course, in 1873, and since then many great champions have enjoyed the thrill of winning the title on the most famous course in the world. These include J. H. Taylor, James Braid, Bobby Jones, Sam Snead, Peter Thomson, Bobby Locke, Jack Nicklaus and, more recently, Severiano Ballesteros.

Old course

Length 6933 yd (6340 m)
Par 72
Course record 65 – Neil Coles (British Open, 1965)
65 – Nick Faldo (PGA Championship, 1979)
65 – Greg Norman (Dunhill Cup, 1985)

St Andrews (USA)

The oldest golf club in the United States, it is hardly surprising that the idea came from a Fife immigrant, John Reid, who developed a three-hole course on his cow pasture, and called it after Scotland's famous club.

That was in 1887. Their next course was a six-hole affair in a slightly larger pasture and in 1892 they moved to an apple orchard. The growing band of enthusiasts that moved to the larger six-hole course became known as the 'Apple Tree Gang'. Two years later they were on the move again, to a nine-hole course, and in 1897 they moved to the club's present site at Mount Hope, Ardsley-on-Hudson, New York.

Because of its length and design, St Andrews is not suitable for championship golf. It was, however, the home of two tournaments in 1894 which, prior to the formation of the US Golf Association, masqueraded as the US Amateur and US Open championships.

St Nom-La-Breteche

Situated near Versailles, and 15 miles from Paris, the original St Nom-La-Breteche course was laid out by British designer, Fred Hawtree. A second 18-hole course was subsequently added.

It was selected as the venue for the 1963 World Cup competition which was won by the United States, represented by Arnold Palmer and Jack Nicklaus. Since the inauguration of the Lancôme Trophy in 1970, one of Europe's leading events, St Nom-La-Breteche has been its permanent home. It has also housed the French Open on three occasions since 1965.

There are two courses at St Nom-La-Breteche, the Red and the Blue.

Red course
Length 6712 yd (6137 m)
Par 72
Course record 62 – Ramon Sota (1965)

St Pierre

The laying out of a golf course around Chepstow filled a gap the sport needed in that part of Britain. The club was only opened in 1962 but the site, on the Chepstow–Newport Road, was ideal for a golf course, and designer C. K. Cotton used the natural facilities to their fullest. There was also a mansion within the grounds which could be easily converted into a clubhouse, and country club.

Cotton brought the course up to such a fine standard that it was ready for championship play in 1971. It staged that year's Welsh Professional Championship and also played host to the Dunlop Masters. It was the home of the Masters on seven more occasions, the last being in 1983 when the event was discontinued.

By the mid-1970s St Pierre, one of Britain's first new championship courses since the end of the war, had been extended to 36 holes with the addition of what became the New course. The original course is called the Old course.

Old course
Length 6700 yd (6126 m)
Par 72
Course record 63 – H. Henning (Silk Cut Masters, 1983)

Sammy

A defunct club, similar to a jigger, that was used mainly for short approach shots to the green.

Sand Iron

See Wedge.

Sanyo Open

Although the Sanyo Open has only been part of the European Tour since 1982, it has developed into one of the Tour's leading tournaments, carrying prize money of £120,000.

The first event was held at Barcelona's Sant Cugat club, but all subsequent Sanyo Opens have been at the El Prat club, also near Barcelona.

Winners

Year	Name	Venue	Score
1982	N. Coles	Sant Cugat	266
1983	D. Smyth	El Prat	279
1984	S. Torrance	El Prat	281
1985	S. Ballesteros	El Prat	272

Most wins
No man has won more than one title

Lowest score (72 holes)
266 – Neil Coles (1982)

Sarazen, Gene

Gene Sarazen enjoyed a playing career in excess of 50 years and bridged the gap between Vardon and Nicklaus. Small for a golfer, his main attribute was his consistently accurate hitting. He was also lethal with fairway woods, and developed a sand wedge which was to be his saviour on many occasions.

Gene Sarazen in 1936 during the British Open at Hoylake.

Gene competed in his first US Open in 1920 and two years later, at the age of 20, he took the title to become the youngest ever winner. The following year he came to Britain for the first time and won the North of England title. He went on to Troon to attempt to qualify for the Open, but suffered the embarrassment of failing . . . he was the reigning US champion at the time! (Gene nostalgically returned to Troon in 1973 when he took part in the British Open at the age of 71 and he will be remembered by millions of television viewers who saw him hole his tee shot at the famous Postage Stamp hole.)

He was runner-up in the 1928 British Open but won the title on the only occasion it was played at Prince's, Sandwich, in 1932. Gene won the US Open that year which made him the second man after Bobby Jones to win both titles in the same year. In 1935 he won the US Masters, to become the first man to win all four of the world's leading tournaments—a feat still only held by a handful of golfers.

Regularly playing competitive golf beyond the age of 60 'The Squire', as Sarazen is known, was made an honorary member of the Royal & Ancient Club, and has maintained his contact with the sport via journalism and television broadcasting.

Career highlights
British Open 1932
US Open 1922, 1932
US PGA 1922, 1923, 1933
US Masters 1935
Ryder Cup 1927, 1929, 1931, 1933, 1935, 1937

Scandinavian Open

Sweden is gradually producing some fine top quality professional golfers, many of whom must have been inspired by the Scandinavian Open which was first held in 1973.

By far the country's leading event, the Open has always attracted an international field and no fewer than four British Open winners have won the title.

Played at a variety of different courses, it seems to have found its permanent home at the Sven Tumba Golf and Country Club, Stockholm, which has been the venue of the Open since 1983.

Winners

Year	Name	Venue	Score
1973	R. Charles	Drottningholm	278
1974	A. Jacklin	Bokskogen	279
1975	G. Burns	Bokskogen	279
1976	H. Baiocchi	Drottningholm	271
1977	R. Byman	Drottningholm	275
1978	S. Ballesteros	Vasatorp	279
1979	A. W. Lyle	Vasatorp	276
1980	G. Norman	Vasatorp	276
1981	S. Ballesteros	Linkoping	273
1982	R. Byman	Linkoping	275
1983	S. Torrance	Sven Tumba	280
1984	I. Woosnam	Sven Tumba	280
1985	I. Baker-Finch	Sven Tumba	274

Most wins
2 – Severiano Ballesteros (1978, 1981)
2 – Bob Byman (1977, 1982)

Lowest score (72 holes)
271 – Hugh Baiocchi (1976)

Schenectady Putter

The first centre-shafted putter (qv) and was so called because its inventor, an American called Wright, lived in Schenectady, New York State.

Walter Travis won the Amateur Championship at Sandwich with one of these putters in 1904, which resulted in them being banned nearly 50 years.

Score Cards

Score cards are used in all stroke-play competitions.

At the commencement of the round, cards are exchanged by players who do *not* mark their own card. At the end of the round both players must sign the card, and it is the responsibility of the player whose name appears on the top of the card, to make sure it has been marked correctly. A player who hands in an incorrectly marked card is liable to be disqualified.

One of the most famous incidents of a wrongly-marked card was in the 1968 US Masters when Tommy Aaron marked Roberto de Vicenzo as having scored a four instead of a three at the 17th hole in the final round. De Vicenzo would have forced a play-off with Bob Goalby had the card been correctly marked (disqualification was not compulsory). De Vicenzo has never since won the Masters.

The first time official score cards were used in the British Open was in 1865.

Scratch Golfer

A scratch golfer is one who needs no handicap.
See Handicaps.

Semi-Rough

The part of the course between the fairway and the rough. It is so called because the grass is not as long as the rough, and not as short as the fairway.

Seniors Golf

Players are regarded as 'seniors' once they reach the age of 50 and are eligible to take part in specially organized tournaments.

A Seniors Tour exists in the United States with over 25 tournaments in the calendar. The top money winner in 1985 was five-times British Open Winner Peter Thomson who won over £300,000—a figure way above his best year as a regular tournament player.

The Senior Golfers' Society of Great Britain was formed in 1926 but eligibility to the Society, unlike the professional senior, is only open to golfers over the age of 55.

British and American senior professionals have national championships, and the World Seniors Championship (discontinued in 1978) was a 36-hole head-to-head match-play competition between the winners of the two titles. It was first held in 1954 and, for the first three years, because the British Championships were not introduced until 1957, the British entrants were nominated by the British Association of Golf Writers.

The first winner of the British Senior Professional Tournament, in 1957, was John Burton. Between 1957 and 1966 it was a 54-hole event but since then has been played over 72 holes.

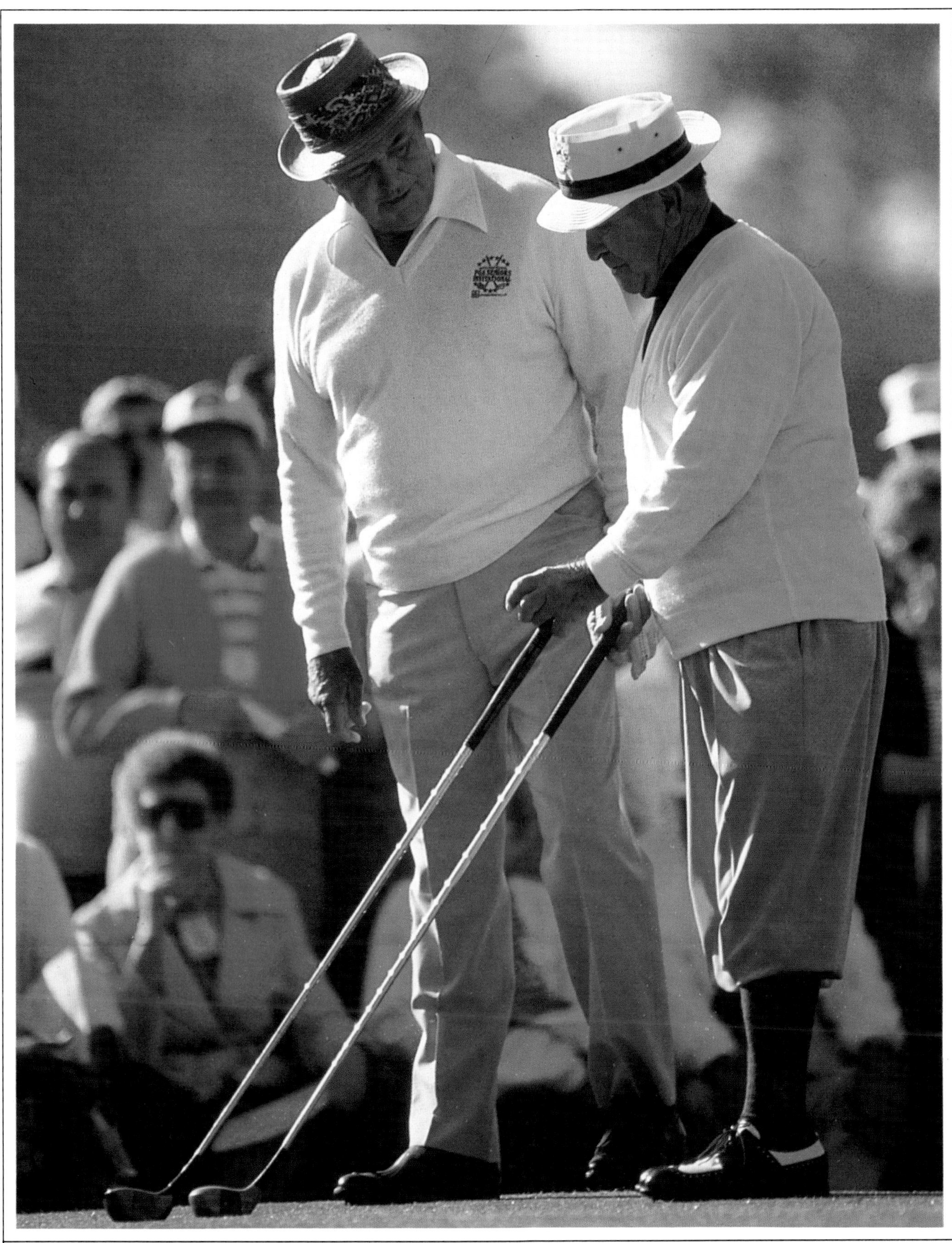

Two grand old men of golf who have enjoyed successful careers as Seniors players – Sam Snead (left) and Gene Sarazen.

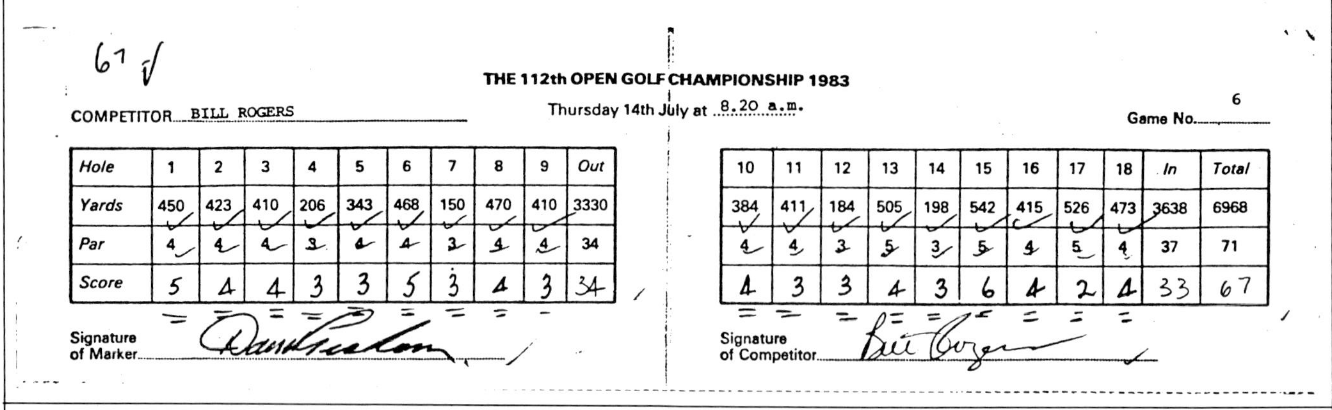
THE 112th OPEN GOLF CHAMPIONSHIP 1983

COMPETITOR BILL ROGERS

Thursday 14th July at 8.20 a.m.

Game No. 6

Hole	1	2	3	4	5	6	7	8	9	Out
Yards	450	423	410	206	343	468	150	470	410	3330
Par	4	4	4	3	4	4	3	4	4	34
Score	5	4	4	3	3	5	3	4	3	34

Hole	10	11	12	13	14	15	16	17	18	In	Total
Yards	384	411	184	505	198	542	415	526	473	3638	6968
Par	4	4	3	5	3	5	4	5	4	37	71
Score	4	3	3	4	3	6	4	2	4	33	67

Signature of Marker

Signature of Competitor

A copy of Bill Rogers' card after the first round of the 1983 British Open at Royal Birkdale, showing his rare albatross at the 526-yd (481-m) par-5 17th hole.

World Seniors Championship (winners)

1954	G. Sarazen	1967	J. Panton (GB)
1955	M. Dutra	1968	C. Harper
1956	B. Kenyon (GB)	1969	T. Bolt
1957	A. Watrous	1970	S. Snead
1958	N. Sutton (GB)	1971	K. D. Nagle (GB)
1959	W. Coggin	1972	S. Snead
1960	D. Metz	1973	S. Snead
1961	P. Runyan	1974	R. de Vicenzo
1962	P. Runyan	1975	K. D. Nagle (GB)
1963	H. Barron	1976	C. O'Connor (GB)
1964	S. Snead	1977	C. O'Connor (GB)
1965	S. Snead	1978	J. Jiminez
1966	F. Haas, Jnr		

Event discontinued after 1978.

Unless stated all winners were reigning US Seniors champions.

Most wins

5 – Sam Snead (1964, 1965, 1970, 1972, 1973)

Biggest winning margin

7 & 6 – Al Watrous beat John Burton (1957)

7 & 6 – Sam Snead beat Syd Scott (1964)

British Senior Professional Tournament

(winners since 1970)

1970	M. Faulkner	1978	P. Skerritt
1971	K. D. Nagle	1979	C. O'Connor
1972	K. Bousfield	1980	P. Skerritt
1973	K. D. Nagle	1981	C. O'Connor
1974	E. Lester	1982	C. O'Connor
1975	K. D. Nagle	1983	C. O'Connor
1976	C. O'Connor	1984	E. Jones
1977	C. O'Connor	1985	N. C. Coles

Most wins

6 – Christy O'Connor (1976, 1977, 1979, 1981, 1982, 1983)

Lowest score (72 holes)

268 – Kel Nagle (1975)

Shaft

The part of the club which is not the head. The grip, at the top, forms part of the shaft.

Shank

The part of the club, at the heel-end of the club-head, near the socket, into which the shaft is fitted. When a player strikes the ball with this part of the club, which the inexperienced golfer does with frustrating regularity, he is said to have 'shanked' the ball.

Shinnecock Hills

One of the oldest surviving golf courses in America, the club was formed in 1891 and the course laid out the following year by Scot Willie Dunn, who became the club's first professional. Situated at Southampton, Long Island, the clubhouse is the oldest in the United States.

In 1896 the course was used as the venue for the US Open, but that was the only occasion.

When Dunn laid the course out, it was the nearest any in the United States had come to resembling a Scottish links course. It was named after a tribe of Indians that once inhabited part of Long Island.

Length 6697 yd (6124 m)
Par 70
Course record 65 – Mark Calcavecchia (US Open, 1986)

Shoes

Spiked golf shoes, as worn today, were only introduced in the 1920s. Prior to that flat-soled shoes, or boots, were worn. But these did nothing to help the stance in wet conditions. Spiked shoes were the answer, and after the Second World War, shoes with removeable spikes were introduced.

Today most shoes are made of leather and good quality shoes can vary between £30 and £100 in price. Modern technology has seen the introduction of a golf shoe with a rubberized 'dimple' sole. But as yet it has to prove itself and, more importantly, gain the support of greenkeepers.

Silk Cut Masters

When Dunlop pulled out of golf sponsorship in 1982, after 36 years continuous sponsorship of their Masters, Silk Cut stepped in as a replacement. They only sponsored the event for one year, however, before it disappeared from the European PGA calendar. The event was staged at St Pierre and was won by Ian Woosnam with a score of 269.

Singapore Open

The Singapore Open was first held at the Royal Island golf club in 1957. It was a match-play event for the first two years of its life, but became a stroke-play event in 1959. The Open was not contested in 1960 but, upon the formation of the Far East Tour (now the Asia Tour) in 1961, Peter Thomson, who has done so much for golf in the Far East, was responsible for getting it re-started. And it has been contested every year since.

All playings of the Open have been at the Singapore Island Country Club and played over either the Bukit or Island course.

Australian David Graham, during the 1968 Open, shot a round of 62 to equal the Far East Tour record set by his fellow Australian Kel Nagle seven years earlier.

Winners (since 1970)

Year	Name	Venue	Score
1970	Hsieh Yung Yo	Bukit	276
1971	H. Yasuda	Bukit	277
1972	T. Kono	Bukit	279
1973	B. Arda	Bukit	284
1974	E. Nival	Bukit	275
1975	Y. Suzuki	Island	284
1976	K. Uchida	Bukit	273
1977	Chi-San Hsu	Bukit	277
1978	T. Gale	Bukit	278
1979	Lu Hsi Chuen	Bukit	280
1980	K. Cox	Bukit	276
1981	M. Aye	Island	273
1982	Hsu Cheng San	Bukit	274
1983	Chien-Soon Lu	Bukit	279
1984	T. Sieckmann	Island	274
1985	Chen Tze-Ming	Bukit	274
1986	G. Turner	Bukit	271

Most wins

2 – Frank Phillips (1961, 1965)
2 – Hsie Yung Yo (1968, 1970)
2 – Ben Arda (1967, 1973)

Lowest score (72 holes)

271 – Graham Turner (1986)

Slice

When the ball veers sharply to the right of its intended target the ball is said to have been sliced. The most common cause is by playing across the back of the ball from right to left as a result of playing an 'out to in' shot. See diagram on page 72.

Snead, Sam

Samuel Jackson Snead was one of the greatest naturally talented golfers of the 20th century. His swing was one of the finest ever seen, which many aspiring golfers attempted to copy. He won all the world's major titles except one—the US Open. He took the British Open in 1946, and won both the US PGA and the US Masters three times.

Sam Snead appeared in seven Ryder Cup matches; he is seen here helping the United States to a narrow victory at Wentworth in 1953.

However, he was runner-up in the US Open on four occasions: to Ralph Guldahl, by two strokes, in his first Open in 1937; ten years later he lost the play-off, by one stroke, to Lew Worsham; in 1949 it was Cary Middlecoff who beat Snead by one stroke; and in 1953 he was no match for Ben Hogan, who won by six strokes.

A professional since 1934 (aged 22) Sam Snead was still playing on the US Tour in the 1980s. In 1974 he was joint third in the US PGA championships—37 years after he first played in it. In 1979 Snead shot a round of 67 in the Quad Cities Open to become the first man to compile a round lower than his age on the US PGA Tour. Fourteen years earlier, at the age of 52, he became the oldest winner on the US Tour when he won the Greater Greensboro Open.

Altogether Snead won over 150 tournaments, including a record 84 on the US Tour.

Career highlights

British Open 1946
US Masters 1949, 1952, 1954
US PGA 1942, 1949, 1951
World Cup (team) 1956, 1960, 1961, 1962
World Cup (individual) 1961
Ryder Cup 1937, 1947, 1949, 1951 (capt), 1953, 1955, 1959 (capt), 1969 (non-playing capt)

Sole

The sole of the golf club is the part that rests on the ground.

Sotogrande

The Club de Golf Sotogrande, on Spain's Costa del Sol, is very popular with both British tourists and the many British residents in the area.

Designed in 1964 by Robert Trent Jones, it was a purpose-built golfing centre and property development. The apartments and villas are still much sought after.

Two 18-hole courses and a nine-hole course now exist, and, while the longest of the two 18-hole courses can be lengthened, it is not basically a championship course. The only major event to have been held here was the 1966 Spanish Open won by Roberto de Vicenzo.

Championship course

Length 6849 yd (6263 m)
Par 72
Course record 66 – Roberto de Vicenzo, Spanish Open, 1966

South African Open

The South African Open goes back to 1909 when Lawrence Waters won the 36-hole event at Kimberley with a score of 147.

South Africa's two outstanding golfers, Bobby Locke and Gary Player, have won the title 22 times between them. Locke first won it as a 17-year-old amateur in 1935, and 20 years later he won it for the ninth time. Player won his first title in 1956, the year after Locke last gained the title. And between then and 1981 he has won it a record 13 times.

Two South African Opens were held in 1976 when its timing altered. It is now an early year event played in January or February.

Winners (since 1970)

Year	Name	Venue	Score
1970	T. Horton	Durban	285
1971	S. Hobday	Mowbray	276
1972	G. Player	Johannesburg	274
1973	R. Charles	Durban	282
1974	R. Cole	Johannesburg	272
1975	G. Player	Mowbray	278
1976	D. Hayes	Houghton	287
1976	G. Player	Durban	280
1977	G. Player	Johannesburg	273
1978	H. Baiocchi	Mowbray	285
1979	G. Player	Houghton	279
1980	R. Cole	Durban	279
1981	G. Player	Johannesburg	272
1982	C. Bolling	Johannesburg	278
1983	C. Bolling	Cape Province	278
1984	A. Johnstone	Houghton	274
1985	G. Levenson	Durban	280
1986	D. Frost	Johannesburg	275

Most wins

13 – Gary Player (1956, 1960, 1965, 1966, 1967, 1968, 1969, 1972, 1975, 1976, 1977, 1979, 1981)

Lowest score (72 holes)

272 – Bobby Cole (1974)
272 – Gary Player (1981)

Southerly Course, most

The most southerly golf course in the world is at Stanley, on the Falkland Islands. The most southerly in the British Isles is situated near Hugh Town on St Mary's, Scilly Isles. The most southerly on the British mainland is the Cury Helston Club near Mullion, six miles south of Helston in Cornwall.

Southport and Ainsdale

Popularly known as the S & A, the Southport and Ainsdale links are just one of the many fine links along the coastline between Formby and Southport in Merseyside.

The club was formed in 1906 with a nine-hole course, but had to move shortly afterwards to make way for a housing development. The present site was laid out in 1923 with the assistance of James Braid who designed a completely new course.

Southport and Ainsdale has staged many major, and national, championships. But the most famous event to be staged on the links was the Ryder Cup. It has twice been held at the club, in 1933 and 1937, the first on either side of the Atlantic to stage two consecutive matches on home soil. It was at the S & A that Great Britain and Northern Ireland registered one of their rare wins, in 1933, which turned out to be their last until 1957.

Two large bunkers are a feature, particularly the Gumbley's bunker at the par-5 16th hole.

Gary Player won the South African Open a record 13 times between 1956 and 1981.

Length 6603 yd (6038 m)
Par 73
Course record 67 – John Hammond (British Open qualifying, 1967)
67 – David Russell (British Open qualifying, 1983)
67 – David Vaughan (British Open qualifying, 1983)

Spade Mashie

Another name for the obsolete mashie niblick.

Spanish Open

Golf first appeared on the Spanish mainland in 1904, some 13 years after the Las Palmas Club was opened on Gran Canaria. The first Spanish Open was held at the Polo Golf Club, Madrid in 1912 and won by Frenchman Arnaud Massy, the 1907 British Open winner.

Now very much part of the European Tour it receives sponsorship from Benson & Hedges, and carries prize money in excess of £100,000.

Madrid's Puerta de Hierro club staged the Open 25 times between 1917 and 1955 but since then the championship has been held on a variety of Spanish courses, thus giving the Spanish public the opportunity to see the host of international stars that have been attending the event since the 1950s.

The 1975 winner was Arnold Palmer who, in winning the title, won his only European Open title, apart from the British Open.

Winners (since 1970)

Year	Name	Venue	Score
1970	A. Gallardo	Nueva Andalucia	284
1971	D. Hayes	El Prat	275
1972	A. Garrido	Pals	293
1973	N. Coles	La Manga	282
1974	J. Heard	La Manga	279
1975	A. Palmer	La Manga	283
1976	E. Polland	La Manga	282
1977	B. Gallacher	La Manga	277
1978	B. Barnes	El Prat	276
1979	D. Hayes	Torrequebrada	278
1980	E. Polland	Escorpion	276
1981	S. Ballesteros	El Prat	273
1982	S. Torrance	Club de Campo	273
1983	E. Darcy	Las Brisas	277
1984	B. Langer	El Saler	275
1985	S. Ballesteros	Vallromanos	266
1986	H. Clark	La Moraleja	272

Most wins
6 – A. de la Torre (1916, 1917, 1919, 1923, 1925, 1935)

Lowest score (72 holes)
266 – Severiano Ballesteros (1985)

Spoon

An obsolete wooden club designed for playing off fairways. The spoon was slightly smaller, with a deeper club-face, than the brassie, and was equivalent to a present-day No 3 wood.

Stableford

Type of competition which was first played at the Wallasey links on the Wirral in 1932. The system of scoring was devised by Dr Frank Stableford, a notable surgeon and fine golfer.

To provide a bit of respite from stroke-play or match-play competitions he drew up a scoring chart whereby each player competed against a fixed score for each hole. The one with the most points at the end of the round was declared the winner. In a singles event, a handicapped player is allowed seven eighths of his handicap, and the strokes taken in accordance with the stroke index (qv).

The scoring system for a Stableford competition is as follows:

A hole completed in more than one over fixed score	0 pts
A hole completed in one over fixed score	1 pt
A hole completed in fixed score	2 pts
A hole completed in one under fixed score	3 pts
A hole completed in two under fixed score	4 pts
A hole completed in three under fixed score	5 pts

Stance

The position a player takes up when addressing the ball. While the terrain often dictates his or her stance, one of three normal stances should be adopted: the closed stance, open stance and straight stance. The first two are covered separately in this encyclopedia. The straight stance is a half-way position between the two and is adopted when both feet are square to the intended line of flight.

Taking up the correct stance is important in playing all shots, and the varying clubs call upon different stances. One simple rule in deciding the correct stance is to line the club-head up with the back of the ball, before taking up a stance.

Standard Scratch Score (SSS)

Each golf course has a Standard Scratch Score (SSS). It is the number of strokes a scratch golfer would be expected to complete a round in when playing from the competition tees, and in summer playing conditions. The score is fixed according to the length of the course as decided by the National Union of Golf Clubs. The SSS is different to the par for a course as it does not decide what score each hole should be completed in, but decides one score for all nine or eighteen holes.

The SSS was first put into operation in Great Britain and Northern Ireland in 1926.

A course measuring between 6601 and 6800 yd (6036–6218 m) would have a standard scratch score of 72. But this would be altered at the discretion of the council after taking into consideration natural hazards, size of the greens, the terrain and other features unusual to that particular course.

Stewards

During championships, stewards are to be found around the golf course. They are appointed by the tournament committee and their main duty is to maintain proper crowd control. They are also there to provide general assistance to the viewing public.

Stroke

The forward movement of the club made with the *intention* of hitting, and moving, the ball. A stroke that misses the ball, when the intention was to hit it, still counts as one stroke.

Stroke Index

Each hole on a golf course is graded according to its difficulty and given a number between 1 and 18: the stroke index. The most difficult hole on a course is No 1 while the easiest is No 18.

The allocation of the index is made by a club committee and its purpose is to identify at which holes players with high handicaps receive strokes over smaller-handicap players in match-play and Stableford competitions.

An example of how this works can be shown by looking at two players, A and B, who are playing each other in a Stableford event. Player A has a handicap of 8, while player B has a handicap of 16. Each player is allowed seven-eighths of his handicap. Therefore player A is allowed a stroke at seven holes, while B would be allowed a stroke at 14 holes. Therefore at the holes with an index 1–7 player A would be allowed to deduct one stroke from his gross score, while player B would be allowed a stroke at the holes numbered 1–14 on the stroke index.

Stroke Play

A stroke-play competition, also known as medal-play, is one whereby the player's net score for the round is taken into consideration, and compared with that of the other competitors.

The first stroke-play competition was in May 1744 when the Gentlemen Golfers of Edinburgh (now the Honourable Company of Edinburgh Golfers) played for a silver club presented by the City of Edinburgh.

Stymie

The word stymied is now used in the English language, meaning 'to be put in a hopeless position'. It was derived from a golfing term, which meant the same.

During match-play events it was permissable to stymie

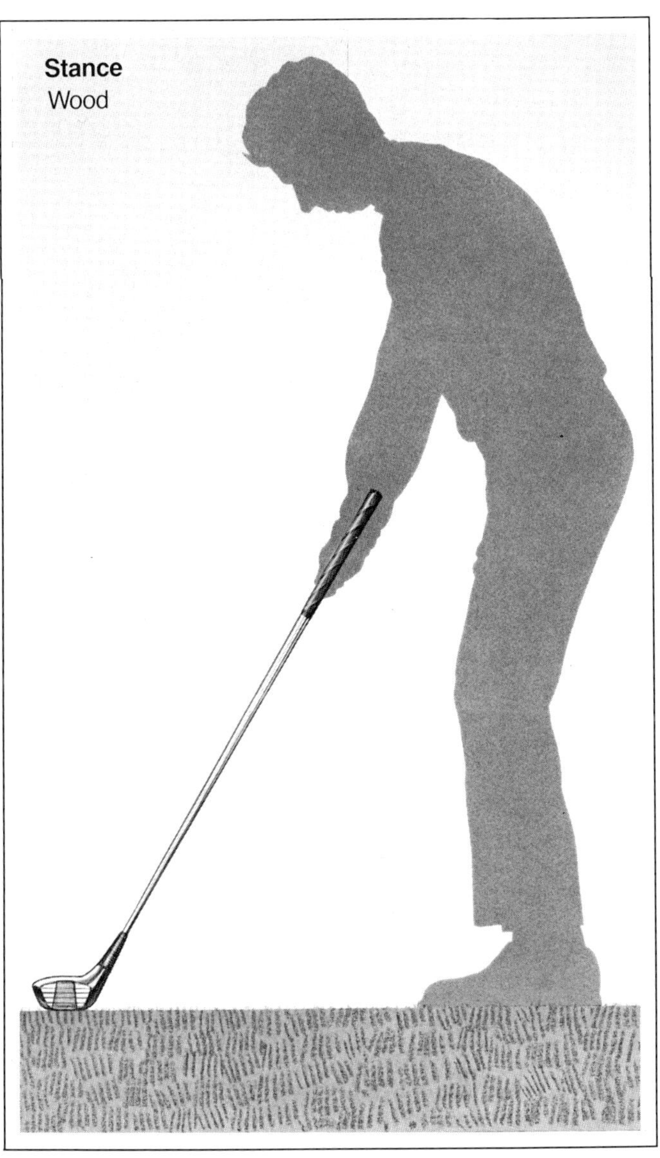

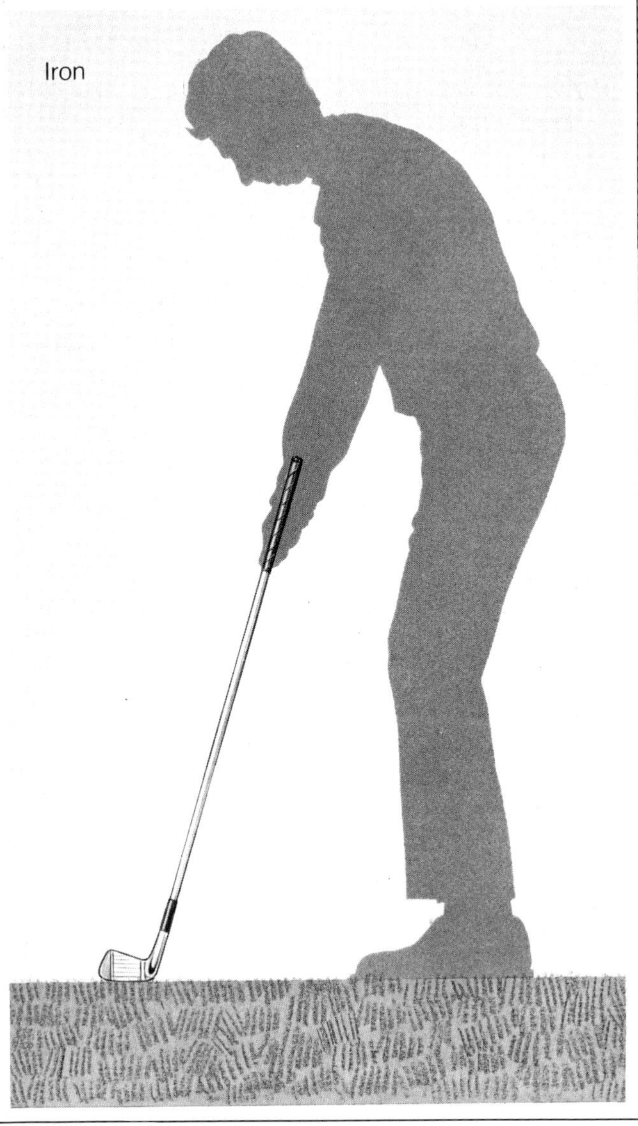

one's opponent by placing your ball between his and the hole on the putting surface, thus preventing him from playing a direct shot.

A very tactical shot, naturally it brought about many controversial moments. When G. P. Roberts won the final of the 1951 English Amateur Championship by laying a stymie for his opponent, H. Bennett, at the 39th hole, the R & A decided to take some action: the stymie was banned; the USGA followed suit. The rules were changed to allow a ball, in such a situation, to be removed while the player furthest from the hole plays his stroke.

Sudden Death

When a match ends up level, the players involved in the tie usually have to play-off to decide a winner. It can either be over an agreed number of holes, or on a sudden-

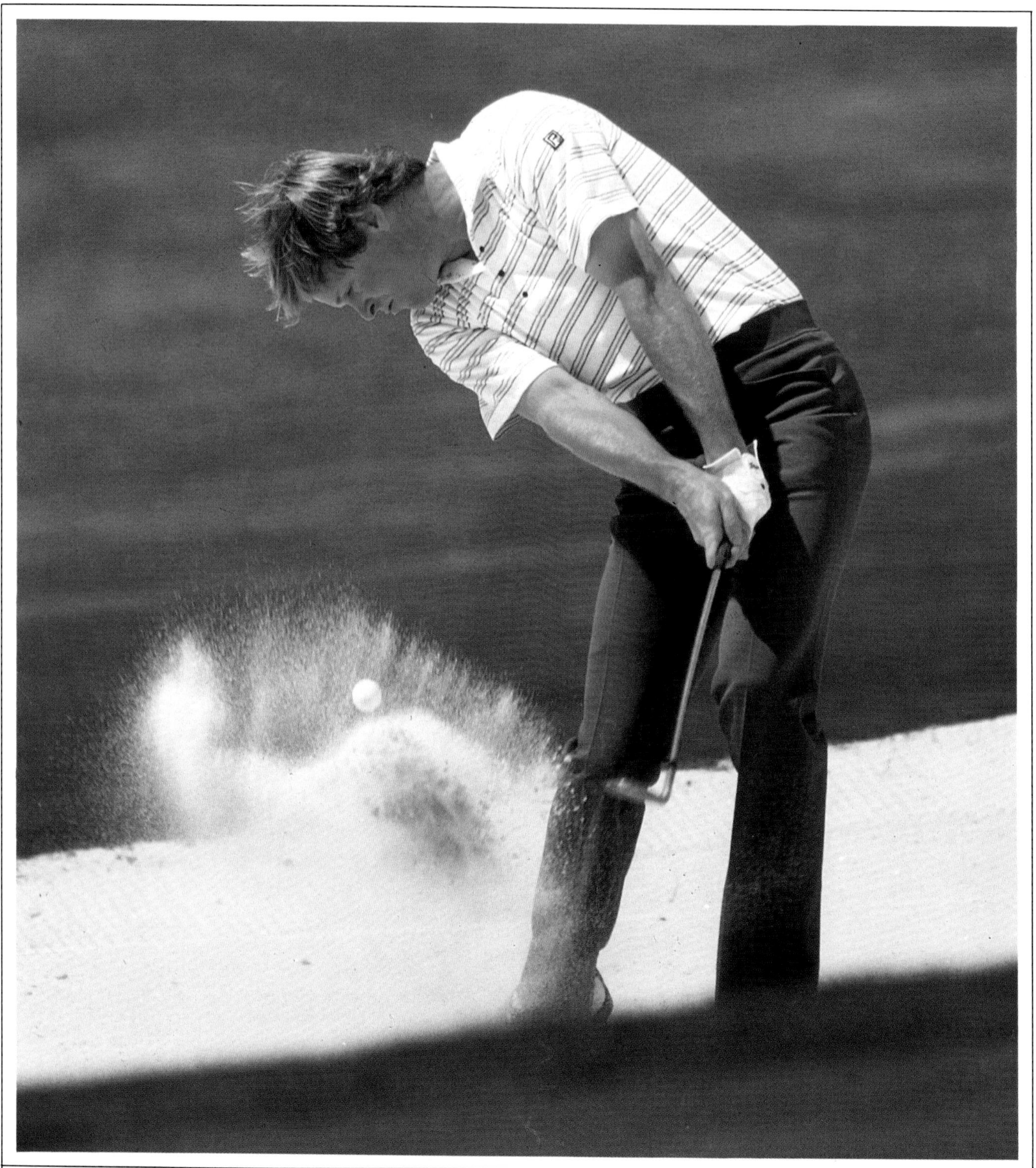

Johnny Miller won the first Sun City Million Dollar Classic and received prize money worth £265,000.

death basis—in other words, the first one to win a hole, wins the match.

If more than two people are involved then the one(s) with the highest score at each hole are eliminated.

In the 1977 United States PGA championships, Lanny Wadkins beat Gene Littler at the third extra hole in the play-off. This was the first time a sudden-death play-off had been used to decide the outcome of one of the four major championships.

See also Extra Holes, Play-Off.

Sun City

Sun City is a leisure complex built in the late-1970s. It is situated in the Pilanesberg range of mountains in Bophuthatswana, on the border with Botswana. Included in the multi-million pound complex is a small-game park, man-made lake, casino, night club, restaurant, hotel and a golf course designed by Gary Player.

So successful was the idea, that the majority of the investment was returned in the first year of opening.

Every December the world's leading golfers arrive in Sun City for the Million Dollar Challenge. First held in 1981, the event started on 31 December and finished on 4 January 1982. It carried the richest first prize in golf when Johnny Miller's winning cheque was worth £265,000. Only five men, Miller, Lee Trevino, Jack Nicklaus, Gary Player and Severiano Ballesteros took part in the first tournament. Today, ten of the world's top golfers are invited to play and the first prize is still worth over £200,000 depending upon exchange rates at the time. Since 1984 five women have participated in a 54-hole satellite tournament. In 1985 that carried a first prize of £45,000.

Winners (Men)

Year	Name	Score
1982	J. Miller	277
1983	S. Ballesteros	274
1984	S. Ballesteros	279
1985	B. Langer	278

Winners (Women)

Year	Name	Score
1984	K. Whitworth	213
1985	P. Rizzo	216

Most winners (Men)
2 – Severiano Ballesteros (1983, 1984)

Lowest score (72 holes)
274 – Severiano Ballesteros (1983)

Sunningdale

Founded in 1900, Sunningdale is one of the most popular clubs in southern England, with the Old and New courses providing some of the finest golf in Surrey.

The Old course, as it was later to be called, was laid out by Willie Park in 1900, and the New course was designed by Harry Colt in 1922.

One of golf's most prestigious clubs, it has been fortunate to have had two future Kings of England as captains: Edward VIII and George VI, when they were the Prince of Wales and Duke of York respectively. Sunningdale has also been used to stage important events, notably the Dunlop Masters, and the qualifying competitions for the British Open. The Old course, small for a championship, is used for the popular Sunningdale Open Foursomes which have been held since 1934.

Sunningdale holds a special place in Gary Player's heart, for it was at the course in 1956 that he won his first major professional event. He is also the professional course record holder for the New course with a 64.

Old course
Length 6563 yd (6001 m)
Par 70
Course record 63 – Norman von Nida (Dunlop Masters, 1948)
63 – Manuel Pinero (European Open, 1982)

New course
Length 6676 yd (6105 m)
Par 70
Course record 64 – Gary Player (Dunlop tournament, 1956)

Swing

The motion of the club-head from the moment it leaves the address position, making contact with the ball, to the follow-through, after contact with the ball.

No two players swings are alike but many professionals have 'text-book' swings. One of the best was the famous American Sam Snead. One of the finest swings in more recent years has been that of American Tom Weiskopf.

Swiss Open

Since 1983 the Swiss Open has been called the Ebel European Masters–Swiss Open Championship. This was because the president of the Swiss Open organizing committee decided to be one move ahead of other European Opens by adding the word Masters to their title.

The first Swiss Open was played at Engen in 1923, and the 36-hole event was won by Alec Ross. Up to 1939 a different venue was chosen most years, but since then all Swiss Opens have been held at the country's best known course at Crans-sur-Sierre.

Many European PGA records have been established during the Swiss Open over the years. It was during the 1971 event that Italy's Baldovino Dassu recorded a round of 60—the lowest ever on the Tour. And in 1978 José-Maria Canizares registered the lowest nine-hole total of 27. Jerry Anderson won the title with a 261 in 1984, just one stroke short of the European record. And in the 1983 event Sandy Lyle compiled a record-equalling ten birdies in one round.

Winners (since 1970)

Year	Name	Score
1970	G. Marsh	274
1971	P. M. Townsend	270
1972	G. Marsh	270
1973	H. Baiocchi	278
1974	R. J. Charles	275
1975	D. Hayes	273
1976	M. Pinero	274
1977	S. Ballesteros	273
1978	S. Ballesteros	272
1979	H. Baiocchi	275
1980	N. Price	267
1981	M. Pinero	277
1982	I. Woosnam	272
1983	N. Faldo	268
1984	J. Anderson	261
1985	C. Stadler	267

Most wins
3 – Alec Ross (1923, 1925, 1926)
3 – Auguste Boyer (1930, 1934, 1935)
3 – Marcel Dallemagne (1931, 1937, 1949)
3 – Dai Rees (1956, 1959, 1963)
3 – Harold Henning (1960, 1964, 1965)

Lowest score (72 holes)
261 – Jerry Anderson (1984)

T

Takeaway
The first movement of the club-head when taken back from the ball at the commencement of the swing. Although it only lasts a few inches, if incorrect the whole swing, and stroke, can ultimately be wrong.

Target Golf
Many driving ranges (qv) have targets marked out on their fairway, and often competitions are arranged with the intention of playing a ball as near the centre of the target as possible. This type of competition is designed to improve lofted shots that require maximum amount of backspin.

Taylor, John
John Henry Taylor, known as J.H., was the youngest member of the Great Triumvirate at the turn of the century.

Taylor, James Braid and Harry Vardon won the British Open 16 times between them in a 21-year spell between 1894 and 1914: Taylor won it five times. His first, in 1894, made him the first non-Scottish professional to hold the title.

He did a lot to improve the status of the professional golfer and was one of the founders of the Professional Golfer's Association (PGA). For his outstanding services to golf Taylor was made an honorary member of the Royal and Ancient Club in 1949.

Apart from his five British Open wins, Taylor also won the German and the French Opens twice. And in 1900 he came close to winning both the British and US Open titles when he finished second to his great contemporary Vardon in the American championship. He beat Vardon by eight strokes to win that year's British Open at St Andrews.

Taylor was honoured with the non-playing captaincy of the Ryder Cup team at Southport and Ainsdale in 1933, leading them to a rare win. The next British success came 24 years later.

Hailing from Northam in North Devon, Taylor's first involvement in golf was as a caddie at the Westward Ho! course. After spending most of his career as the professional at the Royal Mid-Surrey club, he retired to Northam where he died in 1963 at the age of 92. He was the last survivor of the Great Triumvirate.

Career highlights
British Open 1894, 1895, 1900, 1909, 1913
French Open 1908, 1909
German Open 1912
Ryder Cup 1933 (non-playing captain)

Tee
(1) The marked out area at the start of each hole, from where the initial drive is made. Also known as the teeing ground, the area is normally raised and rectangular. The teeing ground should contain two markers, and the drive should be made from between, and behind them. The teeing ground normally contains three sets of tee positions: Normal tees for club members, Medal tees for competitions, and Ladies' tees.
(2) The small wooden or plastic peg upon which the ball is placed on the teeing area is also called a tee.

Until the late 1920s golfers, seeing the need for an artificial aid to assist driving, used to tee their ball up on a small pile of sand. But around 1928 wooden pegs were introduced for this purpose. They have now been replaced by plastic tees, although it is still possible to acquire wooden ones.

It is not compulsory to use a tee on the teeing ground, but it is beneficial, particularly when driving with a wooden club. A tee must not be used on any part of the course other than the teeing ground.

Television
Golf, like many other sports, has grown as a result of television coverage. And because of the attention shown

by TV, the sport has benefited as a result of attracting sponsors which, in turn, has seen prize money rise.

Television first showed a serious interest in golf in the late 1950s and the coverage it gave to the sport, together with the appeal of such men as Arnold Palmer, expanded the US Tour enormously in just a few years.

In Britain, unsuccessful attempts had been made to broadcast golf commentaries on the radio, including part of the 1939 Amateur Championship with Henry Longhurst at the microphone. But it was not until the introduction of television that it became a 'broadcastable' sport.

Television and Radio 'Firsts'

First Broadcast
June 1939 from Coombe Hill, Surrey. Bobby Locke and Reg Whitcombe took part in a specially organized 72-hole competition for a £500 first prize.

First Live Televised British Open
1955 from St Andrews—won by Peter Thomson.

First Live Televised US Open
1954 from Baltusrol—won by Ed Furgol.

First Colour Golf Transmission
1967 from Akron, Ohio when part of the World Series of Golf was broadcast.

First Televised Hole-in-One (Britain)
1967 Dunlop Masters at St George's, Sandwich, by Tony Jacklin.

Texas Open

The Texas Open holds the distinction of having more US PGA Tour records set during it than any other event. Some of these include: the record low score for 72 holes (257) by Mike Souchak in 1955. His victory by 27 strokes also equalled the Tour record for the biggest win and his second nine holes during the first round totalled just 27 strokes, which was also a record.

Souchak's 257 beat the old record of 259 which was held by Byron Nelson and Chandler Harper. The latter established his record-equalling score in the 1954 Texas Open. Harper also created a Tour record for the lowest score in three consecutive rounds—189. Ron Streck created a 36-hole record of 125 during the 1978 Open and in 1951 Al Brosch created a then record for 18 holes, with a round of 60 which was equalled in the Texas Opens of 1954 and 1955 by Ted Kroll and Mike Souchak respectively.

Most of the above records were set at the Brackenridge Park Golf Course, San Antonio, but today's Texas Open is played over the tougher Oak Hills course, also at San Antonio. First held in 1922 it is the fourth oldest championship in the United States after the Open, Western Open, and PGA Championship.

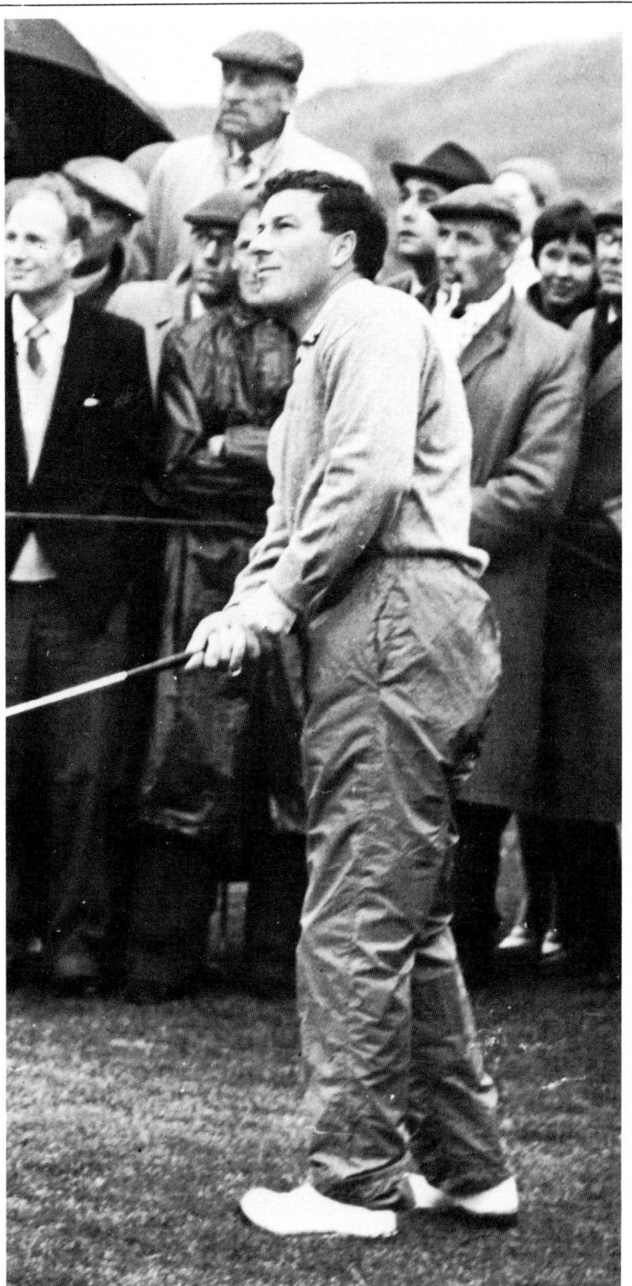

Peter Thomson on his way to winning his fourth British Open title, at Lytham in 1958.

Winners (Since 1970)

Year	Name	Score	Year	Name	Score
1970	R. Cerrudo	273	1978	R. Streck	265
1971	Not held		1979	L. Graham	268
1972	M. Hill	273	1980	L. Trevino	265
1973	B. Crenshaw	270	1981	B. Rogers	266
1974	T. Diehl	269	1982	J. Haas	262
1975	D. January	275	1983	J. Colbert	261
1976	B. Baird	273	1984	C. Peete	266
1977	H. Irwin	266	1985	J. Mahaffey	268

Most wins
3 – Arnold Palmer (1960, 1961, 1962)

Lowest score (72 holes)
257 – Mike Souchak (1955)

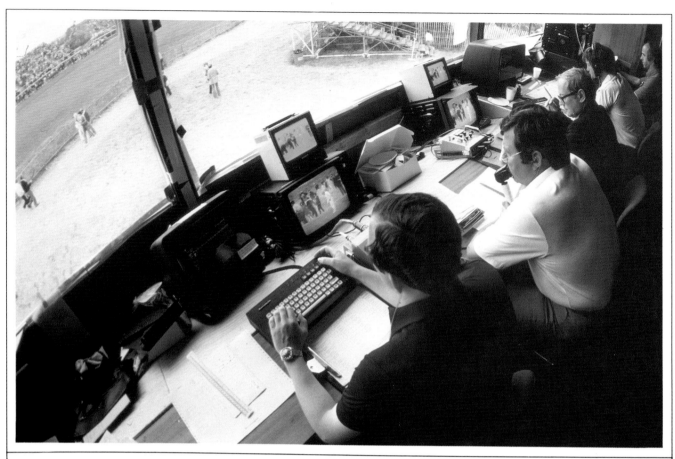

Peter Alliss, Harry Carpenter and the remainder of the BBC television team at the 1981 British Open, Sandwich.

Christy O'Connor, Jnr, won the 1985 Tooting Bec Cup thanks to a round of 64 during the British Open at Sandwich.

Texas Wedge

The American term used to define a shot played with the putter from *off* the putting surface. This stroke is quite effective if the ground is hard, and the grass short, where the use of a lofted club might see the ball go beyond the hole.

The expression was first used by Texan golfers who employed this type of shot because of the frequent dry conditions they experienced at their courses.

Thin Hit

A ball is said to be 'hit thin' when hit with the sole of the club. Consequently the ball will not reach any great height during its flight, and will travel well short of its intended distance. If, however, thin contact is made with a lofted club while attempting to play an approach shot, the result will be the opposite, and invariably the ball will travel beyond its intended target.

Thomson, Peter

Australian Peter Thomson has done more to promote golf in the Far East and Asia than any other man—the flourishing Asia Golf Circuit that now exists bears witness to this.

Peter's experience extends way beyond promoting the sport. He was one of the great players of the 1950s and

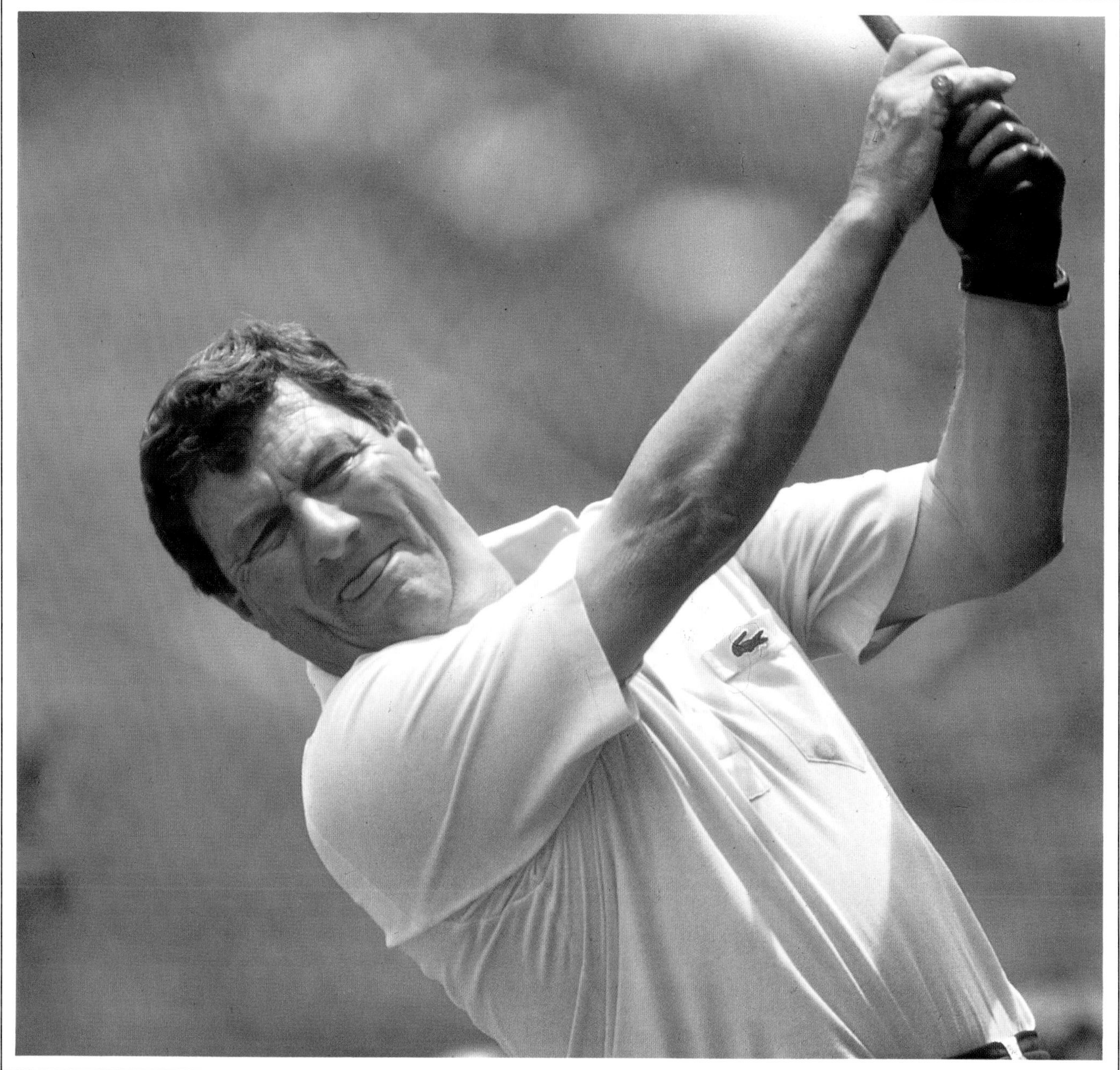

Australian Peter Thomson headed the 1985 US Seniors Tour with winnings in excess of those won in any single year when he was a regular tournament player.

early 1960s. Thomson turned professional in 1949 at the age of 20, and by 1976 he had won the national Open championship of no fewer than nine countries. Ironically he never made it in the United States as a tournament golfer, and consequently was not regarded as one of the 'all-time' greats of the sport.

However, despite his failings in America, he was British Open champion five times, a modern record shared only by Tom Watson. His first victory was at Royal Birkdale in 1954. He then proceeded to win the title three years in succession—the first man since Bob Ferguson, 74 years earlier, to achieve the feat. His fifth and final title was in 1965, again at Birkdale.

He gave up tournament golf in 1979 to take up politics in Australia but, perhaps fortunately, he was not elected as planned, and he returned to golf.

Today he is getting his financial rewards from the game by enjoying life on the United States Seniors tour, of which he was the top money winner in 1985 with over $350,000—far more than he ever won in any one season during his 'non-senior' days.

For his services to golf Peter Thomson has been awarded the MBE.

Career highlights

British Open 1954, 1955, 1956, 1958, 1965
World Cup (team) 1954, 1959
Australian Open 1951, 1967, 1972

Three-ball
A match involving three players who compete against each other. Each plays his own ball.

Threesome
A threesome match is when one player plays against two who take alternate shots at the same ball.

Tie
A match that ends with the scores level, after all the holes have been completed. The final result can remain a tie or, more commonly, be resolved by playing extra holes.
See Play-Off.

Toe
The part of the club-head furthest from the shaft is called the toe, or nose.

Tooting Bec Cup
The Tooting Bec Cup was given to the British Professional Golfers' Association in 1901 and up to 1922 was played as a 36-hole stroke-play competition at different venues. The first winner was J. H. Taylor and the last was George Duncan. James Braid won it a record four times, including three in succession from 1902.

Since 1924, however, the Cup has been presented to the player resident in Great Britain and Ireland who records the lowest round in the British Open. The first recipient of the new award was Ernest Whitcombe for his round of 70 at Hoylake. The first man to receive the Cup for a round of 65 or less was Eric Brown in 1958, for his 65 at Lytham. Christy O'Connor, Jnr, won the Cup with a new record of 64 in 1985, while his uncle, Christy O'Connor, Snr, and Neil Coles have both won the award three times.

Winners (since 1970)

Year	Name	Score	Year	Name	Score
1970	N. Coles	65	1977	T. Horton	65
1971	P. Oosterhuis	66	1978	G. Cullen	67
1972	H. Bannerman	67	1979	B. Longmuir	65
	A. Jacklin	67	1980	K. Brown	68
	G. Hunt	67		B. McColl	68
1973	N. Coles	66		E. Darcy	68
1974	J. Garner	69	1981	G. Brand	65
	P. Townsend	69	1982	A. W. Lyle	66
	J. Morgan	69	1983	D. Durnian	66
1975	M. Bembridge	67	1984	S. Torrance	66
	N. Coles	67	1985	C. O'Connor, Jnr	64
	B. Gallacher	67			
1976	M. James	66			

Top
A ball is said to have been 'topped' when the club strikes the top half of it. The most common cause of topping a ball is the player moving his or her head during the swing. As a result the ball will not leave the ground properly.

Topspin
Topspin, if correctly applied to the ball, will give it extra run once it lands. To impart topspin, however, is not something the ordinary club golfer can do with ease as it necessitates striking the ball in an upward manner, causing the ball to rotate in a forward motion while in flight.

Tournament Players' Championship
The Tournament Players' Championship carries one of the biggest prizes on the United States Tour. Its prize money of over $900,000, including a large first prize ($144,000 in 1985), is bigger than any of the world's four majors. If it were not for the fact that it lacks tradition, it would surely have been the 'Fifth Major' by now.

Played at the Tournament Players' Club, Sawgrass, near Jacksonville, Florida, the headquarters of the US PGA Tour, it was first played in 1974, and attracts one of the best fields for any tournament either side of the Atlantic.

The 1985 winner, Calvin Peete, was the first black golfer to win such an important tournament.

Winners

Year	Name	Score	Year	Name	Score
1974	J. Nicklaus	272	1981	R. Floyd	285
1975	A. Geiberger	270	1982	J. Pate	280
1976	J. Nicklaus	269	1983	H. Sutton	283
1977	M. Hayes	289	1984	F. Couples	277
1978	J. Nicklaus	289	1985	C. Peete	274
1979	L. Wadkins	283	1986	J. Mahaffey	275
1980	L. Trevino	278			

Most wins
3 – Jack Nicklaus (1974, 1976, 1978)

Lowest score (72 holes)
269 – Jack Nicklaus (1976)

Trap
The American word for bunker.

Trevino, Lee
Most sports have, and need, a character like Lee Trevino. He provides the crowds with entertainment at the same time as giving them a first class sporting display.

Born in Dallas, of Mexican parents, 'Supermex' was Rookie of the Year in 1967 and the following year certainly made his presence felt on the US Tour when he won the US Open by four strokes from Jack Nicklaus. He won the title with four rounds all under par—the first time this had been achieved in the history of the championship. In 1971 he enjoyed one of the most successful 21 days ever seen in the history of golf when he won the US, Canadian, and British Open titles. He is the only person to have won all three titles in one year.

His 1971 British Open success, at Birkdale, in which he was involved in a four-day battle with 'Mr Lu' (Lu Liang Huan), was followed by further success the following year at Muirfield. Again it was Nicklaus' challenge he had to beat off to win the title.

Tragedy nearly struck golf's joker in 1975 when he was struck by lightning. The after effects resulted in Trevino undergoing back surgery which hindered his game considerably; it was not until the 1980s that he returned to his old form.

Loved by the British crowds, Trevino enjoys playing in Britain, but he had to endure one of his less pleasant trips to these shores as the non-playing captain of the American Ryder Cup team in 1985. The United States lost the Cup for the first time since 1957.

Career highlights

British Open 1971, 1972
US Open 1968, 1971
US PGA 1974, 1984
World Cup (team) 1969, 1971
(individual) 1969
Ryder Cup 1969, 1971, 1973, 1975, 1979, 1981, 1985 (non-playing capt)

Trick shot specialist Paul Hahn shows off one of his many shots in London in the early 1950s.

Trick Shots

Golf, like many other sports, has given the opportunity for the occasional extrovert to take advantage and turn it into a fun sport. One such exponent is American Paul Hahn, who is by far the world's best known golf 'trick-shot' expert.

A former tournament golfer, he soon took advantage of his ability to communicate with galleries with his quick-witted humour, and moved away from tournament play to the entertainment side of golf.

He has made golf fun, but has added an amazing array of trick shots to his repertoire, many of which the normal professional golfer would never contemplate playing.

Occasionally a professional will be seen playing what appears to be a trick-shot during a tournament. But any such stroke is as a result of his previous shot being a bad one.

Trolley

A relatively new innovation on the golf course, the trolley is a metal framed object with two wheels upon which the golfer puts his bag and clubs. It is pulled by hand and makes the transportation of the clubs easier. In America it is called the Caddie Car.

During the winter months, to protect the fairways, trolleys are often banned, or only those with wide wheels allowed. Consequently, many trolleys have two sets of wheels that can be inter-changed depending upon conditions. Trolleys are *not* permitted on the putting surface and teeing area.

Trolleys became common after the Second World War, and were popularized by Lord Brabazon. A form of trolley was, however, first seen at the turn of the century when a golf bag with wheels was introduced.

Tunisian Open

In the mid-1970s Tunisia possessed just one golf course, at Tunis. Now, as a great testament to the growth of the sport in a country with an ideal golfing climate, the Tunisian Open has recently been the first event on the European Tour each year—even though it is in Africa!

The Open was added to the European calendar in 1982 and that first championship, together with all subsequent ones, was held at the El Kantaoui course at Sousse. Sadly the event was removed from the 1986 calendar.

Winners

Year	Name	Score
1982	A. Garrido	286
1983	M. James	284
1984	S. Torrance	282
1985	S. Bennett	285

Most wins
No man has won more than one title.

Lowest score (72 holes)
282 – Sam Torrance (1984)

Turnberry

The Turnberry Hotel Golf Club, founded in 1903, became, in 1977, the latest course to be used for a first

British Open. On that occasion Tom Watson beat Jack Nicklaus by one stroke and records galore were broken.

Watson's 268 was eight strokes better than the old championship record; Mark Hayes' second round 63 was a championship best; and Watson's last two rounds of 65 and 65 were the lowest 36-hole aggregate in the history of the British Open.

Overlooking the Isle of Arran and the infamous Ailsa Craig, the championship course at Turnberry is called the Ailsa Course. The other 18-hole course is known as the Arran Course.

Had not two world wars intervened, Turnberry could well have been a British Open course many years earlier. But during both hostilities the course was used as an airfield, and was extensively damaged during the Second World War. Only remarkable surgery by designer Mackenzie Ross turned it into a great course; however, it was not until 1951 that Ailsa re-opened.

After being chosen as the venue for the 1960 Home International championships, Turnberry was then selected as host to the Amateur Championship and has since staged most major events including the Walker Cup. It is to play host to the British Open a second time in 1986.

Ailsa Course
Length 6956 yd (6361 m)
Par 70
Course record 63 – Mark Hayes (British Open, 1977)

How the public see Trevino . . .

and how his opponents see him – displaying power and determination.

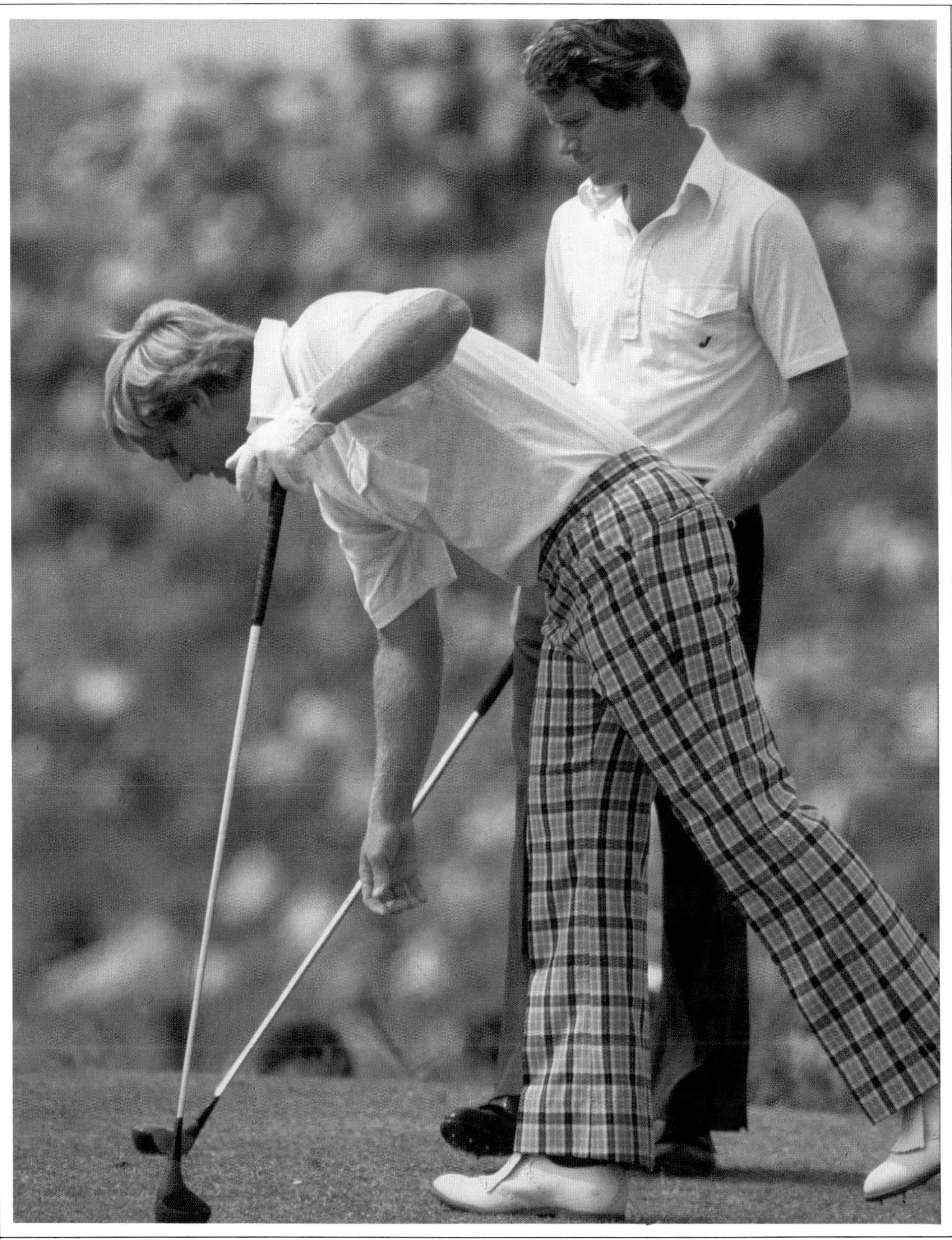

Tom Watson and Jack Nicklaus engaged in a classic confrontation during the first British Open at Turnberry in 1977. Watson eventually won by one stroke.

U

United States Amateur Championship

The first official United States Amateur Championship was held at Newport, Rhode Island in 1895, although two unofficial championships had been held before that date.

Charles Blair Macdonald, a former student at St Andrews University, was the event's first winner. He was succeeded as champion by his son-in-law, H. J. Whigham.

The only British winner of the title has been Harold Hilton who, in 1911, threw away a six-stroke lead over Fred Herreshoff before winning at the first extra hole.

Originally a match-play event the format was changed to stroke-play in 1965, but then reverted to match-play conditions in 1973.

Two men have won the US Amateur title and US Open in the same year. They were Charles Evans Jnr in 1916 and Bobby Jones in 1930.

Some of golf's greats have won the Championship over the years, including Jones, Arnold Palmer and Jack Nicklaus. In recent years current professionals Lanny Wadkins, Craig Stadler, Jerry Pate and Hal Sutton have all won the title. The 1981 winner was Nathaniel Crosby, son of Bing.

United States Golf Association

The United States Golf Association (USGA) was founded in 1894 as the Amateur Golf Association of America. Its first secretary was Henry O. Tallmadge. Like the Royal and Ancient Club in Britain, the USGA is the governing body for the sport in the United States. Also like the R & A it is responsible for the organization of all national championships, including the Open. The two governing bodies, both sides of the Atlantic, liaise well on all matters relating to the rules of golf.

United States Masters

The youngest of the world's four major championships, it is unlike the other three majors in that it is played on the same course each year, the beautiful Augusta National, in Georgia. Also unlike the other three, the Masters is an invitation only event.

The Augusta course and the Masters itself were the brainchild of one of America's greatest golfers, Bobby Jones. And, despite the fact that he had been retired four years, he came out of retirement for the first championship in 1934 to compete and help boost the attendance.

As part of his prize the Masters Champion is presented with a green jacket, one of golf's most treasured prizes.

US Amateur Championship

Winners (Since 1946)

Year	Name	Venue	Score
1946	S. E. Bishop	Baltusrol	37th hole
1947	R. H. Riegel	Pebble Beach	2 & 1
1948	W. P. Turnesa	Memphis	2 & 1
1949	C. R. Coe	Rochester	11 & 10
1950	S. Urzetta	Minneapolis	39th hole
1951	W. J. Maxwell	Saucon Valley	4 & 3
1952	J. Westland	Seattle	3 & 2
1953	G. Littler	Oklahoma City	1 hole
1954	A. Palmer	Detroit	1 hole
1955	E. H. Ward	Richmond	9 & 8
1956	E. H. Ward	Lake Forest	5 & 4
1957	H. Robbins	Brookline	5 & 4
1958	C. R. Coe	San Francisco	5 & 4
1959	J. Nicklaus	Broadmoor	1 hole
1960	D. Beman	St Louis	6 & 4
1961	J. Nicklaus	Pebble Beach	8 & 6
1962	L. E. Harris	Pinehurst	1 hole
1963	D. Beman	Des Moines	2 & 1
1964	W. Campbell	Canterbury	1 hole
1965	R. Murphy	Tulsa	291
1966	G. Cowan	Ardmore	285
1967	R. Dickson	Colorado	285
1968	B. Fleischer	Columbus	284
1969	S. Melnyk	Oakmont	286
1970	L. Wadkins	Portland	279

Year	Name	Venue	Score
1971	G. Cowan	Wilmington	280
1972	M. Giles	Charlotte	285
1973	C. Stadler	Inverness	6 & 5
1974	J. Pate	Ridgewood	2 & 1
1975	F. Ridley	Richmond	2 holes
1976	B. Sander	Bel-Air	8 & 6
1977	J. Fought	Aronimink	9 & 8
1978	J. Cook	Plainfield	5 & 4
1979	M. O'Meara	Canterbury	8 & 7
1980	H. Sutton	North Carolina	9 & 8
1981	N. Crosby	San Francisco	37th hole
1982	J. Sigel	Brookline	8 & 7
1983	J. Sigel	North Shore	8 & 7
1984	S. Verplank	Oak Tree	4 & 3
1985	S. Randolph	Montclair	1 hole

Most wins
5 – Bobby Jones (1924, 1925, 1927, 1928, 1930)

Lowest score (72 holes stroke-play)
279 – Lanny Wadkins (1970)

Biggest Winning Margin (Match-play)
12 & 11 – Charles Blair Macdonald (1895)

Horton Smith, the first winner of the United States Masters tournament in 1934.

Gary Player helping Fuzzy Zoeller on with the coveted Green Jacket after winning the 1979 Masters.

To win the Masters ranks high on any professional golfer's list of achievements, and no man has achieved more than Jack Nicklaus. He first won the title in 1963 as a 23-year-old, the then youngest winner of the title (Severiano Ballesteros was two months younger when he won in 1980), and went on to win the title on four more occasions.

Only three overseas golfers have won the Masters: South African Gary Player, Spain's Severiano Ballesteros (twice), and the 1985 winner Bernhard Langer of West Germany.

Winners

Year	Name	Score	Year	Name	Score
1934	H. Smith	284	1962	A. Palmer	280
1935	G. Sarazen	282	1963	J. Nicklaus	286
1936	H. Smith	285	1964	A. Palmer	276
1937	B. Nelson	283	1965	J. Nicklaus	271
1938	H. Picard	285	1966	J. Nicklaus	288
1939	R. Guldahl	279	1967	G. Brewer	280
1940	J. Demaret	280	1968	B. Goalby	277
1941	C. Wood	280	1969	G. Archer	281
1942	B. Nelson	280	1970	B. Casper	279
1943–45	Not held		1971	C. Coody	279
1946	H. Keiser	282	1972	J. Nicklaus	286
1947	J. Demaret	281	1973	T. Aaron	283
1948	C. Harmon	279	1974	G. Player	278
1949	S. Snead	282	1975	J. Nicklaus	276
1950	J. Demaret	283	1976	R. Floyd	271
1951	B. Hogan	280	1977	T. Watson	276
1952	S. Snead	286	1978	G. Player	277
1953	B. Hogan	274	1979	F. Zoeller	280
1954	S. Snead	289	1980	S. Ballesteros	275
1955	C. Middlecoff	279	1981	T. Watson	280
1956	J. Burke	289	1982	C. Stadler	284
1957	D. Ford	282	1983	S. Ballesteros	280
1958	A. Palmer	284	1984	B. Crenshaw	277
1959	A. Wall	284	1985	B. Langer	282
1960	A. Palmer	282	1986	J. Nicklaus	279
1961	G. Player	280			

Most wins

6 – Jack Nicklaus (1963, 1965, 1966, 1972, 1975, 1986)
4 – Arnold Palmer (1958, 1960, 1962, 1964)
3 – Jimmy Demaret (1940, 1947, 1950)
3 – Sam Snead (1949, 1952, 1954)
3 – Gary Player (1961, 1974, 1978)

Lowest score (72 holes)

271 – Jack Nicklaus (1965)
271 – Ray Floyd (1976)

Lowest individual round

63 – Nick Price (1986)

Best performance by a British golfer

Joint 3rd – Peter Oosterhuis (1973)

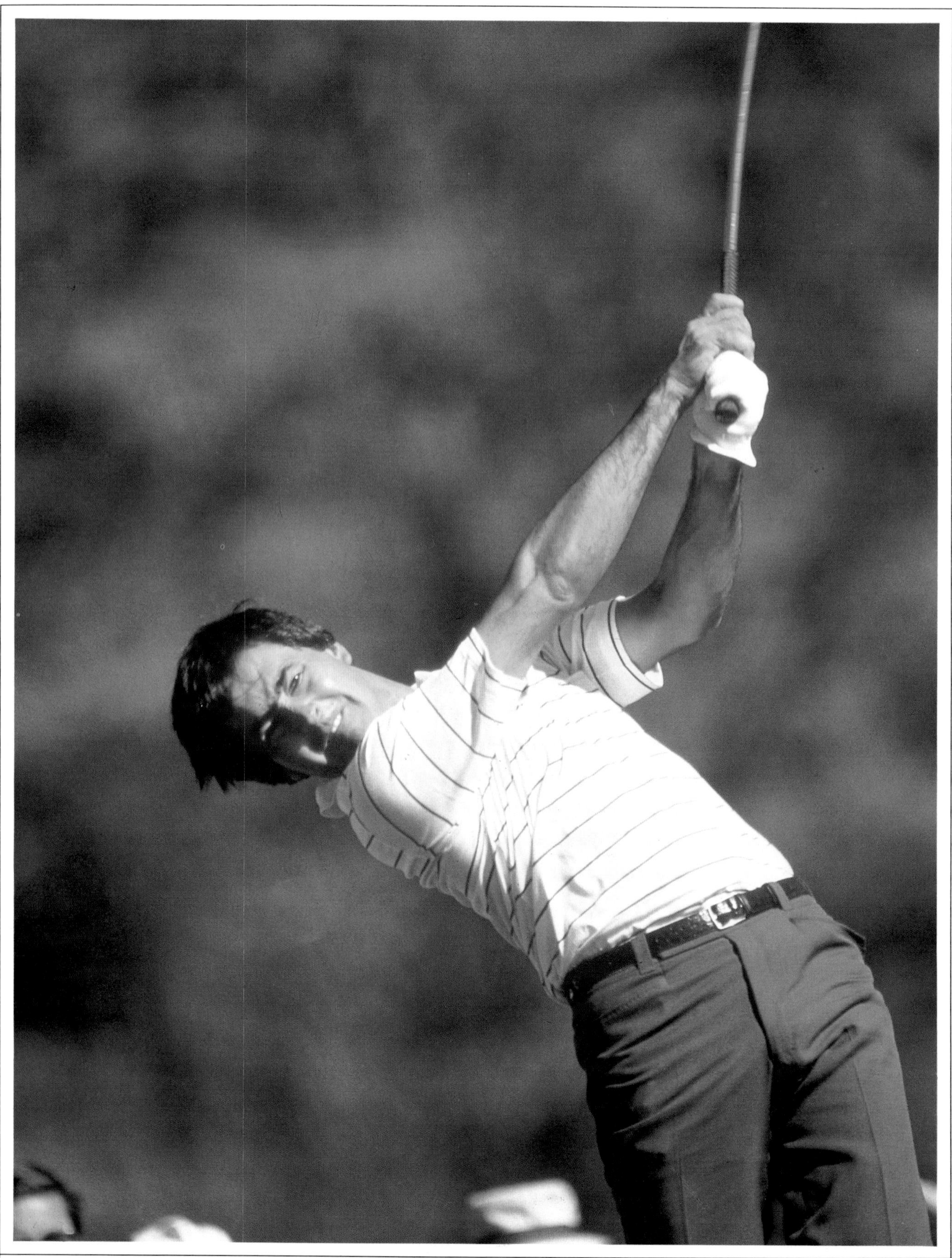

Severiano Ballesteros, Gary Player and Bernhard Langer are the only non-American winners of the US Masters.

Jack Fleck proudly displaying the US Open trophy he won in 1955, beating the favourite, Walter Hagen.

United States Open

The first official US Open was held at Newport, Rhode Island in October 1895. Although it is a stroke-play competition, there was a match-play event in 1894, won by Willie Dunn, which is regarded as the forerunner to the Open.

Unlike the British Open, the rota of courses used for the US Open is much larger. And while the British Open has been staged on just 14 courses, nearly 50 have housed the US championship.

The first winner of the title, and the $150 cheque, was English exile Horace Rawlins. British golfers, exiled in the United States, dominated the Open in its first 16 years and it was not until 1911 that an American-born golfer, Johnny McDermott, won the title.

Over the years the US Open courses have been made deliberately difficult, but despite that a host of surprise winners have emerged. One of them was Francis Ouimet, the 1913 winner.

Held at Brookline, Massachusetts, three men were involved in a play-off: the legendary Harry Vardon, another leading British professional, Ted Ray, and 20-year-old Ouimet, who lived a 'three-iron shot' away from Brookline. It was the local boy who surprised everyone by becoming the first amateur to win the title. He beat Ray by five strokes, and Vardon by six. Perhaps more significantly it ended British domination of the championship. Ted Ray did go on to win the title in 1920, but it was 50 years before another Briton, Tony Jacklin, took the title.

For sheer emotion the 1950 Open must be the most outstanding. Ben Hogan, barely a year after a near-fatal car crash, shot a tremendous round of 69 to win a three way play-off. He was still suffering great pain and discomfort from his injuries.

Although it lacks the same tradition as the British Open, or the appeal of the US Masters, it is still the most prestigious, in terms of financial reward, to any golfer.

Arnold Palmer, in all his successful years as a professional golfer, has only won the US Open once, in 1960.

Tony Jacklin, and family, celebrate his famous victory in the 1970 US Open, the first Briton to win the title for 50 years.

United States Open

Winners

Year	Name	Venue	Score
1895	H. Rawlins	Newport	173(a)
1896	J. Foulis	Shinnecock Hills	152(a)
1897	J. Lloyd	Chicago	162(a)
1898	F. Herd	Myopia Hunt	328
1899	W. Smith	Baltimore	315
1900	H. Vardon	Chicago	313
1901	W. Anderson	Myopia Hunt	331
1902	L. Auchterlonie	Garden City	307
1903	W. Anderson	Baltusrol	307
1904	W. Anderson	Glen View	303
1905	W. Anderson	Myopia Hunt	314
1906	A. Smith	Onwentsia	295
1907	A. Ross	Philadelphia	302
1908	F. McLeod	Myopia Hunt	322
1909	G. Sargent	Englewood	290
1910	A. Smith	Philadelphia	298
1911	J. McDermott	Chicago	307
1912	J. McDermott	Buffalo	294
1913	F. Ouimet(*)	Brookline	304
1914	W. Hagen	Midlothian	290
1915	J. Travers(*)	Baltusrol	297
1916	C. Evans, Jnr(*)	Minikahda	286
1917–18 Not held			
1919	W. Hagen	Brae Burn	301
1920	E. Ray	Inverness	295
1921	J. Barnes	Columbia	289
1922	G. Sarazen	Skokie	288
1923	R. T. Jones(*)	Inwood	296
1924	C. Walker	Oakland Hills	297
1925	W. MacFarlane	Worcester	291
1926	R. T. Jones(*)	Scioto	293
1927	T. Armour	Oakmont	301
1928	J. Farrell	Olympia Fields	294
1929	R. T. Jones(*)	Winged Foot	294
1930	R. T. Jones(*)	Interlachen	287
1931	B. Burke	Inverness	292
1932	G. Sarazen	Fresh Meadow	286
1933	J. Goodman(*)	North Shore	287
1934	O. Dutra	Merion	293
1935	S. Parks	Oakmont	299
1936	T. Manero	Baltusrol	282
1937	R. Guldahl	Oakland Hills	281
1938	R. Guldahl	Cherry Hills	284
1939	B. Nelson	Philadelphia	284
1940	L. Little	Canterbury	287
1941	C. Wood	Colonial	284
1942–45 Not held			
1946	L. Mangrum	Canterbury	284
1947	L. Worsham	St Louis	282
1948	B. Hogan	Riviera	276
1949	C. Middlecoff	Medinah	286
1950	B. Hogan	Merion	287
1951	B. Hogan	Oakland Hills	287
1952	J. Boros	Northwood	281
1953	B. Hogan	Oakmont	283
1954	E. Furgol	Baltusrol	284
1955	J. Fleck	Olympic	287
1956	C. Middlecoff	Oak Hill	281
1957	D. Mayer	Inverness	282
1958	T. Bolt	Southern Hills	283
1959	B. Casper	Winged Foot	282
1960	A. Palmer	Cherry Hills	280
1961	G. Littler	Oakland Hills	281
1962	J. Nicklaus	Oakmont	283
1963	J. Boros	Brookline	293
1964	K. Venturi	Congressional	278
1965	G. Player	Bellerive	282
1966	B. Casper	Olympic	278
1967	J. Nicklaus	Baltusrol	275
1968	L. Trevino	Oak Hill	275
1969	O. Moody	Champions	281
1970	A. Jacklin	Hazeltine	281
1971	L. Trevino	Merion	280
1972	J. Nicklaus	Pebble Beach	290
1973	J. Miller	Oakmont	279
1974	H. Irwin	Winged Foot	287
1975	L. Graham	Medinah	287
1976	J. Pate	Atlanta	277
1977	H. Green	Southern Hills	278
1978	A. North	Cherry Hills	285
1979	H. Irwin	Inverness	284
1980	J. Nicklaus	Baltusrol	272
1981	D. Graham	Merion	273
1982	T. Watson	Pebble Beach	282
1983	L. Nelson	Oakmont	280
1984	F. Zoeller	Winged Foot	276
1985	A. North	Oakland Hills	279
1986	R. Floyd	Shinnecock Hills	279

(a) over 36 holes (*) indicates amateur

Most wins

4 – Willie Anderson (1901, 1903, 1904, 1905)
4 – Bobby Jones (1923, 1926, 1929, 1930)
4 – Ben Hogan (1948, 1950, 1951, 1953)
4 – Jack Nicklaus (1962, 1967, 1972, 1980)

Lowest score (72 holes)

272 – Jack Nicklaus (Baltusrol, 1980)

Lowest rounds

63 – Johnny Miller (Oakmont, 1973)
63 – Tom Weiskopf (Baltusrol, 1980)
63 – Jack Nicklaus (Baltusrol, 1980)

British winners (excluding Britons who became naturalized Americans)

1900 – Harry Vardon
1920 – Ted Ray
1970 – Tony Jacklin

Most frequently used courses

6 – Baltusrol
6 – Oakmont
5 – Oakland Hills
4 – Inverness
4 – Merion
4 – Myopia Hunt
4 – Winged Foot

United States PGA Championship

The US PGA Championship, although one of the world's four major tournaments, is, perhaps, the least prestigious of all the 'majors'.

Part of the US PGA calendar since 1916, the year the US PGA was formed, it is one of the oldest events but admittance is restricted to golfers on the US Tour. An attractive part of winning the PGA title, apart from the £125,000-plus first prize, is exemption from pre-qualifying for PGA events for life.

Between 1916 and 1957 the championship was a match-play event, and the first final was contested by Jim Barnes and Jock Hutchinson, two Britons resident in America. Barnes won by one hole.

By the mid-1950s match-play events were less popular and consequently the championship lost a lot of its appeal to both players and spectators. As a result it was made into a stroke-play event.

The actual trophy presented to the winner is one of the finest seen in any sport, and Walter Hagen has the distinction of winning it the most times—five.

Walter Hagen earned himself the reputation as master of match-play when he started a run of 22 consecutive matches in the US PGA without defeat. The run started in 1924 and ended in the quarter-finals in 1928 when he lost to Leo Diegel. In between he won the title four times. When he lost in 1928 he was asked for the trophy back by the PGA. He replied saying that he'd left it in the back of a taxi in 1925! It was, however, recovered . . .

One of the PGA's all-time great matches was the 1930 final between Tommy Armour and Gene Sarazen. Having been neck-and-neck for 35 of the 36 holes, Armour holed from 14 ft (4 m) at the 36th. Sarazen then had a similar putt, but missed by inches.

Winners

Year	Name	Venue	Score
1916	J. Barnes	Siwanoy	1 hole
1917–18	Not held		
1919	J. Barnes	Engineers	6 & 5
1920	J. Hutchison	Flossmoor	1 hole
1921	W. Hagen	Inwood	3 & 2
1922	G. Sarazen	Oakmont	4 & 3
1923	G. Sarazen	Pelham	38th hole
1924	W. Hagen	French Lick	2 holes
1925	W. Hagen	Olympia Fields	6 & 5
1926	W. Hagen	Salisbury	5 & 3
1927	W. Hagen	Cedar Crest	1 hole
1928	L. Diegel	Five Farms	6 & 5
1929	L. Diegel	Hill Crest	6 & 4
1930	T. Armour	Fresh Meadow	1 hole
1931	T. Creavy	Wannamoisett	2 & 1
1932	O. Dutra	Keller	4 & 3
1933	G. Sarazen	Blue Mound	5 & 4
1934	P. Runyan	Park, NY	38th hole
1935	J. Revolta	Twin Hills	5 & 4
1936	D. Shute	Pinehurst	3 & 2
1937	D. Shute	Pittsburgh	37th hole
1938	P. Runyan	Shawnee	8 & 7
1939	H. Picard	Pomonok	37th hole
1940	B. Nelson	Hershey	1 hole
1941	V. Ghezzi	Cherry Hills	38th hole
1942	S. Snead	Sea View	2 & 1
1943	Not held		
1944	B. Hamilton	Manito	1 hole
1945	B. Nelson	Morraine	4 & 3
1946	B. Hogan	Portland	6 & 4
1947	J. Ferrier	Plum Hollow	2 & 1
1948	B. Hogan	Norwood Hills	7 & 6
1949	S. Snead	Hermitage	3 & 2
1950	C. Harper	Scioto	4 & 3
1951	S. Snead	Oakmont	7 & 6
1952	J. Turnesa	Big Spring	1 hole
1953	W. Burkemo	Birmingham	2 & 1
1954	C. Harbert	Keiller	4 & 3
1955	D. Ford	Meadowbrook	4 & 3
1956	J. Burke	Blue Hill	3 & 2
1957	L. Hebert	Miami Valley	2 & 1

Year	Name	Venue	Score
1958	D. Finsterwald	Llanerch	276
1959	B. Rosburg	Minneapolis	277
1960	J. Hebert	Firestone	281
1961	J. Barber	Olympia Fields	277
1962	G. Player	Aronimink	278
1963	J. Nicklaus	Dallas	279
1964	B. Nichols	Columbus	271
1965	D. Marr	Laurel Valley	280
1966	A. Geiberger	Firestone	280
1967	D. January	Columbine	281
1968	J. Boros	Pecan Valley	281
1969	R. Floyd	NCR, Dayton	276
1970	D. Stockton	Southern Hills	279
1971	J. Nicklaus	PGA National	281
1972	G. Player	Oakland Hills	281
1973	J. Nicklaus	Canterbury	277
1974	L. Trevino	Tanglewood	276
1975	J. Nicklaus	Firestone	276
1976	D. Stockton	Congressional	281
1977	L. Wadkins	Pebble Beach	282
1978	J. Mahaffey	Oakmont	276
1979	D. Graham	Oakland Hills	272
1980	J. Nicklaus	Oak Hill	274
1981	L. Nelson	Atlanta	273
1982	R. Floyd	Southern Hills	272
1983	H. Sutton	Riviera	274
1984	L. Trevino	Shoal Creek	273
1985	H. Green	Cherry Hills	278

Most wins (Match-play)
5 – Walter Hagen (1921, 1924, 1925, 1926, 1927)

Most wins (Stroke-play)
5 – Jack Nicklaus (1963, 1971, 1973, 1975, 1980)

Biggest winning margin (Match-play)
8 & 7 – Paul Runyan beat Sam Snead (Shawnee, 1938)

Lowest score (72 holes, stroke-play)
271 – Bobby Nichols (Columbus, 1964)

Lowest individual round
63 – Bruce Crampton (Firestone, 1975)
63 – Gary Player (Shoal Creek, 1984)

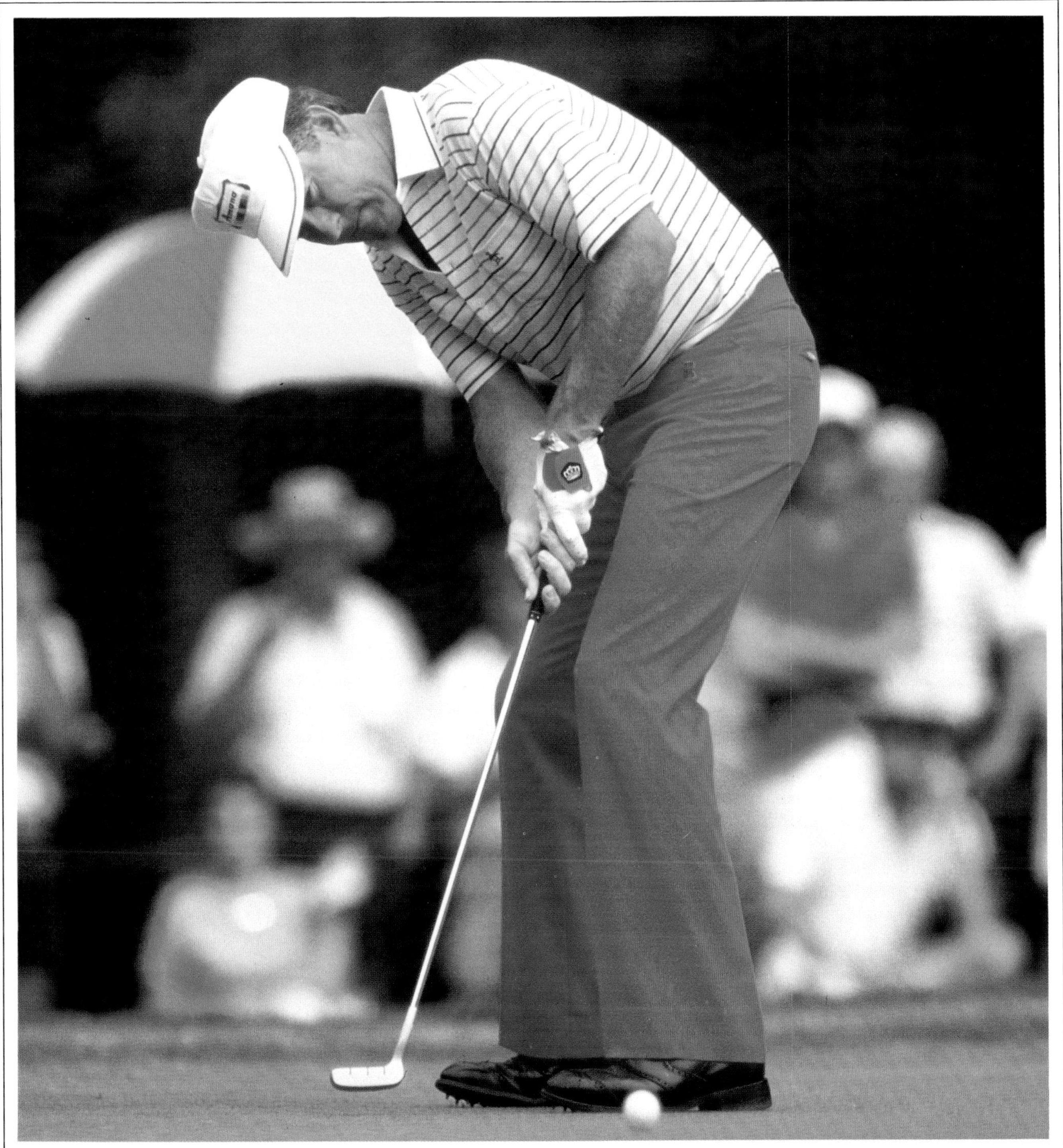

Dave Stockton, the 1976 winner of the United States PGA championship, seen here during the 1984 event.

United States PGA Tour

Strictly speaking the US Tour has been in existence since 1899 when the first Western Open was held. But the forerunner of today's PGA Tour can be traced back to the 1920s when club professionals, after busy summer months, would meet up to play a series of competitions on the West Coast, Texas and in Florida. By the spring they would have moved to the East coast before returning to their clubs for the summer months.

People like Walter Hagen, Gene Sarazen and Bobby Jones, already household names, were attracting a lot of publicity on these tours. By the end of the 1920s the Los Angeles Open, Pensacola Open and Texas Open had joined the Western Open as permanent fixtures on the tour. In the 1930s the Phoenix Open, Bing Crosby Pro-Am, US F&G Classic and Greensboro Open were added.

After the Second World War the tour became more structured and organized. When television showed an interest in PGA events in the late 1950s, they had an enormous effect on prize money as a result of the television rights.

The touring professionals took over the control of tour events in 1968 when they formed the Tournament Players Division. In October 1980 the PGA Tour moved its headquarters to Ponte Vedra, Florida.

So many professionals wanted to join the circuit that a satellite tour had to be introduced which saw the establishment of the PGA School. That school still exists today and players who finish outside the top 125 money-winners, except those exempt players, have to take part in the School to gain admittance to the following year's tour, known as 'getting one's ticket'. The top 50 in the School get their ticket. Britain's Peter Oosterhuis knows only too well the embarrassment of having to take part in the satellite circuit, as he finished outside the top 125 in 1985, and then failed to get his ticket at the PGA School.

The events on the 1985 tour, which carried prize money in the region of $20 million, were:

Bob Hope Classic
Phoenix Open
Los Angeles Open
Bing Crosby National Pro-Am
Hawaiian Open
Isuzu–Andy Williams San Diego Open
Doral–Eastern Open
Honda Classic
Hertz Bay Hill Classic
USF & G Classic
Panasonic Las Vegas Invitational
Tournament Players' Championship
Greater Greensboro Open
The Masters
Sea Pines Heritage Classic
Houston Open
MONY Tournament of Champions
Byron Nelson Classic
Colonial National Invitation
Memorial Tournament
Kemper Open
Manufacturers Hanover Westchester Classic
US Open
Georgia–Pacific Atlanta Classic
St Jude Memphis Classic
Canadian Open
Anheuser-Busch Classic
Miller High Life QCO
Canon-Sammy Davis, Jnr–Greater Hartford Open
Western Open
PGA Championship
Buick Open
NEC World Series of Golf
BC Open
Bank of Boston Classic
Greater Milwaukee Open
LaJet Classic
Texas Open
Southern Open

US Tour Records

Most wins in career
84 – Sam Snead

Most official wins in one year
18 – Byron Nelson (1945)

Most consecutive victories
11 – Byron Nelson (March–August 1945)

Lowest score (72 holes)
257 – Mike Souchak (Texas Open, 1955)

Lowest score (54 holes)
189 – Chandler Harper (Texas Open, 1954)

Lowest score (36 holes)
125 – Ron Streck (Texas Open, 1978)

Lowest score (18 holes)
59 – Al Geiberger (Memphis Classic, 1977)

Lowest score (9 holes)
27 – Mike Souchak (Texas Open, 1955)
27 – Andy North (BC Open, 1975)

Oldest winner
52 yr 10 mth – Sam Snead (Greater Greensboro Open, 1965)

Youngest winner
19 yr 10 mth – Johnny McDermott (US Open, 1911)

Leading money-winners (since 1968)

		$
1968	Billy Casper	205,169
1969	Frank Beard	164,707
1970	Lee Trevino	157,038
1971	Jack Nicklaus	244,491
1972	Jack Nicklaus	320,542
1973	Jack Nicklaus	308,362
1974	Johnny Miller	353,022
1975	Jack Nicklaus	298,149
1976	Jack Nicklaus	266,439
1977	Tom Watson	310,653
1978	Tom Watson	362,429
1979	Tom Watson	462,636
1980	Tom Watson	530,808
1981	Tom Kite	375,699
1982	Craig Stadler	446,462
1983	Hal Sutton	426,668
1984	Tom Watson	476,260
1985	Curtis Strange	542,321

Most times leading money-winner
8 – Jack Nicklaus (1964, 1965, 1967, 1971, 1972, 1973, 1975, 1976)

Walt Disney World Classic
Pensacola Open
Seiko–Tucson Matchplay Championship
Kapalua International
USA v Japan Team Matches
Skins Game
JC Penney Classic
Chrysler Team Invitational

United States Women's Open Championship

This event is the leading championship in women's golf. Although it does not attract the biggest first prize (around $40,000) on the US LPGA circuit, it remains the most prestigious of all the Tour events.

Patty Berg was the first winner in 1946 when, after a stroke-play qualifying competition, it became a match-play event. That was the only occasion match-play rules were adopted. Since then the event has been a 72-hole stroke-play competition.

One of the greatest all-round sportswomen, Mildred Zaharias (qv) won the title on three occasions, in 1948, 1950 and 1954. Her third victory was remarkable because she overcame major cancer surgery in 1953 to win.

There have only been two non-American winners of the title. France's Catherine Lacoste in 1967, and Australia's Jan Stephenson in 1983.

Winners

Year	Name	Venue	Score
1946	P. Berg	Spokane	5 & 4
1947	B. Jameson	Greensboro	295
1948	M. Zaharias	Atlantic City	300
1949	L. Suggs	Maryland	291
1950	M. Zaharias	Wichita	291
1951	B. Rawls	Atlanta	293
1952	L. Suggs	Bala	284
1953	B. Rawls	Rochester	302
1954	M. Zaharias	Peabody	291
1955	F. Crocker	Wichita	299
1956	K. Cornelius	Duluth	302
1957	B. Rawls	Mamaroneck	299
1958	M. Wright	Bloomfield Hills	290
1959	M. Wright	Pittsburgh	287
1960	B. Rawls	Worcester	292
1961	M. Wright	Springfield	293
1962	M. Lindstrom	Myrtle Beach	301
1963	M. Mills	Kenwood	289
1964	M. Wright	San Diego	290
1965	C. Mann	Northfield	290
1966	S. Spuzich	Hazeltine	297
1967	C. Lacoste(*)	Hot Springs	294
1968	S. M. Berning	Moselem Springs	289
1969	D. Caponi	Scenic-Hills	294
1970	D. Caponi	Muskogee	287
1971	J. Gunderson-Carner	Erie	288
1972	S. Berning	Mamaroneck	299
1973	S. Berning	Rochester	290
1974	S. Haynie	La Grange	295
1975	S. Palmer	Northfield	295
1976	J. Carner	Springfield	292
1977	H. Stacy	Hazeltine	292
1978	H. Stacy	Indianapolis	289
1979	J. Britz	Brooklawn	284
1980	A. Alcott	Richland	280
1981	P. Bradley	La Grange	279
1982	J. Alex	Del Paso	283
1983	J. Stephenson	Broken Arrow	290
1984	H. Stacy	Salem	290
1985	K. Baker	Springfield	280

(*) denotes amateur

Most wins

4 – Betsy Rawls (1951, 1953, 1957, 1960)
4 – Mickey Wright (1958, 1959, 1961, 1964)

Lowest score (72 holes)

279 – Pat Bradley (1981)

V

Vardon, Harry

The third member of golf's Great Triumvirate that reigned supreme between 1894 and 1914, Harry Vardon was perhaps the most successful of the three. His record six British Open wins and one US Open certainly put him ahead of his two contempories, Braid and Taylor.

Vardon can rightly be looked upon as the 'father of modern golf' as he brought new techniques to the golf swing. His famous grip, named after him although he did not invent it, is regarded as the correct one by many leading golfers. And his tour of the United States in 1900, when he won the Open, has had a lasting effect on the game: it united golfers and golf fans on both sides of the Atlantic. His techniques have been imitated by many golfers over the years.

Born at Grouville, Jersey, in 1870, his first professional post was at Ripon, Yorkshire. His younger brother Tom was professional at St Annes—the other side of the Peninnes—at the time and he encouraged Harry to make the move north. From Ripon Harry moved to Bury and then Ganton. In 1903 he moved to the South Herts Club and spent the remainder of his career there until his death in 1937. He was the first of the Great Triumvirate to die.

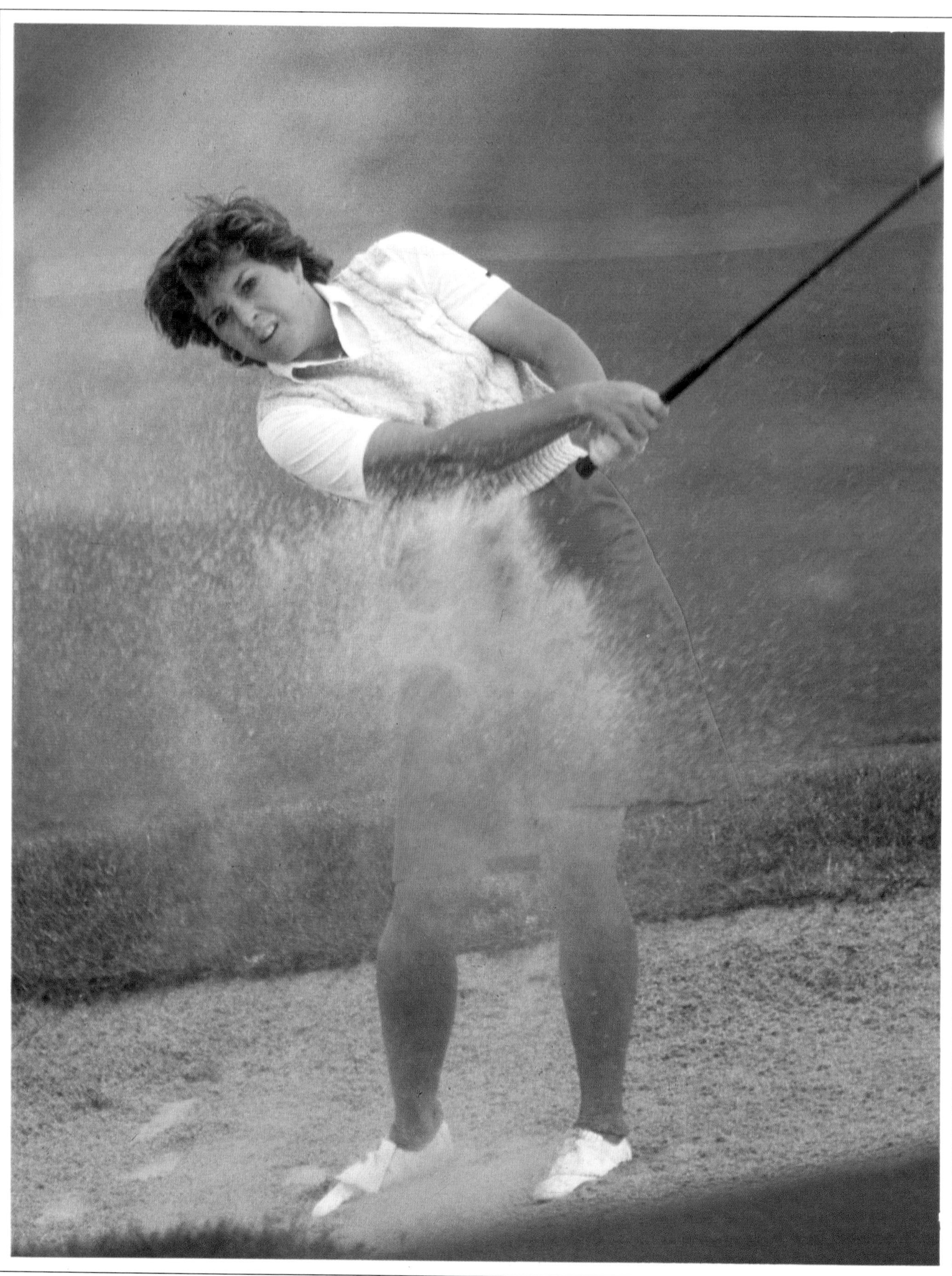

Hollis Stacy on the way to winning her third US Women's Open title in 1984.

Career highlights
British Open 1896, 1898, 1899, 1903, 1911, 1914
US Open 1900
German Open 1911
French Open 1912, 1914

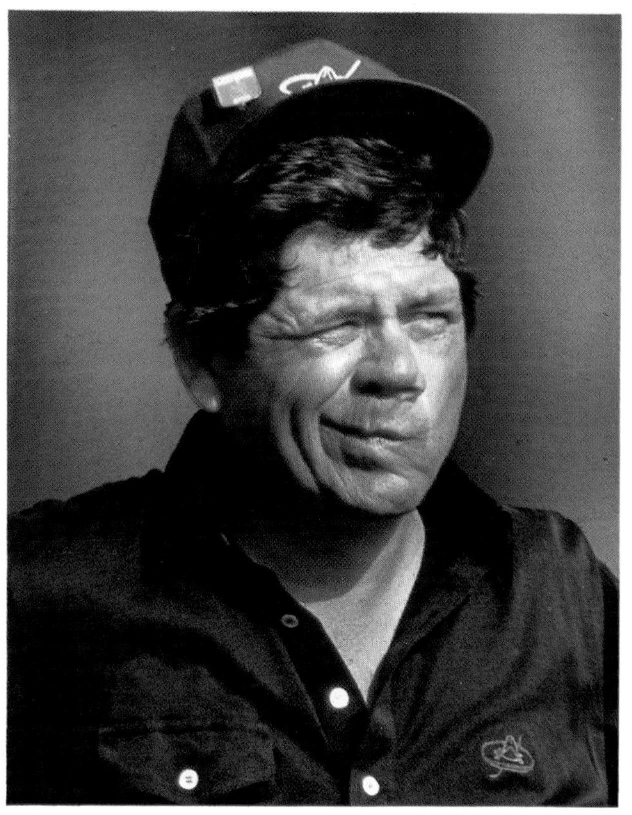

Five times winner of the American Vardon Trophy, Lee Trevino was also the first man to win it three years in succession between 1970 and 1972.

Vardon Trophy

The great Harry Vardon is remembered in the United States and Britain by annual Vardon Trophies.

In the US it is awarded to the PGA member with the lowest stroke average in PGA Tour co-sponsored or approved events during the season.

The Vardon Trophy was awarded for the same reason in Britain until 1971; since then it has been awarded to the PGA member who heads the official money winning list.

The first Vardon Trophies were presented in 1937, and the American version succeeded the Harry A. Radix Trophy, which had been in existence for three years.

Winners (Since 1970)

	US	Britain
1970	Lee Trevino	Neil Coles
1971	Lee Trevino	Peter Oosterhuis
1972	Lee Trevino	Peter Oosterhuis
1973	Bruce Crampton	Peter Oosterhuis
1974	Lee Trevino	Peter Oosterhuis
1975	Bruce Crampton	Dale Hayes
1976	Don January	Severiano Ballesteros
1977	Tom Watson	Severiano Ballesteros
1978	Tom Watson	Severiano Ballesteros
1979	Tom Watson	Sandy Lyle
1980	Lee Trevino	Sandy Lyle
1981	Tom Kite	Bernhard Langer
1982	Tom Kite	Greg Norman
1983	Ray Floyd	Nick Faldo
1984	Calvin Peete	Bernhard Langer
1985	Don Pooley	Sandy Lyle

Most wins (USA)
5 – Bill Casper (1960, 1963, 1965, 1966, 1968)
5 – Lee Trevino (1970, 1971, 1972, 1974, 1980)

Most wins (Britain)
4 – Peter Oosterhuis (1971, 1972, 1973, 1974)

W

Wadkins, Lanny

American Lanny Wadkins has a cool temperament, ideal in a crisis. Understandably he has gained representative honours in both American Walker Cup and Ryder Cup teams.

The 1970 US Amateur Champion, he won the title with a championship record of 279. Ironically, when he won his first and only major professional title, the 1977 US PGA, he did so with the event's *highest* ever total—282.

Lanny turned professional in 1971, but shortly before getting his professional ticket, he finished second in the prestigious Heritage Classic, one of the best results by an amateur in recent years on the US Tour. His first professional year saw him win the Rookie of the Year award, thanks to winnings of $116,616.

In his 1977 US PGA win (the first PGA Championship to be held at Pebble Beach) he beat seasoned-campaigner Gene Littler at the third extra hole in a sudden-death play-off, the first time it had been used to decide one of the major championships.

Lanny's brother Bobby is also a professional golfer. He won the inaugural European Open at Walton Heath in 1978.

Career highlights
US PGA 1977
US Amateur 1970
British Open (best) jt 4th – 1984
Walker Cup 1969, 1971
Ryder Cup 1977, 1979, 1983, 1985

Walker Cup

In 1921 an international match between teams of amateurs from the United States and Great Britain was held on the Royal Liverpool links at Hoylake. The following year the two countries met at Long Island in the first match for the Walker Cup.

An annual event until 1924, it is now played every two years. The trophy was presented by George Herbert Walker, a former president of the United States Golf Association, and it became popularly known as the Walker Cup even though its proper title is The United States Golf Association International Challenge Trophy.

Teams consist of not more than ten players and a captain, and the venue for each competition alternates between the two countries.

The match consists of four foursomes and eight singles matches over 18 holes on each of two days. This format has been adopted since 1963; prior to that play consisted of four foursomes over 36-holes on one day, and eight singles, also over 36-holes, on the second day.

Great Britain's record in the Walker Cup is worse than that in the Ryder Cup. They have won only two, and tied one, of the 30 contests. The last win was under Michael Bonallack's captaincy at St Andrews in 1971. Over the years the United States have inflicted some heavy defeats on the British team, including two 11–1 defeats. The first was in 1928 when Bobby Jones led the winning team, and in 1961 when Jack Westland led the Americans. In 1936 Great Britain failed to win a match for the one and only time in the event, although they did halve three matches.

Results

1922 Long Island, New York
USA 8 W. C. Fownes, capt
GB & NI 4 R. Harris, capt

1923 St Andrews, Scotland
USA 6½ R. A. Gardner, capt
GB & NI 5½ R. Harris, capt

1924 Garden City, New York
USA 9 R. A. Gardner, capt
GB & NI 3 C. J. H. Tolley, capt

1926 St Andrews, Scotland
USA 6½ R. A. Gardner, capt
GB & NI 5½ R. Harris, capt

1928 Chicago GC, Illinois
USA 11 R. T. Jones, Jnr, capt
GB & NI 1 W. Tweddell, capt

1930 Royal St George's, Sandwich
USA 10 R. T. Jones, Jnr, capt
GB & NI 2 R. H. Wethered, capt

1932 Brookline, Massachusetts
USA 9½ F. D. Ouimet, capt
GB & NI 2½ T. A. Torrance, capt

1934 St Andrews, Scotland
USA 9½ F. D. Ouimet, capt
GB & NI 2½ M. Scott, capt

1936 Pine Valley, New Jersey
USA 10½ F. D. Ouimet, capt (*)
GB & NI 1½ W. Tweddell, capt

1938 St Andrews, Scotland
GB & NI 7½ J. B. Beck, capt
USA 4½ F. D. Ouimet, capt (*)

1947 St Andrews, Scotland
(Should have been held in USA, but the Americans agreed to play at St Andrews)
USA 8 F. D. Ouimet, capt (*)
GB & NI 4 J. B. Beck, capt

1949 Winged Foot, New York
USA 10 F. D. Ouimet, capt (*)
GB & NI 2 P. B. Lucas, capt

1951 Royal Birkdale, Southport
USA 7½ W. P. Turnesa, capt (*)
GB & NI 4½ R. Oppenheimer, capt

1953 Kittansett, Massachusetts
USA 9 C. R. Yates, capt (*)
GB & NI 3 A. A. Duncan, capt (*)

1955 St Andrews, Scotland
USA 10 W. C. Campbell, capt (*)
GB & NI 2 G. A. Hill, capt (*)

1957 Minikhada, Minnesota
USA 8½ C. R. Coe, capt (*)
GB & NI 3½ G. H. Micklem, capt (*)

1959 Muirfield, Scotland
USA 9 C. R. Coe, capt
GB & NI 3 G. H. Micklem, capt (*)

1961 Seattle, Washington
USA 11 J. Westland, capt (*)
GB & NI 1 C. D. Lawrie, capt (*)

1963 Turnberry, Scotland
USA 14 R. S. Tufts, capt (*)
GB & NI 10 C. D. Lawrie, capt (*)

1965 Baltimore, Maryland
USA 12 J. W. Fischer, capt (*)
GB & NI 12 J. B. Carr, capt

1967 Royal St George's, Sandwich
USA 15 J. W. Sweetser, capt (*)
GB & NI 9 J. B. Carr, capt

1969 Milwaukee, Wisconsin
USA 13 B. J. Patton, capt (*)
GB & NI 11 M. Bonallack, capt

1971 St Andrews, Scotland
GB & NI 13 M. Bonallack, capt
USA 11 J. M. Winters, Jnr, capt (*)

1973 Brookline, Massachusetts
USA 14 J. W. Sweetser, capt (*)
GB & NI 10 D. M. Marsh, capt

1975 St Andrews, Scotland
USA 15½ E. R. Updegraff, capt (*)
GB & NI 8½ D. M. Marsh, capt

1977 Shinnecock Hills, New York
USA 16 L. W. Dehmig, capt (*)
GB & NI 8 S. C. Saddler, capt (*)

1979 Muirfield, Scotland
USA 15½ R. Siderowf, capt (*)
GB & NI 8½ R. Foster, capt

1981 Cypress Point, California
USA 15 J. Gabrielsen, capt (*)
GB & NI 9 R. Foster, capt (*)

1983 Royal Liverpool, Hoylake
USA 13½ J. Sigel, capt
GB & NI 10½ C. Green, capt (*)

1985 Pine Valley, Philadelphia
USA 13 J. Sigel, capt
GB & NI 11 C. Green, capt (*)

(*) indicates non-playing captain

Wins
United States – 27
Great Britain – 2
Tied – 1

Records – 36 hole matches
Biggest Winning Margins (Team)

USA	– 10: won 11–1 at Chicago, Illinois, 1928
	– 10: won 11–1 at Seattle, Washington, 1961
GB & NI	– 3: won $7\frac{1}{2}$–$4\frac{1}{2}$ at St Andrews, 1938

Biggest Winning Margin (Foursomes)

USA	– 9 & 8: E. H. Ward & J. Westland beat J. D. Langley & A. H. Perowne (1953)
	– 9 & 8: C. R. Coe & W. J. Patton beat M. Bonallack & A. H. Perowne (1959)
GB & NI	– 6 & 5: C. J. H. Tolley & R. H. Wethered beat F. D. Ouimet & J. D. Sweetser (1923)

Biggest Winning Margins (Singles)

USA	– 13 & 12: R. T. Jones, Jnr beat T. P. Perkins (1928)
GB & NI	– 9 & 8: G. B. Peters beat R. Smith (1938)

Records – 18 hole matches
Biggest Winning Margins (Team)

USA	– 8: won 16–8 at Shinnecock Hills, 1977
GB & NI	– 2: won 13–11 at St Andrews, 1971

Biggest Winning Margin (Foursomes)

USA	– 7 & 6: B. Lewis & J. Holtgrieve beat M. Lewis & M. Thompson (1983)
GB & NI	– 6 & 5: P. Baker & P. McEvoy beat R. Sonnier & J. Haas (1985)

Biggest Winning Margins (Singles)

USA	– 9 & 7: S. Hoch beat J. Buckley (1979)
GB & NI	– 7 & 5: J. B. Carr beat R. H. Sikes (1963)

Most appearances

USA	– 8: Francis Ouimet (1922–34) (Ouimet was also non-playing captain in 1936, 1938, 1947 and 1949)
GB & NI	– 10: Joe Carr (1947–67) (In addition, Carr was captain in 1965, but did not play)

Walton Heath

Founded in 1904, Walton Heath was fortunate to have the legendary James Braid as its professional from then until his death in 1950.

Two 18-hole courses, the Old and the New, provide fine golf at Walton-on-the-Hill in Surrey which, surprisingly for an inland course, is affected by strong winds.

The club was owned by the Carr family, owners of the *News of the World*, for many years. Consequently it was the home of the News of the World British Match-Play Championship between 1903 and 1969, when they discontinued their sponsorship.

Being a parkland course, admission money could not be charged. The club, however, eventually passed ownership from the Carr family to its members and they sought an Act of Parliament which granted permission to enclose the course and charge admission money for one week of the year. Consequently professional championship golf returned to Walton Heath in 1978 when Bobby Wadkins won the inaugural European Open.

Old course
Length 6813 yd (6230 m)
Par 73
Course record 65 – Peter Townsend (Pro-Am, 1976)

Water Hazards

The rules of golf define a water hazard as: 'Any sea, lake, pond, river, ditch, surface drainage ditch, or other open water course (whether or not containing water) and anything of a similar nature.'

The margin of a water hazard is deemed to extend vertically upwards, and all water hazards should be defined by yellow stakes or lines. This does not apply to lateral water hazards.

See also Hazards, Lateral Water Hazards.

Watson, Tom

Tom Watson succeeded Jack Nicklaus as the world's most successful golfer. His record of five British Open wins (just one short of Harry Vardon's record), two US Masters titles, and one US Open success, all in a space of eight years, confirm his dominance. In addition he was top money-winner in the United States four years in succession between 1977 and 1980, and when a decline took him to third, fifth and then 12th there was much talk that he was on his way out. But Watson defied all the critics by topping the list for the fifth time in 1984 with $476,226.

Born in Kansas City in 1949, he was only six years old when his father first introduced him to the sport. He turned professional in 1971 and won his first US PGA Tour event, the Western Open, in 1974. Since then he has won over 30 events on the Tour to put him in the all-time top ten.

Watson's first major championship was the 1975 British Open when he beat Australian Jack Newton in a play-off. Two years later he won the first Open to be held at Turnberry, with a championship record score of 268, after a nail-biting battle with Jack Nicklaus. Three months earlier he had been involved in another close battle with Nicklaus—to win the US Masters.

His third British Open success was in 1980 when he won by four strokes from Lee Trevino at Muirfield. Watson was again champion at Troon two years later when he beat Britain's Peter Oosterhuis by one stroke. And at Birkdale in 1983 Watson won his fifth Open, and his first in England. In between he had won the Masters for the second time and in 1982 completed the rare British/US Open double when he won his first American Open title, at Pebble Beach. Once more it was his great rival Nicklaus who occupied the runners-up position.

The former psychology graduate from Stanford

University has now won nearly $4 million from golf and, when time permits, he escapes from the golf course to enjoy his pastimes of hunting and fishing.

Career highlights
British Open 1975, 1977, 1980, 1982, 1983
US Open 1982
US Masters 1977, 1981
Ryder Cup 1977, 1981, 1983

Wedge

In the 1930s, Gene Sarazen devised a club with a deep face and flanged sole for playing out of bunkers. This club was later modified and is today known as the wedge.

There are two forms of wedge; the sand wedge (also known as sand iron) and pitching wedge. The sand wedge has a slightly deeper face than the pitching wedge. The design of the pitching wedge enables the golfer to play lofted shots from the fairway to the green, and get the ball to stop on landing. In the case of the sand wedge, one can get under the ball to propel it out of the sand and on to the green, without too much run upon landing.

Weiskopf, Tom

One of golf's nice guys, Tom Weiskopf has been on the professional circuit for over 20 years. He turned professional in 1964 and became one of the most consistent golfers on the US Tour.

Possessor of one of golf's finest swings, his consistency kept him in the top 20 money-winners in the US throughout most of the 1970s. In 1973 he enjoyed his most successful year. Not only was he third in the money list with a personal best tally of $245,463, but in an eight-week period he won five events: The Colonial National, Kemper Open, Philadelphia Classic, Canadian Open, and the British Open.

The previous year, at Wentworth, he had enjoyed a 4 and 3 victory over fellow American Lee Trevino in the final of the World Match-Play Championship. He was back in Britain in 1973 for the Open at Troon and led from start to finish to win his first, and only, major. He also equalled the championship record of 276.

American majors have eluded Weiskopf, however, although he once finished second in the US Open, and four times was runner-up in the Masters.

Since the late 1970s Tom's position on the US money-winning list has declined dramatically, but that is attributable to the fact that he has been spending more time with his family, and taking part in his favourite pastime —hunting elk. He has also turned his attention to golf course design, and is an expert summarizer for CBS television.

Career highlights
British Open 1973
Canadian Open 1973, 1975
World Match-Play 1972
Ryder Cup 1973, 1975

Wentworth

Mention Wentworth and most golfers will immediately think of the World Match-Play Championship. Admittedly the event has been played over the Surrey course since its inception in 1964, but other important events have been held at the club. In 1926 Great Britain defeated the United States in an international match. This turned out to be the forerunner of the Ryder Cup, held for the first time the following year. The Ryder Cup itself came to the Virginia Water course in 1953 and the Canada Cup (now the World Cup) was played at the course in 1956—the only occasion it has been held in England. Wentworth was also the venue for the first Curtis Cup match in 1932.

One of the newest of the clubs in the London area, Wentworth was only opened in 1924 and now has two 18-hole courses, the East (which was the first of the two) and the West—the latter, because of its severe trek of nearly 7000 yd (6400 m), is known as the Burma Road. There is also a short nine-hole course. Although the West course was added in the 1930s it was not until after the war that it became recognized as a championship course. Its 17th hole is regarded by Arnold Palmer as one of the best par-5s in championship golf.

West course
Length 6945 yd (6351 m)
Par 72
Course record 64 – Howard Clark (Whyte and Mackay PGA, 1984)

Westchester Classic

The Westchester Classic, or to give it its full title, the Manufacturers Hanover Westchester Classic, is a mid-season tournament played over the West Course at the Westchester Country Club, Harrison, New York.

First introduced into the US PGA Tour in 1967, it now carries a first prize of $90,000 out of a total prize fund of $500,000.

Jack Nicklaus was the first and second winner, while Julius Boros, aged 48, won the next title. He nearly won the title again in 1975 but lost the play-off to Gene Littler. The Westchester Classic has fond memories for Tom Weiskopf: during the 1974 event he surpassed career earnings of $1 million when he finished third.

Winners (since 1970)

Year	Name	Score	Year	Name	Score
1970	B. Crampton	273	1978	L. Elder	274
1971	A. Palmer	270	1979	J. Renner	277
1972	J. Nicklaus	270	1980	C. Strange	273
1973	B. Nichols	272	1981	R. Floyd	275
1974	J. Miller	269	1982	B. Gilder	261
1975	G. Littler	271	1983	S. Ballesteros	276
1976	D. Graham	272	1984	S. Simpson	269
1977	A. North	272	1985	R. Maltbie	275

Most wins
2 – Jack Nicklaus (1967, 1972)

Lowest score (72 holes)
261 – Bob Gilder (1982)

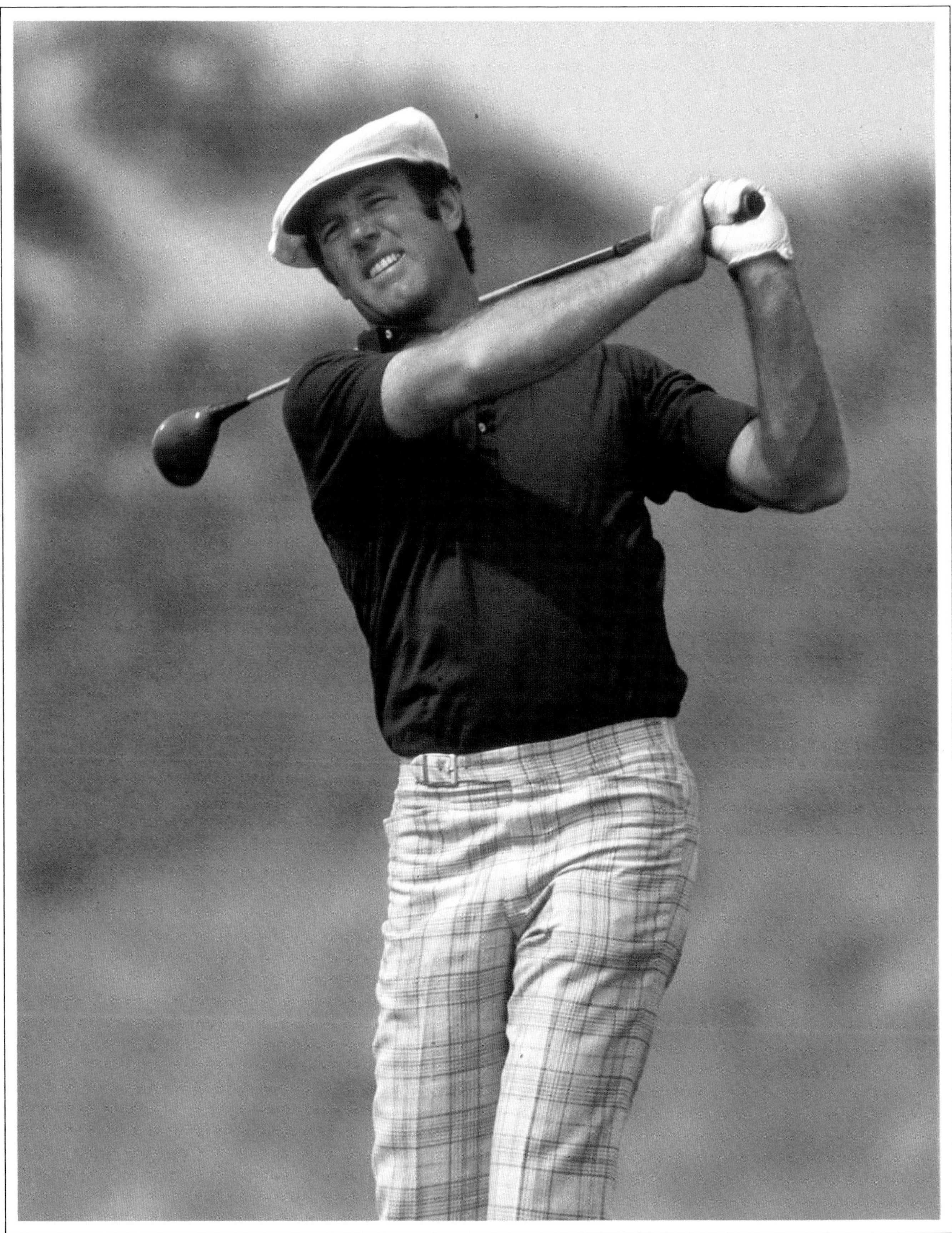

After 20 years on the US Tour, Tom Weiskopf is spending more time these days engaging in his favourite pastime – big game hunting.

Western Open

After the United States Open, the Western Open is the oldest continuous professional event in America. Held in either July or August at the Butler National Golf Club, Oak Brook, Illinois, the first competition was in 1899, four years after the Open. It was won by Willie Smith of Scotland, who also took that year's US Open.

Tom Watson has won the Western Open on three occasions. His first win, in 1974, was his first success on the US Tour.

Scott Verplank struck a mighty blow for amateur golfers when he won the title in 1985. He beat Jim Thorpe in a play-off to become the first amateur to win on the US Tour since 1954 when Gene Littler won the San Diego Open. Verplank became the second amateur to win the Western Open. The first was Charles Evans, Jnr, who won in 1910, one of just two occasions the championship was contested on a match-play basis.

Unlike most other US events it does not attract commercial sponsorship. Its long tradition maintains it as one of the top events on the US Tour.

Winners (Since 1970)

Year	Name	Score
1970	H. Royer	273
1971	B. Crampton	279
1972	J. Jamieson	271
1973	B. Casper	272
1974	T. Watson	287
1975	H. Irwin	283
1976	A. Geiberger	288
1977	T. Watson	283
1978	A. Bean	282
1979	L. Nelson	286
1980	S. Simpson	281
1981	E. Fiori	277
1982	T. Weiskopf	276
1983	M. McCumber	284
1984	T. Watson	280
1985	S. Verplank (*)	279

(*) denotes amateur

Most wins
5 – Walter Hagen (1916, 1921, 1926, 1927, 1932)

Lowest score (72 holes)
268 – Sam Snead (1949)
268 – Juan Rodriguez (1964)

Winged Foot

Situated north of New York, at Mamaronech, Winged Foot is one of America's most famous golf clubs. Founded in the 1920s by members of the New York Athletic Club—it was from their emblem that the club took its name—Winged Foot has two 18-hole courses, the East and the West. While the West is the longer, as well as being the championship course, many members regard the East as the better of the two.

The US Open has been played at Winged Foot on four occasions. The first was in 1929 when Bobby Jones won his third title, while Billy Casper was the next winner, in 1959. Hale Irwin took his first title in 1974 and ten years later Fuzzy Zoeller beat Greg Norman in a play-off to win his first Open.

Other major events have been held at Winged Foot including the US Amateur Championship, US Ladies' Championship, and the Walker Cup.

West course
Length 6930 yd (6337 m)
Par 70
Course record 64 – Jug McSpaden (Goodall Tournament, 1946)

Winter Rules

During the winter months, club committees normally issue local rules in order to protect the course from adverse weather conditions.

The most widely adopted are the introduction of preferred lies (qv), the banning of trolleys (qv) or the insistence that they have wide wheels, and the laying out of winter greens, normally on the fairway and in front of the existing green. Winter greens are inferior to the quality of the normal greens, but act as an adequate temporary replacement.

Women's World Amateur Team Championship

Played by amateur teams of not more than three players, the Women's World Amateur Team Championship was introduced in Paris in 1964 and is held every two years.

They play for the Espirito Santo Trophy, named after Mrs Ricardo Santo of Portugal who donated it. The tournament is over four days, with each team member playing 18 holes per day; the aggregate score of the best two each day counts towards the team total.

The United States have dominated the event, like most other golf team competitions, with nine wins from the 11 championships so far.

Results

Year	Winners	Venue	Score
1964	France	France	588
1966	United States	Mexico	580
1968	United States	Australia	616
1970	United States	Spain	598
1972	United States	Argentina	583
1974	United States	Dominican Republic	620
1976	United States	Portugal	605
1978	Australia	Fiji	596
1980	United States	United States	588
1982	United States	Switzerland	579
1984	United States	Hong Kong	585

Most wins (Team)
9 – United States

Most wins (Individual)
3 – Jane Banstenchury-Booth – US (1968, 1970, 1972)

Lowest aggregate team score
579 – United States (1982)

Lowest individual score (72 holes)
289 – Marlene Stewart (Canada) 1966

Tom Watson (right) and Jack Newton were all-square after 72 holes at the end of the 1975 British Open and both pose with the trophy. After an extra round, it became Watson's for the first time.

Woods

A golfer is allowed to carry a maximum of 14 clubs in his bag. Normally this number is made up of ten irons (including the putter) and four woods.

Wooden-headed clubs have been replaced by nylon, or other composite, heads, but are still referred to as woods.

At one time the wooden clubs had splendid names like brassie, spoon and baffy but today, woods, like irons, are numbered according to the degree of loft of the club-face. The No 1 wood, the driver (qv), has the smallest angle, approximately 10 degrees, and so on.

Until the 1970s it was rare to see anything higher than a No 4 wood. Now No 5, and even up to No 8, woods are to be found. The latter would have an equivalent loft to that of a No 7 iron.

Naturally, with having bigger, solid heads, one can obtain greater distance with wooden clubs, and they are popular for playing long second shots from the fairway. But the average club golfer has difficulty in playing such a shot. In fact many club golfers dislike using the driver, and prefer to drive with a No 2 wood.

Equivalents of Old-Named Wooden Clubs to Modern Day Ones

No 2 wood – Brassie
No 3 wood – Spoon
No 4 wood – Baffy

World Amateur Team Championship

First held in 1958, the World Amateur Team Championship is contested every two years and the winning team receives the Eisenhower Trophy named after and presented by the former United States President Dwight D. Eisenhower (qv).

Participating nations consist of four-man teams of amateur players and each plays 72 holes over four days. The best three scores count towards the team's aggregate score. Again, the event has been dominated by the United States who have won the trophy on nine occasions.

Some famous names have appeared in winning American teams over the years. Jack Nicklaus was a member of the first United States team to win the trophy in 1960. Tom Kite and Lanny Wadkins were both members of the

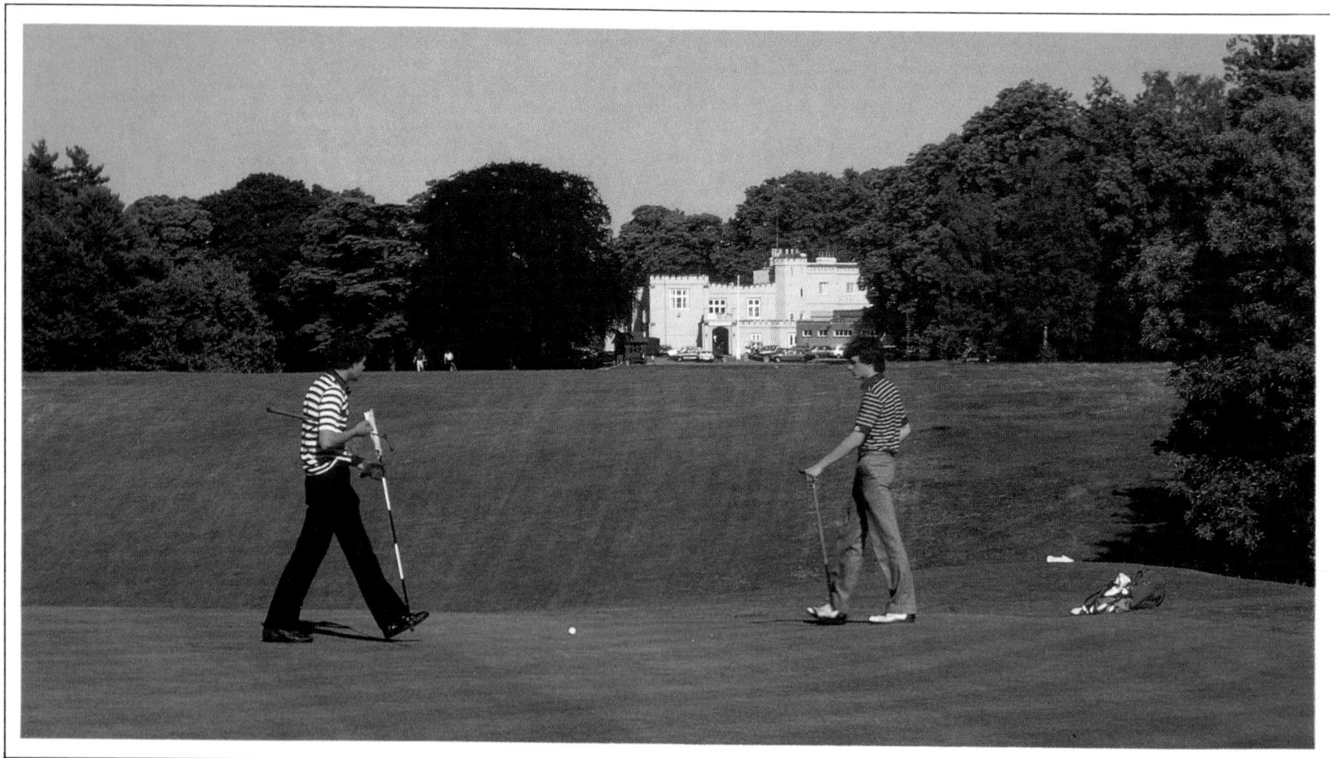

View of the Wentworth clubhouse from the green of the 1st hole on the West course.

World Amateur Team Championship

Year	Winning Team	Score	Venue	Leading Individual	Score
1958	Australia	918	Scotland	B. Devlin (Australia)	301
				R. Jack (Scotland)	301
				W. Hyndman (US)	301
1960	United States	834	US	J. Nicklaus (US)	269
1962	United States	854	Japan	G. Cowan (Canada)	280
1964	GB & Ireland	895	Italy	Min Nan Hsieh (Formosa)	294
1966	Australia	877	Mexico	R. D. B. M. Shade (GB)	281
1968	United States	868	Australia	M. F. Bonallack (GB)	286
				M. Giles (US)	286
1970	United States	857	Spain	V. Regaldo (Mexico)	280
1972	United States	865	Argentina	A. Gresham (Australia)	285
1974	United States	888	Dominican Republic	J. Pate (US)	294
				J. Gonzalez (Brazil)	294
1976	GB & Ireland	892	Portugal	I. Hutcheon (GB)	293
				T. M. Chen (Taiwan)	293
1978	United States	873	Fiji	R. Clampett (US)	287
1980	United States	848	USA	H. Sutton (US)	276
1982	United States	859	Switzerland	L. Carbonetti (Argentina)	284
1984	Japan	870	Hong Kong	L. Carbonetti (Argentina)	286

Most wins (Team)
9 – United States

Most wins (Individual)
3 – Vinny Giles, US (1968, 1970, 1972)
3 – Jay Sigel, US (1978, 1980, 1982)

Most wins of individual title
2 – L. Carbonetti, Argentina (1982, 1984)

Lowest score (Team)
834 – US (D. Beman, J. W. Nicklaus, W. Hyndman, R. Gardner), 1960

Lowest individual score (72 holes)
269 – Jack Nicklaus, US (1960)

1970 winning team, while Ben Crenshaw and Mark Hayes were in the team two years later. Since then top professionals Jerry Pate, Curtis Strange, Gary Koch, Hal Sutton and Bob Clampett have figured in winning teams.

World Cup

American industrialist John Jay Hopkins saw, in the early 1950s, that more and more countries were playing golf. He therefore felt the sport was ready for another professional international team competition. There was only the Ryder Cup at the time, and that only involved professional players from Great Britain and the United States.

So, in 1953, seven nations responded to his invitation to send two-man teams to Montreal for the first Canada Cup, as it was then called. (It became the World Cup in 1967).

Argentina won the first title when their team of Roberto de Vicenzo and Antonio Cerda beat Canada by ten strokes. Cerda was the first winner of the individual title.

Although carrying a grand title, it does not match up to its name in prestige, and in recent years many leading golfers have snubbed the event. The format is four 18-hole stroke-play rounds for each team member (in 1953 it was over two rounds each), and their aggregate scores count towards the team total.

Results

Year	Winning Team	Score	Venue	Leading Individual	Score
1953	Argentina	287	Canada	A. Cerda (Argentina)	140
1954	Australia	556	Canada	S. Leonard (Canada)	275
1955	United States	560	US	E. Furgol (US)	279
1956	United States	567	England	B. Hogan (US)	277
1957	Japan	557	Japan	T. Nakamura (Japan)	274
1958	Ireland	579	Mexico	A. Miguel (Spain)	286
1959	Australia	563	Australia	S. Leonard (Canada)	275
1960	United States	565	Ireland	F. van Donck (Belgium)	279
1961	United States	560	Puerto Rico	S. Snead (US)	272
1962	United States	557	Argentina	R. de Vicenzo (Argentina)	276
1963	United States	482(a)	France	J. Nicklaus (US)	237(a)
1964	United States	554	Hawaii	J. Nicklaus (US)	276
1965	South Africa	571	Spain	G. Player (South Africa)	281
1966	United States	548	Japan	G. Knudson (Canada)	272
1967	United States	557	Mexico	A. Palmer (US)	276
1968	Canada	569	Italy	A. Balding (Canada)	274
1969	United States	552	Singapore	L. Trevino (US)	275
1970	Australia	544	Argentina	R. de Vicenzo (Argentina)	269
1971	United States	555	USA	J. Nicklaus (US)	271
1972	Taiwan	438(b)	Australia	Min-Nan Hsieh (Taiwan)	217(b)
1973	United States	558	Spain	J. Miller (US)	277
1974	South Africa	554	Venezuela	B. Cole (South Africa)	271
1975	United States	554	Thailand	J. Miller (US)	275
1976	Spain	574	USA	E. Acosta (Mexico)	282
1977	Spain	591	Philippines	G. Player (South Africa)	289
1978	United States	564	Hawaii	J. Mahaffey (US)	281
1979	United States	575	Greece	H. Irwin (US)	285
1980	Canada	572	Colombia	A. W. Lyle (Scotland)	282
1981	Not held				
1982	Spain	563	Mexico	M. Pinero (Spain	281
1983	United States	565	Indonesia	D. Barr (Canada)	276
1984	Spain	414(b)	Italy	J.-M. Canizares (Spain)	205(b)
1985	Canada	559	USA	H. Clark (England)	272

(a) play curtailed to 63 holes
(b) play curtailed to 54 holes

Most wins (Team)
16 – United States

Most wins (Individual)
6 – Arnold Palmer, USA (1960, 1962, 1963, 1964, 1966, 1967)
6 – Jack Nicklaus, USA (1963, 1964, 1966, 1967, 1971, 1973)

Most wins of individual title
3 – Jack Nicklaus, USA (1963, 1964, 1971)

Lowest score-team (over four complete rounds)
544 – Australia (B. Devlin & D. Graham), 1970

Lowest individual score (72 holes)
269 – Roberto de Vicenzo (Argentina), 1970

World Match-Play Championship

With a cast of just 12 leading players, the end-of-season World Match-Play Championship at Wentworth attracts large crowds, and has done so every year since its inception in 1964.

Originally just eight invited players took part. All matches, played on a knockout basis, consist of 36 holes; 18 in the morning and the same in the afternoon.

The first prize money of £50,000 was bettered only by the British Open on the European PGA Tour in 1985.

One of the dominating figures of the World Match-Play Championship is Gary Player. In the ten years from 1965 he won it five times, and was defeated in one other final. Only the record of Seve Ballesteros, with four wins since 1981 can compare with the South African's achievement.

During the 1979 championship, Japan's Isao Aoki lifted the biggest prize of his career—and he was the beaten finalist! A hole-in-one at the second won him a special prize of a flat and furnishings valued at £55,000. The event has had three sponsors over the years: Piccadilly sponsored it between 1964–76; Colgate took over for 1977 and 1978; and since 1979 the sponsors have been Suntory.

Winners & Runners-Up

Year	Name	Runner-up	Score
1964	A. Palmer	N. Coles	2 & 1
1965	G. Player	P. Thomson	3 & 2
1966	G. Player	J. Nicklaus	6 & 4
1967	A. Palmer	P. Thomson	1 hole
1968	G. Player	R. Charles	1 hole
1969	R. Charles	G. Littler	37th hole
1970	J. Nicklaus	L. Trevino	2 & 1
1971	G. Player	J. Nicklaus	5 & 4
1972	T. Weiskopf	L. Trevino	4 & 3
1973	G. Player	G. Marsh	40th hole
1974	H. Irwin	G. Player	3 & 1
1975	H. Irwin	A. Geiberger	4 & 2
1976	D. Graham	H. Irwin	38th hole
1977	G. Marsh	R. Floyd	5 & 3
1978	I. Aoki	S. Owen	3 & 2
1979	B. Rogers	I. Aoki	1 hole
1980	G. Norman	A. W. Lyle	1 hole
1981	S. Ballesteros	B. Crenshaw	1 hole
1982	S. Ballesteros	A. W. Lyle	37th hole
1983	G. Norman	N. Faldo	3 & 2
1984	S. Ballesteros	B. Langer	2 & 1
1985	S. Ballesteros	B. Langer	6 & 5

Most wins

5 – Gary Player (1965, 1966, 1968, 1971, 1973)

Biggest winning margin

11 & 9 – Tom Watson v. Dale Hayes (1st Round, 1979)

Biggest winning margin (Final)

6 & 5 – Severiano Ballesteros v. Bernhard Langer (1985)

World Series of Golf

Carrying a first prize of $126,000, the NEC World Series of Golf is one of the richest tournaments in the United States. It is played each year, normally in August, at the Firestone Country Club, Akron, Ohio. The club was constructed in the mid-1920s by Harvey Firestone, Snr, who had the course laid out for use by employees at his Firestone Tyre and Rubber Company.

The first World Series was played in 1962 when just four men took part in a 36-hole exhibition. This format remained until 1975. The following year it became a 72-hole stroke-play competition involving the winners of all

One of the all-time greatest women golfers – Mickey Wright.

Winners (Since 1970)

Year	Name	Score
1970	J. Nicklaus	136
1971	C. Coody	141
1972	G. Player	142
1973	T. Weiskopf	137
1974	L. Trevino	139
1975	T. Watson	140
1976	J. Nicklaus	275
1977	L. Wadkins	267
1978	G. Morgan	278
1979	L. Hinckle	272
1980	T. Watson	270
1981	B. Rogers	275
1982	C. Stadler	278
1983	N. Price	270
1984	D. Watson	271
1985	R. Maltby	268

Most wins
5 – Jack Nicklaus (1962, 1963, 1967, 1970, 1976)

Lowest score (72 holes)
267 – Lanny Wadkins (1977)

Lowest score (36 holes)
135 – Jack Nicklaus (1962)

US Tour events, including the three majors, and winners of important events in other countries, thus ensuring a quality field.

Jack Nicklaus was the winner of the new-style event, just as he was the winner of the original tournament in 1962.

Wright, Mickey

Mickey Wright must surely rank as one of the greatest of all women golfers. Her record of four United States Women's Open and four Ladies' PGA titles is ample evidence.

Born in San Diego as Mary Kathryn Wright in 1935, her father had decided they were having a boy, to be named Michael, and so she was called Mickey. She turned professional in 1954, after winning the amateur title, and added a new dimension to ladies' golf in the United States. Her long and powerful hitting was something not seen before. She won the US Women's Open on four occasions and won 82 tournaments throughout her career, including a record 13 in 1963. She was the top US money winner four times between 1961–4. Mickey finished playing tournament golf in 1978.

Career highlights
US Women's Open 1958, 1959, 1961, 1964
US Ladies' PGA 1958, 1960, 1961, 1963
US Women's Amateur 1954

Youngest Players

The following have been the youngest winners of major championships:

British Open
17 years 160 days – Tom Morris, Jnr (Prestwick, 1868)

United States Open
19 years 319 days – John McDermott (Chicago, 1911)

United States Masters
23 years 4 days – Severiano Ballesteros (1980)

United States PGA
20 years 172 days – Gene Sarazen (Oakmont, 1922)

The youngest competitor in the **Ryder Cup** was Nick Faldo who was just 20 years 58 days when he made his debut in 1977.

Ronan Rafferty is the youngest person to have appeared in the **Walker Cup**. He was just 17 when he competed in 1981.

Marko Vovk of Yugoslavia was just 15 when he represented his country in the 1979 **World Cup** in Athens.

John Beharral (1956) and Bobby Cole (1966) were both 18 years 1 month old when they won the **British Amateur Championship**.

Jack Nicklaus was just 19 years 39 weeks old when he won the **US Amateur Championship** in 1959, but he was not the youngest winner of the title. Robert A. Gardner was three months younger when he won in 1909.

The youngest winner of the **US Women's Amateur Championship** is Laura Baugh who was just 16 years 81 days when she won the title in 1971.

In the 1930s Pam Barton won the **French Ladies'** and **British** and **American Women's Championships**—all before she was 20.

David Robertson, who was banned for 20 years by the PGA European Tour in 1985 for alleged cheating during the qualifying competition for the British Open, was the youngest winner of the **British Youths Championship**. He was 17 years 49 days old when he won the title in 1974. The maximum age limit for the event was 22. Robertson was only 16 when he first represented Scotland the previous year.

The youngest player to represent **England** at international level is Paul Downes who was 16 when he made his debut in 1976.

Severiano Ballesteros was only 19 years 4 months old when he won the 1976 **Dutch Open** to become the youngest winner on the European PGA Tour. Paul Way was also 19 years 4 months when he won the same title in 1982.

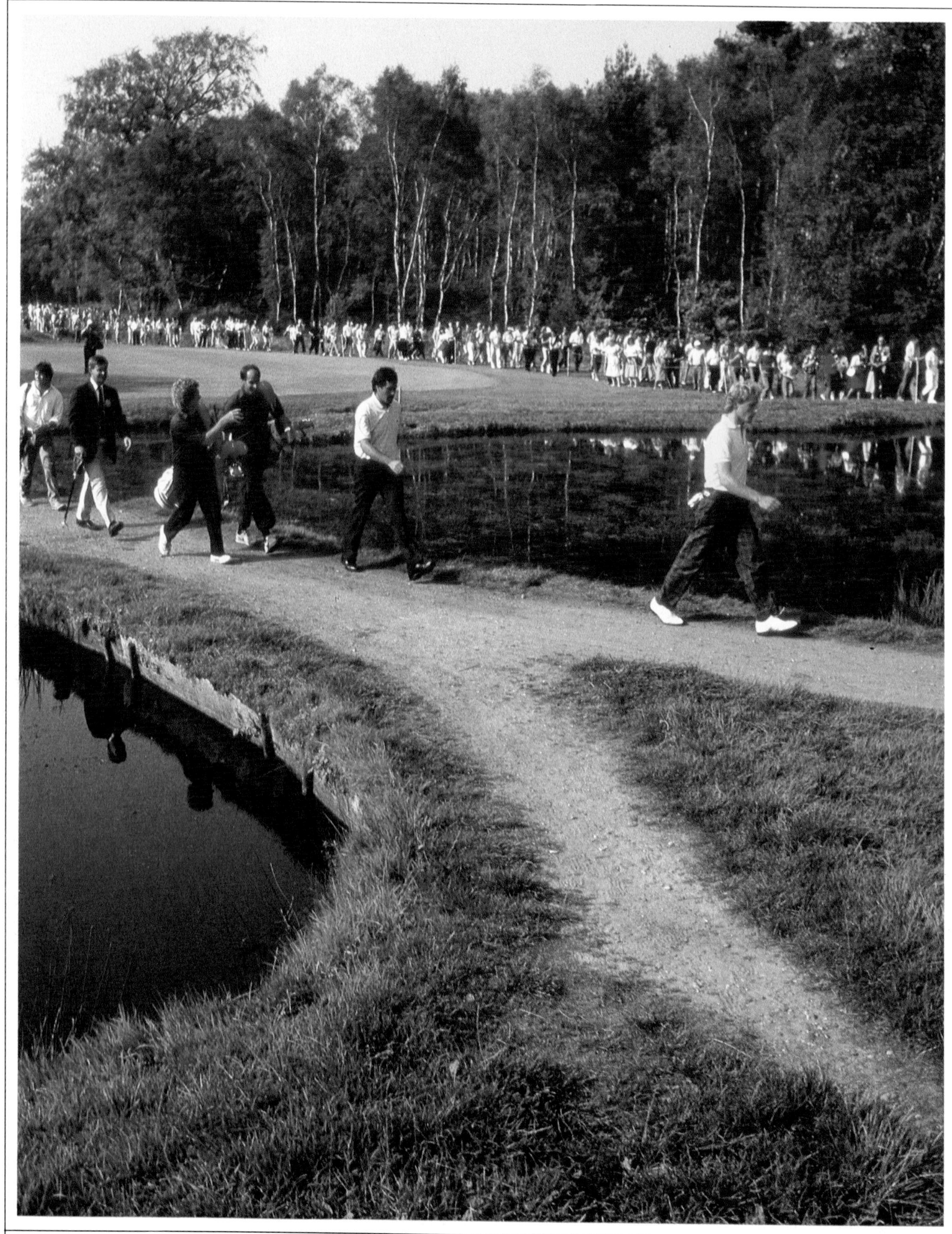

Bernhard Langer and Severiano Ballesteros, Europe's leading players, met in the 1984 and 1985 World Match-Play finals. They are seen here making their way to the 8th hole during the 1985 final, which Ballesteros won.

Z

Zaharias, Mildred

Mildred Zaharias (neé Didrikson) was not only the greatest female golfer of her time but also one of the world's most outstanding athletes.

Nicknamed 'Babe' because she was good at baseball (Babe Ruth was her idol), she was also an All-American Basketball player. But it was at track and field athletics that she first excelled.

At the 1932 Los Angeles Olympics she won three gold medals, in the 80 metres hurdles, javelin and high jump. She was only 18 at the time. Two years earlier, at 16, she had broken the world javelin record. Although she had qualified for five Olympic events, the rules allowed her to participate in only three, otherwise her medal tally would probably have been higher.

After her athletics days were over she turned to golf, encouraged by her wrestler husband, George Zaharias.

Her record at the new sport outweighed her track and field achievements. She won the US Women's Amateur Championship, and then became the first American to win the British Ladies' Amateur Championship. She turned professional in 1947 and went on to win the US Ladies' Open title on three occasions. Her final one, in 1954, was one of golf's great emotional moments. The year before she had undergone major cancer surgery but returned to win the Open, by 12 strokes. Sadly the cancer returned and on 17 September 1956 she died aged just 42.

Career highlights (Golf)

Ladies' British Open Amateur 1947
US Women's Amateur 1946
US Women's Open 1948, 1950, 1954

One of the world's greatest all-round sportswomen, Mildred Zaharias, during the 1951 Graphic Tournament at Wentworth.

Zoeller, Fuzzy

Fuzzy Zoeller first swung a golf club at the age of three. Two years later he entered his first tournament! It is hardly surprising therefore that he developed into one of America's leading players.

He first hit the headlines in 1976, his second year on the US Tour, when he equalled the 25-year-old all-time Tour record by registering eight consecutive birdies in the Quad Cities Open.

But it was in 1979 that Fuzzy Zoeller rose to prominence. He won his first Tour event, the Andy Williams San Diego Open, and then went on to become the surprise winner of the Masters. A win that even surprised him . . .

Going into the last round he trailed Ed Sneed by six strokes and he was sitting in the club-house, tied second place with Tom Watson, watching Sneed play the last hole. All he needed was a par to win the title, but Sneed shocked everyone by bogeying the hole and creating a three-way play-off which Zoeller won.

His second major victory was also after a play-off. That was in 1984 when he beat Greg Norman by eight strokes to win the US Open. That was his only win in 1984 as he slipped from second, in 1983, to 40th in the money-winning list. But he spent part of the season suffering from a recurring back injury.

Zoeller returned to the top 20 in 1985 with winnings of over $240,000 which put him in 12th place.

Career highlights

US Masters 1979
US Open 1984
British Open (best) jt 8th – 1982
Ryder Cup 1979, 1983, 1985

BIBLIOGRAPHY

Benson & Hedges Golfer's Handbook (Macmillan, 1985)
Encyclopedia of Golf Webster Evans (Robert Hale, 1980)
The Guinness Book of Golf Facts and Feats by Donald Steel (Guinness Superlatives, 1980)
Pro-Golf '85 (PGA European Tour, 1985)
The Shell International Encyclopedia of Golf edited by Donald Steel and Peter Ryde (Ebury Press & Pelham Books, 1975)
The Tour Book 1985 (US PGA Tour, 1985)
World Atlas of Golf (Mitchell Beazley, 1976)